Language Acquisition and
Communicative Choice

Language Acquisition and Communicative Choice

Essays by Susan M. Ervin-Tripp

Selected and Introduced
by Anwar S. Dil

Stanford University Press, Stanford, California

Language Science and National Development

A Series Sponsored by the
Linguistic Research Group of Pakistan

General Editor: Anwar S. Dil

Stanford University Press
Stanford, California
© 1973 by Susan M. Ervin-Tripp
Printed in the United States of America
ISBN 0-8047-0831-2
Original edition 1973
Last figure below indicates year of this printing:
85 84 83 82 81 80 79 78 77 76

Contents

Acknowledgments

The Linguistic Research Group of Pakistan and the General Editor of the Language Science and National Development Series are deeply grateful to Professor Susan M. Ervin-Tripp, Life Member of the Group, for giving us the privilege of presenting her selected writings as the seventh volume in our series established in 1970 to commemorate the International Education Year.

We are indebted to the editors and publishers of the following publications. The ready permission on the part of the holders of the copyrights, acknowledged in each case, is a proof of the existing international cooperation and goodwill that gives hope for better collaboration among scholars of all nations for international exchange of knowledge.

Second Language Learning and Bilingualism; with Charles E. Osgood. Excerpted from Chapter 6 in Psycholinguistics: A Survey of Theory and Research Problems, 1954-1964, ed. by Charles E. Osgood and Thomas A. Sebeok (Bloomington: Indiana University Press, 1965), 139-146, with permission of the publisher.

Learning and Recall in Bilinguals. The American Journal of Psychology 74, 3. 446-451 (1961), with permission of the publisher, the University of Illinois Press.

Semantic Shift in Bilingualism. The American Journal of Psychology 74, 2. 233-241 (1961), with permission of the publisher, the University of Illinois Press.

Language and TAT Content in Bilinguals. Journal of Abnormal and Social Psychology 68, 5. 500-507 (1964), with permission of the publisher. ©1964 by the American Psychological Association, Inc.

An Issei Learns English. The Journal of Social Issues 23, 2. 78-90 (1967), with permission of the Society for the Psychological Study of Social Issues.

On Becoming a Bilingual. Originally appeared as a "Commentary" on the paper "How and Where Did Persons Become Bilingual," by R. M. Jones, in Description and Measurement of Bilingualism: An International Seminar, ed. by Louis G. Kelly (Toronto: University of Toronto Press, 1969), pp. 26-35, with permission of the publisher.

Structure and Process in Language Acquisition. Monograph No. 23, The Report of the Twenty-First Annual Round Table Meeting on Languages and Linguistics (Washington, D.C.: Georgetown University Press, 1970), pp. 313-353, with permission of the publisher.

The Development of Meaning in Children's Descriptive Terms; with Garrett Foster. Journal of Abnormal and Social Psychology 61, 2. 271-275 (1960), with permission of the publisher. ©1960 by the American Psychological Association, Inc.

Changes with Age in the Verbal Determinants of Word-Association. The American Journal of Psychology 74, 3. 361-372 (1961), with permission of the publisher, the University of Illinois Press.

The Connotations of Gender. Word 18, 3. 249-261 (1962), with permission of the Editor and of the Johnson Reprint Corporation.

Navajo Word-Associations; with Herbert Landar. The American Journal of Psychology 76, 1. 49-57 (1963), with permission of the publisher, the University of Illinois Press.

Imitation and Structural Change in Children's Language. New Directions in the Study of Language, ed. by Eric H. Lenneberg (Cambridge, Mass.: The MIT Press, 1964), pp. 163-189, with permission of the publisher. © 1964 by the Massachusetts Institute of Technology.

Some Strategies for the First Two Years. Cognitive Development and the Acquisition of Language, ed. by Timothy Moore (New York: Academic Press, 1973), with permission of the publisher. © 1973 by The Research Foundation of State University of New York.

An Analysis of the Interaction of Language, Topic, and Listener. American Anthropologist 66, 6, Part 2, The Ethnography Of Communication, ed. by John J. Gumperz and Dell Hymes (1964), pp. 86-102, with permission of the American Anthropological Association.

Children's Sociolinguistic Competence and Dialect Diversity. Early Childhood Education: The Seventy-First Yearbook of the National Society for the Study of Education, ed. by Ira J. Gordon (Chicago: University of Chicago Press, 1972), pp. 123-160, with permission of the National Society for the Study of Education.

The Structure of Communicative Choice. The major sections of this essay are from two published essays: "On Sociolinguistic Rules: Alternations and Co-occurrence," in Directions in Sociolinguistics: The Ethnography of Communication, ed. by John J. Gumperz and Dell Hymes (New York: Holt, Rinehart and Winston, 1972), pp. 218-250, © 1972 by Holt, Rinehart and Winston, Inc.; and "Sociolinguistics," in Advances in Experimental Social Psychology, ed. by Leonard Berkowitz (New York: Academic Press, 1969), Vol. 4, pp. 91-165, © 1969 by Academic Press, Inc. The previously published material appears here with permission of the publishers; minor revisions have been made and new material added.

The Editor completed major portion of the work on this volume while he was in residence as Visiting Scholar in Linguistics at Stanford University (1969-72). He is especially grateful to Professor Charles A. Ferguson, Chairman of the Committee on Linguistics, for arranging library and office facilities.

Grateful acknowledgments are extended to Dr. Afia Dil of the Department of Linguistics, California State University, San Diego, for her help in many ways. Thanks are also due to Professor Robert D. Tripp of the Department of Physics, University of California, Berkeley, for his generous cooperation. The financial assistance from the University of California, Berkeley, to cover part of the typing expenses of the manuscript is gratefully acknowledged. Typing of the camera-ready manuscript has been done by Patricia Jean Ford and Ruth Spiering of San Diego. They certainly deserve a word of appreciation for a job well done.

This volume is affectionately dedicated to Alexander, Catherine, and Nicholas, the author's children who have been such willing speakers and collaborators.

EDITOR'S NOTE

These essays have been reprinted from the originals with only minor changes made in the interest of uniformity of style and appearance. A few changes in wording have been made in consultation with the author. In some cases bibliographical entries and notes have been updated. Footnotes marked by asterisks have been added by the Editor.

Introduction

Susan Moore Ervin was born in Minneapolis, Minnesota, on June 29, 1927. After graduating from Vassar College, where she acquired a broad general education in art history, languages, and the social sciences, she went to the University of Michigan for graduate work in social psychology. On completing her doctoral course requirements she left for Washington, D. C., where she worked first for the American Psychological Association and later at the Bureau of Social Science Research. After receiving her Ph. D. degree in 1955 she spent the next few years at Harvard University teaching courses in statistics and child language and doing research, notably for the Southwest Project in Comparative Psycholinguistics under the direction of John B. Carroll. In 1958 she went to teach at the University of California, Berkeley, where she has been Professor of Rhetoric since 1968.

As a senior member of the research team at the Language-Behavior Research Laboratory and the Institute for Human Learning at Berkeley, she has worked in close collaboration with John J. Gumperz in sociolinguistics and Dan I. Slobin in psycholinguistics. Among the fruitful results of their collaboration is A Field Manual for Cross- Cultural Study of the Acquisition of Communicative Competence (1967). She has served as a member of the Sociolinguistics Committee of the Social Science Research Council (1965-70), and is currently a member of the editorial boards of the Journal of Child Language, the International Journal of the Sociology of Language,

and the monograph series Language, Thought, and Culture: Advances
in the Study of Cognition. She has been a Life Member of the Linguistic Research Group of Pakistan since 1968.

Susan Ervin showed an early interest in languages. By the
time she graduated from Vassar, she had acquired French, German,
Spanish, Latin, and Greek because it was "such fun and seemed such
a natural thing to do." It was at the University of Michigan, where
she heard a bilingual friend complain that two languages made for a
sort of dual personality, that she first became interested in exploring
why for some individuals and groups bilingualism is such a critical
problem while for others it is not. A Czech colleague at the Bureau
of Social Science Research sharpened her interest in this subject, and
she applied to the Social Science Research Council for a predoctoral
fellowship to study the bilingual behavior of speakers of English and
French.

As part of her fellowship she participated in the Linguistic
Institute and the Seminar in Psycholinguistics held at Indiana University during the summer of 1953. The eight-week seminar brought together some half dozen eminent linguists, psychologists, and communication specialists, including Joseph H. Greenberg and Charles E.
Osgood, and an equal number of younger scholars, including Sol
Saporta, for a pioneering exploration of the points of intersection between the linguist's conception of language as a structure of inter-
related formal units, the psychologist's conception of language as a
system of habits relating signs to behavior, and the communication
specialist's conception of language as a means of transmitting information. Susan Ervin's contributions to the now classic report
Psycholinguistics: A Survey of Theory and Research Problems,
edited by C. E. Osgood and T. A. Sebeok (1954), reflect her deepened
understanding of language learning and bilingual behavior.

After following up a number of related problems in her dissertation, she continued her post doctoral research work at Harvard
University. A summer spent among the Navajo Indians for the Southwest Project gave her a rich experience of research with informants
in real-life situations and made it clear that other language and culture groups could be very different from her own. Also during her
Harvard period she pursued her interest in child language studies,

an area in which her contacts with John Carroll and Roger Brown
proved stimulating.

A new element was added to her research experience at
Berkeley, where from 1959 to 1965 she was directly involved in programs of teaching and learning English as a second language. She
came to believe that the study of language acquisition by children and
of second language learning, viewed in the context of the overall process of language acquisition, was fundamental to any general theory
of human learning and behavior. Her growing concern with the social
dimensions of language, for which she acknowledges her debt to her
good friends Dell Hymes and John Gumperz, is reflected in much of
her recent work, notably her 1972 paper on children's sociolinguistic
competence and dialect diversity.

In her postscript in this volume, Susan Ervin-Tripp (she
added the 'Tripp' after marrying the Berkeley physicist Robert D.
Tripp) writes about the great joy of listening to children and bilinguals and learning from innovators in the study of language. Her
zest for exploring language phenomena, both in her own experiments
and research projects and in the work of other scholars, is refresh-
ingly evident in her teaching as well as in her research reports and
review articles.

A casual look at her list of publications could give the impression of a wide scatter of topics — identification, motivation,
memory storage and retrieval, word association, translation equivalence, semantic shift, and so on— but a closer look reveals her
continuing search for an understanding of the basic language phenomena
of human life. Her distinguished articles on child language and bilingualism published over the past two decades have earned her a place
of honor among the leading scholars in these fields. In recent years
at least two of her sociolinguistic essays, "An Analysis of the Interaction of Language, Topic, and Listener" (1964) and "Sociolinguistics"
(1968), have been recognized as among the most significant contributions in this emerging area of interdisciplinary study. Her current
major research activities involve field work in Switzerland for a
study of the structure of human communication with the speech act
as its basic unit, and preliminary investigations in Yugoslavia for a
comparative research project on children's language learning.

Susan Ervin-Tripp is the first woman to be represented in
the Language Science and National Development series. Given the
growing contribution of women scholars to the field of language
science, we may not only hope but confidently expect that she will be
the first of many.

Anwar S. Dil

School of Human Behavior
U. S. International University
San Diego, California
March 17, 1973

**Language Acquisition and
Communicative Choice**

Part I. Bilingualism

1 | Identification and Bilingualism

Language learning occurs for the child and for the immigrant within a context of social learning. An examination of this context and some of the psychological processes that seem to be involved in socialization or acculturation may help us to understand certain aspects of language learning which have not seemed clear in other descriptions. In particular, we need to account for three phenomena: age changes in success in learning languages, the fact the language forms are learned which do not contribute to comprehensibility— that learning can go very far, and that what is said, as well as how to say it, is learned. We need to understand why language learners learn much more than intelligibility for instrumental purposes.

A fundamental concept in the description of the social context of language learning is identification. This is a term used to refer to the adoption of features of another's behavior as stable and relatively permanent elements of the behavioral patterns of the learner. In general, identification will be distinguished here from imitation only in terms of degree with respect to three dimensions— pervasiveness, or the variety of behavior affected, permanence, and also perhaps susceptibility to voluntary control. Imitation is considered narrower, less permanent, more voluntary. The term identification has been applied to the adoption of qualities of the model such as mannerisms and style of dress, social roles insofar as social positions permit, and standards of conduct. [1]

One of the principal conditions for the occurrence of identification apparently is the relative dependence of the learner on the model. The most significant identifications therefore occur at a very

early age. In the state of dependence, the model is an agent in satisfying the needs of the child, and for this reason the satisfactions experienced by the child become associated with the various stimuli
such as speech and gestures which are provided by the adult who cares
for him. At an early age, a child responds with evident pleasure to
the faces of other persons. If he is hungry, his crying may stop before he actually receives food, because the sight of a face has become
a sign to him of forthcoming need-satisfaction. Such signs shall be
called secondary rewards.

We may expect that as the child matures, the recollection
of these secondary rewards may afford pleasure, so that in a state
of need, the image of the parent's face may be momentarily soothing
too. As the child's motor capacities increase, he may be capable
himself of creating stimuli like those he recollects, and in this way he
can provide his own gratification. At this point the simulation of
parental secondary rewards may be one of the few gratifications within
the child's muscular control. Each time such actions occur acciden-
tally, they provide pleasure for the child, and they will tend to be
repeated more and more often. They would be particularly gratifying when the child is in a state of moderate need, as in the temporary absence of the caretaker.

This description clearly applies to speech. The babbling of
the child not only gives muscle pleasure but provides a secondary reward in letting him hear sounds like those his mother makes. Gradually we would expect fine-grained phonetic similarity to develop between features of the infant's vocalizations and that of the adult, within the range, of course, of the child's muscular capacities. Of all
the behavior which the child adopts from adults, the learning of
speech seems most easily to be explained in this way because the
auditory stimuli of mother and child are so available for comparison.

In addition to the secondary reward experienced in the absence of the model, there are various direct rewards given by others
when behavior imitative of adults has occurred. Imitation may also
facilitate skill learning which helps the child in satisfying his own
needs. So we find small children, at the beginning of first or
second language learning, often repeating after another speaker, or
rehearsing to themselves snatches of what they have heard. Eventually,

the child learns that imitating others is gratifying, and under favor-
able conditions he is likely to acquire a generalized tendency to imitate others, particularly the parents, resulting in what we have called
identification. Not only speech, but walking, dressing, and the other
complicated acts that a child learns in his early years may involve
the secondary reward experienced in imitating the parent. Instrumental learning alone could not explain the acquisition of complicated and
persistent styles of behavior, or the imitating of the favorite gesture
of another in a particular situation.

One source of evidence supporting this explanation is provided by Mowrer's observations of talking birds (8). He reports that
optimal learning occurs when the birds are isolated from their kind
and reduced to a state of extreme dependence on the trainer. The
birds first began recognizably vocalizing in the absence of the trainer,
and often stopped when he reappeared. This prior stage of learning
seems to select sounds sufficiently from the bird's total repertoire
so that the trainer can reward those he wishes to, and elicit imitation.

In summary there appear to be two processes in the early
acquisition of speech and other learning of adult behavior: first,
imitation in the absence of the model because of the secondary reward
involved in being reminded of the gratifications received from the
model; second, direct reward of imitative behavior. Both of these
processes create a generalized tendency to identify with the model.
Sears' research on identification has indicated that it varies in degree
with the degree of prior nurturance, the kind and severity of demands
by the parents, and the contingency of reward and punishment on success in fulfilling parental demands. Loving, consistent, and fairly
strict parents presumably create the maximum degree of identification, as measured by Sears in terms of adoption of parental qualities, roles, and moral standards (10).

Identification may be a medium for the acquisition of certain
aspects of speech similarity, but in addition, through language, it
may aid in the evolution of the sense of self and of conscience.
Language serves two functions relevant to the self-observing process so crucial to conscience. First, it supplies labels for acts of
the child so that he can refer to himself as he might to someone
else's behavior. In other words it facilitates treating his own

behavior as an object. Secondly, his speech sounds like the speech
of others, so that the verbal reactions to one's own behavior, or to
someone else's, are likely to be similar to what the child thinks a
parent would say. To the extent that this occurs even in the absence
of other persons, it can be explained as a consequence of identification. We would expect that in addition to the non-verbal moral learning of children, there may be auditory imagery associated with reward and punishment, and originally perceived as external in origin.
These phrases which convey adult opinion become the bearers of
the teachings, admonitions, and ideals of the "significant others", and
the child may even parrot them back at a model who violates his own
rules. Vivid examples of children whose conscience was clearly verbal and derived from imitation of adults are given by Reik (9) and by
Murray, quoted in Witmer (11).

The first identifications of course are likely to be directed
toward the parents in a society with nuclear families. Eventually,
however, the child goes outside of the family for new partial identifications, as soon as peer culture becomes important to him. In traditional families, this process might be particularly marked in early
adolescence, when new biological and social demands lead to the trying out of varying patterns of behavior. Anna Freud gives a vivid
description of this aspect of adolescence:

> The changeableness of young people is a commonplace.
> In their handwriting, mode of speech, way of doing their
> hair, their dress and all sorts of habits they are far more
> adaptable than at any other period of life. Often a single
> glance at an adolescent will tell us who is the older friend
> whom he admires. (3)

Since the conditions conducive to identification vary from generation to generation as child-rearing practices change and as the
social environment of children changes, it is unwise to make generalizations about specific ages. However, Einar Haugen has remarked
that he found that about the age of fourteen marked a point of decline
in the ability to learn a foreign language adequately. For most individuals, the point of shift should be that time when the individual
has reached a relatively stable and mature level in his personal development, so that he no longer has need for relating to others through

total identifications. He then becomes less able to acquire those aspects of second language skills which are most dependent on identification with the speakers of the language. Of course there is great individual variation, but for many persons this point would be reached around adolescence, in our society.

Obviously normal adults do not readily surrender their earlier identities, and adult identifications are likely to be partial, involving, in a sense, the acquisition of new roles (7). In general, we would expect adult identifications in the sense of permanent personality changes to occur under conditions of extreme dependence or stress, such as combat; emotional closeness with another person who is a source of gratification; or difference in social position in its widest sense, when the other person performs a role or occupies a position that is desirable. The desire to be like another person need not be conscious. In our society the desire for social advancement is so readily accepted that often it may be more readily reported than other desires to emulate. One should take care to use some indirect tests to ascertain the direction of desires to emulate others.

Now let us turn to the possible implications of this material for bilingualism and second language learning. In the first place the age at which a language is learned is as we know of considerable significance in terms of later skill in using the language. One might expect that the two bodies of meaning in a coordinate bilingual (2) might show the effects of differential development of knowledge and skills at the two ages. In particular, the earlier language may show continuing childhood associations peculiar to the age of the child, not to the social environment in which the language was learned. These differences then would pervade all systems of meaning regardless of the cultures involved.

For example, the child's framework of meanings is usually highly body-oriented. His dependence on others for satisfying his recurrent physical needs, his problems of learning muscular control, and his circumscribed experience with the world, tend to make the representations of body processes and parts loom large in his framework of symbolic relationships. Since he knows more about his body, so to speak, than about the external world, it appears that in his contacts with new objects outside of himself he often associates them symboli-

cally with body parts or products. Children have been observed to
have idiosyncracies in these associations, some directing them toward buildings, others toward machinery, food, clothing, or animals
(6). Of course we all make these symbolic comparisons in adult
life, but the prevalence of these bodily associations in children's
thinking might result in a difference in meanings for adult speech
when one of the languages of a bilingual was learned at an age when
this process was pronounced. This aspect of meaning may account
in part for the feeling that one's mother tongue is symbolically richer than a language learned as an adult.

Secondly, the fact that languages are learned at different
ages may be reflected in the way the language is spoken. When we
mention age, of course, we encounter the hazard of confusing the
results of earlier learning with the effects of longer practice. Let us
suppose, however, that we are dealing with persons whose use of a
later dominant language has at least equalized practice for both languages. One would expect the kind of age factors mentioned earlier in
connection with adolescent identifications to affect those features of
language which matter the least for intelligibility. The need for intelligibility obviously will force anyone to learn over a certain period of time if he is forced to have important discourse with monolinguals, but phone substitution and stylistic features may more
successfully resist change. We all know immigrants who have failed
to learn them in forty years of residence here. Sometimes this
learning does not occur in a child immigrant, and it is possible to
discover what differences in his social relations may be related to
this failure. Here is a case of a child who spoke with as heavy an
accent as his parents:

> John was an 8 year old boy who had come to the United
> States from Germany at the age of three. John had an
> excessive admiration for his father and competed with
> him desperately. He readily adopted his father's opinions,
> including his disapproval of American education and culture.
> He went to school, but failed to develop friendships. In
> the course of time and analysis, the feelings which had led
> to a strong identification with his father changed. He shifted
> the focus of his interests outside of the family, took up

baseball, played with the neighborhood gang, and began
to speak the dialect of his pals. He was still able to mimic
his father's accent at will. (1)

Studies of speech might be made within the context of data
on other indices of identification. Such studies would be most fruitful if done with children before identifications are so diffuse as to
obscure the origins of the behavior that occurs. Dialect differences
between parents , or between parents and others in the environment;
sex differentiated linguistic features; and most clearly the speech of
parents who speak a foreign language in the home or speak English
with an accent all provide opportunities for such research.

The social relationships peculiar to the age at which a language was spoken may affect the way it is spoken; they will also
clearly affect the meanings associated with the language. It has been
noted above that the verbalized prohibitions and ideals of the parents
or parent-substitutes may be recalled by the child and gradually
assimilated as though he himself had said them. It has been observed
that in the earlier stages of this process there may be considerable
rigidity and literalness in interpreting rules. This is most likely to
happen under the conditions of nurturance and consistent strictness
described earlier, and is apparently related to the power of the adult
who imposes rules, and to the apparent arbitrariness and irrational-
ity of the world in which the child lives. Under these circumstances,
we would expect the meanings learned at this time to include this
moralistic quality. It is frequently observed, for example, that
obscenities in the mother tongue are much more obscene in connotation. It would be expected that factors which are conducive to identification would result in a stronger moralistic connotation for the language of the identification-object. For example, in general if there
were a language difference between parents it would be stronger
for the language of the like-sexed parent.

Even in the case of second-language learning by adults some
of the values of the speakers must be acquired. It is a necessary
consequence of oral use of language that our range of meanings becomes adapted to those utilized by the interlocutor. To maintain a
totally compound system would bring about lack of intelligibility,
and simple concept learning will guarantee some acquiring of new

meanings, if the old ones are sufficiently inadequate, and the speaker learns that they are inadequate. In addition, in conversing the learner may learn longer messages, propositions containing value judgments and beliefs. This seems to be the case with the Japanese-American whose case will be examined in detail below. There is evidence (5) that overt verbalization which does not conform with one's convictions can somewhat change these convictions. Thus language-learning can lead to acculturation in a profound way.

It is not only children who have strong emotional ties. Marriage to a person in the new culture, raising children who must be socialized in the new language, can deeply alter the knowledge of values and the emotional significance of the new language forms. The more varied and the more emotional the situations in which the languages are used, and the more the learner has developed a tendency to identify with native speakers, the more likely it is that the quality of responses of native speakers, and their selection of a stimulus context for response will be perceived by the learner and become a part of his own meaning system. Thus identification may not only facilitate certain kinds of phonological learning, but may facilitate appropriate application of many lexical items; in particular it would lead to more apt use in live situations, with the emotional connotations peculiar to the acquired culture.

The following case is taken from a study of differences in the interpretation of ambiguous stimuli by bilingual persons when they are speaking the two languages on separate occasions. The subject was a 27 year old Japanese-American, born in this country but educated in Japan between the ages of 8 and 14. He used only Japanese with his parents, and with a few friends, but he spoke English with his siblings, except for a period in an internment camp after his return to this country. He has had virtually no translating experience. On the whole one would expect to find a coordinate system since there has been considerable contact with monolinguals in both languages and he does relatively little language mixing.

There were two tasks, a sentence-completion test and a Thematic Apperception Test, with the English sessions occurring six weeks after the Japanese. The tests were administered by another Japanese-American. The following are paraphrased summaries of themes from the stories told to the T. A. T. pictures:

1. Jap: A wife calls her husband to dinner. "An expression is acting on her face that she intends to prepare something which the husband is very much fond of, in order to surprise him. The husband is holding the papers and is smoking. He is now making himself comfortable. Being called by his sweet wife he stands up slowly..."

Eng: A maid is calling her boss to the phone.
(The picture shows a woman opening a door and looking in a room.)

2. Jap: A girl is drinking in a cabaret in order to forget a man. She is "crying aloud in her pain" and past days "haunt her without order like a collapsed kaleidoscope." She commits suicide.

Eng: A girl "pressed by economic necessities, had degraded herself to the very bottom of women's morality" and keeps coming home drunk. "I feel great pity inasmuch as she is just one of those millions who suffered on account of man's inability to keep society one whole piece." (The picture shows a girl leaning against a door with her face hidden in one hand.)

3. Jap: A son comes home ill and dies before his mother, who goes mad with grief.

Eng: A young man was invited in off the highway when he was lost by a hypnotist, who robbed him. (The picture shows a boy lying down with someone bending over him.)

4. Jap: A woman weeps over her lost fiancé and thinks of suicide.

Eng: A girl tries to complete a sewing project for class. (The picture shows a figure from the back, sitting on the floor, the head buried in a couch or bench.)

It can readily be seen that there is much more emotion in the Japanese stories. The characters are more often members of

the family, and the themes more often concern close personal ties.
Only three of the English stories involved people in the same family
or emotionally related, whereas eight of the Japanese stories concern
family relationships, and two more a love relation. Love, unfaith-
fulness, loss of loved ones appear in many Japanese stories, but in
the English stories there are only two references to such feelings—
in one case a child feels neglected, and in another a man loves his
dog. In general the English stories seem abstract and cold, the relationships formal. This was also noticeable in the sentence completions:

> Jap: Most women/are two faced.
> Eng: Most women/make excellent mothers and good wives.
>
> Jap: Mothers/enjoyed their cherry-blossom picnic.
> Eng: Mothers/are the best creation of God.
>
> Jap: Responsibility/is only half-way liked.
> Eng: Responsibility/must go hand in hand with freedom.

In general the differences are those one would expect when the primary
emotional relationships are in one language and the other language is
used chiefly for formal situations, such as school and impersonal
contacts.

However there is a more fundamental difference to be found.
There are consistent differences between the conflicts encountered
by the characters in the two languages, so that in reading the two
sets of material one might think they were the products of two different people. The most common theme in the Japanese stories is
the child's debt to his parents, with ensuing guilt or fear of disap-
pointing them. In the corresponding English stories such themes
do not appear.

> 5. Jap: A child is worrying about having broken a violin
> for which his parents made great sacrifices, and he fears
> punishment.
>
> Eng: A child is disgusted because he hasn't been playing
> well.

6. Jap: A student feels in conflict about being sent to college. Her mother is sick, and the father works hard without much financial reward. "Nevertheless, he continues to work diligently, without saying anything, praying for the daughter's success. Also he is a husband who never complains to his wife."

Eng: A sociology student observing farmers at work is "struck by the difficulty of farm life." (The scene shows a farm, with a farmer plowing in the background, a woman leaning against a tree, and in the foreground a girl carrying books on her arm.)

7. Jap: A son feels tremendous remorse and the mother disappointment over something he's done. There is a long description of feelings.

Eng: A son comes to tell his mother he's been drafted. Only factual details of the circumstances are described.

The second principal difference is the greater emphasis on achievement in Japanese.

Jap: If the work is too hard/ he says "well, this is merely..." and as if whipping himself, he works all the harder.

Eng: If the work is too hard/ for me, I'll just quit.

Jap: I like to read/ about sociology.

Eng: I like to read/ comics once in a while because they sort of relax my mind.

Jap: My greatest pleasure/ is to graduate from graduate school.

Eng: My greatest pleasure/ is to be able to lie on the warm sands of the beach out west.

This man's reactions were sufficiently different in English as to give a completely misleading impression of his feelings and past

experiences. Here are some quotations from a report written prior
to the translation of the Japanese material, purely on the basis of the
English stories, the English sentence-completions, and an English
Rorschach test. It was quite lengthy and the writer believed there
was fairly consistent evidence supporting the analysis.

> The subject's moral code is clearly defined.... He is preoc-
> cupied with work and kindness and conscientiousness but
> he is not especially guilty over deviations.... No one really
> gets punished or suffers for misdeeds.... One gets the im-
> pression of a conscience geared rather to the external evi-
> dences of its operation, towards the approval of others,
> than to an internalized value system.... His value system
> appears to have been acquired rather late.... The subject
> is markedly concerned with external success.... There is
> no evidence of an especially warm relationship to the parents;
> there seems rather to have been neglect....

The subject went to an American school until the age of eight
and to an American high school and college. He spoke English with
his siblings as a child and again after adolescence. It is not inability
to speak English, but apparently the markedly different nature of his
relationships with others during the period when he used the two
languages which accounts for the appearance of a "double personality."

In concluding, let me raise three questions concerning
second language learning which have been suggested by the above
material. Is it possible to make some sort of classification with
respect to the features necessary for intelligibility in both the first
and the second language? If we can say that phone substitutions are
usually unimportant for intelligibility, then it seems that we may
expect phone substitutions to be learned in a different way than other
features. In the adult learning situation, there may be less feedback about errors than in the child's situation. Therefore the
adult learner must rely on his own ability to imitate the sound made
by the other person. Here it seems that the social and psychological incitements to imitation and to identification may account for some
of the marked individual differences in attainment.

Can feedback from speakers of the second language be so reduced that the learning of features necessary for intelligibility is delayed? This seems to have happened in certain colonial situations when the language of the subject group required tonal distinctions which Europeans failed to learn. The social situation may have prevented feedback just because of the marked status differential in the eyes of the learner. Certain cultural factors, such as extreme courtesy, might reduce feedback. Personality factors may inhibit perception of the cues provided by others. On the other hand, one would expect that people with a certain kind of manipulative relationship with others would have highly developed sensitivity to such cues. Specific studies would be in order.

If adult identifications are less pervasive, one might say that a new identification is an adoption of a new role, and does not necessarily hinder one's capacity to revert to another role in an appropriate situation. On the other hand, there may be persons who because of their particular personality structure, or because of unpleasant experiences in the original group, replace one set of attitudes and standards with another, and become deculturated with respect to the first culture. Are there features of language learning which vary together with these differences in type of adaptation to the new culture? It would be appropriate to study both the language behavior in the new culture and in the old in order to relate them to the fate of the earlier patterns of non-verbal behavior.

NOTES

Unpublished paper presented at a conference on bilingualism sponsored by the Social Science Research Council Committee on Psycholinguistics, Washington, D. C., in 1954.

[1] This summary is drawn from a report of current research at the Psychology Colloquium of the University of Michigan in 1950–51 by Robert R. Sears. Some hectographed material has been prepared by the Harvard Laboratory of Human Development concerning this research.

REFERENCES

1. Buxbaum, Edith. The role of a second language in the formation of ego and superego. Psychoanalytic Quarterly 18. 279–289 (1949).

2. Ervin, Susan and C.E. Osgood. Second language learning and bilingualism. [In this volume, pp. 15-23.]

3. Freud, Anna. The ego and the mechanisms of defense. London: Hogarth, 1948.

4. Haugen, Einar. Personal communication.

5. Janis, I.L. and B.T. King. The influence of role playing on opinion change. Journal of Abnormal and Social Psychology 49. 211-218 (1954).

6. Kubie, L.S. Body symbolization and development of language. Psychoanalytic Quarterly 3. 430-444 (1934).

7. Mead, G.H. Mind, self, and society. Chicago: University of Chicago Press, 1934.

8. Mowrer, O.H. Learning theory and personality dynamics. New York: Ronald Press, 1950.

9. Reik, Theodore. Psychoanalysis of the unconscious sense of guilt. International Journal of Psychoanalysis 5. 14-20 (1924).

10. Sears, Robert. Current research on identification. Psychology colloquium, University of Michigan, 1951.

11. Witmer, Helen (Ed.). Teaching psychotherapeutic medicine. New York: Commonwealth Fund, 1947.

2 | Second Language Learning and Bilingualism

In Collaboration with Charles E. Osgood

When, after becoming a practical expert in his own, first language, a person starts learning a second language, new sets of decoding and encoding habits are being formed in competition with the old. When the bilingual shifts from language to language, similarly, two systems of decoding and encoding habits come into conflict to a greater or lesser degree. The fact that the same general principles found to be important elsewhere in this section* also are significant here justified discussing second language learning and bilingualism in the present context. Since the seminar** did not devote much time to these topics, however, only a brief sketch of the thinking of some of us on these problems is offered. The reader is referred to recent books by Uriel Weinreich and Einar Haugen[1] for excellent treatments, undertaken from the linguistic point of view, but with very considerable psychological and sociological sophistication.

Compound and Coordinate Language Systems

Both second language learning and bilingualism involve the acquisition and utilization of two linguistic codes. The messages produced in the two or more languages employ differently constructed and organized units, different grammatical rules, and different and

---

*Diachronic psycholinguistics, pp. 126-63. In Psycholinguistics, ed. by Charles E. Osgood and Thomas A. Sebeok. Bloomington: Indiana University Press, 1954.

**The Summer Seminar on Psycholinguistics sponsored by the Social Science Research Council held at Indiana University in 1953.

equally arbitrary lexical systems, excepting occasional cognates.
To the extent that phonemic systems are different, two sets of differentiations and constancies on the decoding side and two sets of vocalic
skill components on the encoding side have to be maintained. Since
the entire systems of transitional redundancies in two languages are
different, alternative anticipational and dispositional integrations
have to be established. And since the lexical aspects of messages in
two languages are different, alternative sets of semantic decoding
and encoding habits have to be maintained—in other words, alternative
sets of associations between message events and events in the representational system, or meanings.

Perhaps because of dependence on the model provided by
second language learning in school situations, many writers seem to
have assumed that meanings are constant in second language learning
and in bilingualism. The meaning of the object HORSE remains the
same as perceptually experienced. Hence the meaning of its alternative linguistic signs, horse/Pferd, must be the same—all that is
involved is two systems of coding the same meaning. This is the
case under certain circumstances, which establish what we shall call
a compound language system. In such a system, as shown in Figure
1, two sets of linguistic signs, one appropriate to language A ($\boxed{S}_A$),
and the other appropriate to language B ($\boxed{S}_B$), come to be associated
with the same set of representational mediation processes or meanings ($r_m \rightarrow s_m$). On the encoding side, likewise, the same set of representational processes comes to be alternatively associated with two
sets of linguistic responses, one in language A ($\boxed{R}_A$) and the other in
language B ($\boxed{R}_B$). This development is typical of learning a foreign
language in the school situation. It is obviously fostered by learning
vocabulary lists, which associate a sign from language B with a sign
and its meaning in language A. A compound system can, however,
also be characteristic of bilingualism acquired by a child who grows
up in a home where two languages are spoken more or less interchangeably by the same people and in the same situations. In this
instance some compromise representational processes taken from
both languages may be established, with neither having pronounced
dominance.

A very different kind of relation between two languages in
the same nervous system is what we shall call a coordinate language

system. In this case, as shown on the right-hand side of the diagram, the set of linguistic signs and responses appropriate to one language come to be associated with one set of representational mediating processes ($r_{m_1} \rightarrow s_{m_1}$), but the set of linguistic signs and responses appropriate to the other language become associated with a somewhat different set of representational processes ($r_{m_2} \rightarrow s_{m_2}$). This kind of development is typical of the "true" bilingual, who has learned to speak one language with his parents, for example, and the other language in school and at work. The total situations, both external and emotional, and the total behaviors occurring when one language is being used will differ from those occurring with the other. The kinds of representational processes developed must then also be different and hence the meanings of the signs. This development can also characterize the second language learner, who, relying as little as possible on translation and immersing himself in the living culture of another language community, comes to speak a second tongue well.

Even within a coordinate system there may be interference between the two sets of processes. Given the likenesses throughout human cultures in the situations and objects dealt with by language, it is certain that the representational processes elicited by translation-equivalent signs in two languages will often be similar. In decoding, this produces a constant pressure on the bilingual to confuse meanings, to interpret a sign in language A as its translation-equivalent in language B would be interpreted. The more similar the signs—cognates, for instance—and the more similar the mediators, the greater this pressure will be. Interference is most likely to occur when the languages are closely related and the cultures or the experiences associated with the languages are alike.

On the encoding side, the more similar the meanings or representational processes, the more errors there will be. These may consist in delays or blocking of response, if the alternative responses in the two languages are quite different. There may be intrusions of responses from the wrong language, if the items in the two languages are similar. These phenomena are often obvious in the compound system, where identical mediators must elicit alternative responses. They may take subtle forms in the coordinate bilingual, resulting merely in minute delays or shifts in response frequencies in comparison with monolinguals. Compromise formations usually result, depending upon relative habit strengths in the two languages in vocalic skills, lexical associations, and transitional patterning.

In spite of the pressures for interference, there are many instances of remarkably pure bilingualism, in which the speaker, once launched in a given language, in an appropriate situation, and speaking of events associated with that language, will experience no difficulties and perform like a monolingual. There are at least three general predictive factors to be considered for the coordinate bilingual. In the first place, the feedback stimuli from previous utterances in a given language are more associated with mediators appropriate to that language than another, unless considerable language mixture has occurred in past usage. Secondly, the current interpersonal situation will affect interference in speech as much as it does features of style or dialect within one language. Hearer bilingualism, the relative prestige of the languages, momentary feelings toward the hearer will alter the general availability of responses in each language or even lead to deliberate use of interference by a speaker. Finally, stimuli arising from the scenes, objects, and people present during the formation of a language will also be associated more strongly with mediators appropriate to that language. Hence bilinguals report that when they are with, or even think about, their parents or their home, the parental language becomes more available. A bilingual under emotional stress may revert to the language spoken when comparable emotions have been experienced in the past.

For any semantic area we would expect speakers of more than one language to distribute themselves along a continuum from a pure compound system to a pure coordinate system. How would one measure or index the location of particular individuals along this continuum? At one extreme, the meanings of translation-equivalent signs are identical, and at the other the meanings of translation-equivalent signs are different. Furthermore, the semantic differences involved tend to be connotative rather than denotative. The semantic differential* seems particularly appropriate as a tool here. It could be used to measure coordinateness within a semantic area or

---

*Cf. Section 7.2.2, Measurement of connotative meaning, by Charles E. Osgood, pp. 177-83. In Psycholinguistics, op. cit.

to make a general estimate if appropriate samples could be devised. If a sample of pairs of translation equivalent signs were given to a varied group of two-language speakers for differentiation against an appropriate form of the semantic instrument, with D between profiles of the pairs computed for each speaker, the average D (difference in meaning) should vary directly with the degree of "coordinateness" of the language systems within each speaker. The validity of this measure could be estimated against such criteria as frequency of interference in ordinary conversation, fluency measures, and translation facility, to which we now turn our attention.

Translation under Compound and Coordinate Systems

In the process of translating from one language to another, linguistic signs in one language ($\boxed{S}_A$) must be decoded and equivalent or related linguistic responses must be made in the other language ($\boxed{R}_B$). The behavioral situations are quite different, depending on (a) whether the translator maintains compound or coordinate languages in his nervous system, and, if the former, (b) whether he is translating to or from his dominant language. The upper diagram in Figure 2 represents the translation process for a compound language system. Solid lines show translation <u>from</u> the dominant language, and dashed lines show translation <u>to</u> the dominant language. The lower diagram represents the translation process for a coordinate language system; the encircled numbers represent alternative translating circuits at different stages in the development of translating fluency in the coordinate system.

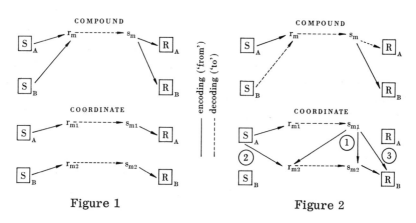

Figure 1   Figure 2

Compound system translating. When the product of an ordinary foreign language course in high school, let us say, translates from his native English into the other language, we have the situation represented by the solid lines in the left-hand diagram. Encoding the foreign forms involves direct response competition, since both are associated with a single set of American culture meanings. The "same" mediated stimulus must elicit a response (foreign language output) quite different from the dominant response (English language output) in the habit hierarchy. The task would be impossible were it not for differences in the total stimulus pattern for the translator. Such differences may be brought about by the "set" to translate, the feedback of foreign cues from preceding output, distinctive dispositional tendencies (once the foreign language grammar and syntax has become sufficiently learned), and unique associations with the use of the second language. These cues must be sufficient to counteract the stronger English response tendencies in the presence of s_m. An analogous situation exists for the external context, thoughts about events that occurred in the context of language A, or a conversation with a language A monolingual. For learning to occur, r_{m_2} must also be elicited, perhaps because a language B monolingual describes or refers to situations or objects represented by s_{m_1} but using language B signs. Generally, it would appear that a learned association between s_{m_1} and r_{m_2} probably only develops in situations in which some generalization between s_{m_1} and s_{m_2} also occurs. Learning then facilitates the appropriate translation. Whether through generalization, learning, or both, the translation is such that the meanings elicited in monolinguals in languages A and B are as similar as possible.

The ideal translator or interpreter accomplishes a transformation of signs through a three-person channel (monolingual A—coordinate translator—monolingual B) such that the representational processes of all three, or the meanings of the signs, remain unchanged. Obviously, the more the cultures, or the situations and objects discussed differ, the less rapidly the interpreter can encode. He is delayed by lack of quick generalization to similar meanings in the other language, or by conflict between several partially appropriate meanings. Interference in decoding may be produced by semi-cognates, similar or identical forms with varying meanings.

The above description treats the coordinate translator as though he were translating for the first time, but the translation process itself brings about new learning. Practice may reduce the capacity for cross-cultural translation, as we will demonstrate. Three different kinds of short-cuts may develop in the proficient translator or interpreter. In encoding, a linguistic response in language B must repeatedly occur in close sequence with the representational process appropriate to language A, as shown by pathway (3). This produces the same kind of interference discussed earlier, in the compound system, since s_{m_1} may elicit different responses depending on whether the speaker is supposed to speak language A or to translate it. Note that the representational process of language B has not been elicited at all. The second short-cut may consist in direct decoding into language B by pathway (2). The representational process appropriate to language B occurs soon after presentation of the linguistic sign in language A when there is frequent translation. This sign in language A must therefore become associated with a mediation process appropriate to language B, and it will compete with the process appropriate to language A, and, to the extent that they are similar, will lead to elimination of the meaningful discrimination in decoding. Finally, the mediation process may be only secondary, the response in language B being directly associated with hearing of a sign in language A, without intervention of a meaning process. This is most likely to happen for simultaneous interpreters who always use the same translation for the same word or phrase.

If a coordinate bilingual is hired to interpret in one direction only, from language A to language B, we must predict that (a) he will gradually develop an appropriate set of translation meanings for the signs in language A, and (b) he will lose his ability to speak language A. In other words, he will become a perfect A-to-B translating machine, while retaining his proficiency in language B—thus, a sort of dual-input speaker of language B. If a coordinate bilingual translates frequently in both directions, he must gradually (a) lose the distinctiveness among the mediation processes appropriate to each language and (b) suffer increasing confusion in encoding. In other words, the very process of two-way translating tends to transform a coordinate system into a compound system. It would be interesting to test these predictions on a sample of professional translators over time, using the type of experimental design suggested earlier with the semantic differential. This transformation can be minimized by refreshing the monolingual associations in both languages, of course.

Grammatical and skill levels

We have emphasized the semantic aspects of second language learning and bilingualism because these aspects have been relatively neglected. There is a great deal of carefully analyzed information on purely linguistic aspects of bilingualism, phonemic, morphemic, and grammatical interactions and the like, and the interested reader is referred to the two sources given at the beginning of this report. For the most part previous work has reported the occurrence of certain phenomena without attempting to relate frequencies of occurrence to the learning experiences of the speaker. Grammatical aspects should be particularly profitable to study from this standpoint. Being organized on largely unconscious levels on the basis of transitional redundancies, these aspects of encoding should be especially difficult to learn and, once learned, should be equally difficult to suppress when trying to master a second language. For the coordinate bilingual, on the other hand, two alternative grammatical systmes once established should provide for greater stability and independence between the two language systems.

We have considered here only the aspects of bilingual speech which reflect the influence of two linguistic codes on each other, omitting consideration of such non-linguistic features as pronunciation and style.* Yet further study of these features would probably be rewarding, especially for psychologists who would be interested in their sensitivity to differences in the attitudes of bilinguals and second-language learners toward the respective speech communities.

Research proposals

(1) Indexing degree of coordinateness of language systems. The possible use of the semantic differential as a means of determining

---

* Cf. Section 4.1, Within band organization, pp. 74-88. In Psycholinguistics, op. cit.

the degree of separateness of meanings for translation-equivalent signs has already been discussed. (A comparison with responses of monolinguals is suggested in section 7.4.3.1.* This would determine not only semantic areas in which a compound system exists, but the language community for which the meanings are appropriate.) (2) Influence of bilingualism on perception and meaning. One of the writers[2] is now engaged in research of this nature. Subjects varying in degree of bilingualism tell stories in response to the Thematic Apperception Test (a series of rather ambiguous situational pictures), (a) in language A after preliminary instructions in that language, and (b) after an interval of several weeks, in language B after similar preparation. The expectation is that ways of perceiving these pictorial signs, their meaning to the subject, will vary with the language being used, and with the degree of coordinateness of the systems in a given subject. (3) Measuring the transitional proficiencies of second language learners and bilinguals. The "Cloze" procedure developed by Wilson Taylor and described briefly in section 5** seems adaptable to problems in this area. Passages in languages A and B, as translated by maximally facile coordinate translators, could be mutilated (every fifth word deleted, for example) and given to subjects with varying degrees of bilingualism or varying amounts of second language training. In the former case, the more nearly equal the correct "fill-in" scores for languages A and B, the more "truly" bilingual in the coordinate sense the subject; in the latter case, the more nearly equal the scores in A and B, the greater the learning of the second language. This technique has two advantages; first, by its nature it samples all of the subtle contextual factors of both semantic associational and grammatical-dispositional levels; second, by using each subject's own performance in his most proficient language as a criterion, it eliminates individual differences in intelligence, language abilities, and the like. (4) Measuring interference between languages under varying conditions. Three factors were cited above in accounting for the degree of interference in encoding—feedback, the interpersonal situation, and differential past experience. Encoding with these conditions varied can be studied to see how conditions influence the amount and the kind of borrowing.

---

* Psycholinguistics, op. cit., pp. 195-97.
** Psycholinguistics, op. cit., pp. 93-125.

3 | Learning and Recall in Bilinguals

Natural bilinguals supply an opportunity to explore the effects of a type of verbal training too prolonged and complex to be easily duplicated in a laboratory. In the following study, the effects on memory of varying the languages used in learning and recall are investigated.

A bilingual may be said to be dominant in the language in which he has greater facility in naming common objects. One might expect that recall would be most complete in the dominant language. It is not obvious, however, that this superiority would be true for material learned in another language and recalled later in the language then dominant.

A model for bilingual recall is suggested by studies of mediated associations. Bastian has shown that the learning of eagle-sickness, for instance, facilitates later acquisition of eagle-health, presumably through the covert mediation of sickness-health.[1] Similar response-mediation can occur during naming of non-verbal stimuli. In a study of color-naming, the author showed that the names offered by bilinguals differ from those given by monolinguals, and that these were the names with the shortest response-time, or their translations.[2] A covert response seems to mediate a translation when response-language is restricted by instructions.

Similarly, it may be expected that in the naming of pictured items it will be found that: (1) the language of shorter reaction-time is the language of covert response when overt language is restricted; (2) covert responses in a different language from that used in the overt responses reduce recall in the latter language; (3) spontaneous translation is more probable into the dominant language than into the subordinate language.

In the following discussion, major items are those normally named more quickly in the dominant language and minor items are those named more quickly in the subordinate language.

The first two hypotheses lead to the prediction that major items will be recalled best when named in the dominant language and recalled in that language, as in Sector D of Table 1. Similarly, for minor items recall will be facilitated in Sector A. If covert practice had no effect, then there would be no difference between major and minor items.

Spontaneous translation into the dominant language at the time of recall would facilitate recall in Sector C for both kinds of items. When would recall be worst? Presumably in Sector B, where items must be learned in one language and recalled in another, without the help of translation into the dominant language. This condition should be especially poor for major items, which are not even covertly practiced in the language of recall in Sector B. When items are pooled, Sector C should be optimal and B worst.

Table 1.   Predicted Recall under Different Conditions

("Minor" and "Major" refer to the type of items learned. Conditions marked "plus" are above the mean of all conditions.)

Language of recall	Naming language	
	subordinate	dominant
Subordinate	A	B
	Minor+	Minor−
		Major−
Dominant	C	D
	Minor+	Major+
	Major+	

The above predictions might be compared to those based on other premises. If skill in the response-language alone mattered, then dominant recall should always be superior. If overt practice alone mattered, then the conditions in which the language is switched—Sectors B and C—would always be inferior. In neither case would major and minor items be different.

In a preliminary experiment on 16 "English-dominant" and 16 "Navaho-dominant" Navahos, tested on the reservation, sets of pictures were named and recalled under the four conditions described in Table 1. The pictures were half of Indian and half of Anglo objects. It was found that better recall occurred whenever S was asked to recall in his dominant language ($p < 0.05$). Sector B was worse than all other conditions combined ($p < 0.03$) and Sector C was better than the other conditions combined ($p < 0.05$). Since Ss paced themselves, they were exposed longer to the items most difficult to name in the designated language. This varying exposure-time makes interpretation somewhat difficult. It was, however, clear that the pattern of ease of recall for the Navaho-dominant was the mirror-image of that of the English-dominant. Thus the pattern was the same regardless of which particular language was dominant.

Method

General. In the experiment reported below Italian-Americans were first given tests to establish control over individual differences. After an initial interview, they were given a language-dominance test to determine their relative skill in Italian and English, and an intrusion-test of spontaneous translation in recall. The learning experiment took place several weeks after the initial tests. The Ss, 32 in number, were assigned in a factorial design, according to dominant language, high or low intrusion-score, language of learning in the experimental session, and language of recall in the experimental session. There were two Ss in each cell of this design.

Language-dominance test. A set of 120 drawings of simple objects namable in both Italian and English was presented in a six-page booklet to each S. He was instructed to name the first three pages in English, then the next three in Italian. Then the procedure

was repeated, reversing the order. The total response-time in Italian
and in English for each set of three pages was recorded, together with
the number of items S could not name. The difference in the response-
times in log seconds for the naming of the same sets of puctures in
English and in Italian constituted the test of relative dominance. As
a validation, a similar test constructed for Navahos had yielded a correlation of 0.72 between English dominance and years of schooling.
Schooling is the principal, but not the only source of English training
for Navahos. In addition, other evidence on the background of the
Italians supported the validity of the test.

Intrusion-test. To permit control over individual differences
in the probability of spontaneous translation between the two languages,
a further test was constructed. Six pages of five pictures each were
presented, and Ss named alternate pages in each language. At the
end, they were asked to recall as many pictures as possible. The
proportion of switches to the other language than the one in which the
picture was named was used as a measure of intrusions for each language. This measure was used for a balanced design, a high-intrusion
and low-intrusion S being assigned to each experimental condition.

Learning. To guarantee that all Ss could name the pictures
readily in both languages, the 18 pictures in the learning experiment
were chosen from the 120-picture test of language-dominance. Only
those pictures were selected which all Ss had named on both languages.
This criterion guaranteed that the pictures were unambiguous, and that
the terms were all common in both languages. While the actual
exposure-time during naming in the test of language-dominance was
not controlled, it is highly probable that these items, being the easiest,
were named the most rapidly of the items in the test, hence effects
on the learning task several weeks later would be minimal.

At the learning session, S was instructed to name the pictures
in a specified language, and told that he would be asked to recall them
later. Instructions were in English, due to the dialectal variations
of Italian, but Ss had heard E speak standard Italian. The series was
in the same order for all Ss, and was shown twice, with a 6-sec.
interval between items. The response-time for naming each item was
recorded. During the interval between learning and recall, Italian
adjectives were assigned to Italian nonsense-words. After 6-min.

Ss were instructed to recall as many items as they could in a specified language. There was no time-limit on the period of recall.

Classification of items. After the collection of the data, the items which were easier to name in Italian than in English were identified empirically. For the Italian-dominant Ss, six items were found which had shorter latencies in Italian than in English. These were Items 2, 5, 7, 11, 14, and 15 of the 18-item list. The six items named relatively faster in English were Items 3, 4, 6, 10, 12, 13. This categorization was based on a comparison of average latencies for the same items for the group which named in Italian and the group which named in English. Within each group, when the rank-order of latencies for different items was compared, the order was appropriate—for example, the Italian items had the shortest latencies for the group speaking Italian and the English items the longest. There was a rank-order correlation of 0.60 between the latencies of these 12 items in the group speaking English and in that speaking Italian. This consistency suggested that a stable set of major and of minor items had been identified. These six items in each group were used in the analysis of results reported below.

In the English-dominant group, only three items were named more quickly in Italian than in English, and the rank-order of latencies of the items within the two groups was uncorrelated. No separate analysis of major and minor items was, therefore, possible for the English-dominant Ss.

The design did not counterbalance order of pictures. Since the major pictures were farther from the middle of the list for the Italian-dominants than were the minor pictures, they should have been remembered better, if the items were otherwise equated.[3] The predictions at issue concerned comparisons between conditions within each set of items separately, however, and across conditions serial order of items was constant.

Subjects. Interviews and tests were given to Italian-Americans in Boston, aged 20-80 yr. The extreme groups in dominance in the two languages were selected to comprise two groups of 16 Ss.

It was found that the two groups differed in many important respects. The Italian-dominants were older. None had come to this country before the age of 9 yr. They spoke Italian most of the time. None of the English-dominants came to this country after the age of 6 yr. and most were born here. They spoke English in school, with friends and siblings, learning Italian from older relatives but mixing it liberally with English. They were thus compound bilinguals whereas the Italian-dominants, who learned Italian from monolinguals, were more coördinate and thus less likely to have associative links between the languages.[4]

Results

There were no significant differences in recall under the various conditions for the English-dominant Ss. The Italian-dominant Ss did however, display differential recall under various conditions. Minor (English) items were most often recalled when they had been named in English, regardless of the language of recall, (F = 9.1), and there was an interaction between the language of learning and of recall (F = 5.8), with language-switching reducing recall.[5] These differences are significant at the 5% level.

Discussion

The results have supported the analysis of covert naming during learning. If covert naming were unimportant, there would be similar patterns of facilitation for major and minor items. In the Italian-dominant group, however, Condition A was facilitative only for minor items and Condition D for major items (see Table 1). If there is only an overt effect of practice there should have been equal facilitation for all items in both conditions.

The significantly lower recall of major items in Condition B also demonstrates the presence of covert naming, since this is the only situation in which there is assumed to be neither covert practice in the language of recall nor translation.

Table 2.   Mean Number of Items Recalled

Recall	English-dominant (N = 16)		Italian-dominant (N = 16)	
	Sub. naming	Dom. naming	Sub. naming	Dom. naming
Subordinate	9.50	11.25	7.50	5.50
Dominant	9.00	9.25	9.00	6.75

Table 3.   Mean Number of Major and Minor Items Recalled

(Ambiguous items were excluded from this analysis, hence the
totals do not equal those in Table 2.)

(Italian-dominant Ss)

Recall	Minor items		Major items	
	Sub. naming	Dom. naming	Sub. naming	Dom. naming
Subordinate	2.50	1.50	2.25	1.25
Dominant	3.75	1.75	2.50	3.50

The differences were significant only for the Italian-dominant
bilinguals, and in the pilot study, for the Navahos, who had learned
and used the languages under "coördinate" conditions, separating the
audiences and settings of use. Such conditions maximize differences
of meaning,[6] and minimize the probability of intrusions.[7] For the
English-dominant compound bilinguals, however, strong associative
relationships between the two languages were likely as a result of
the fact that the languages were used interchangeably with the same
speakers and situations. Practice in one language then induces practice in the other by mediated generalization, and consequently recall-
conditions would not differ.

This finding places an important restriction on the generality
of language-effects on recall. Language will differentially influence

recall only if the speaker addresses monolinguals frequently enough so that there is minimal probability of cross-language association.

Would these findings also apply to incidental learning? Probably so, since there is greater generalization under intentional learning.[8] Response-generalization extending to the other language would destroy the differential effects found in this study, so it seems reasonable to assume that under incidental conditions the differences would be at least as great. Indeed, it has been reported by Doob that for verbal statements there is differential recall under conditions of incidental learning, when languages of learning and recall are varied.[9]

Summary

Italian bilinguals were tested for recall of pictorial material using English and Italian during learning and during recall. Pictures easier to name in the bilingual's more fluent language were recalled significantly more often in that language regardless of the language of learning. Optimal circumstances for recall of such pictures were learning and recall in the dominant language, if exposure-time during learning was controlled. The worst condition for recall was learning in the dominant language and recall in the other language.

Pictures easier to name in the bilingual's less fluent language were recalled equally well in either language, but learning in the subordinate language was superior.

Thus it appears that under natural conditions, where material would be learned in the language most appropriate to it, the optimal recall-language is always the language dominant at the time of recall. These differences between conditions appeared only for coördinate bilinguals, who had had an opportunity to learn both languages from monolinguals.

These differences fit the following assumptions: (a) there are covert responses in the language of easier naming, when overt language is restricted; (b) covert responses in the same language as the overt response strengthen recall in that language; (c) spontaneous translation is more probable into the dominant language.

NOTES

This research was supported by the Social Science Research Council as part of the 1955-56 Southwestern Project in Comparative Psycholinguistics, directed by John B. Carroll.

[1] J. R. Bastian, Response chaining in verbal transfer, Minnesota studies in the role of language in behavior, Technical Report No. 13, 1957, 44-45.

[2] Susan Ervin, Semantic shift in bilingualism, The American Journal of Psychology, 74, 1961, 233-241.

[3] James Deese, Serial organization in the recall of disconnected items, Psychol. Reports, 3, 1957, 577-582.

[4] Susan Ervin and C. E. Osgood, Second language learning and bilingualism, in C. E. Osgood and Thomas Sebeok (eds.), Psycholinguistics, J. abnorm. soc. Psychol., Suppl., 49, 1954, 139-146; W. E. Lambert, J. Havelka, and C. Crosby, The influence of language-acquisition contexts on bilingualism, J. abnorm. soc. Psychol., 56, 1958, 239-244.

[5] In the analysis of variance, third-order interactions and within-S variance were pooled as an estimate of residual variance. For the resulting $1/9$ df., $F_{0.05} = 5.12$, and $F_{0.01} = 10.56$.

[6] Lambert, Havelka, and Crosby, op. cit., 242.

[7] Discrepancy of skill in two languages, as assessed by a test of language-dominance, is only reflected in intrusions in speech where there is a relatively frequent conversation with bilinguals, according to evidence of Ervin, The verbal behavior of bilinguals: The effect of language of report upon the Thematic Apperception-Test stories of adult French bilinguals, Unpublished Doctoral dissertation, University of Michigan, 1955, 155.

[8] Leo Postman and P. A. Adams, Studies in incidental learning: VI. Intraserial interference, J. exp. Psychol., 54, 1957, 153-167.

[9] L. W. Doob, The effect of language on verbal expression and recall, Amer. Anthropol., 59, 1957, 88-100.

4 | Semantic Shift in Bilingualism

It has long been known that languages differ widely in their systems of categories for naming colors. Roberts and Lenneberg, in contrasting the English and Zuni systems, noted that bilingual Zuni terminology differed from that of monolinguals.[1] In this paper a method of prediction of bilingual color-terminology is proposed, on the basis of a simple theory of verbal mediation. The material is presented both as a test of an extension of this theory,[2] and as an explanation for the phenomenon of semantic interference, or shift in the meaning of terms under the influence of a second language.[3]

The semantics of color must be described in probabilities, both for individual usage and in a language community. It is likely that any system of categories applied to continuous physical dimensions has this property, both because of the difficulty in learning sharp discriminations, and because the perceptual conditions for speakers and reinforcing hearers are rarely identical. At the center of categories, where the probability of a particular name is at its peak, reaction-time is consistently shorter, as is shown in comparison of Figure 1 A with 1 B. Marbe's law thus applies to naming as well as to word-associations.[4] Brown and Lenneberg have shown that high correlations occur between measures of interpersonal agreement in naming (commonality), intrapersonal agreement, and speed of reaction, in monolinguals.[5]

Bilinguals, however, have available a larger set of possible responses. If a bilingual is asked to name colors in a particular language, he must suppress intrusions from the wrong language. If implicit responses occur in the suppressed language, response-probabilities in the overt language will be altered. Two circumstances

would increase the probability of such prior implicit responses:
(1) greater fluency in the suppressed language; (2) greater commonality for the primary name in the suppressed language than in the
overt language. The latter condition would occur if a color were near
a category-boundary in the overt language but central to a category
in the suppressed language, or if a single term were dominant in the
suppressed language for a color-range named by several terms in
the overt language.

If an implicit response occurs in the suppressed language,
it mediates a response in the overt language. When two responses
have often been emitted in the presence of the same external stimulus, they acquire a chained relation to each other, in the sense that
one later may elicit the other without the presence of the external
stimulus. Synonym word-associations in monolinguals and translation-
responses in bilinguals are examples. Experimentally, A-C, A-B
training has been shown to produce C-B and B-C linkage.[6] The most
probable terms in translation are not necessarily directionally sym-
metrical, since one term in one language may refer to the range of
several terms in the other.[7]

It should be possible, knowing the response-probabilities of
names in the two languages, a speaker's relative fluency, and trans-
lation-probabilities, to predict semantic shifts in terms.

Method

Subjects. On the Navaho reservation, 28 monolinguals, 21
English-dominant bilinguals, and 13 Navaho-dominant bilinguals were
tested. Most of the Ss were women, with ages ranging between 17
and 70 years. The English monolinguals tested were 41 San Quentin
prisoners, chosen for their low education. The Navahos were screened
for color-blindness after naming, by having them sort chips if deviant
categories were used. The San Quentin prisoners were given the
Ishihara test before color-naming.

Test of language dominance. Prior to the color-naming,
the bilinguals were given a picture-test for relative speed of naming
in the two languages, and those with faster responses in Navaho were

designated as Navaho-dominant. This test is described in greater
detail elsewhere. It has been validated by a correlation of 0.72 with
years of school, the chief source of training in English, and by its
significant relation to items recalled in the two languages in a recall-
test. The speed obtained in the experiment reported below, when
colors were named, did not correlate with the other indicators of
language-dominance.

Stimulus-materials. A set of the Farnsworth Munsell 100
Hue test was prepared with acetate protectors for the color caps.
These colors are designed to differ in hue but are the same in satura-
tion and brightness. Distances are perceptually equal between the
hues.[8] For testing purposes, every third chip was used.

Procedure. The colors were presented in random order,
but with no colors adjacent in the hue-sequence in immediate sequence
in testing. Ss were tested first in Navaho and later during the same
day in English. They were told to talk as if they were naming the
color to a friend.

Navaho instructions were tape-recorded. They were prepared by an experienced interpreter, and literally and freely back-
translated before a final version was recorded. An interpreter was
present to answer questions. Both the name offered and the reaction-
time were recorded. If no name was given in 30 seconds, the chip
was inserted into the series and presented later.

Data-analysis. The reaction-times were converted into
log. seconds and then the scores for each individual were standardized, to adjust for inter-individual differences. Names were tallied
according to the head term in a construction. These were identified
in Navaho by suffixes and in English either by suffix or order. Thus
blue-green was a green and greenish blue was a blue. Where a pause
occurred, as in blue...green, only the first term was counted. No
other mergers of terms were used.

Results

(1) Monolingual. The key points of difference between the
monolingual groups were first established as a basis for predicting

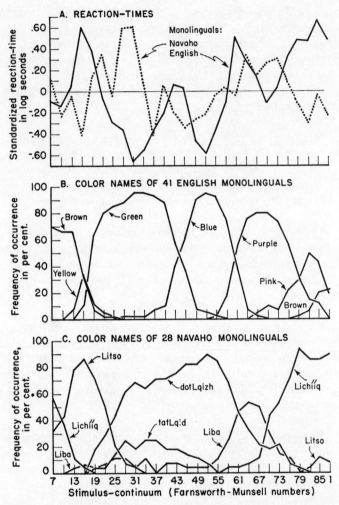

Fig. 1. Diagrammatical display of semantic shift in bilingualism.

points of semantic shift. The major differences between the two
monolingual groups were as follows.

(a) <u>Yellow</u>. The yellow range is more difficult to name in
English. The Navaho term <u>Litso</u> occurs over a wider range than
<u>yellow</u> and reaches a much higher strength at its peak.[9] Color 16
was the peak in both languages, but 89% of the Navahos called it <u>Litso</u>,
whereas 34% of the Anglos called it <u>yellow</u>. The color is more desat-
urated than a good yellow, and is called tan, beige, green, and brown.
English monolinguals took longer to name Color 16 than any other
color except 84. Their reaction-time was considerably longer than
that of the Navahos ($p < 0.0001$). On Color 16, implicit naming in
Navaho would be predicted for bilinguals when speaking English, increasing the probability of <u>yellow</u>.

(b) <u>Yellow boundary</u>. The boundary between yellow and green
is nearer green in Navaho than it is in English. For English monolinguals the transition is at Color 17; for Navaho, at Color 23.

It may be expected that at Color 17 the Navaho term will intrude for bilinguals speaking English and at Color 25 the English
response will intrude at the Navaho sessions. Since the translation
terms of <u>Litso</u> is less ambiguous than that for <u>green</u>, the impact of
English intrusion at Color 25 should be less than that of Navaho at
Color 17. Responses to the intermediate colors should be determined
by the dominant language of the speaker, since these colors are near
a boundary in both languages. Thus a Navaho-dominant speaker should
more often have an implicit Navaho response when speaking English
than an English-dominant speaker, and hence call the intermediate
colors <u>yellow</u>.

The intrusion of <u>green</u> when bilinguals speak Navaho should
cause maximal interference farther into the yellow range for the
English-dominant than for the Navaho-dominant bilinguals. The intrusion of <u>Litso</u> at the English session should also have the effect of
producing delay for the Navaho-dominant farther into the green range
than for the English-dominant. In brief, the peak delay should be
farther toward the green hues in the Navaho-dominant in both languages.

(c) DotLqizh. One term in Navaho, dotLqizh, refers to the range of three in English: green, blue, and purple. Though modifiers and some distinctive terms occur in this range, making terminological distinction possible, dotLqizh is the dominant term for the entire range from 25 to 67.

In English, the term green reaches a peak in the area of Colors 31-34, being used by 95% of the Navaho monolinguals. The corresponding Navaho term, tatLqid has a peak of 25% at Colors 34 and 37. The transition between green and blue occurs between Colors 44 and 45; there is no such point of shift in Navaho, since the distinctive term for green is of such low frequency. Thus the Navaho who learns English must learn a new discrimination—the transition between green and blue. It would be expected that the greater his knowledge of English, the more stable this discrimination would be, and the closer it would come to the English norm for the transition.

In Navaho, if green mediates his response, he may increase the frequency of its translation-terms, whatever these may be. These terms would be less likely to occur beyond Color 45, since blue would then mediate the response.

(d) Purple. The term purple has no corresponding category in Navaho. The large domain of dotLqizh reaches a transition to Lichíiq (red) at Color 69, in English the peak of the category of purple. Purple is bounded on one side with blue, with a transition between Colors 60 and 61, and on the other side with pink, with the transition at Color 79.

When bilinguals speak Navaho, there should be no influence from English because mediation by purple has no unambiguous translational term. In English, however, the domain of purple should be reduced by the mediation of dotLqizh and Lichíiq which have other, more probable, translational terms. This effect should be stronger in Navaho-dominant bilinguals.

(e) Gray. Navahos translate Liba as gray. Liba occurred throughout the entire range of hues with low frequency, but was offered by 46% of the Navahos for Color 61. Gray was used rarely in

English, its maximal frequency, 7%, occurring at Colors 64 and 67. If Liba mediates a response in English to Color 61, the frequency of gray should be increased in bilinguals speaking English, especially Navaho-dominant bilinguals. There would be no effect of English on Navaho, since Color 61 is at the blue-purple boundary.

(2) Bilingual results. The results for bilinguals are presented separately for each of the differences reported. Reported probabilities are one-tailed.

(a) Yellow. The proportion of Navaho bilinguals using yellow as a name for Color 16 was significantly greater ($p < 0.0005$ by X^2) than the proportion of monolinguals naming the color yellow ($p < 0.0005$ by X^2). The lack of competing vocabulary does not seem a suitable explanation, since the chief competing term in the English monolinguals was brown (32%), and this term was used elsewhere by 38% of the Navaho-dominant and 52% of the English-dominant bilinguals.

(b) Yellow boundary. At Color 24, the prediction that green would mediate an increase in the probability of its translation-terms in Navaho was not borne out. At Color 18 however, Litso and yellow did predominate (see Table 1). For Color 21, in Navaho, but not in English, there was a significantly greater probability of using the terms for green (tatLqid and dotLqizh) for the English-dominant than for the Navaho-dominant bilinguals, ($p < 0.03$ by X^2). If the transitional point from yellow to green was estimated for every S. however, the average transition was different in English, being nearer green for the Navaho-dominant bilinguals ($p < 0.05$ by the t-test).

In further support of the different boundary for the two bilingual groups, in both languages the English-dominant bilinguals showed peak reaction-times farther toward the yellow direction than the Navaho-dominant bilinguals. In English this difference appeared in comparison of Colors 18 and 21, and in Navaho in Colors 21 and 24, ($p < .05$ by X^2).

(c) DotLqizh. In speaking English, the English-dominant bilinguals had more intra-individual and inter-individual agreement as to the blue-green boundary than the Navaho-dominant bilinguals.

Five per cent of the former and 58% of the latter group showed over-lap—that is, called a color green that was bluer than a color called blue. The most extreme case listed the colors from Nos. 24 to 70 as purple, purple, green, green, blue, green, green, green, green, blue, green, green, purple, green, and the rest purple. These were all hues which in Navaho could be called dotLqizh.

If an hypothetical transition-point for each S was calculated as the midpoint between the first blue and last green, the Navaho-dominant speakers had significantly greater variability, (p < 0.01).

There was no evidence of an increase in occurrence of tatLqid or of modifiers of dotLqizh among the bilinguals when naming colors in the green range. One reason for this is that the younger Navahos do not know the word tatLqid (p < 0.005 by the t-test); though learning theoretically should increase the occurrence of the translation-term, perhaps the weak initial strength of this term works against the effect. [10]

Among the Navaho-dominant bilinguals, there was signifi-cantly less variability in the use of translations of green than among the Navaho monolinguals, (p < 0.05). This finding suggests that if blue mediates a response, the probability of dotLqizh (a high-probability translation) is increased, but that if green mediates, either dotLqizh or tatLqid may be offered.

(d) Purple. If only the responses are counted which are either blue or purple, significantly more bilinguals call Color 63 blue

Table 1. Color Names and Response Times of Bilinguals

Domi-nance*	Re-sponse	Color											
		15			18			21			24		
		Y	G	log. sec.	Y	G	log. sec.	Y	G	log. sec.	Y	G	log. sec.
English	English	76%	0%	-.12	62%	0%	.08	48%	14%	-.21	10%	43%	+.12
Navaho	English	69%	0%	.19	62%	8%	-.14	46%	15%	.22	8%	62%	.30
English	Navaho	95%	0%	.15	67%	14%	.02	43%	57%	.63	14%	76%	.17
Navaho	Navaho	92%	0%	.00	69%	15%	.17	69%	15%	.18	24%	54%	.76

*Among the Ss, 21 were English dominant and 13 Navaho dominant.

than purple, (p < 0.0005 by X^2). If violet, lavender, and purple be compared to red and pink as responses to Color 78, significantly more bilinguals chose the latter names (p < 0.03 by X^2). Thus for bilinguals the category of purple and its variant names was more limited than in monolinguals. There was no evidence that the effect was significantly stronger in the Navaho-dominant bilinguals.

(e) Gray. In the range of Colors 57 to 69, the term gray was not only used more often by bilinguals than by monolinguals, but significantly more Navaho-dominant than English-dominant used it at least once (p < 0.05 by X^2).

Discussion

Support for the treatment of bilingual naming in terms of implicit responses linked by translation to overt speech has been shown in a variety of situations. These situations can be stated in a more generalized form.

(1) In a domain where one language had a single high-probability name and the other had none, the high-probability term and its translation dominated in bilinguals in both languages (Case a).

(2) Where the two languages differed in the boundary between two categories, both of which have translational terms, the bilingual's dominant language determined his boundary in both languages (Case b and a).

(3) Where a category in one language covered the domain of two categories in the other language, the boundary-point in the latter language was variable and reflected the degree of learning of that language (Case c).

(4) A domain divided into two categories in one language was divided into three in the other, with the added category straddling the boundary in the two-category language; bilinguals reduced the size of the middle category when speaking the language with three categories (Case d).

We began with the assumption that the vocabulary available in the two bilingual groups would be comparable and that the difference would be due to over-all response-strength differences between Navaho and English in the two groups. This assumption was mistaken. There was evidence that English vocabulary becomes richer in color terms, with a significant relation between the language dominance score and the probability of using such terms as <u>lavender</u> and <u>violet</u>, ($p < 0.005$ by <u>t</u>-test), which have lower frequency in English than <u>purple</u>. [11]

In the native language of the bilinguals, the same differential appears, with the older Navahos having a richer color vocabulary. The age-difference was significant with both <u>tatLqid</u> and <u>Liba</u>, though a higher proportion of the bilinguals used the latter term. Some of the English-dominant, young, bilinguals who used these terms did so incorrectly, by monolingual standards. Thus one S used <u>tatLqid</u> for Color 18 and 63 but for nothing in between; therefore, the probabilities of terms as translations may not be exactly predictable from monolinguals because knowledge of the vocabulary may not be identical.

It seems likely that processes similar to those found for colors would occur in semantic shifts in other domains of meaning, such as emotion-terms. It remains to be seen whether semantic shift in the case of referents forming discrete categories, rather than referents on a continuous dimension, can be as simply explained.

These findings do not imply that there is any difference in the color vision of bilingual and monolingual Ss at the time of immediate perception. Lenneberg's Zuni research showed no difference in Zuni and Anglo color-perception when there was simultaneous display of colors. [12] Both the arrangement of colors in order and tests of limens showed that acuity is not influenced by verbal categories. In conditions where verbal mediation may be expected to occur during performance, it is obvious, however, that bilinguals and monolinguals will differ.

Summary

Semantic shift was examined in the color-naming of Navaho bilinguals, in comparison with two monolingual groups. It was found

that the categories for color used by the bilinguals differed systematically from the monolingual norms. The differences could be predicted on the basis of an assumption of verbal mediation by the re-
sponse-term which is most rapid. Where the response-language
is restricted, the mediating term may be translated by the most
probable term. The explanation accounted for four types of monolingual norm-conflict: a term of high probability for a referent in
one language and not in the other; a difference in boundary between
two similar categories; use of two categories in one language for the
range of one category in the other; and the use of three categories in
one language for the range of two in the other.

NOTES

This study was made possible by the sponsorship of the Southwest
Project in Comparative Psycholinguistics, of the Social Science Research Council, under the direction of J. B. Carroll. The assistance
of Arnold Horowitz, Herbert Landar, and Albert Silverstein, who
collected the monolingual data, is gratefully acknowledged. Figure 1
has appeared in Herbert Landar, S. M. Ervin, and A. E. Horowitz,
Navaho color categories, Language, 36, 1960, p. 380, and is reproduced by permission of the Linguistic Society of America. The latter
article presents a later phonemic version of color terminology.
   [1] E. H. Lenneberg and J. M. Roberts, The language of experience, Internat. J. Amer. Linguistics, Memoir 13, 1956, 22.
   [2] J. P. Foley, Jr., and M. A. Mathews, Mediated generalization and the interpretation of verbal behavior: IV. Experimental
study of the development of inter-linguistic synonym gradients, J.
exp. Psychol., 33, 1943, 188-200; W. A. Russell and L. H. Storms,
Implicit verbal chaining in paired-associate learning, ibid., 49, 1955,
287-293; J. R. Bastian, Response chaining in verbal transfer, Studies
in the Role of Language in Behavior, Technical Rep., 13, 1957, 44-
45.
   [3] Semantic shift has been discussed by linguists, especially
Uriel Weinreich, Languages in Contact, Linguistic Circle of New
York, 1953, 47-62; and Einar Haugen, The Norwegian Language in
America, University of Pennsylvania Press, 1953, Vol. 2, 459-474.
   [4] According to Marbe, the more common responses in word-
association have shorter latencies. There is a summary of Marbe's

work and later substantiations in C. E. Osgood, Method and Theory in Experimental Psychology, Oxford University Press, 1953, pp. 722-723.

[5] R. W. Brown and E. H. Lenneberg, A study in language and cognition, J. abnorm. soc. Psychol., 49, 1954, 454-462.

[6] P. M. Kjeldergaard and D. L. Horton, An experimental analysis of associative factors in stimulus equivalence, response equivalence, and chaining paradigms. Studies in Verbal Behavior, University of Minnesota, No. 3, 1960, 21-36.

[7] S. M. Ervin, Information transmission with code translation, J. abnorm. soc. Psychol., Suppl., 49, 1954, 185-192.

[8] Dean Farnsworth, The Farnsworth-Munsell 100 hue and dichotomous tests for color vision, J. opt. soc. Amer., 33, 1943, 568-576.

[9] In transcribing the Navaho words, the following conventions have been used: "L" refers to a voiceless lateral spirant—a breathy, whispered "l"; "q" refers to a glottal stop or glottalized release—the initial consonant when "Ann" is shouted, or the consonant between the two syllables of the negative "hunh-unh"; "zh" refers to the final consonant of "rouge"; and acute accents refer to raised pitch.

[10] In a personal communication, Herbert Landar, who has been studying medical terms intensively, has pointed out a reason for the low frequency of tatLqid. The word can be analyzed at ta-, "water," and -tLqid, "flatus." Some Navahos will not use the word tatLqid in polite conversation for this reason, though the meaning of the combined term is "moss, algae, or water-scum." It is likely that the more acculturated Navahos would be more sensitive about this, hence the English-dominant would be least likely to use it.

[11] E. L. Thorndike and Irving Lorge, A Teacher's Word Book of 30,000 Words, 1944. Purple is rated 2 B, violet 3 A, lavender 8. Both violet and lavender were rare among the San Quentin prisoners.

[12] E. H. Lenneberg, Color naming, color recognition, color discrimination: a re-appraisal, 1961.

5 | Language and TAT Content in Bilinguals

Spoken language is, almost without exception, learned in a social setting. This setting includes material and behavioral referents for speech, rewards for speaking in a certain way about specific topics, and feelings towards those who hear and towards those who provide models of speech. Speakers in different language communities will have different things to say, and we may expect that learning a language carries with it learning of content.

Bilinguals provide a natural control for the investigation of content differences. Lambert, Havelka, and Crosby (1958) have shown that for "house," "drink," "poor," and "me," semantic-differential meanings differed for French-Canadian bilinguals. The pooled differences were significant only for those who learned the two languages in different physical settings. Since different social surroundings may occur in the same region, it is possible that the meanings of emotion or social-role terms might differ even for childhood bilinguals who learn two languages in the same physical surroundings.

With the purpose of studying content differences in speech, the present study compared two sets of Thematic Apperception Test (TAT) stories told by bilinguals about the same pictures at a French session and at an English session. The choice of languages was dictated by necessity (the author's ability to speak English and French) but it should be recognized that the languages and language community chosen were in some respects poor for testing the hypothesis of systematic content difference. The relationship of French and English makes generalization between them more likely; middle-class French and American cultures have many similarities; many of the bilinguals

in the Washington, D. C. , French community speak both languages
with the same interlocutors. For all of these reasons content differences would be minimal.

Since economy precluded testing appropriate monolingual
control groups, predictions regarding TAT differences were based
on data about culture differences made available by Maccoby (1952)
and by Métraux and Mead (1954), corroborated by other informants.
Since that time, Wylie (1958) has confirmed some of the generalizations. A set of assumptions regarding the relation between TAT content and culture permitted specific predictions.

These assumptions were derived principally from Sanford's
(Sanford, Adkins, Miller, Cobb, et al. , 1943) study of the relation
between school children's TAT stories and ratings of their behavior.
In interpreting his findings, he proposed that: behavior that does
not conflict with social sanctions appears in fantasy only if there is
insufficient ability or opportunity for overt expression (e. g. , achievement and dominance); behavior conflicting with social sanctions
appears more often in fantasy expression; ambivalent cultural pre-
scriptions lead to more primitivism in fantasy than in nonfantasy expression.

Because of the possibility, suggested by experimental work
with the TAT, that the testing conditions might influence the extent
to which content conflicted with social sanctions, it was decided to
conduct testing individually, orally, and face-to-face. In these conditions, while socially prohibited needs might be expressed, it seemed
that the form of expression might be governed by cultural differences
in preferred modes. Otherwise there was the risk that a greater pro-
hibition of a certain form of behavior in one of the two cultures would
have ambiguous implications for predicting TAT thematic differences.

Specific predictions of differences were these:

1. For women, greater achievement need in English. This
difference was based on the ambivalence of American education for
women toward the role of housewife, in contrast with the French view,
and on the greater sex-role difference in France.

2. More emphasis on recognition by others in English. This prediction was based on Kluckhohn's (1949) remark that emphasis is less on fulfillment and more on external success in America than in Europe. Riesman (1950) has made a statement which implies the contrary: he states that other-directed persons (such as Americans) want to "cut everyone down to size who stands up or stands out in any direction." The hypothesis of culture difference between France and America is thus a weak one.

3. More domination by elders in French stories. Parents were said to be more influential in selection of wives and jobs in France.

4. More withdrawal and autonomy in French stories. A characteristic mode of aggression reported within French families was silent withdrawal to do as one wished, perhaps contrary to the wishes of another. Wylie (1958) reported that both children and adults after a disagreement tended to withdraw, and quoted a French child: "What we really do when we're angry is to go away from each other and not speak anymore [p. 199]."

5. More verbal aggression toward parents in English stories. Verbal attacks on elders are more strictly prohibited in France than in the United States, though Wylie reported considerable variation between families in the extent to which threats of punishment for verbal disrespect were carried out.

6. More verbal aggression toward peers in French stories. There is considerable admiration for verbal prowess in France. Wylie (1958) reports that this was true even in a rural village. French education emphasizes skill in oral argument, and children "are allowed to threaten and insult each other as much as they like [p. 50]."

7. More physical aggression in English stories. In France, children are immediately separated by adults if they begin to fight, and both are punished, according to Wylie, regardless of the culprit (p. 81). Presumably the culture difference would be greater for men than for women, since physical aggression is prohibited for American as well as French girls. However, there were too few men in the sample to permit a breakdown by sex.

8. More guilt in French stories and more frequent attempts
to escape blame in English stories. This prediction was based in
part on the age difference for acquisition of the two languages, on
the assumption that a language learned in childhood would be more
strongly associated with internalized values than one learned during
adult life. Further, Métraux and Mead's (1954) informants reported
greater emphasis in France on internal control of behavior by adults,
rejection of social pressure as a legitimate basis for action, and more
strictness and consistency in child rearing.

In terms of the evidence of culture difference, the strongest
evidence, most widely confirmed, concerns the forms of aggression
preferred. The weakest evidence concerns the difference in the need
for recognition.

Method

Subjects

Sixty-four adult French persons, raised in metropolitan
France in middle-class families, were found in Washington, D. C.
All had lived in the United States for more than 4 years and had
learned English primarily from Americans. All of them spoke both
languages fluently, the average number of years in the United States
being 12. Forty were or had been married to Americans. The mean
age was 38 years. Two-thirds were women.

Background Interview

An extensive interview determined how English was learned,
how often and to whom both language were spoken, and how much contact there had been with Americans. Scores from this interview were
used to evaluate contact, amount of mixture, or switching of languages
with the same interlocutors, degree of current French usage, education, and attitude toward linguistic interference. Details of this interview and other methodological information can be found in Ervin
(1955).

Language Dominance Test

As a test of relative skill in French and English, a tape-recorded word-association test was constructed. The language of the stimulus word was varied at random in a list of words in various semantic domains, with frequency of the words in the respective languages matched. The subjects were instructed to offer orally an association to each word in the same language as the stimulus word. The score consisted of the median French reaction time in log seconds minus the median English time, when corrections had been made for translation responses and other language switches. The average subject, according to this test, was slightly French dominant. [1]

Materials and Procedure

Nine standard TAT pictures which elicit themes related to the hypotheses were selected: 1, 2, 3BM, 8BM, 6BM, 4, 13MF, 7BM, and 18GF. They were presented in the above order. Subjects were given instructions to tell what was happening, what had happened in the past, what would happen in the future, and what the characters were thinking and feeling. In addition, at the second session, they were instructed to tell a different story if they recalled the first. Stories were to be 3 minutes long; a 3-minute glass was turned before the subject as he began each story.

The same examiner appeared at both sessions, speaking only French at the French session from the moment the subject appeared. The instructions were tape recorded in the appropriate language, and all responses were tape recorded. Analysis of content and of linguistic features was based on a verbatim typescript.

Design

Two groups were matched on the basis of sex, age, education, and language dominance. In addition, it was found that they were matched, on the average, in years in the United States, age at which English was learned, amount of contact with Americans, and amount of language switching. One group was instructed to tell French stories at the first session, and the other group told stories in English. There was a 6-week interval between the sessions for each subject.

Content Analysis

A quantitative system of analysis was adapted from those devised by McClelland, Atkinson, Clark, and Lowell (1953) and by Aron (1949). Each time a theme appeared in a story with a new actor (hero) and target of action, it was given a quantitative score. Thus a theme might be scored several times if in a given story the actor or object changed. If a picture "pulled" a particular theme—e. g., physical aggression in 18GF—each occurrence of the theme received a lower base score than if it was a rare theme for that picture. If there was more than a simple occurrence of the theme—if there was adjectival or adverbial elaboration, addition of details, or repetition of the theme—the value might be increased by one or two points.

The reliability scores reported are product-moment correlations based on scores by picture for each theme. In the abbreviated category definitions below, reliabilities are presented in parentheses. The first is the reliability (product-moment correlation) of scores by two different coders, and the second the intracoder reliability with a 2-month interval. Since all coding in both languages was done by the author, the intracoder reliability is important.

Achievement (.77, .88). The hero is industrious. He fantasies hard work, studiousness, invention, attainment, accomplishment, reaching a career goal. He wants to accomplish great things. He prepares for or has achieved a profession, or a skilled occupation.

Recognition (.90, .81). The hero fantasies greatness, public acclaim, recognition by others, applause, prestige, renown. He seeks approval, boasts, performs in public, competes, strives to rise in status as a primary goal. He is a master; he is great.

Dominance (.84, .84). The hero tries to influence another by pleading or persuasion. He leads, directs, guides, advises, cajoles, but does not bring undue pressure, threaten withdrawal, or argue.

Withdrawal and autonomy (.69, .74). The hero does something bad, violates moral standards, or acts in a way contrary to the wishes of love objects. He makes them suffer or knowingly disappoints them. He expresses anger or dislike by turning away from, snubbing, or rejecting a love object.

Verbal aggression (.88, .87). The hero verbally expresses scorn, contempt, disdain. He quarrels, is involved in a misunderstanding or discussion (a more disputatious term in French than in English, but scored as verbal aggression in both languages).

Physical aggression (.81, .93). The hero fights, attacks physically, or injures, or kills another human being.

Guilt (.44, .73). The hero evaluates on the basis of moral principle. He avoids or regrets out of duty, moral standards, religious scruples. He resists temptation, or experiences anguish or regret. (The results will not be reported for this category because of the low reliability.)

Escaping blame (.70, .99). The hero seeks to avoid external censure or punishment by refraining from reprehensible acts, or by resorting to denial, deceit, or flight. He verbally defends himself against censure, proclaims his innocence, justifies his action.

Translation Control

Since there was a possibility of systematic bias in the scoring in the two languages, one of each subject's stories in each language was translated. These translations were given the appearance and style or originals, and were indistinguishable except by checking a code number. In the first phase of coding, the originals were removed, and the translations were mixed with the untranslated versions of each story for coding. In the second phase, 2 months later, the originals of the translated stories were mixed with other copies of previously coded stories for the intracoder reliability check.

Three kinds of checks were used to test coder bias. First, the intracoder reliabilities were compared for stories scored in the same language twice, and for stories scored in the original and in translation. It was found that achievement was scored more reliably when the story was in the same language both times. Reliability correlations differed at the .05 level. Escaping blame was scored more reliably in the same language at the .01 level. Thus it appeared that changing language might have led to different scoring standards. Such a difference might not be significant if it was unrelated to the hypotheses.

The total amount of each variable found in the originals and in the translations of the same stories were then compared to see if the differences in reliability were systematic. There were no significant differences.

Finally, the frequencies of the variables in all the stories coded in the first phase were compared to see if the stories coded in translation differed from those coded in the original language. There were no significant differences for any of the variables.

Results

Content frequencies for each subject were weighted by the reciprocal of the total length in each language, since the stories in French were usually longer. The distributions of the variables were very skewed, medians of zero occurring for all but three variables. These distributions reflected the fact that some themes were readily elicited by the pictures, others not so readily. One might characterize the pictures as differing in their power to bring out thematic material above a threshold of overt speech. Presumably other pictures might have elicited responses from all subjects, and allowed a measure of session differences for all subjects for each theme. In order to make an analysis of variance possible in spite of the skewed distributions, the assumption was made that subjects who gave no responses relevant to a given theme at either session were randomly distributed as to session differences. Since the relative strength of their responses was in effect not measured, there was no way of knowing whether appropriate pictures would have elicited more thematic material in French or in English. In calculation of the analysis of variance, for each theme, subjects were removed who never used the theme at either session. For Physical Aggression and Withdrawal-Autonomy this adjustment was not necessary, and all subjects were included. The remaining frequencies were transformed to the logarithm of X + 1.

The analysis of variance was a Lindquist (1956) Type I design, with the group to which the subject was assigned a between-subject effect, and the session and language as within-subject effects. Because of the four-celled Latin-square design, there was confounding of certain types of interaction. The effects of language in this design appear as an interaction of session with group, since Session I is in French for one group and in English for the other. There is likely to be an interaction of language with session for certain variables, however, and this interaction cannot be isolated.

With these limitations, three variables showed significant language effects in the predicted direction: Verbal Aggression to Peers, Withdrawal-Autonomy, and Achievement. In addition, there was a significant group difference in Recognition, with no effect of language at all.

The following stories will illustrate the difference between the French and English versions by the same subject, a 27-year-old Frenchwoman, married to an American, who spoke English with her husband and child. Most of her friends were Americans. She was a full-time clerk, using English for the most part in her work. The stories were told for Picture 4 in the Murray series.

[French, first session] She seems to beg him, to plead with him. I don't know if he wants to leave her for another woman or what, or if it's her who has...but she seems to press against him. I think he wants to leave her because he's found another woman he loves more, and that he really wants to go, or maybe it's because she... she's deceived him with another man. I don't know whose fault it is but they certainly seem angry. Unless it's in his work, and he wants to go see someone and he wants to get in a fight with someone, and she holds him back and doesn't like him to get angry. I don't know, it could be many things....

Table 1. Weighted Content Differences in TAT Stories

Content variable	N^a	32 French-first M^b		32 English-first M		df	F for language^c
		F_1	E_2	F_2	E_1		
Achievement (women)	21	14.3	26.6	21.1	25.1	1/40	6.148*
Recognition	24	4.7	4.8	7.3	8.3	1/46	—^{d}
Dominance to Younger	27	5.3	4.4	4.8	3.2	1/52	2.051
Withdrawal–Autonomy	32	30.5	24.8	25.5	21.0	1/62	9.234**
Verbal							
Aggression to Elders	17	3.6	4.4	1.5	2.2	1/32	1.682
Aggression to Peers	20	5.1	4.9	4.7	3.2	1/38	5.333*
Physical Aggression	32	10.8	15.3	12.3	11.0	1/62	1.709
Escaping Blame	16	2.3	3.2	2.3	3.8	1/30	3.926

a N in each group after cases with zero in both sessions had been removed.

b Means for the weighted raw scores of the total sample of 32 in each group.

c Lindquist's Type I analysis, with Language as a within–subject effect, and a within–subject error term derived from the within–subject sum of squares minus Session and Language.

d The Group effect here had an F of 5.503, p<.025.

* p < .05.

** p < .01.

[English, second session] Oh, that one. In the past, well I think it was a married couple, average, and he got out of the Army and got himself a job or something like that or has decided he would go to college. He's decided to get a good education and maybe after he would have a better job and be able to support his wife much better, and everything would come out for the best. He keeps on working and going to college at night some of the time. Now let me see. He finally decided that was too much. He found he was too tired, he was discouraged and something went wrong with his work. The boss told him that, well, his production had decreased or something like that, that he didn't get enough sleep or something like that, that he couldn't carry on studies and working at the same time. He'd have to give something up, and he's very discouraged and his wife tries to cheer him up. Now, let me see. And eventually he'll probably keep on working his way through and finally get his diploma and get a better job and they will be much happier and... well, his wife will have helped him along too and as he was discouraged and all and was willing to give up everything, she boosted him up. That's all.

In French the picture elicited a variety of themes of aggression and striving for autonomy. In English the heroine supports the husband in his achievement strivings.

The subject below was a 33-year-old bachelor, with higher education in both countries. Most of his friends were Americans, but he used French in his work. The picture was 13MF.

[English, first session] Now this is a horrible story. This is one of those, one of those things that happen in married life when the husband suddenly finds out his own intelligence, his own way of living, his own... life altogether has gone to pieces. There is no weapon around in the room. But there is the hand which have murdered. There is the guilt of having in a moment of horrible passion, of aberration of mind when she was telling him that she loved the other, that he was more intelligent, that he was more beautiful, that he let himself go and put his fingers around her neck. And her laughter became more and more raucous. He had pressed down his thumbs and then he has gotten up, has dressed. The horror of the moment becomes entirely obvious to him. He knows that the next thing he will have to do is to go to the police and report it—maybe to flee, maybe

to take his car and drive away. What kind of a life that will be. Constantly this thing in front of him. A dead body in the bed half-naked.
Over the sheets. Police. Discovery. Warrants. Sirens. Shame.
Flight. And perhaps prison and perhaps death. All this goes through
his mind as he wonders where to go.

[French, second session] That's not a scene of a household
but of a false household. There are sometimes false households with
love, and there are those with hatred. This is a false household with
hatred. They detest each other, and cannot separate. They are held
together by physical attraction as much as by their quarrels, quarrels
which change their life from an everyday life, a life which becomes
infernal and at the same time different. If they had no quarrels they
would be nearly dead with boredom, and when they are separated they
desire only to see each other. He is still young, she already older,
and it is she basically who holds him. He, too young, doesn't want
to marry. She, older, wants only one thing, a home. Then, to oblige
this man to live with her, to found this home she wants, she tries to
hold him, to live with him at any price even if it is torture for both.
Their joy, their only joy is physical contact, and even this joy has
dangers of torture, of horror because for them this physical life is
a bond, a terrible bond, of which he particularly is aware. This is
how the woman holds him. He detests her and yet cannot detach himself. What we see here is the night when he has slept with her another
time, dressed, and while she sleeps, he wants to leave, to leave forever, to forget this inhuman life, tear the bonds which...one becomes
enslaved to this woman. He hides his eyes still, an instant of reflection, then takes his two books and goes out the door forever.

The last two stories contrast aggression by physical assault
with aggression by quarreling and escape. Certain characteristics
of the English story reflect mass media models.

Discussion

There are several alternative explanations for the differences
in content, none of which can as yet be excluded. One explanation is
that the subjects interpreted the instructions to speak a particular
language as an instruction to tell a story appropriate to that language.

Such an alternative could be tested by giving instructions to give appropriate stories, while the language is held constant. No such control was used.

A second possibility is that language affects classification of stimuli (Ervin, 1961b) and presumably recall of experience through the classification (Brown and Lenneberg, 1954), and that bilinguals have systematically different recall of past experience in two languages. If we extrapolate findings from recall of simple pictured objects (Ervin, 1961a), we would expect that use of the weaker language would have a strong biasing tendency toward recall of experiences originally codified in that language and appropriate to its culture.

Third, the thematic differences may reflect the respective mass media. Those who use projective tests to assess individual differences usually dismiss this explanation and point out that selective reading, viewing, and recall are pertinent to differences. But such an argument cannot be used when cross-cultural comparisons are at issue, since exposure is not then entirely self-selected but is culturally imposed, and there is little doubt that there are systematic differences in thematic frequencies in the mass media in different countries.

A fourth alternative is that the differences are not due merely to contrasts in the mass media, but to more pervasive differences in the verbal preoccupations and values expressed verbally in the two cultures. Thus it may be said that story themes may reflect the gossip, verbalized personal experiences, and verbal evaluations of the behavior of oneself and others which have been experienced in the two cultural settings.

It should be noted that much value learning comes from verbal sources; condemnation of murder is learned not by punishment for murder, but by verbal learning of what is classified as murder (not killing in war, for instance), and by learning emotional attitudes toward verbal descriptions of murder and what happens to murderers; only in part is it learned by generalization of punishment for committed aggressive acts. Nobody concerned with education, propaganda, advertising, or the study of opinion change through role playing would dismiss the possibility that verbal sequences may affect other behavior as well, and thus create consistency with nonverbal behavior. Some of the effect of verbal sequences on other behavior may come through what has come to be known as verbal mediation. Self-control through verbal mediation has been studied in relatively few situations (e.g., Luria, 1961). Since the origins of such mediation may lie in verbal training conditions in early childhood, which vary widely, we can expect significant group and individual differences in the extent to which verbal training affects nonverbal behavior.

Finally, quite aside from such mediational effects, it is possible that a shift in language is associated with a shift in social roles and emotional attitudes. Since each language is learned and usually employed with different persons and in a different context, the use of each language may come to be associated with shift in a large array of behavior. Presumably such changes would have to be assessed nonverbally, at least in part through physiological measures, to separate changes in emotional state from the verbal statements by which attitudes are usually judged.

The above explanations can be summarized as attributing content changes with language to different interpretation of instructions, differences in perception and in recall of experience, to the effects of mass media; to differences in verbally expressed values; and to role or attitude shifts associated with contacts with the respective language communities.

Do these findings mean that our subjects have two personalities? The answer seems to be yes, at least to the extent that personality involves verbal behavior and perhaps further. This is a result no more surprising than any other shift in behavior with social context. It happens that bilinguals have available an additional dimension of potential variation in behavior in comparison with the alternative roles available to monolinguals.

But language is a very important dimension. It is not yet clear whether the differences found in bilinguals are merely a special case of biculturalism, or whether the fact that language is a medium not only for social behavior but for internal storage of information and self-control implies that bilinguals have a means of insulating sets of alternative behavior more pervasive than mere contrasts in behavior for different social situations or audiences.

Our basis for choosing between these explanations is at present slight. The fact that certain variables yielded stronger content differences than others may provide a clue. For this purpose, we may exclude Recognition, for which the evidence for an actual culture contrast on which to base a prediction was from the start precarious. The largest differences appeared in Autonomy, Verbal Aggression against Peers, and Achievement in Women. The smallest appeared in Physical Aggression, Domination by Elders, and Verbal Aggression against Parents. One feature that the first three share is that they are likely to be the preoccupations of adults, in contrast with the second three. Quite simply, adults who move to the United States from France may observe cultural contrasts in those domains of interpersonal relations that they observe directly in consequence of the roles into which they are cast as adults. If some of this learning is second hand, from the mass media, then it selectively reflects adult concerns. Physical aggression is certainly a common feature of the mass media in this country, yet the contrast in the amount mentioned in the French and English stories was not significant.

Not all of the subjects displayed content differences of the sort found in the averages. Too little data on individual acculturative experiences were available to account for the individual differences. Presumably some people are attracted to a second culture because they are already deviant in their own; others never adapt to a new culture but merely translate the familiar into a new language. Ervin and Osgood (1954) had suggested earlier that "coordinate" bilinguals who learned both languages in distinct settings should display these differences more than those who learn in one setting. All of the bilinguals in this study were coordinate bilinguals by this criterion but there was a wide range in their actual learning. Of all the variables measured—amount of switching with interlocutors, amount of linguistic interference in the stories from the other language, contact with Americans, attitude towards assimilation, having children reared here—none correlated markedly with the degree of contrast found. Thus the clarification of both the nature of the contrast we observed grossly and the individual process by which the differences develop must await later research.

NOTES

This study was conducted with the support of a predoctoral training fellowship from the Social Science Research Council. The author wishes to acknowledge the help of her dissertation committee chairman, T. M. Newcomb, and of those who scored the extensive data for linguistic interference and content, Jacqueline Frank, Colette Gougenheim, Dorothy Lipson, and Georgiana Smith. The advice of R. T. Bower and Ivor Wayne, and the facilities they made available at the Bureau of Social Science Research in Washington, D. C., are gratefully appreciated.

[1] Superior language dominance tests have since been constructed. Literate subjects may use a machine devised by Lambert (1955) which measures reactions to printed words. A pictorial test, measuring time in naming simple objects, was used by Ervin (1961a).

REFERENCES

Aron, Betty. A manual for analysis of the Thematic Apperception Test. Berkeley, Calif.: Willis E. Berg, 1949.

Brown, R. W., and Lenneberg, E. H. A study in language and cognition. J. abnorm. soc. Psychol., 1954, 49, 454-462.

Ervin, Susan M. The verbal behavior of bilinguals: The effect of language of report upon the Thematic Apperception Test stories of adult French bilinguals. (Doctoral dissertation, University of Michigan) Ann Arbor, Mich.: University Microfilms, 1955, MicA 55-2228.

Ervin, Susan M. Learning and recall in bilinguals. Amer. J. Psychol., 1961, 74, 446-451. (a)

Ervin, Susan M. Semantic shift in bilingualism. Amer. J. Psychol., 1961, 74, 233-241. (b)

Ervin, Susan M., and Osgood, C. E. Second language learning and bilingualism. J. abnorm. soc. Psychol., 1954, 49 (Pt. 2), 139-146.

Kluckhohn, C. Mirror for man. New York: McGraw-Hill, 1949.

Lambert, W. E. Measurement of the linguistic dominance of bilinguals. J. abnorm. soc. Psychol., 1955, 50, 197-200.

Lambert, W. E., Havelka, J., and Crosby, C. The influence of language-acquisition contexts on bilingualism. J. abnorm. soc. Psychol., 1958, 56, 239-244.

Lindquist, E. F. Design and analysis of experiments in psychology and education. Boston: Houghton Mifflin, 1956.

Luria, A. R. The role of speech in the regulation of normal and abnormal behavior. New York: Liveright, 1961.

McClelland, D. C., Atkinson, J. W., Clark, R. A., and Lowell, E. L. The achievement motive. New York: Appleton-Century-Crofts, 1953.

Maccoby, Eleanor. Some notes on French child-rearing among the Parisian middle class. Cambridge: Harvard Laboratory of Human Development, 1952. (Ditto)

Métraux, Rhoda, and Mead, Margaret. Themes in French culture. Stanford: Stanford University Press, 1954.

Riesman, D. The lonely crowd. New Haven: Yale University Press, 1950.

Sanford, R. N., Adkins, M. M., Miller, R. B., Cobb, E. A., et al. Physique, personality, and scholarship: A cooperative study of school children. Monogr. Soc. Res. Child Develpm., 1943, 8.

Wylie, L. Village in the Vaucluse. Cambridge: Harvard University Press, 1958.

6 An Issei Learns English

In the years since the second world war, large numbers
of American servicemen have brought home Japanese wives. These
women, who are Issei, or first-generation, have been exposed to
English intensively. Few of their husbands know any Japanese. Few
of the women have the intention of teaching their children Japanese.
They are scattered about rather than clustered residentially, so that
in many cases their friendships are with Caucasians.

They maintain Japanese primarily through reading or friendships with other war brides whom they meet through the war brides
clubs or through employment in Japanese restaurants. Since there
are two other Japanese communities in the area, comprised of earlier
immigrants and of the young business and official groups, one might
expect ties with other Japanese. But the other immigrants are mainly
older and of rural background. Furthermore, interracial marriages
are sufficiently unpopular in Japan to inhibit friendships between the
war brides and other Japanese.

I have investigated two aspects of the acquisition of English
in this special group of Issei: Why do some learn English faster than
others, and why do some learn what to say as well as how to say it
in English ?

I will use in this report several different types of measures
of English mastery. Relative fluency is a measure of comparative
speed in naming pictures of simple objects in Japanese and in English.
This measure has been found before (Ervin 1961), to be a useful and
valid device for assessing purely oral skills, but it does not, of
course, take into account any grammatical skills at all. Morphology

was a test based on a purely verbal version of the device Jean Berko
(1958) used with children which asks for the plural, past tense, or
possessive of a number of nonsense syllables. For example, one
might say "I have a nizz. There are two of them. What are they?"
The interest in this measure was whether the speaker inflected the
form or not. Japanese does not have inflectional suffixes for nouns
so the women often omit them in English. Prosody was a score for
appropriate stress and intonation patterns in reading sentences designed to test typical contrasts in English. Phonemes were measures
of the success in distinguishing English phonemes in pictures or in
sentences containing key words like ship and sheep, light and right,
and hat, hot and hut. Subphonemes were allophonic contrasts like
vowel length before final consonants, pronunciation of consonant clusters, and syllabic nasals of wooden and mountain. These were treated
separately from phonemic errors on the grounds that subphonemic
errors were less likely to lead to misunderstanding of messages.

Many factors should be related to ease in acquiring English.
The most important of these are the amount of contact with English
including, separately, hearing and speaking the language. In addition
it was believed that certain variables of an attitudinal type might be
important, in view of Lambert's work (1965) which showed differences
between students who varied in level of motivation to learn a second
language. Attitudinal variables should have more effect on the features
least important for intelligibility.

The number of women in this study was small. Thirty-six
Issei women were tested on a variety of tests for a total of around
nine hours per woman. In the correlational analysis resulting from
the large array of data, there is some problem in sifting causal relations from simple co-occurrences.

Relative Fluency

Basically English dominance, results in terms of naming
speed, seems to be a function of exposure to English. There is a
relation of .42 to over-all exposure, and both the number of years in
the United States and the age of children are related to fluency in
English.

On the other hand, some beliefs about oneself are related to low English fluency. The women who judged themselves to be relatively conservative, and those who still yearned to visit or live in Japan, had relatively low fluency in English.

The naming measure is also a relatively good predictor of associate fluency in <u>both</u> languages. (Associate fluency refers to the number of word associations given in each language in the test described below.) Evidently the women who have greater verbal fluency in Japanese succeed in learning English more rapidly.

Morphology

Second language learners can successfully communicate in spite of quite deviant grammar in certain respects. Many Japanese women speak English without the usual English inflectional affixes. They omit subjects or objects when these are obvious from context. In many situations of encounter between speakers of two unrelated languages, we find stable pidgins developing. Listening to the "transitional pidgin" of the Issei, and struck by its surprising success in terms of conveying messages, one must ask why these women ever go beyond this stage of learning.

Pidgins typically develop when both parties to a transaction are satisfied with or derive benefit from using this special language. On the other hand, if there is sufficient contact with monolingual norms for the deviance of a pidgin to be disapproved, if there is sufficient contact to allow at least one group to become bilingual, and if there is social equality so that relative rank is not marked by the use of pidgin, bilingualism or even language shift may result from contact. Since the condition of the Issei women is one that makes for bilingualism or language shift, we expect that under the pressure of contact and standard English norms they will gradually shift toward standard English.

Morphological omissions in English are similar to phonemic errors in that they can occasionally result in misunderstanding. Learning of morphology and learning of phonemes go hand in hand ($r = .70$). The strongest predictors of morphological skill are schooling and reading ($p < .05$)[1] which is hardly surprising.

Phonemic System

In every language some sound differences alter messages; others simply indicate dialect, style, accent or mood. Phonemic distinctions are those which can give a different message. The greater variety of word forms and phonemes in English present serious difficulties to Japanese who wish to learn English. Among the most frequent sounds in English are /l/ and /r/, indistinguishable to a Japanese, who imitates both as a flap, as in a stereotyped British very. Japanese has five vowels; American English has at least nine. The Japanese confuse ship and sheep, pool and pull, cat, cot, and cut. Since /v/ and /th/ don't exist in Japanese, substitutes are made.

The astonishing result of this study is that the highest predictor of phonemic mastery, even in naming pictures, is reading, ($p < .01$) though exposure to English in school and on jobs, ($p < .05$), and correction by others are also significant predictors, ($p < .05$). On the other hand, movies, TV and radio are unrelated with phonemic skills and, indeed, phonemic scores are slightly lower for regular moviegoers.

There are two quite different interpretations of the finding that reading is the best predictor of phonemic mastery. One possibility is simply that people who read a lot care more about language, are more motivated to learn, and are more disturbed by failure to be understood, to understand or to meet the norms for English.

Another possibility is that reading helps to supplement oral training. Since many of the phonemic distinctions which cause trouble for the Japanese have spelling correlates, reading is in fact not unrelated to phonemic training. Teachers find that children who have phonemic confusions in discrimination or articulation have trouble reading. If two words have a distinctive spelling, their phonemic distinctiveness in listening could be sought, and in articulation better remembered. In this view, distinctive spelling could accelerate learning. Which of these is the better explanation can only be discovered by experimental manipulation.

Prosody and Accent

In addition to phonemic differences, some measures were
included which related to aspects of English less crucial to the intelligibility of messages. One problem with these measures is that they
are often more difficult to assess reliably, since the native speaker's
ear judges phonemic errors most acutely and tends to disregard
features of speech which are not essential to intelligibility. Both of
these measures have some relation to phonemic scores (prosody,
$r = .41$; phonetic accuracy $r = .55$).

Prosody appears to have some relation to attitudinal variables,
in that women with poor prosody scores were more likely to report
that it is important to be attractive ($p < .01$) and that jobs are important and may require an accent ($p < .05$). Voices with more Japanese
accent were also judged less favorably than samples of American
voices ($r = .33$) by women with better English prosodic pattern.

The phonetic scores were better ($p < .05$) for women who said
it is important to be a good wife and mother, and if one knows English
one can understand the family better. On the whole, prediction of
both measures was poor.

Attitudes

I had expected that attitudinal variables might prove to be
related closely to the acquisition of prosody and phonetic patterns in
English, and included items bearing on both the advantages and disadvantages of an accent and on attitudes about language purity or mixture.
Most of the Issei, unlike the French-born bilinguals in an earlier
study (Ervin, 1955), do not feel there is anything wrong with language
mixture. However, Ss whose pronunciation was poor generally see
both more advantages and disadvantages attached to an accent. These
findings render the technique suspect because if it had assessed real
and possibly effective differences in motivation, I would have expected
a relation between good pronunciation and belief that accents are
disadvantageous. In conclusion, I think that the attitudes reported
arise from the woman's skills at the time of the interview. The

French informants who had more language mixture in their speech
also approved of it more. Their judgment may rationalize the fact.

Language and Content

Content Shifting

The recent work of Blom and Gùmperz (1966) has revealed
that language switching is a subtle and pervasive process. In groups
of friends in a Norwegian village they found that the introduction of
topics of a general sort as opposed to local questions led to an unconscious increase in the use of the standard Norwegian lexicon. One
might think that this kind of tie between form and content can only
be effective when the forms are not sharply distinct, as in dialect
variation where co-occurrence restrictions may be less than in language variation. The observation of the natural speech of many bilinguals belies this belief.

Our concern here will be with the reverse facet of this tie of
form and content, i. e. , with the effect of language choice upon content.
Within the life of a bilingual individual who has moved from one linguistic milieu to another the two languages may have been used in
distinctive physical and social environments and at different parts of
the life cycle. If there are differences in social experience and beliefs in the two cultural milieux we might expect that language shift
will be accompanied by a shift in content. These changes might be
due to differences in the perception or recall of experience associated
with the two languages, or to differences in verbally expressed values
in the two cultures. In other words such a bilingual, in becoming
competent in two cultures, learns to associate particular kinds of
content with each language.

What might we expect the content differences associated with
language to consist of? The simplest possible assumption is that the
differences between content in the two languages of a bilingual might
be similar to differences between two monolingual groups. This is
at least a starting point. In an earlier study with French who came
to the United States as adults, predictions were made about content
differences in Thematic Apperception Test latent themes. For some

variables the themes of the stories changed with language in the direction predicted as likely for monolinguals (Ervin, 1955 and 1964).

In the present study, monolingual norms were obtained for a series of verbal measures. These were Thematic Apperception Test stories, word associations, sentence completions, semantic differentials and story completions. The monolinguals were similar in age, education and social class to the bilingual women. Two groups of bilingual women were studied, the Issei described earlier, and a sample of Kibei Nisei, or second generation Japanese American who returned to Japan for education.

For each type of content, a system was devised for scoring distance from American norms, distance from Japanese norms, and relative dominance of the two distance scores. Thus for stories, sentence completions and word associations, responses were weighted by their frequency in the norm group. For example, on the TAT card MF13, a score of 3 Japanese and 18 American is given for a guilt theme, since 3 Japanese women and 18 Americans said the man felt guilty; in Japan the more common theme was failure. For the semantic differentials a deviation score was devised. While the differences in norms were in some cases surprising, the procedure was completely mechanical and required no judgment about the typicality of the responses.

An analysis of the monolingual norms for story completion led to some curious findings. For example one story ran: "A father died leaving many debts. His only son, earning his own living is studying. " One might guess that the Japanese would feel a greater obligation to maintain the family good name in such a case. However, about half the Japanese said that the student finished his studies before repaying, and another 13 per cent never repaid; almost all of the Americans said the student repaid soon by leaving school or working part time. After the fact, one can see that two differences are involved. One is the close tie in the Japanese industrial system between school and job through personal networks, which would make interrupting a highly competitive school career unthinkable; the other is the difference in student economics. The point of the illustration, however, is that the monolingual norms in some cases match a stereotype and in some cases sharply deviate from it.

Content Shifts for Each Task

The most clear-cut effect of language was on word associations and sentence completions. When speaking Japanese, both Issei
and Nisei gave associations more typical of women in Japan; when
speaking English, the Issei gave typically American associations.
The over-all effect was that content shifted with language for both
groups.

Some concepts, of course, are typically more Japanese
while others are more American. Thus, mushrooms and New Year's
Day are typically Japanese, while kitchen, plate and marriage are
more typically American. There is not so much shift with language in
connection with these words since they reflect a kind of domain specialization. Even in Japan, kitchens look American now; but mushrooms have, even in English, a rich evocation of the pine forests in
the fall in Japan. On the other hand, tea evokes lemon and cookies
in English, and in Japanese the utensils of the tea ceremony.

As expected, then, shifting was greater for some words. It
was also greater for those Issei who were more fluent in English.
Evidently learning English brings with it learning appropriate American associates.

Sentence completions also showed a marked relation to language for both groups. In particular the Issei shifted markedly towards the American norms when responding in English. When responding in Japanese both groups increased their Japanese content
scores.

Some of the differences are quite subtle. For instance,
Japanese women more often say "what I want most in life. . . is peace."
Americans say ". . . happiness." "When I am with men. . ." Japanese
women are uncomfortable, American women contented. "When a
husband finds fault with his wife, the wife. . ." in Japan—is defensive,
in America—tries to improve.

For both word associations and sentence completions, though
the change in conformity to American norms with language was considerable (p < .001) for the Issei, the Nisei responses, though differing

in the two languages, were equally close to American norms in both. Possibly the difference between Issei and Nisei lies in the greater separation of two cultures for the Issei. For the Nisei the American milieu has always been bilingual, since often their families mix languages. But since they were in Japan during the conservative, nationalistic thirties, traditional Japanese culture is uniquely tied to the Japanese language for them, even more than for the Issei who knew post-war Japan.

For story completions, both groups again showed an increase in Japanese solutions when the Japanese language was used. But American solutions did not depend on language. For example, "it is closing time, but the boss is still in his office. An office girl finished her work, but as usual many of the other workers are still remaining." The typical American solution has the girl leave without asking; in the Japanese solutions she waits without asking. Frequently the women commented about the difference in customs. One Issei gave this solution in Japanese: "I think that since she is a working person I guess she will not be able to leave until her boss goes home. She will wait." And in English: "Well sometimes she have to work, boss say to her...I think he say wait, well she does wait." In this case, there is neither a typical American nor a typical Japanese solution at the second session.

The semantic differential results indicated that the effect of language depended on the concept being judged; in the Thematic Apperception Test stories there was no over-all shift with language at all.

Set

One way to account for these effects is to attribute them to self-instructions. If the women can guess what typical responses are, they may be able to shift content with language because the change in language implies a difference in what they ought to say. We sought to separate this feature from language by holding language constant and asking some subjects to give typically Japanese responses at one session and typically American responses at the other.

For some words, set did produce an effect on word association responses. For example, New Year's Day drew quite different

responses from one woman under different sets—"New Year's cele-
bration, New Year's greetings, New Year's cards, New Year's house
visiting, New Year's eve," vs. "New Year's Eve party, champagne,
holiday, New Year's resolution." Most women could simulate typical
Japanese responses appropriately but not typically American responses,
perhaps because they don't know them. The over-all effect was to
increase relative dominance of Japanese under the Japanese set and
decrease it under the American set.

For the completions also, the Japanese scores could be
increased. In addition there was change for some stories in the
American score. Evidently the stereotype of the norms varied from
story to story. The two examples we have given of the student with
his father's debts and of the office girl leaving at the end of the day
illustrate cases where the norms do not conform equally to a stereotype.

In the case of the semantic differential, an American set was
effective for some concepts, but not for all. For sentence completions, set affected only American scores, and for the TAT, an American set makes stories more Japanese!

It thus appears that the subjects were able to manipulate
proximity only to the Japanese norms on those measures where there
had been an effect of language, with the exception of sentence completions. The over-all increase in American score in English testing
for word associations and story completions in the Issei is thus unex-
plained by set.

Individual Differences

I have suggested that learning what is typically American
content may be part of the competence to be acquired along with the
English language itself. The Issei might be expected to have as wide
a range in this kind of mastery as was found in their phonological
skills.

What kind of woman shifts scores with language? In order
to classify them, I ignored how deviant from the norms each woman

was and simply looked at how close to each norm group she was at each session, and gave her a relative score.

A woman who moves to the United States might simply learn English and in effect translate her Japanese responses into English. Such a woman should, if she was relatively close to typical Japanese responses in Japan, give such responses in both languages. We shall call her J-dominant. J-dominant women are pictured as shy, conservative and lacking contacts in the United States.

A woman who moves to a different social context in the United States and learns new content appropriate to English would alter content with language. These women are called shifters. They probably have maintained contacts in Japan, and also are fairly acculturated in their behavior in America, but without strong preferences.

Some women may become (or have become) Americanized even in their behavior in Japanese. They will be called A-dominant. They probably have a strong identification with American women, show a high degree of acculturation and prefer American contacts.

The J-dominant on word associations do appear to be conservative. They would rather be Japanese than American, they serve Japanese food at home, believe in lucky days ($p < .01$), and wean their children late. But it is hard to distinguish shifters from A-dominant. The shifters wean their children early, have a separate room from the children, like driving a car, and are A-dominant on sentence completions. They are dependent on others and believe it is important to have many acquaintances, ($p < .01$). The A-dominant identify with American women more than the others ($r = .51$), and prefer them as friends ($r = .35$). They go to American movies a lot, and know their neighbors but not their in-laws. They even expect their children to first-name adult friends.

The J-dominant on the TAT were similar in that they weaned their children late, have a typical Japanese New Year's, and are least acculturated. But most of their friends are American. A-dominants have closer friends in America, and have a more American New Year's. Shifters tend to be more acculturated on a few scales. They wean their children early, and have adopted American customs of

courtesy and seldom follow such Japanese customs as bowing. They
have many Japanese friends, but unlike the A-dominant they lack
close friends in America, and are not affectionate. Their high shift
score arises largely from being more typically Japanese in responses
at the appropriate session.

The problem situations or story completions showed some
marked differences between the groups. The J-dominant write to
Japan and prefer Japanese friends though they have been married a
long time ($p < .01$). They don't read American magazines ($p < .01$)
and hence may simply not know American norms for solutions. For
them, comfortable living is paramount ($p < .01$). The A-dominant
does read American magazines ($p < .01$), is highly dependent ($p < .01$),
and was encouraged in her American trends because the closest family
member favored her marriage. Her husband doesn't like her Japanese
ties ($r = .66$), doesn't ask her questions about Japan, and doesn't like
to hear her speak Japanese. Shifters on the other hand are not dependent.

The J-dominant and shifters on sentence completions have
no marked characteristics. The A-dominant are married to men
who like the Japanese language, clothes and women, but they have
high contact and are relatively acculturated. They have some definite
verbal attitudes about values, saying it is important to be attractive,
have many acquaintances, do well in a profession, be a good wife
and mother and raise children a special way.

Some common themes showed in the results, though there
were variations for the different verbal measures. The J-dominant
were typically more conservative, more closely tied to Japan, and
less acculturated. The particular measures revealing these features
varied. Many said they would rather be Japanese than American.

The A-dominant were the reverse. Generally the A-dominant
identified with American women more than the others, and preferred
them as friends. They had close friends here, and were sometimes
quite dependent on them. Their families did not oppose their marriages. They learned a good deal about America from the mass
media, going to movies and reading magazines a lot.

The shifters, like the A-dominant, were more acculturated.
But they often lacked Caucasian friends here, sometimes lacking any

close friends here. Perhaps this is the key difference between shifters and A-dominant who have become completely "Americanized."

It is evident that the knowledge demanded to give American responses varies for the different tests. The word associations could be shifted simply by enumerating different objects; far subtler differences in preoccupations are revealed in the TAT's and sentence completions. The only conspicuous source discovered for American content is American magazines. Women who read them had high scores in both languages for American content.

The Bilingual and Monolingual Norms

This study began with a model of a bilingual as a person with access to two sets of norms, both of which must be learned. When the norms are linguistic, and the two languages with which he has contact are both standardized languages with which he maintains contact through reading if not orally, such a model may have some appropriateness. But even in language, new norms develop for bilinguals[2] if they use either of their languages primarily with other bilinguals. Their sense of what is "correct" itself changes. Some French informants in the United States even asked me what was correct French. Since actual speech is likely to change even faster than beliefs about language, any group cut off from a monolingual community and low in reading, rapidly loses its ability to shift between two sets of monolingual norms. In the French study every informant, no matter how educated and committed to the maintenance of French and no matter how often he returned to France, showed evidence of English influences in his French, often subtly through semantic categories, frequency of cognates or word order.

In the case of content, there is no norm in the sense of a standard of correctness. Within each monolingual community there is diversity. An Issei who marries an American and emigrates must be deviant herself. Though she might know what average or typical behavior is, there is no reason to assume that she responds this way herself. Besides, of course, it is not clear what average she might be reflecting—the Japanese woman of the time she emigrated, or her contemporary in Japan, certainly changed with the years. In some cases I found that Navaho and Anglo monolinguals in the American southwest (Ervin-Tripp, 1964) were more alike than bilinguals on semantic differentials. For example, both Anglos and Navaho monolinguals think highly of doctors. Navaho bilinguals have, like the monolinguals, had contact with doctors in the hospitals, but in addition to recognizing their medical effectiveness, they are aware through their knowledge of English that some Anglo doctors have contempt for Navahos, and speak rudely to and about them. Bilinguals may thus be deviant from both groups.

Secondly, in all bilingual groups there is some specialization of function by language, so that the two languages taken together have the full range of functions for the bilingual individual that a single language has for a monolingual. Thus the bilingual women reported that they knew of their husband's work chiefly through English. The current specialization of functions and topics is closely tied to the fact that in their life histories the two languages were not learned at the same time. It cannot then be expected that they will have acquired knowledge of verbalized values and content in the same way as women who grew up here speaking English. Some content they can learn as adults; the story completions reflect themes discussed for adults in the women's magazines. But some of the subtle differences in TAT themes, such as the preoccupation with guilt or with failure, may reflect differences which can only be learned through childhood socialization, rearing children here, or decades of close association with Americans. As was pointed out (Ervin, 1964) with the French TAT protocols, the themes that showed most marked shift were those most obvious to adults (e.g., achievement).

In this report of initial results, I sought to characterize why some women learn English faster than others, and why some show more content shift than others. The strongest predictors of simple fluency were found to be contact with the language through the number of years in the United States. But for mastery of English morphological rules and pronunciation, reading of English was important, either because of its relation to values about correct use of language, or because of a direct influence on awareness of distinctions between words.

Marked shifts in content with shift in language were found in a variety of verbal measures. These changes appear to be due to more than self-instruction to give typical responses, because when such instructions were given, the women were unable to make their answers more American, except on sentence completions. Thus set may be a partial but not an adequate explanation for the fact that responses were more typical of the Japanese when given in Japanese and more typical of Americans when given in English.

Women who gave typically American responses in both languages differed on other measures—of conservatism, identification with Americans and acculturation—from women who gave typically Japanese responses in both. Thus the content data were consistent with other differences in these women's behavior and were not particularly tied to the language being spoken. In one case, story or problem solutions, American themes seem to have been learned from the mass media. At this point in the analysis, the only difference that can be found between those who adopt American content only in English and those who do so also in Japanese is that the latter have stronger friendships here. Since the women who changed content with language were not the same for all the measures of content, I cannot conclude that there is a separate group of women who display two somewhat different selves in the two languages. This kind of shifting with context evidently occurs for most of the women some of the time.

NOTES

This research was conducted at the Institutes of Human Development and Human Learning under a grant from the National Science Foundation. I am indebted to Yaeko Nishijima Putzar for a major role in all phases of the study and to Naomi Quenk, David Stimpson, and Jean Goodman as well. Professor Katsuo Sano supervised collection of the norms in Japan.

[1] Unless otherwise indicated Mann-Whitney U-Tests were used.

[2] Blom and Gumperz (1966), and Gumperz show that where bilinguals have been interacting mainly with other bilinguals for a long time the model for each of their languages is not monolingual usage of those languages, but rather the modified forms of those languages as spoken by the bilinguals themselves.

REFERENCES

Berko, Jean. The child's learning of English morphology. Word,
    1958, 14, 150-177.
Blom, Jan-Petter and John Gumperz. Some social determinants of
    verbal behavior. Unpublished paper presented at the annual
    general meeting of the American Sociological Association,
    1966.
Ervin, Susan M. Semantic shift in bilingualism. American Journal
    of Psychology, 1961, 74, 233-241.
Ervin, Susan M. Language and TAT content in bilinguals. Journal
    of Abnormal and Social Psychology, 1964, 68, 500-507.
    [In this volume, pp. 45-61.]
Ervin, Susan M. The verbal behavior of bilinguals: The effect of
    language of report upon the Thematic Apperception Test
    stories of adult French bilinguals. (Doctoral dissertation,
    University of Michigan) Ann Arbor, Mich.: University
    Microfilms, 1955, MicA 55-2228.
Ervin-Tripp, Susan M. Navaho connotative judgments: the metaphor
    of person description. In D. Hymes and W. E. Bittle (eds.),
    Studies in southwestern ethnolinguistics. The Hague, Mouton,
    1967, 91-116.
Ervin-Tripp, Susan M. An analysis of the interaction of language,
    topic, and listener. American Anthropologist, 1964, 66,
    No. 6, Part 2, 86-102.
Gumperz, John J. On the linguistic markers of bilingual communica-
    tion. Journal of Social Issues, 1967, 23, No. 2, 48-57.

Lambert, Wallace E. Psychological approaches to the study of lan-
    guage. Part II. On second-language learning and bilingual-
    ism. Modern Language Journal, 1965, 47, 114-121.

7 | On Becoming a Bilingual

Bilingualism is an achievement that arrives by many routes. The bilingual-in-process might be a child growing up in a bilingual adult milieu, member of a bilingual family, or of a monolingual minority. He might be an adult who has moved to a different linguistic environment. The learning process might be casual or systematic pedagogy. The differences in what the learner hears, what he is expected to say, and how much formal correctness is demanded from the start make for radical differences in the process of acquisition according to age and milieu.

Pedagogy and Age

Phonology. There is strong evidence that for children under eleven language is sound, for adults, sense. Children generalize more between words alike in sound, give more clang associations, confuse the meanings of similar-sounding words. (Ervin-Tripp 1967: 62-63) In adults, similar behavior appears in feeblemindedness and under drugs. One might say that for adults language is transparent, since adults rapidly penetrate the surface of an utterance to its meanings, to a network of connected thoughts. (Sachs 1965) Children attend more to the surface, just as they also connect speech more to the immediate situation in which it occurs.

The basis for this difference between children and adults is unknown. If this difference is neurological, (Lenneberg 1967) or if it lies in the loss of an ability (like the traditional notion of eidetic imagery) then there is a clear pedagogical implication: children must be exposed to different teaching methods than adults, since their abilities differ. If the difference in behavior is a consequence of shift of set or attention (like the shift from color-sorting of blocks to form-sorting), or if the difference is a result of the adults' greater richness and skill in semantic association, then the implications are quite different. First, one would have to find out what the age curve is, for specific items, to see if an age difference in learning rate affects new sounds where there is no negative transfer, and if the curve matches the generalization curve mentioned above. If so, then one might seek to simulate in adults the conditions of attention to sounds that are common in child use of language. In one experiment, attention to sound was increased by simply delaying semantic information (glosses) for a few days. Phonological skill in this group was no better than in a control group with no delay. [2]

Lexicon. Children's lexicon is composed almost entirely, in Osgood's terms, of signs rather than assigns. (Osgood, Suci & Tannenbaum 1957 p. 8) New words are normally learned in the context of visual-motor activity, whereas much of the adult's vocabulary is learned in a purely verbal context so that its meanings are verbal. Asher has claimed dramatic increases in learning rate and retention when adults were treated like children with respect to learning context, i. e. when they were taught to recognize words referring to actions they performed and objects they handled. (Asher 1965)

Grammar. Differences between adults and children in grammatical capacity may arise from limitations in memory and "programming capacity" rather than limitations in the character of the grammatical rules they can process. That is, the differences may be more quantitative than qualitative. At six, there do appear to be some limits in the grammatical rules used by English-speaking children. There are some specific details of the English system to be worked out, such as nominalizations of verbs, pronominalizations, participial verb complements, and semantically complex structures like "if" and "so" clauses, and perfect aspect. [3]   Children do not know the rules involving rare structures, or those used in various styles. But it is impressive to see in a variety of studies in different languages how early most grammatical patterns and sociolinguistic variations are acquired. [4]

In order to know whether control of a grammatical pattern in one language will facilitate learning an analogous pattern in another language, one needs an underlying theory of the logical structure of grammatical rules. The results from studies of grammatical development have so far not been stated in a sufficiently abstract form, transcending the specific structures of each langue, and even of langage. The emphasis of general cognitive research on children has been on development before two and after five, so we know little about the cognitive operations children develop during this age period, which is most critical for language. But judging from the child language diaries it appears that there must be, by school age, an extraordinary capacity for grammatical learning. There is no evidence of basic intellectual barriers to learning new language structures quite early, provided (a) the semantic distinctions are not difficult ones, such as the conditional, and (b) the training input is not too complex quantitatively, in terms of the amount of imbedding, or the co-occurrence of new meanings with new grammatical structures. It may be that even these limitations are sufficiently inconvenient so that from the standpoint of learning grammatical patterns, unlike the learning of sounds, early teaching is no distinct advantage.

Imitation. Studies of input-output relationships in imitations appear to be a fruitful way to characterize the linguistic system as it changes. Here I shall draw on some pioneering work of Charles Welsh, who has been developing a process model of utterance imitation for a two-year-old child. This model can predict the output for any input. While processing models have been offered before, [5] the convenience of imitation is that both input and output are fully specifiable.

The Welsh model[6] contains first a phonological analyzer. Both segments and phonotactic patterns are analyzed according to the child's rules. For example, the child may consistently convert "banana" to ['mana], and "gramma" to ['ŋama] and "gun" to [ŋ ət] through a general analyzer which perceives all nasals as in initial position but preserves other features of the initial consonant. [7]

The second component in the model is a dictionary with category markers, which assimilates what is heard to familiar words, within certain limits. Thus "Chomsky and Veritas are crying" became "Cynthia and Tasha cry" but "cui bono is the quarter" became "cui bona a quarter." If the sentence is less than five words long, a new item could enter the child's dictionary, receiving the category marker inferred from its position.

The third component is an auditory storage device for holding material while further analysis occurs. In one model[8] this analysis consists of predictions, rather like a Markov chain. In Welsh's
current thinking, there is a set of pre-analyzed templates in the form
of category sequences. The surface structure of the sentence, in
terms of category markers, is scanned and the appropriate template
is selected, which includes "encounter-operate rules" for what to do
when standard order (e.g. English S-V-O) is violated. It is these
templates which result in the return of "The boy the chair hit was
dirty" as "Boy hit the chair was dirty," and "The man who I saw
yesterday runs fast" as "I saw the man and he run fast," and "The
pencil and some paper are here" as "Some pencil here and some
paper here."

An analysis of such rules at various stages of second language learning would prove highly enlightening. [9] One can expect that
there might be sharp changes in comprehension and imitation as new
templates or new encounter-operate rules are acquired. [10] It is important to note that these models are not logical models of the rules
of a language, such as those of a linguist, but an attempt to characterize the processing algorithms of real speakers. They will therefore contain quite different components and types of rules.

Imitation is often used as a pedagogical device, and it is
frequently considered both a necessary and sufficient account of language learning. Recent evidence suggests that it is neither, at least
in terms of structural learning. (Ervin 1964 pp. 163-190) Spontaneous imitations of two-year-olds, whose linguistic systems are
undergoing rapid change, are as simple as or simpler syntactically
than their free speech. Many adults and some children learn languages without any overt imitation, as well as without correction, to
a degree beyond that required for intelligibility. Thus we do not in
fact know how to account for the fact that the linguistic system changes
very rapidly, except to refer to changes in the system of comprehension. For example, children may say " otherbody" before they
say "somebody," "tomorning" before they say "tonight," and "do-ed"
before any regular past tense. This evidence suggests that children's
structural analysis of what they hear, rather than any rote imitation,
is the key to systematic change. [11]

Elicited imitation in the classroom probably has two values:

motor drill and the manipulation of attention. The first, of course, refers to peripheral skill in articulating sequences. The second is more interesting. It may be that elicited imitation is like disconfirmation in logical or cognitive development. Disconfirmation can draw attention to features hitherto ignored as noisy or irrelevant. Short simple sequences might be repeated to a point which violates former processing rules, thus forcing the rule system to change. The imitation of verses, songs, and dialogues, advocated by Jones, thus has value only if there is evidence that the learner comprehends the components and produces imitations that are phonologically or grammatically superior to free speech. Even this kind of practice may not succeed in altering the structures for sentence production, of course. If the imitations used in the classroom are consistently filtered through the existing processing device of the pupil without any effect on that device, then they are not pedagogically useful for learning the linguistic system, though they may have other uses.

Social Milieu of Learning

The above discussion pertains to school teaching of second language or of the mother tongue. In almost all respects other circumstances of bilingual acquisition are dissimilar: in social support of the two languages, values, norms of correct usage, and sociolinguistic rules for speech. I shall touch on each of these points briefly.

By social support of bilingualism, I mean that the learner hears speech in several languages outside the classroom, either because he moves between two monolingual communities or because there are consistent rules governing alternations in a bilingual community.

Social support appears to be of greater importance to children than to adults. It is a common complaint of sojourners abroad that their children both learn and forget languages too readily, whenever the linguistic milieu is changed. It could be that when the milieu is reinstated there would be marked savings on re-learning, so that there is not so much "forgetting" as lowered availability. On this point we sorely need systematic research. Perhaps children's selection of linguistic variety is more dependent on the social milieu and less dependent on private motives than the adult's. Adults can sometimes alter the language used to a given interlocutor at will. In addition, their rich inner speech and their access to reading may provide a form of support, FLES programs may have serious problems in the event that there is continuous exposure to a language neither in the school nor outside.

Values play an important role in determining whether a given condition of social support will produce or sustain learning. At a gross level, beliefs about the ease or appropriateness of becoming bilingual may affect the probability of child or adult learning. In India it is assumed that children will readily become multilingual; in the United States bilingualism is taken as a matter of course only where the second language is English. Speech markers of social identity carry a strong value which may promote or retard learning. Labov, for example, has noted that the speech features of women teachers in New York may not be learned readily by working class boys, who fear a threat to their "machismo." (Labov 1965b)

In addition to altering the effects of a fixed social milieu, the learner's values may lead him to increase or decrease exposure to the second language. Thus Japanese women married to Americans learned fluency as a simple function of years in the United States, but beyond the needs of rudimentary communication there were vast differences in the degree of learning of phonology and grammar and even of American ideas, related largely to their values and education. (Ervin-Tripp 1967a)

Values should enter prediction at two points. If circumstances do not guarantee exposure, values may lead to seeking out conditions for listening and inner speech. If the social milieu provides support, then the social meaning of linguistic markers will determine how far second language learning progresses beyond lexical alternations and the basic syntax necessary for intelligibility.

Primary Language Data

Any full analysis of the process of learning must contain realistic specification of the actual input system, or in this case the "primary language data," including the stable and variable features, the social meaning of each variable, and the co-occurrence rules. While other papers in this seminar have dealt more fully with the specification of norms, I wish to emphasize that it is the norms of the <u>face-to-face community</u> which influence bilingual speech (Blom and Gumperz 1966; Gumperz 1964).

In school learning, for example, the pupil may never use L_2 in a monolingual setting, nor learn the sociolinguistic rules of that setting. Even in social milieux where two monolingual communities are nearby, there usually is at least a bilingual belt between, and only interpreters and travelers would have occasion to frequent both communities, with resultant constraints on their linguistic behavior.

Probably most bilinguals live among others like themselves; they may have contact with only one or with no monolingual community. The bilingual is likely to be exposed to a single set of semantic and phonetic ranges for many linguistic categories. An American Indian child in the Southwestern United States hears about him a form of English with inter-vocalic glottal stops and simplified final consonant clusters. The Canadian francophone hears considerable common lexicon in both speech varieties, so that "sink", "hotel", and "table" are shared, but "homme" and "man" are not. One is likely to find maximal separation of varieties and maximal co-occurrence restrictions only in the highly self-conscious, carefully monitored formal and written registers. (Gumperz 1967)

Even in bilingual communities maintaining considerable linguistic separation, there may be sociolinguistic convergence. American Nisei have not learned Japanese speech etiquette, and appear rude in Japan; American Lebanese may lack classical Arabic allusions appropriate to formal situations; the familiarity and status distinctions carried by the second person pronoun or inflection of the verb in many languages may be lost by American bilinguals so that the speaker sounds presumptuous. Thus even if the classical "true bilingual" existed, he might be a social boor.

Interference

In all studies of language learning, there must be some way to characterize the linguistic system of the learner. Traditionally, this analysis has consisted of noting from tapes or writing the deviations of the learner's output from some ideal norm. When these deviations can be attributed to structures in another language, they are called interference.

There are at least three general classes of phenomena which have been included in this term. These are features in the systematic norms of the bilingual community, or its language and sociolinguistic rules; systematic features of the learner's language at a particular point in time; and performance errors.

Community norms. In the language of a bilingual community there may be fixed or compound features shared by both linguistic varieties. This is especially likely to be the case with semantic and phonetic features. In the example given above, sink is a lexical item common to both the French and English linguistic milieux for representing the same semantic category.

Second, there may be systematic alternations between the two varieties, which are part of the sociolinguistic norms of the community and carry social meaning which the members can identify. Blom and Gumperz have found that even when speakers can recognize the social meaning of switching, they may not be able to control switching consciously when they talk among themselves. (Blom & Gumperz 1966) They refer to situational switching for the case when the variety is predictable from the interlocutors, setting, or topic. Metaphorical switching occurs within a given situation for connotative purposes.

Learner's idiolect. A newcomer, whether child or adult, to a new linguistic milieu must master a new system. If the milieu is bilingual, he must master as well the rules for alternation between the two varieties. These rules can be characterized by either a linguistic model or a performance model. He must learn general grammatical categories, rules of arrangement of those categories, phonetic and semantic distinctions, and particular morphemes which represent semantic and grammatical categories. It frequently is the case that in lieu of learning all of the new features, he continues to employ the same distinctions, the same grammatical categories, and the same rules of arrangement, and even may import morphemes into the new variety. In the process of learning he may over-generalize newly learned features and alter the initial system accordingly. For example, a Frenchman speaking English may regularly use "who" as the subject of relative clauses, as in "That's the book who is on

the table. " He has a common syntactic rule in both varieties and
merely alternates "qui" and "who" as diamorphs.[12] In such cases,
whether it be L 1 or L 2 which is affected, we speak of interference
because features are used in common in both languages which are not
shared in the speech community from which the norms derive.

However, it also happens that learners employ patterns
common to neither language. When this happens, we may find something analogous to the interesting idiolectal rules in child language
development. A frequent occurrence is the omission or overgeneralization of morphemes in the new variety, even where the appropriate
semantic or syntactic category exists in the primary language. We
might call such instances simplification. By using a reduced set
of distinctions, by omitting inflectional morphemes, the learner cuts
down the task in sentence production. Possibly the morphological
and syntactic simplifications of second-language learners correspond
to some simplifications common among children learning the same
language. [13]

Performance errors. While the speaker may control and
recognize a norm for speech, he does not always realize in his output the rules which he knows. This is true of practiced speakers as
well as learners, of bilinguals as well as monolinguals. Performance
errors are inconsistent, and tend to occur in fatigue or under stress,
or when sentences are long, grammatically complex, or contain
novel lexicon. They arise from overtaxing the "programming capacity" of the speaker. The bilingual's speech system contains more
complex rules, both linguistic and sociolinguistic, than the monolingual's, and therefore his performance errors may violate co-occurrence restrictions socially or linguistically, producing interference.

It would be of great interest to psycholinguists to know whether
there is a non-random distribution of performance errors. For
example, it appears in English texts of Frenchmen that loanshifts
are frequent following cognates. In a system undergoing constant
change, there may be oscillation between rules from two adjacent
stages of development in the learner's dialect. It might be a characteristic feature of performance errors that they include forms of
interference or simplification typical of an earlier stage of learning.
For this reason, it is of value to supplement textual data with tests
in the form of comprehension or imitation measures which provide

richer criteria of those regularities which occur under all conditions of performance. [14]

If the distinctions between different types of interference are correct, then the second kind of analysis, the analysis of the learner's system, is central to an understanding of the process of bilingual learning.

A series of studies in which the social conditions of learning and the primary language data are specified should predict outcomes in terms of the learner's idiolect, or the language of a group of learners. For example, a child of an isolated Italian immigrant couple hears English and Italian morphemes both realized with many Italian phonological features. He is likely, like his parents, to use a common phonological system with lexical alternation. But he may adopt the English phonological system of his peers, interpreting his parents' phonology as idiosyncratic, since it is not uniquely joined to Italian lexicon by co-occurrence restrictions.

The rate of acquisition of different features under specified learning conditions would be of great interest. In my data, semantic compounding is very common, affecting both L_1 and L_2. But among native speakers of French in the United States, the lexicon seems to be the conscious marker of the language being spoken, so little morpheme borrowing occurs when language is controlled by instructions. The rate at which new syntactic rules are acquired varies considerably. Sequences which affect the "basic grammatical relations": [15] modifier-head, subject-predicate, verb-object, are learned very fast and learners rapidly acquire coordinate rules for representing these relations. Thus French bilinguals almost always maintained a difference in noun-adjective sequence for English and French, and Japanese newcomers to English kept S-V-O in English and S-O-V in Japanese. On the other hand, they have great difficulty in maintaining separate rules for adverb placement, and in learning the sub-categorization of English verbs according to objects and complements, so that they say "he put", but never "he them put." Transformations reflecting basic grammatical relations may be learned faster and be more resistant to change than those reflecting secondary relations or subcategorizations.

Differences in the rate of acquisition of new rules, and the

permeability of old rules to convergence with the new, cannot be predicted entirely on the basis of contrastive analysis. The facility with
which the order rules for the basic grammatical relations are learned arises either from their fundamental importance for intelligibility,
or from their role in strategies for listening to the speech of others.
In this respect, as in many others, the problems in the analysis of
the process of becoming bilingual are very similar to those in the
study of monolingual child language acquisition.

NOTES

[1] In second language learning, either positive or negative
transfer may occur, or prior training may be simply irrelevant. Unfortunately, most emphasis has been placed on negative transfer.
For sophisticated application of these psychological concepts to second language learning, see Brière 1966.

[2] Japanese was taught in taped lessons to American students
with structure drills based on a contrastive analysis. For a third of
the sessions no gloss was given. There was no difference in pronunciation between the students who first learned the Japanese sequences without gloss, and those who learned meanings along with
the sequences. See Sawyer et al. 1963.

[3] Menyuk 1963a. In addition sentence imbedding increases
with age, suggesting that children's "programming capacity" increases quantitatively. See, for example, the increasing use of
clauses reported by Templin 1957.

[4] Ervin-Tripp 1967b; Lenneberg 1967; Slobin 1966.

[5] Presidential address of Charles Osgood before the American Psychological Association, (Osgood 1963). This is a general
model which does not yield as specific predictions as an input-output model.

[6] Charles Welsh is a graduate student in psychology at the
University of California, Berkeley, and has presented an outline of
his model informally at the Institute for Human Learning. His dissertation will contain a more fully-developed version.

[7] A nasal anticipation rule is probably common in child language in the second year. For another example of such a rule see
Ervin & Miller 1963.

[8] Thorne et al. n. d. In this computer program, English
sentences were given rapid syntactic interpretations, using only a

dictionary of functions and syntactic category sequence predictions. This might be a hypothetical processing model for actual perception of sentences, as the title implies.

[9] For example, the dictionary might be changed first, by the addition of diamorphs employing similar category-markers in the translation "equivalents."

[10] The template change conveniently accounts for the rapid learning of certain high-frequency phrase structure rules, mentioned below, such as S-V-O order in English. In a phenomenological analysis of learning to comprehend Hebrew during a year in Israel, Robert Epstein, in a term paper, reports bursts and plateaus in comprehension though vocabulary increased at a more constant rate. Epstein suggests these bursts involve shifts in "listening technique," at first involving selective attention (e.g. attention to first and last words) and later "methods of ordering the syntax of sequences." If such sudden shifts can be objectively confirmed, they may correspond empirically to the development of templates or encounter-operate rules.

[11] Ervin-Tripp 1967b. On the learning of semantic shifts, see Earle 1967.

[12] "If two morphemes have phonemic shape or semantic function in common, they will often be identified by bilingual speakers.. .. Such semantic and morphological overlapping has been described as producing a 'compound sign'; in pursuance of my suggestion for the phonemic identification, I shall refer to this as a diamorph." (Haugen 1955) .

[13] For some examples in an inflectional language, see Slobin 1966 .

[14] Examples of such tests can be found in Slobin 1967. This is a draft manual to coordinate studies of first-language acquisition and language socialization in various societies.

[15] It has been argued that these relations apply to the deep structure of sentences, and are universal constraints on grammars. "They supposedly describe an aspect of children's capacity for language. . . . Evidence exists that the basic grammatical relations are honored in children's earliest patterned speech, if not before." This evidence is presented by David McNeill in "The capacity for grammatical development in children," in D. I. Slobin (Ed.) The ontogenesis of grammar: facts and theories, (1971). From a paper presented at a symposium of the American Association of Advancement of Science, December, 1965.

REFERENCES

Asher, James J. 1965. The strategy of total physical response; an application to learning Russian. International Review of Applied Linguistics in Language Teaching (IRAL) 3, 291-300.

Blom, Jan-Petter, and Gumperz, John J. 1972. Social meaning in linguistic structures: Code-switching in Norway. Directions in Sociolinguistics, ed. by J. J. Gumperz and Dell Hymes. New York: Holt, Rinehart and Winston.

Brière, Eugene. 1966. An experimentally defined hierarchy of difficulties of learning phonological categories. Language 42, 768-796.

Earle, M. J. 1967. Bilingual semantic merging and an aspect of acculturation. Journal of Personality and Social Psychology 6, 304-312.

Ervin, Susan M. 1963. Language development. Child Psychology [62nd Yearbook of the National Society for the Study of Education], ed. by H. W. Stevenson, pp. 108-143. Chicago: University of Chicago Press.

Ervin-Tripp, Susan M. 1964. Imitation and structural change in children's language. New directions in the study of language, ed. by E. H. Lenneberg, 163-189. Cambridge, Mass.: MIT Press.

_____ 1966. Language development. Review of child development research, ed. by Lois and Martin Hoffman, vol. 2. pp. 55-105. New York: Russell Sage Foundation.

_____ 1967. An Issei learns English. Journal of Social Issues, 23, 78-90.

J. J. Gumperz. 1964. Linguistic and social interaction in two communities. The ethnography of communication, ed. by J. J. Gumperz and Dell Hymes. American Anthropologist 66, No. 6, part 2, 137-153.

_____ 1967. On the linguistic markers of bilingual communication. Journal of Social Issues 23, 2, 48-57.

Haugen, Einar. 1955. Problems of bilingual description. General linguistics 1, 1-9.

Labov, W. 1965. Stages in the acquisition of standard English in social dialects and language learning. Social dialects and language learning, ed. by Roger Shuy. Champaign, Illinois: National Council of Teachers of English.

Lenneberg, Eric H. 1967. Biological foundations of language. New York: Wiley & Sons.

McNeill, David. 1971. The capacity for grammatical development in children. The ontogenesis of grammar, ed. by Dan I. Slobin. New York: Academic Press.

Menyuk, Paula. 1963. Syntactic structures in the language of children. Child Development 34, 407–422.

Osgood, C. E. 1963. On understanding and creating sentences. American Psychologist 18. 735–751.

Osgood, C. E., Suci, G., and Tannenbaum, H. 1957. The measurement of meaning. Urbana: University of Illinois Press.

Sachs, Jacqueline Strunk. 1967. Recognition memory for syntactic and semantic aspects of connected discourse. Perception and Psychophysics 2. 437–442.

Sawyer, J. Ervin, S. M., Silver, S. D'Andrea, J., and Aoki, H. 1963. The utility of translation and written symbols during the first thirty hours of language study. International Review of Applied Linguistics in Language Teaching (IRAL) 1. 157–192.

Slobin, D. I. 1966. The acquisition of Russian as a native language. The genesis of language; a psycholinguistic approach, ed. by Frank Smith and George A. Miller. Cambridge, Mass.: MIT Press.

Slobin, D. I. (Ed.) 1967. Field manual for the cross-cultural study of the acquisition of communicative competence. Berkeley: University of California, Language-Behavior Laboratory.

Templin, M. 1957. Language skills in children. University of Minnesota Institute of Child Welfare Monograph 26, 94.

Thorne, J. P., Dewar, H. M., Whitefield, H., Bratley, P. n. d. A model for the perception of syntactic structure. Edinburgh: English Language Research Institute.

8 | Structure and Process in Language Acquisition

Wallace Lambert's recent experimental program in which Canadian Anglophones learn French presents a dilemma to American advocates of bilingual education. Lambert took a group of English-speaking children and put them into kindergartens in which for two years French was the sole medium of instruction. The pupils were all monolingual. In an astonishingly short time, their achievements in language and in other subjects were equal to those of French and English monolinguals.

If this could happen, why do Chicanos have problems in our California schools? Since the overt linguistic circumstances seem entirely parallel, it seems to me the differences are social. In the Montreal environment, English-speaking children have no sense of inferiority or disadvantage in the school. Their teachers do not have low expectations for their achievements. Their social group has power in the community; their language is respected, is learned by Francophones, and becomes a medium of instruction later in the school. In the classrooms, the children are not expected to compete with native speakers of French in a milieu which both expects and blames them for their failures, and never provides an opportunity for them to excel in their own language.

If the root problems of Chicano children in our schools are social, rather than linguistic, we can expect that the comparable structure here would provide a fully bilingual program, as in Miami. Thus the Chicano children could see their own language respected as a medium of instruction, and see Anglophones struggling to learn it as they learn English. It would not be surprising if in such fully bilingual programs they eventually learn school English better than

children in schools where English is the sole medium of instruction—
even though they hear and speak less English in the course of the
school day.

I think two major changes have taken place in our views of
language acquisition in recent years. One is that we now are beginning to see the functions of language in the life of the speaker as of
far more importance in its acquisition than we had realized, and the
other is that the mechanical view that practice makes perfect has
given way under the impact of the evidence that speechless children
can have well developed language. Studies of first language acquisition have grown rapidly and undergone some major theoretical
changes. It is my purpose in this paper to bring the current views
of child language acquisition and of language processing strategies
to bear on some issues of second language learning.

If one is to study how people change, how they learn to understand, imitate, or emit sentences, then one must at least start with
some notions of how they handle such linguistic material at a given
point in development. The study of change then is a study of change
either in their processing procedures or in the stored structures—
for example their vocabulary—as it is employed in that processing.

Recent work on children's language acquisition has brought
out strongly that the child is not just a passive vessel of sense impres-
sions. He actively strains, filters, reorganizes what he is exposed
to. His imitations are not exact duplications or even random reductions of input, but reflect knowledge similar to that revealed in his
other uses of language. In this respect, first and second language
learning must be quite alike; the learner actively reorganizes, makes
generalizations, simplifies. Any learning model which predicts language learning on the basis of input without regard to the selective
processing by the learner will not work, except for trivial problems. [1]
And yet most of our rationales for procedures in second language instruction have been based on assumptions that organization of input,
plus practice, will have predictable results.

The processing or strategy analyses currently discussed
differ from linguistic descriptions in that they are concerned with
actual behavior occurring in time, so that questions of how long a

process takes, and what processes are simultaneous make sense.
In testing hypotheses about processing we are concerned to use a maximum range of criteria. Linguists rely on native speakers' judgments of grammaticality, paraphrase equivalence, and structural parallelism. In addition we would use other criteria, such as effects of memory, time to process, mistakes in repetition, and differences between types of performance.

There are at present no processing models in existence except as general schemata. You can imagine that filling in the details will take many years, since the program is so ambitious. I plan to illustrate the relation of such approaches to second language learning in a few instances.

If we begin by looking at processing of the auditory surface, it is important to think about some of the interactions involved. For example, speakers of English interpret pitch and intensity cues to differentiate meanings. But when judges are asked to draw or identify the details of the contours, they often reconstruct on the basis of the full, completed sentence interpretation (Lieberman 1965). It is this reconstruction of which Chomsky and Halle (1968) speak in describing the cyclic rules of stress and the impact of grammar on prosodic judgments. They are not talking about the initial perception and utilization of pitch and intensity. Otherwise it would be totally baffling how infants under one year discriminate these properties and imitate them long before they interpret grammatical features.

It is perfectly clear that lexical, grammatical, and pragmatic contexts can influence the interpretation of phonological features. These interpretations are a final outcome. Any model must account for the fact that a preparatory set or some input information may effect an interpretation powerfully relative to other information. Yet it is the case that people can analyze and remember isolated syllables independent of lexical and grammatical information—how else could we repeat nonsense or expect students to write down new technical vocabulary? Or, for that matter, learn a new language.

The implications of these effects are merely that the overall model will not take the form of a series of equally important, irrevocable decisions ordered from phonology to syntax, but will be far more complex and may include short-term surface structure memory and provisional analyses.

One way of looking at second-language learning is to assume that the first encounters with a second language will be handled by the apparatus of structure and process already available. But there is an additional factor to consider. An adult who has changed his linguistic system only in minor ways—by adding new vocabulary, for example—for many years may not have available ready strategies for change. An adult who has already learned other languages, or a child who is constantly in the process of reorganizing his processing system and adding to his storage at all levels will have quite different approaches to new input. "Learning to learn" is an established notion in psychology. The most adaptable, sensitive language learner we can find is a young child. Surely we can expect that his second language learning will reflect many of the same processes of development as he used to discover his first language. On the other hand, in the case of inexperienced adults we can expect the system to be most adaptable just at the point where it changes most readily in adult life—the lexicon. But we can expect the typical adult to be ready to process both the sounds and syntax of what he hears as if his usual processing devices were appropriate. [2]

Three different kinds of performance have been the bases for making inferences about mental processes. For example, we often use imitation to assess knowledge of language. At a minimum, it can be shown that imitation requires perception, storage, organization of output, and motor output. In addition, before the storage phase there will be interpretation if the material is interpretable.

It is a common practice in reporting imitations to say that speakers "perceive" in a certain way. But I think it is clear that even someone who clearly could hear a difference between two input items might not differentiate them in his own pronunciation.

When a person listens to an utterance, and then answers it, acts on it, paraphrases it, or just stores up its message, we say he has interpreted its meaning. The components of interpreting and imitation are in part the same. In interpreting, components may be perception, short term storage while various kinds of processing occur, and an outcome which may result in immediate action of some kind, in long-term storage of the message, or both. If the outcome options are limited, the surface structure in short-term memory is erased very rapidly, and even linguistic processing may be minimal. There are several kinds of good evidence that when the task is to understand, surface structure features like exact words, passive vs. active, are rapidly forgotten though they must have been utilized for the interpretive task.

In the task of <u>production</u> the processing is far more difficult to analyze because the input is not known. It must overlap with interpretation in including lexical and syntactic processing, but the nature of the input is quite different so it remains to be seen how the processing can be similar. In terms of organization and motor output the processes are like imitation.

It is often pointed out (e. g. Fraser, Bellugi, and Brown 1963) that during language acquisition interpretation appears to be more advanced than production. For example, a child who frequently gives in production nouns unmarked for number may consistently correctly interpret plurality. In the case of phonology, the difference may merely lie in the articulatory demands absent in interpretation. In syntax, there are other reasons. One may be that in organizing the production of a sentence, the speaker must make many explicit choices. He cannot rely on redundancy. He cannot hope mumbling will be correctly interpreted—unless, as we all know, he is in his family or close peer group and can rely on their assumptions regarding his meanings. But the listener frequently expects such a narrow range of alternatives—or in picture tests he may be given such a narrow range—that he need process very little input to know what is going on—he can listen with half an ear. Further, as McNeill has suggested, the time available to the listener is longer since normally nobody paces his decisions, but sentence production forces linear output and the unskilled orator has no preprogrammed material to plug in while he prepares. We have evidence that listeners may still be processing an earlier sentence when exposed to later material.

The comparison of interpreting skill and production skills can of course only be made when topic and structure are carefully controlled; we can find the opposite result if they are not. For example, foreign students with control of topic can produce pre-organized sentences like skilled producers of English. But if you make rapid topical and structural switches you may find their comprehension is poor. At an extreme, some linguists learn questions and greetings in a new language so well they are taken for native speakers—but then nobody shows them the way when they can't understand directions.

These three processes, imitation, interpretation or comprehension, and sentence production are obviously intercalated in various ways. We have reason to believe, for example, that interpretation may routinely accompany imitation since it can often occur very rapidly and does not interfere. We find that children given a series of sentences of various types to imitate will often answer the questions or act out the imperatives if they can easily. If the sentence to be imitated surpasses the memory span for the period of delay before the imitation is to be produced, it is likely to be interpreted first. Then the sentence is put out through the normal sentence production device and looks very similar in many respects to spontaneous utterances. We see in two-year olds that imitations are grammatically like free speech. The Harlem teenagers who worked with Labov, for certain forms like imbedded questions, translated standard English into their normal equivalent when asked to imitate (Labov et al. 1968).

I am sure that the appropriate sentence processing models will not show one route, but many, available to account both for the speed and power of human sentence processing. It is clear that we have heuristic devices which allow us to listen with minimal attention, to process with great rapidity and minimal analysis. But at the opposite extreme we can discover the multiple ambiguities in context-free sentences thrown at us by linguists. If linguists tend to be most impressed with the power of our occasional performance (from which they want to infer competence), psychologists are more likely to want to account for the speed of our usual interaction. But we can't ignore either. The decoding of triply-imbedded sentences can be viewed as a special instance of a logical puzzle, since such sentences even when they are decoded cannot be apprehended like ordinary sentences. But within the range we can call normal sentence processing, there seem to be a family of strategies available to us as a result of task definition, set, or as alternatives when the quickest route fails.

One intuitive clue is the experience of telling a speaker we didn't understand what he said; we may find we have done so by the time he opens his mouth to repeat. In this case it appears that a quick route has failed but an alternative succeeds.

Sound system processing

Children discriminate different terminal contours by the middle of the first year (Kaplan 1970) and can imitate a few months later. The first differentiations that identify speakers from different language milieux seem to be these tonal features and other global qualities of timing and stress (Nakazima 1962). This is the time, near the end of the first year, when parents report that their children seem to converse, read the paper, to talk to their dolls. Bever (in press) has identified meaning in one of these recurrent long sequences, which may indeed be first words, but represent a level of unit analysis different from the conventional word level.

An example from a three-year old Chicano child learning English in nursery school is this (from Hernandez' material).[3]

What's his name?   [hə̂tɪtǽ]

What's his name?   [hə̂sinéⁱ]

The stress-pitch qualities of the contour are retained in both imitations. The first imitation correctly retains basic vowel qualities and locates consonants, the second adds information on sibilant and nasal, differentiating the internal consonants. The simplest structure, CVCVCV, is used. In this case the repetition gives information on the level of difficulty of the features for storage of a relatively complicated sequence, where some selection was required.

In Malmberg's report (1945, 1964)[4] of a 4 1/2 year old Finnish girl moved into a Swedish environment we find that the child produced Swedish words like "marmalad" with the stress on the first syllable as in the Finnish cognate. In this case, since the word is stored as a Finnish cognate, we can suppose that the stored lexicon lacks stress marking since it is predictable, and that in spontaneous production she generates the stress as a feature of her organizational processing in producing sentences. We can expect that any conditions which distract, which make more difficult the task of imitation, might foster reliance on already available organizational strategies and reduce the accuracy of production of timing and prosody.

Children treat prosodic contours as additional material to be stored for imitation. If they are asked to imitate grammatically difficult utterances, some do better if they are produced in a sing-song. One reason may be that easy-to-remember prosodic input may release processing capacities for other tasks. Another reason may be that the additional stress provided by such patterns supplies more stressed vowels as cues for the child.

In a detailed study of the imitations of a well-trained 2 1/2 year old girl, Slobin and Welsh (1968) report the following:

Chómsky and véritâs are crýing—Cýnthia and Tásha crý.
(1)   s í n   tâs a   krái
(2) č ms i an   tâs a   krái

In the second case, we account for the consonants in Cynthia by meta-thesis. The recency effect is clearly illustrated, the retention of the main stress, the conversion of nasality and the features composing the sibilants and fricatives into components allowing recombination— e. g. [m] becomes [n], [s] becomes [š]. The pressures for change relate to stored lexical material, so that this example illustrates another stage of imitation, not merely processing of the surface structure.

Bruce (1956) has presented words at very low intensities to listeners. He found that the guesses were primarily influenced by the stressed vowel. However, if the words presented were drawn from a category, the guessers soon used this additional clue. They guessed words at far below their thresholds in random sequences. But if they chose a wrong guess, they perseverated beyond the con-textless threshold, so that a pre-established hypothesis could make one less attentive to sensory cues. Thus in redundancy conditions the influence of phonetic input may be reduced.

In imitations, vocalic similarity tends to be retained. In addition, nasals tend to be preserved, even if they are displaced, and voiceless friction as well. Miller and Nicely (1955) also found these were acoustically easily identified.

Some of this selectivity is vividly illustrated in a recurrent
sequence of my 35-month old son, which was clearly nonsense to him:

[jao fíyə jáyns wǽs]   or: [wǽyɫθ]

After he had produced it on command with some minor variations, I
finally recognized it as a line he had heard a few times from a story
in which Molly Whipple outwits a giant, who says to her:

If once more thou cross my path
Thou shalt feel the giant's wrath!

He normally of course by this age used definite articles in standard
fashion, so the loss reflects the lack of syntactic processing of the
sentence. The stressed material only was retained .

In sum, it seems possible to predict that certain features
are more salient in unanalyzed input, and hence are preserved in imitation and recall.   They may also be better candidates for perceptual
cues for interpretation:

(1) In English, peak pitch, what is stressed or not
    stressed, and terminal fall or non-fall; Lieberman
    (1965) has shown that the physical signal presents this
    information.
(2) Timing and length in terms of stressed syllables, for
    short utterances within memory span.
(3) Approximate quality of stressed vowels, especially
    unrounded vowels.
(4) Approximate location of marked features such as fric-
    tion and nasal consonants.

As the input becomes longer and more complicated relative to the
hearer's capacities, we can expect that these factors of saliency,
along with locational markedness such as first word, and recency,
will most often show up in imitations (Blasdell and Jensen, in press).

It is common to make a distinction between ability to perceive
contrasts or recognize features, and ability to articulate that sound
with the appropriate constellation of features. But we do not ordinarily
take into account that in almost all the discrimination tasks there may
be various amounts of storage required and that the storage may
affect the retention of phonological information.

A standard way to test perception of contrasts is to use either a same-different judgment between pairs, or to present a third and ask which it matches. In such tasks, short-term storage is required to permit the comparison through time, since dichotic comparison is normally not employed. The amount of informatior that can be retained in these testing conditions can be very high.

In the Haskins laboratory procedures the subjects are well-trained and sophisticated. They know how to sit still, to ignore internal and external distractions, to orient to the acoustic input only. The input is very brief so the memory load is minimal, and even the location of attention within the syllables presented is likely to be highly focussed through long experience with similar stimuli. Even under these optimal conditions, judgments of stimuli which are near on acoustic continua but reflect articulatory discontinuities— e. g. <u>ba</u> vs. <u>ga</u> vs. <u>da</u> are no better than the categorial assignments. That is, the judgments appear to reflect coding into categories, as defined by the phonemic system of English. On the other hand, for vocalic ranges, discrimination is relatively fine, and much information on vowel quality is available in storage for comparisons (Lisker, Cooper, and Liberman 1962).

Why, then, do Spanish speakers often have trouble with classroom or examination aural discrimination of <u>bit</u> vs. <u>beet</u>? Obviously the testing conditions are quite different, and it may be that the additional distractions and anxiety may lead to more reliance on categorial storage than in the Haskins testing conditions.

In this explanation, we raise the question of the difference between what is heard and what is stored. Lengthened delays and more complicated input may demand different types of storage than brief, simple discriminations. More categorial storage reflecting experience with the most useful coding dimensions will occur the longer the delay or the more complex the material. Another distinction in process occurs when storage may be influenced by lexical recognition, in which case comparisons or reproduction may be affected by the analytic dimensions employed in lexical storage. Foreign or nonsense input is less subject to such effects, though the Slobin and Welsh example of "Chomsky and veritas are crying" shows that in complex cases even nonsense can be assimilated to available lexicon.

It is reasonable to assume that some kind of analytic process is necessary to permit matching a relatively fully specified string in immediate memory with the features of lexical items as they are stored. It has been argued by linguists in terms of efficiency that lexical storage contains only the minimal features required to differentiate lexical items, and nothing more. The features specifiable by general phonological rules, including redundancies within segments (e.g. that nasality implies voicing) or phonotactic obligations, need not be stored in the lexicon.

The ready availability of an analytic category set must speed up learning of new lexicon. Paula Menyuk (1968) showed that with age, children were increasingly efficient in recognizing and recalling the semantic association to a referent if the name they were taught to recognize conformed to English rules for monosyllabic words. Messer (1967) showed that by 3 1/2 children say these are more like words than, e.g. [dlek].

The features employed in storage may, of course, be neutralized in production. Roger Brown has used the example of a child who says fis for fish but is indignant when an adult says fis. The child's irritation shows that he has an internal model of the word fish which allows him to recognize it when produced by others and to recognize incorrect production by others.

Edward Hernandez has recently analyzed in detail the phonological development of a bilingual Chicano of three. The child produced a great variety of substitutions for adult /r/s. On internal grounds, such as distributional differences between word-final and intervocalic location, he was able to identify three underlying forms. In certain positions, such as word-finally, the contrasts were neutralized in production. The three underlying forms turned out to correspond to English /r/ and Spanish /r/ and /rr/. For example, in intervocalic position flaps might appear for señores, but never for here is (even though the latter is based on Spanish syntax).

In picture-naming by Japanese who learned English as adults, the second naming was usually better in the cases of the most able speakers, suggesting that they compared their own output to a stored criterion.

When information is coded for purposes of matching to lexical storage, in the case where interpretation occurs, what happens to phonetic information superfluous to interpretation? In some cases it probably is lost, but it clearly is often retained. We employ cues of social class, ethnicity and so on to classify speakers, but generally in a categorical fashion, as Labov has shown (1966). Listeners to lower class speakers from New York assume they always say da for the and fa for far, and lose probabilistic information which is in fact the basis for correct class assignment. As Geohegan has shown (1969) various prosodic and phonological features may be employed in marking rules to indicate deference, affection, distance, and anger. We assume that the decoding of this information, too, may be stereotyped. In "imitation," it is possible that accent, dialect, and mood imitations are in fact reconstructions accomplished via these stereotypes rather than accurate reflections of input features.

If information in lexical storage has been reduced to an efficient minimum, then considerable reorganization arises not only in the process of producing lexical items in isolation, but of course out of the combination which occurs in normal continuous speech. This reorganizing we assume to be a level of processing which occurs prior to the sending of motor commands which are realized as actual motor output.

It is a puzzling fact about the acquisition of English as a second language that the same "input"—e. g. the interdental consonants— may be quite differently realized by speakers with varying first languages. If we take only languages containing both apical stops and sibilants, we find a preference for one or the other to the point that it can be a reliable means of identifying "accent." A possibility proposed by Carter (n. d.) and cited in a stimulating discussion by Kathleen Connors (1968), is that there is a feature hierarchy that differs even though the same features may be present.

Many speakers can hear a difference, and when monitoring their speech carefully are able to articulate the interdental. For these reasons, we assume that it is identified distinctively in lexical storage. Therefore we assume the selectivity occurs whenever in naming, spontaneous speech, or reconstruction during imitation, material in lexical storage is turned into strings of fully specified

motor commands. Presumably also included at this level are some of
the alternation patterns which regulate contrasts between formal and
allegro speech, including which features dominate in assimilations and
simplified output. If this is the case, it should be possible to find instances of language-internal style alternations which will reveal the
greater importance, for example, of continuant properties to a French
speaker relative to a Russian or French-Canadian and thus account
for θ → s and θ → t. This kind of evidence may provide some insight
into language processing, if such adaptations can be isolated proce-
durally.

If experience in a variety of phonological rule systems aids
learning of new rules, then bilinguals should in general have more
ability to imitate sequences which violate the phonological rules of
the languages they already know. Cohen, Tucker, and Lambert (1967)
tested adult bilinguals in this respect by developing monosyllabic test
words which began with consonant clusters not acceptable in either
French or English. The most common error in all groups was simplification by loss of the first consonant. The bilinguals made fewer
errors in imitation than the monolinguals.

Brière was the first to provide systematic experimentation
on the issue of the relative difficulty of different types of new phonological learning in adults. Learning a contrast between cat and cot
requires learning a set of acoustic ranges to be identified as one or
the other class, in a given consonantal context—i.e. learning, not a
discrimination, but the limits for categorial identification, for absolute
judgment. As Harlan Lane has pointed out (1966) the task is similar
to learning semantic ranges. I have examined the progress of learning
narrower and narrower semantic overlap, so that categories have a
relatively steep slope to the 50% overlap point. Of course, even if
one performs this task well, mistakes can be made in recognizing
natural speech. Native speakers may deviate quite far in natural conditions, but are intelligible because of lexical and syntactic information which a new learner may lack.

Kathleen Connors, giving English-speaking children Hindi
words for imitation, found that they recognized the inadequacies of
their imitations. She found that the Hindi /o/ in a CVC context,
which is phonetically close, was imitated on first hearing most often

as English /u/ , next as /o/ , and least often as / ʊ / . It seems clear that some of the time the listeners were storing the information in English categorial ranges.

When a new discrimination is developed, and the coding categories to go with it, the lexicon must be reorganized. In such instances there may be hypercorrections, or there may be layered lexicon in which recently acquired items represent a distinction reliably but older items do not. The latter must be relearned and appropriately tagged.

Is it always the case that perceptual discrimination and categorial absolute judgments precede productive accuracy? This must be the case if the only available route for monitoring the produced form is auditory. Brière has commented (1968) that by articulatory instructions he was able to teach experimental subjects to produce pharyngeal fricatives and initial, heavily aspirated, lenis unvoiced stops before they could be reliably distinguished from laryngeals and other unvoiced stops, respectively. But one would guess that unless kinesthetic feedback is very reliable, the production would not be trustworthy for these consonants. We do know, from vocal training of the deaf, that it is possible to maintain intelligible speech with only kinesthetic feedback. In addition, new lexicon could be added which was learned from reading and produced through motor commands without auditory monitoring.

Brière's data provide information on both discrimination and imitative output, comparing segmental material related in systematic ways to the English mother-tongue. He found shifting of vowel ranges for categories to be the easiest to make in imitative output. New sounds were most difficult, but even they varied. The pharyngeal fricative from Arabic was extremely difficult, as was a back unrounded vowel. On phonemic grounds it is puzzling that back unrounded vowels should be much more difficult than front rounded vowels, even once discrimination has been learned. The typical error was to round the back vowel, rather than produce a front unrounded vowel, as though producing a back vowel was most controllable, but the acoustic impression of lack of rounding was less so. In terms of the unity of a motor set, rounding is much more definable than not rounding, and perhaps more easily under voluntary control.

Brière found also that unvoiced velar fricatives were learned more rapidly than their voiced counterpart. One reason was that apparently the Arabic-speaking judges tolerated a far greater range of variability in [x] as long as the friction was sufficient. Another factor may be the additional complexity in production in adding the voicing command, since voicing is a marked feature in fricatives. Substitutions for voiced fricatives included even the English /r/, which suggests that they are interpreted or decoded as French or German /r/ and translated.

Brière's most interesting finding is that redistribution of existent allophones is of only moderate difficulty. Placing [ŋ] in initial position, employing nasalized [ɛ] before stops, using voiced [h] initially, and fortis unaspirated [t] initially, proved of about the same level of difficulty, given the task of imitating isolated words. In contrast, heavily aspirated, lenis initial [ts] was relatively difficult to learn.

Mrs. Roengpitiya, a Berkeley student (1969), found that English of a Thai student showed no new sounds at all yet in spontaneous speech, but redistributions on the model of English. In both the Brière study and Mrs. Roengpitiya's analysis, phonological rule changes are acquired more readily than sounds employing new feature combinations.

In the following cases, the English form is represented by the Thai phone, not only in syllable initial position, but occasionally in syllable-final position, where it does not occur in Thai:

English	Thai	Examples
voiced affricate [ǰ]	unvoiced [ts]	judge [tsəts]
	[s]	because [bikhɔɔt]~
		[bikhɔɔs]
		rose [root]~
		[roos]
[š], [ž]	aspirated affricate	garage [garaat]~
	[tsh]	[garaatsh]

The speaker appears to have discovered that there are equivalences between English and Thai initial consonants, and in English contexts he replaces the Thai initial consonants with the Thai consonants

which are closest to English! These might be said to be lexical redistributions. They seem to reflect realization of lexicon through the
new organizational process, and new phonological rules, with no
changes yet in the resulting feature combinations available to him as
segmental output. For example, the place names pronounced in Thai
[paaklat] and [tsanburii] when mentioned in an English context receive
initial aspiration, [phaaklat] and [tshanburii].

In sum, it appears that the most permeable processes are
the learning of new discriminations, and the development in imitated
articulation at least of new phonetic locations. Second in difficulty is
the development of new phonological rules. The hardest aspect of
acquisition of a new sound system is the articulation of new feature
combinations, with considerable over-generalization occurring in the
process.

It has commonly been noted that children are more adept than
adults in learning new sound systems. They do not lack problems, of
course—witness, for example, the difficulties of the 4 1/2 year old
child studied by Bertil Malmberg in acquiring voiced stops. And
there are children with articulatory difficulties in their native language
at that age.

On the theory that the attentional focus and learning strategy
applied to a second language is a function of the most recent learning
problems in a prior language, one would expect that most adults attend
primarily to learning a new lexicon. One of the children studied by
Hernandez rejected parallel lexicon in English and Spanish, and
insisted one word could do for both, in the case of new words at least,
such as animal names. Adults, unlike children, have a large invest-
ment in lexical alternations as a means of conveying information.
For children, a great deal of interaction remains affective, and therefore is carried by articulatory and prosodic variations.

Children often hear adult speech which is unintelligible by
virtue of lexicon or grammar. The fact that a foreign language is
lexically or grammatically unintelligible is not distinctive. What is
distinctive is the sound surface. Hernandez noted that some Spanish-
speaking children first "speak English" by using English phonolgical
features with Spanish lexicon and grammar. Similar instances have
observed in English-speaking children.

For a variety of reasons which are not well understood, children show more interest in sounds than do most adults. They play with sounds, make up nonsense games, generalize between words that sound alike more than words alike in meaning.

It was a vivid feature of the difference in Hernandez' corpus between the Chicano child's responses in speaking English and in speaking Spanish, his first language, that he imitated English far more often. In Spanish, he usually replies rather than imitates. The difference, of course, is that he understands English less well. Shipley, Smith, and Gleitman (1969) found that children around two to three exposed to short utterances with nonsense in various locations often spontaneously imitated the nonsense word. In our work on language development in monolinguals, we found imitating was very frequent around two, but diminished later.

One way to describe the function of spontaneous imitation for the learner is that it enables him to hold the strange object a moment longer before him, to look at it from all angles, before it fades from view. Whether from curiosity or delight, children in such cases seem to treat words as they do objects. It is not clear what the effects of this spontaneous behavior may be on learning. Perhaps the new distributional patterns become better recognized in this way. Perhaps the meaning of new lexicon may be learned, for imitation enables the child to tie the arbitrary new sound sequence to a discerned meaning for a moment longer, much as repetition of a new name helps us store it while we stare at its owner.

Experienced language teachers report that in large groups in organized language programs discrimination generally proves not to be a problem, but rather output is the issue, and in output large individual differences persist. The difference between adults and children, and between different adults, might lie in part in the skill in utilizing kinesthetic feedback, and relating it to what is heard, or recalled.

Here is a Chicano child, practicing alone:

      hayuse. ʔayo. xáy xáy xáyú xáyǿ háwaryÛ
      əháwaryú xay xou
      háwryú
      xawyu...

Another child hears him and says:

> hàwiryú
> hâwyú hâweyú

And so on.

Lexical processing

      Information about vocabulary has to be approachable either from phonological input or semantic input, to allow for both interpretation and sentence production. An example of how word-searches in production may work is given in Brown and McNeill's ingenious experiment with the "tip of the tongue" phenomenon (1966). When you try to remember someone's name, you may have the following experience: You may, in the United States, recognize the national origin of the name. Such general categorial groups are efficient for American names; orientals otherwise fluent in English sometimes have trouble remembering American names because they lack a full array of European name-sorting clues. In addition to such semantic groupings, you may remember how many syllables the name had, the location of stress, and the first sound or letter. Brown and McNeill, giving meanings of rare words, evoked partial recall. These same features appeared during recall stages, and in addition final letters; a serial position effect was revealed as is common in arbitrary sequences, and in addition "chunking" of units like suffixes. In accounting for their results, the authors propose (1966: 355) an analogy to a card storage device. "Suppose that there are entries for <u>sextant</u> on several different cards. They might all be incomplete, but at different points, or some might be incomplete and one or more of them complete. The several cards would be punched for different semantic markers and perhaps for different associations so that the entry recovered would vary with the rule of retrieval.... The more accessible features are entered on more cards or else the cards on which they appear are punched for more markers; in effect, they are wired into a more extended associative net."

      The problem, of course, is that if we assume that at one computer "address" there is a matrix of phonological features, enough to separate one lexical item from others, a set of syntactic markers,

and semantic features, we have no way of accounting for partial recall.
It is clear that on the separate, rare occasions of exposure to low
frequency words only a partial array of semantic features and of
phonological features may be stored, and there is, of course, no
reason to assume that they will be identical on all occasions. The
features selected by the device include some we have reason to believe,
from imitative behavior, are most salient to perception. One major
difference is that Bruce's recognition data make vowel quality dominant; Brown and McNeill speak of "first letters." The difference
implies that for perception, vowels may be clearer, but that once
identification and interpretation has occurred, long-term lexical
storage may employ more consonantal information. From the standpoint of informational efficiency, consonants would be better. If
words are rare, and stored primarily via consonants, they should not
be accessible to Bruce's subjects until a signal level is reached that
makes consonantal information audible.

During sentence production anticipations can indicate lexical
selection ahead of time, whereas hesitations occur not only at points
of syntactic encoding but at points of maximum lexical uncertainty.
In Goldman-Eisler's clever experiment (1964) it was found that when
words were clipped from an otherwise intact tape (as they might be
on a bad phone connection) the least predictable items elicited the
longest hesitation pauses both for the original speakers and those who
correctly guessed them.

Interestingly, those morphemes which were most predictable
were also least audible, which of course proves English is the most
efficient of all languages since its stress and timing rules permit
producer economy just when there would be least loss!

In addition to phonological and semantic features of variable
detail, lexical storage must contain information regarding selectional
restrictions. The storage of he contains a restriction to subject position in the surface structure. One might simply assume that the
selection of pronouns for gender and number occurs directly from
semantic information. But what happens when someone speaks of
washing the spinach and uses a pronoun? In French, one would say
lavez-les, in English, Be sure to wash it well. But we would not say
wash them, like a Frenchman. This difference suggests that even

exophoric pronouns, those referring to external referents not previously specified in discourse, may yet require passage through the noun-storage device. Is it possible to use the correct pronoun gender, say in German, but forget the noun? Brown and McNeill's experiment implies that it might be.

In addition to single lexical items there must be similar devices for higher order units of many kinds, like United States of America, how are you, and idiosyncratically frequent sequences.

Processing theories vary in whether they locate lexical processing before or after grammatical analysis in interpretation. Thorne et al (n. d.) describing a device for interpretation of the phrase markers of input sentences, utilize no dictionary at all except a list of finite items like function words and affixes. It is clear that syntactic information could make far more efficient the recognition device for lexicon by narrowing the search. But the process is not assumed by anyone to involve one stage for a whole utterance (except very short ones), and then another stage, but rather it is ordinarily assumed that processing of earlier material co-occurs with input later, and may in fact influence the thresholds for features of that input.

Evidence from child language favors the priority of lexical processing, since children for some years make little use of cues other than order and syntactic features of lexicon in grammatical processing. In handling jabberwocky, for example, they are more influenced by order than by affixes and grammatical morphemes (Porter 1955).

Some years ago, Einar Haugen (1955:7) developed the very fruitful concept of the diamorph. "If two morphemes have phonemic shape or semantic function in common, they will often be identified by bilingual speakers." The identification is manifested in semantic and syntactic shifting, in which the two items are treated as equivalent in meaning, syntactic features, selectional restrictions, and so on. For example, in Je cherche pour le livre the French child carries over the distribution of the English look into French, and in il est un garçon the syntactic features of he and il, which largely overlap, are assumed to be equivalent.

We would in fact assume that a plausible first step in second language learning is to map matched synonyms onto the elaborate structure of semantic and syntactic features already available. This is the classic case of compound bilingualism, with common semantic features and categories employed in both languages. Differentiation of features occurs as the items are experienced in different verbal and nonverbal contexts, just as differentiation within the lexicon of a single language occurs, though some items in early vocabulary, like big and strong, are treated as synonyms by young children. Indeed, such differentiation may be so fine that in bilingual communities supposed translation equivalents may coexist in both codes because the nuances of connotation have added dimensions of discrimination not available to monolinguals. Japanese women in the United States often use the word husband among themselves since it lacks the "lord and master" feature of the Japanese translation.

Some diamorphs reveal features of the syntactic development of second language learners. For example, when a Frenchman says, That's a book who is on the table, we wonder if generally who = qui. A similar case is He held his hat in her hand, in which (if we ignore the anomaly of her for inalienable possession), we find son = his, and sa = her, although of course the basis for gender of possessives is entirely different in the two languages, concerning the possessor in English, the possessed in French.

A 6-year old French child in an English milieu, described by Paul Kinzel (1964) and grammatically analyzed by Kathleen Connors, gives excellent evidence of diamorphs for pronouns, in sentences like these:

> "She is all mixed up." (pendule)
> "I got her." (serviette)
> "I'm going to jump her." (crepe)
> "Who likes them?" (épinards)

Here again we see that pronoun selection requires processing via a gender- and number-marked unit of some sort rather than directly from semantic information.

What is the relation between the stored French lexicon and stored English lexicon for such a child? If the storage of phonological features and of lexicon involves merely an additional tag designating language, register, or affective connotations, then one would assume that the tagging process goes to the morphophonemic matrix only for the lexicon at first, and leaves semantic and many syntactic features unmarked, undifferentiated, appropriate to both codes of a bilingual. Through additional learning, perhaps dependent on differentiated contexts, whether verbal or nonverbal, these semantic feature constellations also could acquire such code and register tags. I would not want to assume that entirely separate environments, e. g. Montreal vs. France, are necessarily required for such differentiation. It is well known that even within the life of linguistic enclaves in the United States there may be quite distinctive usage complexes for items if they have a "home and kitchen" implication in one language, and a "work" implication in the other. Indeed, my work with Japanese bilinguals on this issue suggests that the differentiation of meaning constellations is extremely complex and may not work the same way for different domains of lexicon (Ervin-Tripp 1967).

There has, however, been some confirmation of the effect of acquisition milieu in developing more differentiated semantic systems and associative networks (Lambert, Havelka, and Crosby 1958; Gekoski 1968).

One of the advantages of using feature marking rather than separate locations in the brain as a way of handling code differentiation is that in bilingual communities shifting between languages is frequently a reflection of nuances of social meaning (Gumperz and Hernandez 1969). For this reason, one would not want to make the apparatus for shifting more elaborate than that required for style shifting of monolinguals.

The structure of meaning and hence of lexical mapping appears from the little evidence we have to change a good deal with age. The earliest lexical items at the beginning of language development are global semantically, and change significance with context. For example, the word coat may mean coat, hat, dress, going for a walk, baby carriage, let's go! Gradually both semantic and syntactic specificity increase, the latter depending on the differentiation of syntax and the elaboration of selectional rules. The similarity in these features in the early lexicon of both languages of bilingual children is evident in their ability to switch in midsentence, as in esta Chicqui coming? ves este in here? and Un de tes blooms sont dead.

The semantic complexity of adult lexicon is far greater in terms of elaboration of features, knowledge of distributional probabilities, and analytic abstractness of features, as in the development of taxonomic hierarchies. All of this development takes place within a context of enriched conceptual discrimination, which may affect far more than direct verbal functioning. For these reasons, we can assume that acquisition of new lexicon by adults could occur extremely rapidly. It does not have to wait upon conceptual maturation. To the extent that semantic universals exist, a large part of the work in the acquisition of structure had already occurred. In addition, as we have suggested earlier, adults continue throughout life to add lexical items both in terms of entirely new semantic features and constellations of features, and in terms of stylistic and affective nuances of selection. As Geohegan found in his extraordinary study of address rules in Samal, changes continued to enrich the address alternatives and complexity of rules of selection throughout adult life. This is one domain of language in which children appear to have no particular advantage in acquisition. To the extent that languages acquired in childhood appear to have some semantic differences (e.g. one can be angrier or sadder in one's mother tongue), they may simply reflect the fact that the affective life of the child is different; lexicon acquired in childhood may retain connotations from that time. My work with adult bilinguals has revealed that adults can acquire emotional connotations in the adult language depending on their "resocialization." Child rearing in a second language can have a profound impact, for example, on semantic differentiation and connotative elaboration in that language.

Syntactic processing

The order of relationship in ability between comprehension, imitation, and production of syntax is not the same at all ages. Normally, it is true, comprehension is superior to production for features undergoing change. The reasons have been discussed earlier. However, the relative ease of imitation depends on age, memory span, and the features to be imitated. For example, children below two have very brief productive capacities. The mean utterance length of their free speech shows surprising reliability over samples and grows at a constant rate. After the beginnings of ellipsis, of course, this measure becomes an increasingly poor index of both complexity and level of development because deletions and compressions requiring sophistication may result in a shorter sentence. At the age when produced sentences are short, so are imitations. In other respects as well, such as the number of basic sentence elements present, imitations are like spontaneous speech. Presumably at this stage the immediate rote memory span is quite short, and the processing abilities of the child are so small as not to allow him to generate an imitated sentence longer than his immediate rote span when he imitates.

On the other hand, research on comprehension at this stage suggests that children may attend to connective items they do not produce, such as articles, since their absence or replacement with nonsense disrupts comprehension (Shipley, Smith, Gleitman 1969).

At a certain point, abilities become sufficiently advanced to permit interpretation, storage, and reproduction to allow imitations to well exceed rote memory span. For example, Labov noted that teenage boys who could not imitate I asked him whether he could play baseball, were able to interpret and translate I asked him if he could play baseball into I axed him could he play baseball. They clearly interpreted the sentence as containing an imbedded question and produced their version of such a structure, but believed they had imitated verbatim.

As coding ability for storage increases, learners at first reproduce deviant material according to their own grammar; later, they may be able to store the information about deviance as well, and reproduce it, as though they coded the basic syntax plus footnotes. Some building up of the level of syntactic difficulty in imitated material can be obtained by repeating, or gradually enlarging the complexity of a given utterance (by expansions). As an instructional device for altering grammatical skill this method (which is rather like many drill methods) is no more effective than giving replies, and thus increasing the learner's exposure to relevant heard sentences (Cazden 1965).

Models for syntactic processing have been forced to differentiate "surface structure" processing from deeper levels. It has been repeatedly found that such surface features as subject vs. predicate location of information (e. g. passive vs. active), and prenominal vs. postnominal location of adjectives can make a difference in processing speed, latency in comprehension, and so forth. On the other hand information that requires more complex processing, like agent vs. direct object of action in passive vs. active sentences, or main vs. subordinate clause will alter the same processing measures. Smith has pointed out that the "compression" of information into constituents, which sometimes arises, according to linguists, from reordering and deletion transformation, and sometimes does not, as in complex auxiliaries, can alter ease of imitation. It is obvious that the first level that the listener encounters is surface order and cues as to underlying structure, such as connectives. Sentences can sometimes be interpreted from this information alone with only lexical processing. For instance, truncated passives require minimal analysis because there is only one semantic relation possible.

There is some evidence of the existence of simple order processing heuristics in both children and adults. Troike (1969) has cited the following:

> Coleman had matched groups of speakers
> read, once, passages containing many passives...

The sentence would not mislead a reader were it not for the possibility of interpreting read as +past, but the initial readiness to fall into this trap arises from the structural preference for an agent-transitive verb-object sequence.

In center-imbedded sentences this strategy may also impede solutions.

> The chef cooks oil signed the list.

Compare this sentence to the following:

> The cat the dog chased ate the meat.

Welsh has suggested that following a lexical processing that yields syntactic and semantic features, a kind of storage loop keeps recycling the syntactic markers to subject them to "templates" of "encounter-operate rules." For example, if a noun is encountered,

look for a verb. If the verb is transitive, look for a noun. Interpret
as agent-verb-object. His data from imitations of a 2 1/2 year old
to some extent support this hypothesis.

In answering questions, children seem to employ the NVN
and related strategies. For example, if they hear a question word followed by N+TV, they normally reply with a direct object of the verb,
if the question word is not in their lexical repertoire, for instance
how or when. If they hear a question word followed by an inanimate
noun and an intransitive verb, they are more likely to give a missing
locative phrase. That is, the children act as though they are completing a standard sentence frame (Ervin-Tripp 1970).

Young children often misinterpret passives which contain the
agent. They will understand The cat is chased by the moth to refer
to a picture in which a cat chases a moth. Since passives nearly always have the agent truncated, this unusual sentence sequence elicits
the usual interpretation that the NVN sequence must mean standard
transitive order.

In adult comprehension, Sachs (1967) has found that the formal contrast passive vs. active is forgotten almost as fast as the
particular lexical item of paired synonyms chosen. Lorraine Novinski
(1968) noted that children recognized passives, even in comprehension
instructions, when they otherwise forgot surface details in immediate
recognition tests. In this case it may be that the striking contrast of
surface order was very vivid; it may be even more important to children than to adults, by whom meaning is rapidly interpreted.

The presence of clues to guide the conversion of surface
structure into deep structure may alter the ease of processing. For
example, Shipley and Catlin (1967) compared processing time for
children imitating sentences with relative clauses. They tested
processing time by adding a short list of arbitrary items to be remembered after the sentence. Reduction in recall of the first item on this
list suggested sentence analysis still was going on when this word was
heard. Such reductions happened more often when a relative pronoun
was deleted (e. g. I saw the cat the mouse liked). One child who supplied the pronoun in his imitations did not have the reduction in list
recall either.

118 Language Acquisition and Communicative Choice

The learning of syntax in children clearly begins with their development of analysis strategies in listening, when they are expected to make appropriate reactions to heard material. The evidence we have about their early syntax in a variety of languages suggests that it begins with a set of primitive and universal basic semantic relations: negation, conjunction, agent-action, action-object, attribution, location, identification, possession. Normally, these basic relations are represented by order relations in speech, but of course in inflecting languages children may develop morphological realizations of these relations much earlier than in languages like English, where affixes represent less basic features. Order relations seem to be very apparent to children. Where they are very consistent in adult speech— e. g. location of question words in English—they are the same in child speech. Numerous children have used consistent order in output, when input was less orderly. In the grammars of children I have worked with, it is more likely that action-object order can be permuted than that agent-verb is changed. Order is almost always accurately reproduced in imitations.

The point in the development of English where semantic relations are no longer represented by simple orders in the surface structure is most strikingly the time, around 2-3, when the auxiliary and do system develops. This is also a system of great interest in second language learning since it is peculiar to English.

Klima and Bellugi (1966) have described the development of the negative and interrogative, and their results correspond closely to what we have found in Berkeley in these structures and in ellipsis. The negative goes through three stages: a negator external to the sentence nucleus, an internal negator placed before the predicate, and differentiated into no or not before nouns and adjectives, and these plus some monomorphemic negative verbs like don't or won't before main verbs—finally, the adult pattern. In the interrogative two stages are essentially characterized by use of intonation, and the prefixing of question words to otherwise complete sentences. In the third stage, do is differentiated and inflected for tense. It alternates with modals before main verbs in negatives, and the auxiliary is permuted with the subject in yes-no questions and occasionally in wh-questions. It appears alone with pronouns in ellipsis.

Children who speak other languages seem to have difficulty differentiating the English system from their own, but in some respects they follow the same order of development. Hernandez noted that one of the Chicano children produced no can and no could on the model of Spanish. This order would only occur in English monolinguals at the very early stage when subjects ordinarily are not present.

An excellent analysis by Ravem (1968) of the auxiliary system of his 6-year old Norwegian-speaking son, who acquired English in Scotland, points to compromises between Norwegian and English. In Norwegian and English interrogative and negative sentences, modals are alike. For this reason, an underlying structure might be available to the child for developing the English rule easily, simply generalizing modals to all auxiliaries. But in the early stages, do was omitted, perhaps because it is meaningless.

In English-speaking children before do or copulas are systematically present, negatives are marked by a variety of negators between subject and main verb or predicate. Ravem's son often produced similar sentences: I not looking for edge, I not like that, I not sitting on my chair. In acquiring negatives, the boy followed a developmental sequence similar to English-speaking children, with the negator before the main verb regularly, as in the Norwegian sentence with a modal.

However, in the case of interrogatives, before do appeared, inversion of the main verb and subject occurred as in Norwegian: Drive you car to-yesterday? Like you ice-cream? Like you me not, Reidun? These inversions are not usually found in American children. But like American children, he inverts less often in wh-questions: What you reading to-yesterday? What you did in Rothbury? When the do-form appeared, Say it you not to Daddy? was replaced by Did you not say it to Daddy? The formality of this version probably represents the parental English the child heard.

Thus when do appeared, the child acquired normal English, but prior to that time he employed a negative pattern unlike Norwegian (except for modal sentences) and like younger English-speaking monolinguals. In the case of the interrogative, on the other hand, the Norwegian inversion pattern dominated, whereas at the comparable stage

American children rely solely on intonation without inversion. A good account of the reason for this difference would rest on developmental studies of Norwegian negation and questions. One might guess that in the case of interrogation an inversion locating subject second is a very reliable question cue in listening, particularly important in yes-no questions to indicate meaning from the start of the utterance whether a modal is present or not. Thus the inversion may be a strong and stable pattern by six. In the case of the negative, location is not important to meaning, and a separate rule is used for modals and nonmodalized verbs—one could see English as simpler in this sense. For this reason the child may move more readily to the English order. In other respects we see the same features that we find developmentally in monolinguals.

A rich source of information on the contrast between child bilingualism in a truly bilingual context, and adult second-language learning, appears in the research reported by Lance and his colleagues in Texas (1969). In their studies, the adults showed the usual array of problems arising from processing of English through existent Spanish syntactic rules. However, the authors make the important observation that from one-third to two-thirds of the deviant features of the foreign students' speech could not be traced to identifiable features of Spanish. I found also in doing detailed statistical counts of errors coded according to their relation to French in adult bilinguals that a large percentage had no clear basis of this sort. What are these errors, then? Some are of course production slips of one sort or another. Monolinguals make mistakes, too. These are nonrandom and revealing of production processes. Others are what I would call learner's simplifications. They are developmental features which often are shared with other learners—for instance, lack of tense inflection. Uninverted wh-questions in the Ravem study seem to rep-present this kind of developmental pattern.

Lance points out that almost all of the highly frequent deviations from standard English in the migrant bilingual children in their study were not based on Spanish. Many reflected the local English of their peers. Others seem to be developmentally based since they are common in English monolinguals, possibly at an earlier age. In Hernandez' data, too, Spanish-based structures were rare: no can, here is. The high incidence of switching in the everyday discourse

of the bilinguals in the Lance study corresponds to observations elsewhere (Gumperz and Hernandez 1969). Even where the social inhibi-
tions about switching are low, language alternations are never random.
We have very little evidence on how they are learned as sociolinguistic
regularities.

Socially, there appear to be bases in the structure of
discourse—switches to the language of quotations, boundary markers
for greetings, and for arrivals and departures of participants. Referential content may generate switching; some lexical realizations may
be common to both codes. Social allusions may generate switching.
Where the latter is a conscious rhetorical device its linguistic location may be different, being at points where hesitation pauses for
lexical input are most frequent—e. g. before nouns rather than noun
phrases.

Where social constraints are few, switching may occur at
major constituent boundaries in the case of social allusion and lexicon
may shift with syntax with some vertical cooccurrence of codes. In
some texts, the switches appear largely at underlying sentence boundaries; in others, smaller units may be switched.

In experimental situations where language is controlled by
instruction, on the other hand, we often find that the conscious control exerted affects the output language, the morphophonemic realizations of lexicon, and "switching" when it occurs is at the level of
semantic categories, syntax, or surface order, with a resulting inconsistency in vertical code features. This has been the case in my
research with Japanese and French-English bilinguals.

In communities with a long history of bilingualism, it sometimes happens that for social reasons the output language is constrained
by situation. In these cases, the codes tend to merge except at the
level of the phonemic entries in the "dictionary." Gumperz found
such surface-only switching by situation in Marathi-Kannada bilingualism in India (1967) and Brugner in Slovenian-German bilingualism
in Austria. These seem to be historically different phases of the same
psychological process of merger as my experimental studies showed.

The linguistic units shifted under both constrained and free
conditions consitute excellent evidence of the units in language

processing. For example, in an unconstrained situation, we find nearby in the same narrative in Yiddish and English: <u>un er zol buy-n di haus... zogt er, "vos darf ix keifn"... so di shul bought di haus...</u> (text collected and transcribed by David Argoff). Note that the quotations are more consistently Yiddish, but when the borrowed lexical item <u>buy</u> appears in a Yiddish context it is syntactically integrated with the suffix.

The stages of development in such a systematic separation of affixes has been described by Malmberg for a child learning Swedish after Finnish. At Stage 1, Finnish postpositions were attached to Swedish nouns to designate location. Next, the Swedish case suffix was used, followed by the postposition in Finnish. Next, the postposition was replaced by the Swedish preposition but followed the noun as before. Thus the general syntactic frame remained the same until the fourth stage, but Swedish "diamorphs" gradually replaced their Finnish counterparts until a syntactic restructuring occurred. We do not know what if any switching continued to occur.

Stage 0. $N_F + Gen_F + Po_F$

Stage 1. $N_S + Gen_F + Po_F$

Stage 2. $N_S + Suf_S + Po_F$

Stage 3. $N_S + Suf_S + Pr_S$

Stage 4. $Pr_S + N_S + Suf_S$

The child who lives in a bilingual environment hears a good deal of switching. Then we may need to find out how he comes to tag the features of his two codes and separate them in formal style. We clearly need more process descriptions to see how these changes come about. Malmberg's has the advantage of showing stages, but we know very little about the conditions under which the utterances are produced, and whether the patterns vary so that children develop situationally-controlled switching rules.

Finally, I would like to return to the issue of how the learning takes place. In the case of concurrent learning, as may happen with bilingual children, there is evidence that code separation of lexical material can, in experimental conditions, be better than in successive learning (Lambert and Witelson 1961). In the case of concurrent learning of two languages by children, we simply can assume we are dealing with primary language acquisition. In the case of successive or overlapping learning, we assume that some prior processes and structures will be employed during learning. There are dramatic differences in the learning conditions of natural second language learning and classroom second language learning that must have consequences for the kinds of changes that take place during learning. The evidence from natural learning suggests that manifest speech is largely secondary. That is, as long as the learner orients to speech, interprets it, and learns the form or arrangement that represents the meaning, he learns language as fast as someone speaking. Children have normal language development who cannot or do not speak. The only case where motor practice might have any merits is in articulation of new sounds or in writing letters in a new alphabet.

Secondly, it would appear to be impossible to learn to recognize what contrasts of sound or structure are important, or to learn to interpret either lexicon or structure, unless one knows what is meant. Children do not learn languages spoken as secret languages between adults. They do not learn languages from television, if their parents are deaf and use signs. They normally learn language if they hear simple, repetitive speech, which is what characterizes "baby talk" style or speech to infants, and after the first few months this speech normally refers to meanings that are obvious from context. The first syntactic structures children interpret and produce are those focused on basic semantic relations. These are picked out very early from the complex input.

Is the same true of language-learning adults in natural situations? I have observed that Japanese speakers, who have immense syntactic problems in learning English, for which almost every conceivable order is different from Japanese, do successfully signal basic semantic relations. There are cases when they will slip, and put the verb last.

> Everybody together and "omochi" and "otoso" and other
> many—big dinners, have, enjoy.
> Every day I think come—all over the street and some
> funny comics make—I don't know.

But these order problems are surprisingly few. Far more persistent are subject, preposition, and object deletions which do not disrupt

intelligibility because the contexts make them clear. The assumption
is that in learning to interpret English sentences the basic processing
heuristics which permit identification of subject, verb, and object,
and modifier—head units must be developed very early to permit
even primitive communication to take place. In these respects the
adult seems like the child learning his first language.

But we know that in formal instruction there is frequently
emphasis on structure devoid of semantic context, practiced in instances where meaning is either unclear or trivial—e. g. in transformation drills. So it cannot surprise us when after an hour of practicing turning statements into questions a student intent on getting a
question answered, after class, produces a question that is a word-
for-word translation of his mother tongue and shows no impact whatever of the drill. What means this word, Mrs. Tripp?

Valerian Postovsky, of the Russian department at the Defense
Language Institute at Monterey, recently compared two instructional
methods which differed in the point at which speaking was introduced.
In both, highly discriminative listening was required. For a month
the experimental subjects performed various written drills from
spoken input, but they did not speak except in the first few days when
they were taught the Cyrillic alphabet. They heard speech only from
native speakers. The audio-lingual group had oral drills along with
their usual memorizing of dialogue and written work. They heard
their own speech, and that of fellow-students. Both groups had six
hours a day of class and laboratory drills in addition to homework.
After a month, the experimental group was very superior in morphology, and somewhat superior in vocabulary even when tested by story
telling aloud. Most surprising of all to the believers in oral drill is
the finding that the experimental group had better Russian pronunciation. Most of the items were redistributions of sounds in their repertoire like dark and light [l], [l^y] and so on. This experiment suggests
that a thoughtful incorporation of features we have found in natural
language-learning may improve our pedagogical success. But to do
this adaptation rationally, we need a much more analytic approach to
the stages of development in language processing during learning.
We need to be able to sort out for the adult learner the entirely different kind of processing skills he may need, and not blindly assume that
there is one method for all ends, or even that the superficial features
of skill practiced will inevitably match the knowledge acquired.

NOTES

I am grateful for discussions on the materials in this paper to John Gumperz, Edward Hernandez, John Macnamara, and Martin Braine. Braine's superb paper (1971) on language acquisition aided me in seeing the relation between first and second language learning and how we might connect processing models with learning.

[1] An example of the devastating effects of an automatic operant view of language acquisition is provided in a Russian teaching program supervised by Morton, described by Valerian Postovsky (1970). The taped self-instructional material consisted of writing discriminatory responses to phonemes, words, sentences, and then imitating them, then imitating sentences. Hints of meaning were finally given in the latter stage of the third of four stages in the materials. Students worked six hours a day for seventeen weeks. At the end of the period their Army Language Proficiency Test score in Russian was below the score achievable by random marking. They were subsequently enrolled in the regular Russian program at Monterey, but never caught up with the beginners in that course! Whether because Russian became hateful and meaningless to them, or because they created idiosyncratic meanings for the sounds they heard, this program actually interfered with their acquisition of a meaningful language. The idle brain does the devil's work.

[2] The distinction adult-child may be too sharp here. We have some evidence, mentioned later, that children as young as 4 1/2 may show transfer of earlier grammatical patterns into new languages, and in turn over-generalization back to the first language. We have too few close analyses of changing grammatical systems of children as they learn second languages to speak confidently of age changes.

[3] I am grateful to Loni Takeuchi for translating and summarizing.

REFERENCES

Bever, Thomas. 1970. The cognitive basis for linguistic structure. In R. Hayes, ed., Cognition and language learning. New York, Wiley.

Blasdell, Richard, and Paul Jensen. n. d. Stress and word-position as determinants of imitation in first-language learners.

Manuscript of the Communication Sciences Laboratory.
Gainesville, Florida.

Braine, M. D. S. 1971. On two types of models for the internalization of grammars. In D. Slobin, ed., The ontogenesis
of grammar: facts and theories. New York, Academic
Press.

Brière, Eugene. A psycholinguistic study of phonological interference.
The Hague, Mouton.

Brown, Roger, and David McNeill. 1966. The "tip of the tongue"
phenomenon. Journal of verbal learning and verbal behavior.
Vol. 5: 325-337.

Bruce, D. J. 1956. Effects of context upon the intelligibility of
heard speech. In C. Cherry, ed., Information theory:
third London symposium. London, Butterworth.

Cazden, Courtney. 1965. Environmental assistance to the child's
acquisition of grammar. Unpublished doctoral dissertation.
Harvard University.

Chomsky, Noam, and Morris Halle. 1968. The sound pattern of
English. New York, Harper and Row.

Cohen, Stephen P., G. Richard Tucker, and Wallace E. Lambert.
1967. The comparative skills of monolinguals and bilinguals
in perceiving phoneme sequences. Language and speech.
Vol. 10: 159-168.

Connors, Kathleen. Phonological studies of borrowing. I. Aspects
of a study of sound changes in borrowed words. II. Spontaneous "borrowing" of Hindi words into English. III. Problems with feature substitution and minor strategies. Unpublished ms. University of California Phonology Laboratory.
Berkeley, California.

Ervin-Tripp, Susan. 1967. An Issei learns English. Journal of
social issues. Vol. 23, No. 2: 78-90.

_____ 1970. Discourse agreement: how children answer questions. In R. Hayes, ed., Cognition and language learning.
New York, Wiley: 79-107.

Fraser, Colin, Ursula Bellugi, and Roger Brown. 1963. Control of
grammar in imitation, comprehension and production. Journal of verbal learning and verbal behavior. Vol. 2: 121-135.

Gekoski, William Lee. 1968. Associative and translation habits of
bilinguals as a function of language acquisition contexts.
Report 54. Center for Human Growth and Development.
Ann Arbor, Michigan, University of Michigan.

Geohegan, William. 1969. The use of marking rules in semantic systems. Working paper no. 26. Language-Behavior Research Laboratory. Berkeley, California, University of California. Mimeo.

Goldman-Eislar, Frieda. 1964. Hesitation, information, and levels of speech production. In A. V. S. de Reuck and M. O'Connor, eds., Ciba Foundation symposium: Disorders of language. Boston, Little Brown: 96-111.

Gumperz, John. 1967. On the linguistic markers of bilingual communication. Journal of social issues. Vol. 23, No. 2: 48-57.

_____ and Edward Hernandez. 1969. Cognitive aspects of bilingual communication. Language-Behavior Research Laboratory. Working paper no. 28. Berkeley, California, University of California. Mimeo.

Haugen, Einar. 1955. Problems of bilingual description. General linguistics. Vol. 1, No. 1: 1-9.

Kaplan, Eleanor, and George Kaplan. 1970. Is there any such thing as a prelinguistic child? In John Eliot, ed., Human development and cognitive processes. New York, Holt, Rinehart.

Klima, E. S., and Ursula Bellugi. 1966. Syntactic regularities in the speech of children. In J. Lyons and R. J. Wales, eds., Psycholinguistics papers. Edinburgh, Edinburgh University Press: 183-208.

Labov, William. 1967. The social stratification of English in New York City. Washington, D. C., Center for Applied Linguistics.

_____ Paul Cohen, Clarence Robins, and John Lewis. 1968. A study of the nonstandard English of Negro and Puerto Rican speakers in New York City. Final report. Cooperative Research Project No. 3288. Office of Education, Washington, D. C.

Lambert, Wallace E., J. Havelka, and C. Crosby. 1958. The influence of language acquisition contexts on bilingualism. Journal of abnormal and social psychology. Vol. 56: 239-244.

_____ and Sandra Witelson. 1961. Concurrent and consecutive orders of learning two "languages." Montreal, McGill University. Mimeo.

Lance, Donald. 1969. A brief study of Spanish-English bilingualism.
    Final report. Research Project Orr-Liberal Arts-15504.
    College Station, Texas, Texas A and M.

Lane, Harlan. 1966. Identification, discrimination, translation.
    The effects of mapping ranges of physical continua onto
    phoneme and sememe categories. IRAL, Vol. 4: 216-226.

Lieberman, Philip. 1965. On the acoustic basis of the perception of
    intonation by linguists. Word. Vol. 21: 40-53.

Liberman, Alvin M., Katherine S. Harris, Jo Ann Kinney, and Harlan
    Lane. 1961. The discrimination of relative onset-time of
    the components of certain speech and nonspeech patterns.
    Journal of experimental psychology. Vol. 61: 379-388.

Malmberg, Bertil. 1945. Ett barn byter språk. Nordisk Tidsskrift.
    Vol. 21.

———— 1964. Språket och människan. Lund, Aldus. 98-112.

Miller, George, and Patricia Nicely. 1955. An analysis of percep-
    tual confusions among some English consonants. Journal of
    the acoustical society of America. Vol. 27: 338-352.

Menyuk, Paula. 1968. Children's learning and reproduction of gram-
    matical and nongrammatical phonological sequences. Child
    Development. Vol. 38: 849-859.

Messer, Stanley. 1967. Implicit phonology in children. Journal of
    verbal learning and verbal behavior. Vol. 6: 609-613.

Nakazima, Sei. 1962. A comparative study of the speech develop-
    ments of Japanese and American English in childhood. Studia
    phonologica. Vol. 2: 27-46.

Novinski, Lorraine. 1968. Recognition memory in children for se-
    mantic versus syntactic information. Dissertation. Univer-
    sity of California, Berkeley.

Porter, Douglas. 1955. Preliminary analysis of the grammatical
    concept "verb." Cambridge, Harvard School of Education.
    Unpublished.

Postovsky, Valerian. 1970. Effects of delay in oral practice at the
    beginning of second language learning. Dissertation, Uni-
    versity of California, Berkeley.

Ravem, Roar. 1968. Language acquisition in a second language
    environment. IRAL. Vol. 6: 175-185.

Roengpitiya, Karita. 1969. A contrastive analysis of Thai students'
    difficulties with English. Unpublished. Berkeley, University
    of California seminar paper (Rhetoric 155).

Sachs, Jacqueline Struck. 1967. Recognition memory for syntactic
    and semantic aspects of connected discourse. Perception
    and psychophysics. Vol. 2: 437-442.
Shipley, Elizabeth, Carlota Smith, and Lila Gleitman. 1969. A study
    in the acquisition of language: free responses to commands.
    Language. Vol. 45: 322-342.
_____ and Jane Carol Catlin. 1967. Short-term memory for sen-
    tences in children: an exploration study of temporal aspects
    of imposing structure. Technical report V, Grant No. MH
    O7990. Philadelphia, Eastern Psychiatric Institute.
Smith, Carlota. 1969. Children's control of some complex noun
    phrases: a repetition study. L.S.A. meeting, San Francisco,
    California.
Slobin, Dan, and Charles Welsh. 1969. Elicited imitation as a re-
    search tool in developmental psycholinguistics. Language
    Behavior Research Laboratory. Working paper no. 10.
    University of California, Berkeley.
Thorne, James Peter, Hamish Dewar, Harry Whitfield, and Paul
    Bratley. n.d. A model for the perception of syntactic struc-
    ture. Edinburgh, English Language Research Unit. Mimeo.
Troike, Rudolph C. 1969. Receptive competence, productive com-
    petence, and performance. Round Table Monograph No. 20.
    Washington, D.C., Georgetown University Press.
Walker, Edward. 1969. Grammatical relations and sentence memory.
    L.S.A. meeting, San Francisco, California.

Part II. Language Acquisition

9 | ### The Development of Meaning in Children's Descriptive Terms

In Collaboration with Garrett Foster

Children frequently confuse the names for physical dimensions. If two objects differ in size, they may say one is STRONGER than the other. If they differ in weight, one may be called BIGGER than the other. This is, of course, just what one would expect in the early stages of learning if size, weight, and strength are empirically correlated.

Osgood, Suci, and Tannenbaum (1957) have found correlations of a similar sort in examining the structure of meanings measured by semantic differential scales. Three factors have been found repeatedly—Evaluation, Potency, and Activity. Little attention has been given to the development or origin of these factors. Inspection of the scales defining each factor suggests that two conditions would create correlations. One is verbal conjunction; if whatever is said to be GOOD is also said to be FAIR the scales will be correlated through verbal associations. Secondly, "ecological covariation" (Brunswik, 1947) exists for certain sensory dimensions. We would thus expect BIG, HEAVY, and STRONG to be correlated for all cultural groups.

It is clear that adults can discriminate the sensory dimensions that children confuse verbally. On the semantic differential, however, they are normally asked to extend terms metaphorically, as in judging the size and weight of FREE PRESS or EDUCATION. Even on the semantic differential, the correlation of size and weight scales can be destroyed by inclusion of items like DIAMOND and MIST where a check with sense experience is possible and the usual trait correlation is reversed. To the extent that the semantic differential reflects covariation in experience of traits that are logically independent, we would expect that there would be an increase with age in denotative discrimination of the terms that are correlated on the differential. In the following study, age changes in children's verbal confusions are examined.

The more highly correlated two attributes are, the less probable are encounters with discrepant instances. It is useful to note three different variants on this situation. One category may constitute a subclass of a larger category. Thus, if 98% of a child's encounters with men, in which there is direct address or verbal reference to a man, involve his father, we would expect that the child might at first call all adult males DADDY. Discrepant instances would at first be too few for a differentiation to take place. If there were two adult males in the family such an extension would be unlikely. Thus Leopold (1939) noted that while his daughter called all men PAPA, women had individual names and there was no word for FRAU.

The subclass of a hierarchy of classes is actually an extreme instance of the second variant of correlation, a partial overlap of two classes. The degree of correlation or overlap should predict the probability of two terms being confused. Thus, communism and atheism might be confused by those unaware of discrepancies such as religious communist settlements. From a matrix showing the probability of being right in applying the term COMMUNIST to an atheist, we can see that the higher the correlation of the two terms, the greater the probability of being right, and the greater the likelihood that the two ideologies are called by one term. There are other features that enter into the failure to differentiate terms. One is the relative size of the two categories. If there are more atheists than communists, one is more likely to be wrong in calling an atheist a COMMUNIST than calling a communist an ATHEIST. The extreme case would be that in which the whole size of the class of communists is equal to the overlapping class. That is, for example, all communists are atheists but the reverse is not true. This case is identical with the one cited earlier of hierarchical classes. Other relevant factors are the perceptibility of an attribute or class, the consequences of correct and incorrect class discrimination (which may not be the same for the classes involved), the frequency of the terms in usage, and degree of logical independence.

If the dimensions of reference are continuous attributes rather than classes, then the relation may be described by a scatter-plot rather than a matrix of frequencies. The same observations apply; the probability of being correct in saying that a bigger object is HEAVIER is a function of the attribute correlations.

In adult speakers of English, the differentiation of the attributes weight, size, and strength is such that if speakers can make appropriate tests, they are unlikely to say that the heavier of two like-sized objects is BIGGER. There are, however, situations in which the attribute extension in this simple physical case is appropriate. One is in the situation of prediction, where a value on one attribute only is known. Then it becomes useful to be able to predict the probable value on the other attribute. The second situation is one in which metaphor is exploited in verbal or pictorial communication, and one attribute may be used to suggest another.

Thus, we would expect that correlated attributes would appear in experienced speakers' usage, in situations of prediction and metaphorical extension, but not in denotation where the evidence for attribute discrimination is available.

In new learners, however, one term may apply to both attributes, which are not in fact discriminated, or both terms may appear as interchangeable synonyms for the two undiscriminated attributes.

In the following study two semantic differential factors, Evaluation and Potency, are presented as far as possible in conditions requiring denotative discrimination of three attribute expressions of each. A reduction with age is predicted with respect to the use of the wrong terms when a difference in only one attribute of the correlated set is present.

Method

Subjects. There were two groups of Ss, a group of 16 male and 17 female first grade children, and a group of 18 male and 18 female sixth graders. Both groups were from the same school in a

lower socioeconomic Negro district. To reduce variability, the extremely bright and extremely dull children were excluded, the criterion being the teacher's rating in the first grade, and deviations of
20 points from the norm on available IQ tests in the sixth grade.

Materials. In Part I of the experiment, materials were
selected to vary successively three of the dimensions on Osgood's
potency factor. These three dimensions—weight, strength, and size—
had been found to have loadings of .62 with the rotated factor analysis,
involving concepts rated against scales, and coordinates of 1.68,
1.81, and 1.76, respectively, on another analysis of scales judged
against scales. These were the largest components of the factor in
each case.

The objects used were: (a) opaque salt shakers identical
but for weight, (b) opaque jars identical but for weight, (c) cork balls
differing in size, (d) styrofoam balls differing in size, (e) a pair of
insulated wires with the wire removed from the middle third of one,
leaving it flexible, and (f) a dry sponge and a damp one matched in
size.

In Part II drawings of a girl's face were used to represent
three of four dimensions representing Osgood's evaluative factor.
The pictured dimensions were CLEAN-DIRTY, HAPPY-SAD, and
PRETTY -UGLY. A fourth was included in the questioning: GOOD-
BAD. These had loadings, respectively, of .82, .76, .86
(BEAUTIFUL-UGLY), and .88, and coordinates of 2.38, 2.09, 2.40,
2.29 on the first factor.

Procedure. All of the Ss were individually tested with the
following questions:

> I would like to ask you some questions and you can
> give me the correct answers...OK? [For first graders:]
> It's kind of a game and lots of fun. First I'm going to
> ask about these objects. [2 objects contrasting in weight
> put in subject's hands.] Is one of these heavier and one
> lighter or are they both the same weight? [If says dif-
> ferent] Which is heavier? Is one black and one white or
> are they both the same color? Is one bigger and one
> smaller or are they both the same size? [If says

different] Which is bigger? Is one stronger and one
weaker or are they both the same strength? [If says
different] Which is stronger?

If the child failed to indicate the item that was heavier on
the first question, he was eliminated from the rest of Part I. The
second question, to which the answer was "the same" was to control
set. A similar series of questions was asked about all the items,
starting with the actual contrast as a screening question. One of the
six possible key questions was omitted, concerning perception of
weight in objects differing in size. If weight in the objects were controlled, the smaller object might be called heavier on the grounds of
its scale weight. Because of the ambiguity of the term HEAVY
applied to objects differing in size, the question was omitted.

In the analysis the percentages were computed over the
whole set of responses, which included two for each question for each
child because of the double set of materials. The Ns used in the
significance tests were for the actual number of children tested.

In Part II a similar procedure was followed, with the control
question "Does one picture have red hair and one black hair or are
they both the same?" The questions and pictures were rotated, with
every fourth question a control question.

Results

In Table 1* it can be seen that between 39 and 66% of the
first-grade children offered contaminated responses for the various
dimensions of the physical materials. In the sixth grade the proportion
was reduced to a range between 20 and 44%. While none of the individual changes in percentage was significant, there was a reduction
for every comparison, including the subgroups by sex. A sign test
is significant at the .01 level. The dimension that changes the least
is the response that the heavier object is STRONGER; this is also
the statement of highest frequency at both ages for both sexes. Since
strength is less evident than weight, it is possible that this particular
inference would continue in adult Ss. The inference that a bigger
object is STRONGER is next in probability, supporting the notion that

---

*See p. 384 for Tables 1 and 2.

it is the inferred character of strength that is involved. Size is least often presented as a contaminated response, and it is also the most obvious.

It might be thought that the reduction in the sixth grade is due to a tendency to be more careful about differentiating at all, and thus to an increase in same responses. This was not the case. While the percentage of reversals was relatively low, it increased in the sixth grade. This increase occurred in stating that the heavier was SMALLER, that the stronger was SMALLER and LIGHTER. In the latter case these frequencies probably arise because a wet sponge in usually larger, and contains water. Only boys gave the last reversal, 22% of the boys in the sixth grade saying the stronger was LIGHTER, and no girls. Nine percent of the boys and 28% of the girls said the stronger was SMALLER. In the last case this was a larger proportion than those saying it was larger. It might be argued, then, that the reduction in the last two cases was due to sophistication with respect to one of the objects used.

On the study of the evaluative dimension using faces, almost no reversals occurred at either age. The age differences on Table 2 are striking. It may be noted that they do not occur markedly on three cases. Two of these refer to CLEAN. The frequency of children saying one child was CLEANER than the other for the other attributes was small at both ages. Clean may be said to be the most visible of the attributes. In fact it could be argued that it is the only one with a clear-cut physical criterion.

The third instance of lack of marked change was one in which the proportions were very high at both ages. The smiling face was said to be PRETTIER.

With the CLEANER dimension excluded, the range in the first grade is between 42 and 97% offering a contaminated response. The highest are those offering the smiling face as more GOOD and the cleaner face as PRETTIER. All of the first grade boys gave these responses. In the sixth grade the range is between 14 and 75% with the highest now being the smiling face which is seen as PRETTIER about as often as it was in the first grade. Thus, there is a shift in responses as with the physical attributes, but it is markedly different for the different attributes.

Discussion

The slight rate of change with respect to discrimination of physical dimensions suggests the kind of learning to be expected where the criteria are most obvious.

With the personal attributes the findings are both more extreme and more uneven. It is clear that the only term of those used which designates a simple visible trait—CLEAN—is the one seldom offered to describe any other attribute. This finding agrees with the fact that BIG, the most obvious physical attribute, was less often used with the physical materials to describe other differences.

The other evaluative dimensions refer to more complex traits that are not entirely logically independent. PRETTY may also be said to designate a physical characteristic, but one that adults use both as a constant and a temporary trait, so that a clean smiling face might be deemed prettier than a dirty or frowning one. Thus, while the traits are discriminable they are not independent in the sense that the physical traits are.

HAPPY was used to designate a smiling face, but as children learn the use of the term they may find that it refers to a state of feeling only partially correlated with external evidence. Thus even the smiling-nonsmiling distinction might bear only an imperfect relation to the term HAPPY. One of the largest changes was in the use of HAPPY in describing the prettier girl, and the drop was most extreme in girls—a drop of 53%. The children were from the start, especially the boys, only moderately likely to describe the cleaner girl as HAPPIER.

One possible reason for a drop in the ascription of terms to a correlated difference is a change in metaphorical treatment of pictures. Occasionally children would refuse to say that both children were the same in hair color, but said that one had red and one black hair. The hair in the drawing was white, that is, not filled in in the black-and-white outline picture. Younger children, used to storybook imagination, may be less literal about what is on the page. While this might account for the increase in same responses with age, it does not predict the direction of the ascription, by the first graders, which was in no case in the opposite direction from that predicted.

Does the failure to differentiate on this test imply that the children use the terms as virtual synonyms for an undifferentiated referent? With respect to the physical dimensions, only one child was so extreme as to use the same terms interchangeably for all three attributes on all the materials. But if we examine the faces test and omit CLEAN which seems to fall out of the pattern, it appears that 62% of the children used HAPPY-GOOD-PRETTY synonymously, in the first grade.

We would like to argue that the factors that appear as clusters of correlated terms in the semantic differential studies of adults derive from empirical correlations of attributes. They could, of course, be linked purely by verbal associations, as in "He's a good clean player." If this were the case, differentiation of reference might still be accompanied by semantic differential correlations, since many of the terms on the semantic differential can be applied to the "concept" only metaphorically. DEMOCRACY is clean, fragrant, and sweet only in the poetic sense.

While verbal associations may be one source of such dimensions, we are proposing that the history of concept development in the child provides another source. What remains as a connotative, metaphorical relationship in adults may in many cases start as denotative nondifferentiation. In a sense, the child might be said to acquire first a concept, for instance, of "big-strong-heavy..." in other words, a potency referent. The terms he applies to this referent may variously be BIG, STRONG, HEAVY. He may prefer one of these terms for people, another for boats, another for baseballs. Presumably he will only come to differentiate the terms and apply them appropriately to different stimulus dimensions when uncorrelated instances occur and he is corrected, or hears others differentiate the terms. By chance, the sample he selects may have a 100% correlation and he may not encounter errors immediately.

Summary

The physical dimensions of size, weight, and strength are empirically correlated. If the correlation delays discrimination of these attributes as referents for descriptive terms, then younger children should more often use incorrect terms to describe differences between objects. The terms GOOD, PRETTY, CLEAN, and HAPPY should also be used as synonyms prior to differentiation.

A set of materials was prepared in which size, weight, and strength were independently varied in pairs of objects. First-grade children more often than sixth graders said that the pairs of objects differed on other dimensions in addition to the attribute actually contrasted. In a set of pictures of faces, over half of the youngest children treated GOOD, PRETTY, and HAPPY as interchangeable synonyms. The proportion dropped markedly with age. The more easily identified traits, such as the referents of BIG and CLEAN, were least often confused with other attributes.

The results are interpreted as showing that attributes which have metaphorical and connotative links in adult usage, may be denotatively confused at first. The factors found by Osgood on the semantic differential studies of verbal meaning may actually be the referents for several terms used as synonyms, prior to differentiation of finer distinctions between attributes.

NOTE

The authors acknowledge with gratitude the cooperation of Matt Griffeath, Principal, and the teachers of the Durant School in Oakland, California, in providing facilities and Ss.

REFERENCES

Brunswik, E. Systematic and representative design of psychological experiments. Berkeley: University of California Press, 1947.

Leopold, W. F. The speech development of a bilingual child. Evanston, Ill.: Northwestern University Press, 1939-50.

Osgood, C. E., Suci, G. J., and Tannenbaum, P. H. The measurement of meaning. Urbana: University of Illinois Press, 1957.

10 | Changes with Age in the Verbal Determinants of Word-Association

The earliest investigators of word-association noted that adult associations were usually in the same grammatical class as the stimulus-words, and that such responses had especially short latencies.[1] These findings challenge an explanation of the learning of word-associations through simple contiguity in overt speech. On this basis, the most frequent response to transitive verbs would be <u>the.</u>

A paradigmatic response—that is, a response in the same grammatical class—might arise through similarity of referents, common affixes, or common past verbal contexts.[2] The last determinant has the greatest generality. Even the isolated words offered in an association-test have been encountered before in verbal contexts. Two words may be said to be contextually similar to the degree that their past verbal environments overlap. Contextual similarity thus includes both grammatical and semantic similarity between the stimulus-word and response-word, to the extent that the totality of verbal contexts defines meaning.

Two models could account for the learning of association between contextually similar words. A forward association would predict that repetition of <u>a cup of coffee</u> and <u>a cup of tea</u> would lead to the association of <u>coffee</u> with <u>tea</u> and of <u>tea</u> with <u>coffee</u>, due to their contiguity during competition of the response. A reverse, or mediated association, would be learned with practice of <u>front door</u> and <u>back door</u>. In this case, though, since <u>door</u> mediates the association of <u>front</u> and <u>back</u>, it would be the most likely response in free association. Savings in paradigmatic responses would be expected only in a condition of constrained response. It has been shown that both of these conditions do produce learning.[3]

In the following study, differences with age in the frequency of different types of word-association will be examined with reference to an analysis of learning. The following changes with age are expected.

(1) <u>Decrease in syntagmatic responses</u>. Syntagmatic (sequential) associations are more probable where the variety of contexts following the stimulus-word is low relative to its frequency, reducing the number of competing associates. With age, there is an increase in the length and variety of sentences,[4] so that the relative strength of the average syntagmatic association is less.

Syntagmatic associations refer here to any sequential associate, not necessarily the immediately contiguous one. Since determiners (<u>the</u>, <u>my</u>), pure prepositions (<u>of</u>, <u>from</u>), copulas (<u>is</u>, <u>become</u>), nominative pronouns, and coördinate conjunctions virtually never occur in utterances of one word,[5] they would not be expected as responses on an association-test,[6] and may be eliminated in calculation of the sequential probabilities of stimulus- and potential response-words.

(2) <u>Increase in paradigmatic responses</u>. Paradigmatic associates are more likely when the variety of verbal contexts of a stimulus-term is high relative to its frequency. In addition, as vocabulary increases, children have more contextually similar responses in antonyms, synonyms, and words drawn from the abstraction-hierarchy of the stimulus-word.

(3) <u>Differential shift toward paradigmatic responses</u>. If a word occurs frequently in the final position of a sentence, it has relatively weak syntagmatic associations. Such words are nouns, adverbs, adjectives, and intransitive verbs. On the other hand, adverbs of frequency (<u>always</u>, <u>seldom</u>), transitive verbs, and question-words (<u>when</u>, <u>who</u>) occur less often in final positions. They would be expected to elicit syntagmatic responses at later ages than other categories.

(4) <u>Decrease in clang-responses</u>. Since children have less practice than adults in both verbal and non-verbal associations with words, they are more likely to respond to the immediate sound-prop-

erties of verbal stimuli, as if the words were nonsense. Indeed, children are known to display more generalization between words that sound alike. [7]

Earlier research partially supports these generalizations. Wreschner, using German words, found that age and education were both related to paradigmatic dominance, and that children preferred concrete nouns as responses regardless of the class of the stimulus-word. [8] Inflectional affixes in German confound clang-responses and paradigmatic responses.

Reanalysis of Woodrow and Lowell's data for English reveals that paradigmatic responses increased and syntagmatic responses decreased with age. [9] The range of form-classes included was limited, however, and the list was not confined to cases where the adult primary response was present in children's vocabularies. Age-changes may be merely due to specific changes in vocabulary in such cases, though it is true that these alone should not produce the bias in the direction of change which the data indicate.

Method

Materials. The list of associative words, 46 in number, was chosen from a variety of grammatical classes. Since the work was done in conjunction with a study on learning antonyms, 39 of the items were so chosen that the primary response of adults was coördinate or antonymous. All stimulus-words and primary responses of adults were, according to Rinsland, probably within the vocabulary of the youngest children. [10] The form-classes were alternated within the list and the same order of presentation was used for all Ss.

The closed-alternative test was composed of 35 items, the last ten being omitted for the third-graders. Three kinds of items were alternated on the list to test the relative strength of syntagmatic, paradigmatic, and antonymous responses. In one set the words were grammatically alike (snow, winter, summer), but contained an antonym. In a second set, an antonym was contrasted with a syntagmatic associate, (pillow, soft, hard). In the third group, syntagmatic and paradigmatic associates were contrasted, (fire, hot, warm).

Subjects. Twenty-three Ss were chosen from the kindergarten, 10 from the first grade, 52 from the third grade, and 99 from the sixth grade. In the last two grades, the entire class was tested in a group; in the first two, the children were tested individually.

Procedure. The Ss in the kindergarten and first grade were tested orally; those in the third and sixth grades gave their responses in writing. To keep speed uniform and to help slow readers, E read the words aloud to the older children.

Instructions. The following instructions were given for the word-association test.

When you hear a word, sometimes it makes you think of another word. If you heard cat you might think of milk, or purr, or dog, or black—almost anything. What does cat make you think of? What does eat make you think of? Anything else?

All single word answers were accepted.

For the closed-alternative form also given, the children were told to say or to draw a line showing with which word the middle word of three seemed to go best. An example was given: "Does brother go better with sister or with father?"

Response-analysis of free associates. Both the stimulus-words and the response-words were classified by a method oi defining grammatical class derived from Fries. [11] Test-frames or contexts were established; a word was assigned to a class if it could fit into the frames altered by substitutions from the same grammatical classes as the words in the frame. The same word might fall in several classes—walk is both noun and verb, for instance. In addition, coders were instructed to try to judge probable contexts according to children's usage. Thus people was not classified as a verb.

In the following list of some of the principal classes used in the analysis, the numbers indicate the agreement scores among the coders, obtained by computing the probability that an item coded in the given class by one coder would also be coded in that class by another coder. Disagreements largely stemmed from cases where one coder thought a usage too rare to include.

(1) <u>Nouns</u>, including verbs with '-<u>ing</u>', if they could be preceded by adjectives but not adverbs; 0.97.

(2) <u>Pronouns</u>, excluding possessives; 0.96.

(3) <u>Transitive verbs</u>; 0.87.

(4) <u>Intransitive verbs</u>; 0.87. Since most transitive verbs also occur in intransitive contexts (<u>he likes to eat</u>), coders were instructed not to code as intransitive any verbs which could be made transitive merely by adding an object.

(5) <u>Adjectives,</u> including verbs with -<u>ing</u> and -<u>ed</u> if they can be preceded by modifiers or by both adjectives and adverbs of manner; 0.92.

(6) <u>Adverbs</u>; 0.90.

(7) <u>Nominal adverbs</u>; 0.79. This is a subgroup of adverbs which can occur after certain prepositions, e.g. <u>now</u>, <u>here</u>.

The above comprise Fries' parts of speech. Below are several classes of function words most of which cannot occur alone in an utterance without the presence of some other parts of speech.

(8) <u>Modifiers</u>, which precede adverbs or adjectives; 0.85. Examples are <u>quite</u>, <u>really</u>, <u>too</u>, <u>just</u>, <u>very</u>.

(9) <u>Determiners,</u> which include the traditional articles and possessive pronouns; 0.97. Examples: <u>most</u>, <u>the</u>, <u>my</u>, <u>that</u>, <u>some</u>.

(10) <u>Prepositions</u>; 0.99.

(11) <u>Interrogative words</u> and <u>subordinate conjunctions</u> which were pooled for this analysis because of the large overlap in composition of the classes; 0.87.

<u>Sequential analysis</u>. As an approximation to the sequences of grammatical classes in children's speech, children's books were

Table I

Proportion Choosing Same Grammatical Class on
Closed-Alternative Test

Stimulus - sets (with correct pair marked)	Kindergarten and first grade (N= 33)	Third grade (N= 95)	Sixth grade (N= 56)
fire hot —warm	61	30	48 ★
witch wicked — bad	42	35	56 ⊄
up —high sky	39	42	56 ★
lie — cheat bad	36	47	72 ⊄
black —dark night	27	40	48
trees — grass green	17	—*	18
ball — bat play	66	—	96 ★★
supper eating —drinking	37	—	36
write desk —table	83	—	73
pillow soft —hard	21	15	32 ★
sad —happy fun	15	37 ⊄	52 ★
dark night — day	39	39	45
fast run — walk	36	26	34
go — come here	42	58	70 **
behind back —front	39	47	48
to —from away	27	41	54 **
he him — her	70	42	48
light float — sink	67	63	66
softer —harder stone	24	—	50 ★
played —worked hard	34	—	50

*Some items were omitted at the end of the test in the third grade.
★ Higher proportion than in next youngest group, $p < 0.05$.
⊄ $p < 0.01$. ★★ $p < 0.001$.
**Higher than youngest group, $p < 0.001$, but not different from middle group.

subjected to an analysis of grammatical sequences. One hundred or more cases of items in each class were tallied in sequence from the texts to yield an estimate of the probability of each class given another class, and the probability of occurrence of the class in final position. Tallies were discontinued when it appeared that the probabilities for the given class were stable. Two tallies were noted for each item, one of the class of the word immediately following in the text, and the other of the class of the next word omitting functional words. The only major deviation from Fries' categories was that copulas (is, seems) were treated as function-words.

Results

Closed-alternative test. Of the 9 items where there were no antonyms so that only form-class was at issue, there were 5 showing significant increase with age in the selection of the paradigmatic alternative (Table I). On the 11 items where antonyms were compared with syntagmatic choices, there were 5 significant increases with age. In all, two cases of marked decrease appeared, both involving the smallest sample, where the proportions are least reliable.

Paradigmatic responses in free-association. In counting paradigmatic associates on the free-association test, coders used a simple criterion to isolate the purest instances of paradigmatic responses. Responses were called paradigmatic only (a) if they can occur in the same class as the stimulus-word even if each also occurs in other classes, and (b) if they do not occur in immediate sequence or separated only by a determiner in ordinary continuous speech. Thus, though all are nouns, front-door and table-spoon were not tallied as paradigmatic, nor was game-play. The second restriction was not generalized to all function-words rather than merely determiners, because such a rule would include conjunctions. Almost any pair of words in the same grammatical class might, of course, occur in sequence linked by a conjunction. The restrictive rule was pragmatic in origin and in practice successfully excluded the cases which appeared ambiguous as to paradigmatic or syntagmatic status.

One-tailed tests of significance were made of the increases, and are presented only for adjacent groups except when there was a

Table II

Proportion of Paradigmatic Responses on Free-Association Test

Stimulus-word	Response-class tallied	Kindergarten and first grade (N= 33)	Third grade (N= 98)	Sixth grade (N= 52)
table	N	18	69★★	79
moon	N	69	80	71
boy	N	69	92⟅	98
front	N	57	85⟅	77
night	N	57	74*	83
winter	N	69	77	83
hand	N, TV	48	74★	79
game	N	15	33*	34
build	TV	15	18	48★★
give	TV	15	34*	63⟅
float	TV, IV	33	46	81★★
worked	TV, IV	39	55	58
come	IV	33	71★★	75
walking	TV, IV	30	52*	81⟅
from	P	12	15	44★★
across	P, Adv	12	41★	54
over	P, Adv	36	60★	65
up	P, Adv	63	81*	77
out	P, Adv	42	78★★	77
before	P, Adv, SC	33	78★★	85
always	Adv	12	49★★	75★
there	Adv	18	67★★	58
yesterday	N, Adv	63	90⟅	94
him	Pro	30	76★★	71
these	Pro, D	18	64★★	71
when	Q	12	14	21
softer	A	42	69★	73
hotter	A	51	71*	62
slower	A	57	79★	81
worse	A, Adv	42	86★★	87

*Higher proportion than in next youngest group, $p < 0.05$.

$p < 0.01$.   ⟅ $p < 0.001$.   ★★ $p < 0.0001$.

gradual increase that was not sharply inflected. Of the eight nouns, six showed significant increases between the youngest Ss and those in the third grade (Table II). The remaining two stimulus-words, moon and winter, had a very high proportion of paradigmatic responses in the youngest group. Five of six verbs, and all of the prepositions, adverbs, pronouns, and comparative adjectives showed increases with age. When produced a low proportion of paradigmatic responses at all ages.

The primary responses of adults for most of the stimulus-words was a coördinate or antonymous response. It could be argued that the increase in paradigmatic responses simply represents a learning of a particular type of paradigmatic response, or that it merely represents a culturally stereotyped learning of the primary response or training with conjunctive phrases. There are two tests of this explanation. One consists of examining the words which do not have high-frequency primary responses in the oldest group; namely, game, build, across, when. Three of the four showed age-increases.

A more stringent test consists of examining only responses other than those that are adult primaries, this reducing the sample size in each grade. Fourteen items remain with sufficient cases for a statistical analysis, and of these eight showed significant increases with age in paradigmatic responses.

Thus the shift to paradigmatic responses cannot be regarded simply as due to increased learning of the adult primary and peculiar to coördinate or contrast responses.

Since the number of multiple-word responses decreased with age, it could be argued that the change between the youngest Ss and those in the third grade is largely a result of learning to isolate single words. The phrase-responses were retained in the tallies on the grounds that these were the younger child's version of a syntagmatic response, most often consisting of the stimulus-word embedded in a phrase. For the older children the response was often merely the main, or modified, term of the phrase. Thus, in young children across might elicit across the street; in the third-graders simply street.

If only the single-word responses are tallied as a stringent test, a few of the age-changes disappear and all are of course reduced in magnitude. It remains substantially true even of the single-word responses that paradigmatic frequencies increase.

Syntagmatic responses. The fact that paradigmatic responses increase with age does not demonstrate that the remaining responses bear a systematic relation to the stimulus-words. They might be randomly selected from all grammatical classes regardless of the stimulus-class.

If the response-words in association were a function of immediate succession in texts, 45% of associations to transitive verbs would be determiners, and 51% of associations to intransitive verbs would be prepositions. The actual associative probabilities are, in each case, 2%.

Table III

Probability of Grammatical Classes in Texts and Word-Association
Following Specified Antecedent Classes*

Response-class	Noun, Pronoun		Intrans. Verb		Trans. Verb		Adjective	
	word		word		word		word	
	text	assoc.	text	assoc.	text	assoc.	text	assoc.
Noun, pronoun	.31	(.70)	.68	.35	.92	.75	.79	.56
Intransitive verb	.19	.21	.01	(.46)	.03	.02	.01	.06
Transitive verb	.33	.27	.05	.09★	.01	(.46)	–	.13
Adjective	.13	.17	.06	.18	.02	.02	.16	(.71)
Adverb	.03	.02	.20	.28	.02	.07	.03	.03

*Word-association probabilities include function-words and therefore do not add to unity. Parenthesized values represent uncorrected responses in paradigmatic classes.

★When a verb-response to a verb-stimulus was double-coded as both transitive and intransitive, only the paradigmatic code was counted, thus decreasing the values in these cells. Other double coding was not adjusted.

When function-words are omitted from the textual count, on the grounds that function-words rarely occur in isolation and will, therefore, be improbable as associative responses, then the text-sequential probabilities are as shown in Table III. The associative responses shown below them correspond closely, when corrected so that the probabilities of responses in the same form-class as the stimulus-word are based on the expectations if the responses are syntagmatic.

Since there is no way of knowing from inspection which of these responses were based on substitution and which on sequence, an arbitrary correction was made. The probabilities of same-form-class associative responses were assumed to equal those in the texts.

This table is distorted by two factors. One is not easily modified--double coding was used for many responses, and influenced particularly strongly the classes of nouns and verbs. The second difficulty is that there is a difference in the basal probability of each form-class, regardless of antecedents, in texts and in association. This is to be expected because of the difference between textual frequency and occurrence in single-word utterances. It may be noted that the difference was greatest for nouns and pronouns, chiefly because the latter were much less common in associations than in texts. [12] A correction may be made by transforming the table into deviations from row-means, omitting the diagonal cells. Table III has been presented here in uncorrected form because the correction could be made if desired, yet the raw form may be more useful to other investigators. The product-moment correlation between contingent probabilities in texts and in associations after these corrections was 0.87. This correlation may be interpreted as a measure of the dependence of associations on the class of the stimulus-word, once corrections for paradigmatic probabilities and for differential probabilities of offering a response in text and in isolation have been applied. Thus, most of the variance remaining in the word-associations was due to training in textual sequences.

A few examples may clarify the character of syntagmatic responses. The most common response of changed form-class to across was street, to float was boat, to come was here, to build was house, to game was play, to table was eat, to when was now. The last may be regarded as syntagmatic in the sense that it represents a response to a question.

Some of these responses seem to indicate backward associations, but the question of associational direction cannot be solved readily with these data, and backward associations undoubtedly confound the data of Table III.

There were very similar distributions of probabilities in the three age-groups when contingent associations were separately examined. There was a significant change with age in the direction of increasing frequencies of transitive verbs as responses to nouns and decreasing adjectival responses to nouns. Possibly this change reflects a change in speech away from descriptive sentences.

Sentence-final position. It was expected that words which can occupy the final position in a sentence may have less strong subsequent syntagmatic responses. In terms of the proportion in final position in texts, adverbs were highest (0.36), next nouns (0.20), and intransitive verbs and adjectives (0.14). The probability of occurrence in final position of transitive verbs and function-words was less than 0.03. On these grounds we would expect that build, give, from and when would have strong syntagmatic associations, and thus less paradigmatic dominance. In addition, always, while classed as an adverb, occurs most typically in a pre-verbal position or before an adjectival predicate. It may be seen in Table II that these words all showed late development of paradigmatic dominance, there being a significant increase between the third and sixth grade in paradigmatic responses to build, give, from, and always. The proportion of paradigmatic responses to from and when remained low even in the sixth grade. The proportion of paradigmatic responses in the youngest group was highest for nouns, and next for adjectives.

Clang-associates. Clang-associations are interpreted most broadly as all responses with the same initial consonants, with rhyming vowels, or with similar syllables included. Two exclusions were made from the tally—stimulus-words which had clang-antonyms or inflectional affixes such as -ing, -er, and -ed. With these restrictions, the average number of clang-associates per child decreased from 8.33 in the youngest group, to 2.73 in the third grade and 1.62 in the sixth grade. When only clang-responses which were nonsense words or bore no meaningful link with the stimulus-word were considered, the difference was more marked, the frequencies being 4.39, 0.36, and none, respectively.

Discussion

The marked increase in paradigmatic responses with age might be a result of several factors other than the relative strength of conflicting syntagmatic responses. Older children may have more practice in single-word responses than the youngest. The youngest were tested by an oral technique while the older groups wrote their responses. Yet in the controlled-choice test, all 14 sets showed increases in written paradigmatic responses between the third and sixth grades.

Perhaps the change as a function of age reflects educational experience. First-graders in the schools sampled were using exercise-books practicing substitutions of antonyms and synonyms in sentences. Such exercises were not in use at the time of the study of Woodrow and Lowell, in which the children 9—12 yr. of age showed as high syntagmatic predominance as the kindergarteners in the current study. The widespread use of such materials in this country might account both for the increase in common (usually paradigmatic) responses found by Jenkins and Russell over a 30-yr. period in college students, [13] and for the lower degree of commonality of response in Europeans. [14] Yet this explanation does not suffice completely. Woodrow and Lowell's adult sample did show many paradigmatic responses, and non-literate Navaho adults also markedly prefer paradigmatic primaries. [15] Formal educational practices merely hasten changes which occur with experience even without schooling.

Associational direction. The analysis by classes clearly supports the assumption of predominance of forward associations. There was no evidence, for example, of an increment to noun-adjective or to intransitive verb-noun associative responses arising from backward association, when the textual probabilities are compared to the associative responses. [16]

There is some evidence also for this directional bias in English usage. If a word rarely occurs in the final position of a sentence, it also rarely occurs alone. These classes—nominative pronouns, copulas, and function-words—seem to be the most structurally dependent, apparently because some syntagmatic association is very strong. Thus nouns, intransitive verbs, adjectives, adverbs, and accusative pronouns, which can occur in the final position of a sentence, also appear alone in answers to questions. When, however, questions seem to demand a response in a structurally dependent class, two kinds of answers are given. The answer may be longer than a single word: who's coming? I am. We are. Or the respondent chooses a class that can occur alone: Who's coming? me; whose is it? mine. I, we, or my did not occur alone as a response in spoken texts. The only exception to this pattern is the interrogative-word.

A full test of the hypothesis that frequency of final position is related to an earlier increase in paradigmatic responses should be conducted with stimulus-words which can occur in isolation. Verbs with known positional probabilities would be good candidates for such a study, as would subclasses of adverbs. Adverbs of frequency of occurrence typically precede the verb whereas adverbs of place, manner and absolute time more often occupy sentence-final position.

Of the two models presented earlier, the results of the present study conform to the learning model for forward associations. Can this model also account for other forms of verbal behavior showing similar age-changes? The norms of the Stanford-Binet test and Werner and Kaplan's study of nonsense-words both showed age-changes in definitions. [17] The younger children offered sentences as definitions; the older offered synonyms. Brown and Berko have shown that there is a high correlation between paradigmatic dominance in associations and synonymous definitions, for various grammatical classes. [18] The simple model of forward-association does not seem adequate to account for synonymous definitions of nonsense-words such as those found by Werner and Kaplan, but experimental evidence is not available on this point.

Summary

Children in kindergarten, first, third, and sixth grades were given free-and two-choice associative tests. It was found that there was a significant increase with age in the proportion of responses in the same grammatical class as the stimulus-word, with an earlier increase in words occurring more often in final position in sentences than in words typically medial in sentences. There was a decrease with age in clang-associations. When paradigmatic associates were removed, there was a correlation of 0. 87 between the transitional probabilities of five grammatical classes in word-association, and the five classes in texts with the function-words or connective words eliminated. The functional-words do not ordinarily occur in isolation in speech and virtually never occurred as response-words in association.

These findings support a theory of associations based on training by forward contiguity in speech. Responses in the same grammatical class as the stimulus can be learned on the basis of occurrence in the same preceding verbal contexts. Their predominance over sequential associations from speech could derive from the relative variety of the contexts of the stimulus-word, and from the relative strength of substitutable terms. Both contextual variety and size of vocabulary increase with age and hence responses should come increasingly to correspond in grammatical class to the stimulus-word.

NOTES

These data were collected as part of a project on children's reasoning sponsored by the Higgins Fund. The assistance of Edith Kaplan and Roseanne Mandler is gratefully acknowledged.
[1]Gustav Aschaffenburg, Experimentelle Studien uber Assoziationen: I. Die Assoziation im normalen Zustande, Psychol. Arbeit. 1, 1895, 209-299; B. B. Bourdon, Observatives sur la reconnaissance, la discrimination et l'association, Rev. Phil. France et l'Etranger, 40, 1895, 153-185; C. G. Jung, Studies in Word Association, 1919, 234-235; Paul Menzerath, Die Bedeutung der sprachlichen Geläufigkeit oder der formalen sprachlichen Beziehung fur die Reproduktion, Z. Psychol., 48, 1908, 1-95; Friedrich Schmidt, Experimentelle Untersuchungen zur Assoziationslehre, Z. Psychol, 28, 1902, 65-95; Albert Thumb and Karl Marbe, Experimentelle Untersuchungen über die psychologishen Grundlagen der sprachlichen Analogiebildung, 1901, 1-87; Arthur Wreschner, Die Reproduktion and Assoziation von Vorstellungen, Z. Psychol. Ergbd. , 3, 1907, 329-599.
[2]The syntagmatic-paradigmatic distinction was made in discussion of word-association by J. J. Jenkins, in C. E. Osgood and T. A. Sebeok (eds.) Psycholinguistics, Supplement, J. abnorm. soc. Psychol. 52, 1954, 114-116; Sol Saporta, Linguistic structure as a

factor and as a measure in word association, Minnesota Conference on Associative Processes in Verbal Behavior, 1955, 210-213.

[3]Evidence for the model of forward association was offered by W. E. Jeffrey and R. J. Kaplan, Semantic generalization with experimentally induced associations, J. exp. Psychol., 54, 1957, 336-338, and P. M. Kjeldergaard and D. L. Horton, An experimental analysis of associative factors in stimulus equivalence, response equivalence and chaining paradigms, Studies in Verbal Behavior, 1960, No. 3 (University of Minnesota), 21-34. Response-competition is less likely in a speaker than in a listener anticipating speech sequences. David McNeill has ingeniously suggested that children's slower verbal responses may not create the conditions for paradigmatic contiguity through anticipation.

[4]M. C. Templin, Certain language skills in children, Univ. Minn. Child Welf. Monogr., 1957, No. 26, 76-96.

[5]In an unpublished tally of a day's conversational speech transcribed by W. F. Soskin, function-words were rare, except for question-words, in single-word utterances.

[6]While many functional-words would not appear in isolation in either a text or conversational-count, they are sometimes produced by students as isolated responses in school-exercises. If they occur in isolation as stimulus-words in the association-test itself, their subsequent probability as an isolated response may be increased, as has been reported by Davis Howes, On the relation between the probability of a word as an association and in general linguistic usage, J. abnorm. soc. Psychol., 54, 1957, 84.

[7]B. F. Riess, Genetic changes in semantic conditioning. J. exp. Psychol., 36, 1946, 143-152.

[8]Wreschner, op. cit., 70.

[9]Herbert Woodrow and Frances Lowell, Children's association frequency tables, Psychol. Monogr., 22, 1916 (No. 97), 81.

[10]H. D. Rinsland, A Basic Vocabulary of Elementary School Children, 1954.

[11]C. C. Fries, The Structure of English, 1952, 65-109.

[12]In a day's conversational transcript kindly supplied by W. F. Soskin, pronouns occurred in single-word utterances proportionally less often than any other class except functional words. In proportion to their total frequency, nouns were 7.6 times as probable.

[13]W. A. Russell and J. J. Jenkins, The complete Minnesota norms for responses to 100 words from the Kent-Rosanoff test,

Technical Report 11, University of Minnesota, 1954.

[14] M. R. Rosenzweig, Comparisons among word-association responses in English, French, German, and Italian, The American Journal of Psychology, 74, 1961, 347-360.

[15] Sample of 38 Navahos collected for the Southwest Project in Comparative Psycholinguistics by Arnold Horowitz and Susan Ervin.

[16] If the data in Thumb and Marbe, op. cit., 56-63, are retabulated separately for intransitive and transitive verbs, verb-responses dominate for the former, and nouns for the latter.

[17] Heinz Werner and Edith Kaplan, The acquisition of word meanings: A developmental study, Soc. Res. Child Developm. Monogr., 15, 1952 (No. 51), 84.

[18] R. W. Brown and Jean Berko, Word association and the acquisition of grammar, Child Development, 31, 1960, 1-14. This study also replicated the findings on change with age reported here, which had been first presented in a paper, "Grammar and classification", read at the American Psychological Association, 1957.

11 | The Connotations of Gender

Language may influence the perception and recall of things and events through many aspects of its structure. One source of influence is through systems of classification. Any lexical or grammatical marker constitutes a classifier if it has a greater than chance correlation with semantic determinants or with determinants in the social situation of speech. The lexical contrast of "man" vs. "woman" is a classifier for a semantic difference, and the choice is predictable if we control the referent, by asking informants to name people or pictures of men and women. The contrast of "cat" vs. "kitty" is a classifier correlated with social determinants, and the choice is predictable if we control the audience of speech.

It has been demonstrated clearly by Brown and Lenneberg that a system of lexical classification, English color terminology, systematically influences memory.[1] Such a lexical system is explicit in its semantic correlates, and lexical selections have minimum predictability from the utterance structure alone.

Many grammatical markers also have semantic correlates— English plurality, for example. The peculiarity of such grammatical, in contrast to lexical, classification is that it may be mandatory even when there is no appropriate semantic or social cue, or when the feature is of minimal importance to the speaker. Thus its semantic associations may be attenuated.

If the correlation is perfect, the learning of the linguistic contrast may encourage earlier learning of the associated referential discrimination. Casagrande's finding that young Navaho-speaking children were more likely than were English-speaking

Navaho children in the same community to sort objects on the basis of form   is an example of the influence of a completely consistent classification system, the Navaho verb stems. [2]

A correlation that is less than perfect may both stimulate the learning of referential discriminations and influence the connotations of the exceptional items.   English form classes such as mass nouns and verbs are examples of a less than perfect semantic correlation.   Brown has pointed out that a higher proportion of the conversation of children concerns the tangible, visible world, and that, in their speech, form classes may have greater semantic consistency than in adult speech.   He gave children nonsense words in various linguistic environments, such as "a sib", "some sib," and "sibbing," and demonstrated systematic choice of pictures in accordance with the linguistic markers.   Thus pictures of confetti-like heaps were chosen as "some sib," contoured simple objects as "a sib," and pictures of actions as "sibbing."[3]   Thus the meaning of ambiguous items —the nonsense words— was influenced by the dominant features of meaning of the grammatical class to which they belonged.

The Analysis of Gender

Gender is an instance of an imperfectly correlated grammatical system of classification.   In many Indo-European languages the names of males belong to the masculine gender and of females to the feminine gender.   Whether an animate-inanimate distinction is made varies with the language.   We are concerned here with the assignment of meaning to new items.   Presumably, the connotations of sex difference should generalize to members of the masculine and feminine classes, even if the referent is abstract or inanimate.

Gender systems differ in certain respects. [4]   There is considerable evidence in psychological research about the processes by which stimulus generalization and mediated generalization occur. We shall extend these conclusions to make certain predictions about the effects of differences in gender systems.   Stimulus generalization refers to the extension to a new stimulus of a response learned to another stimulus. [5]   Thus, animals trained to approach, for food,

or to avoid, because of shock, a door painted with a particular hue,
will extend this response, without training, to doors with other hues.
The more similar the hue the greater the transfer of the response.
Mediation refers to the role of intervening responses rather than
simple similarity in generalization. Thus if we shock subjects whenever they see a drawing of some drinking glasses, and later show
them among other drawings, a picture of spectacles, they may show
physiological alarm reactions because they have covertly labelled
both as "glasses." We know that semantic responses are highly
transferable. [6]

On psychological grounds, we may make certain predictions
about semantic generalization in grammar:
(1) The larger the proportion of items, in terms of frequency of usage, which share a specific and observable semantic correlate, the greater the generalization. Thus, in a two-gender system
with masculine and feminine gender, many items will refer to inanimate objects with qualities irrelevant to sex. If a three-gender system places many of these inanimate referents in a neuter class, a
higher proportion of the masculine items may refer to males and
more of the feminine items to females. In the latter system, generalization should be greater.

(2) The less the overlap between classes, the stronger the
generalization. By overlap is meant manifestly inappropriate classification. Latin poeta, agricola, and nauta when they refer to
males are syntactically masculine, but they follow a predominantly
feminine declension. The same is true of Italian il dentista, il poeta,
il propheta, il artista, il messia, which have the feminine final
vowel. Since these nouns are syntactically masculine, the force of
the deviation is somewhat vitiated. It would be expected that such
cases, like deviant verb inflections, might survive only in frequent
forms or in elite groups, since analogy would tend to suppress them
in daily conversation. A few cases of complete overlap appear in
Italian, in which a male referent is named by a feminine form which
is also syntactically feminine: la guida, la guardia, and la tigre.

In evaluating overlap, a consistent direction of prediction
must be used, for example from referent to classifier. Frequency

of the cases should be considered, as well as observability of the sex contrast. Assignment of baby chicks to one class, regardless of gender, is irrelevant inclusion since sex is not evident. It may be that some of the animal classifications mentioned by Bonfante, e.g. la tigre, represent both rarity in observation of the referent and lack of obvious secondary sex differences. [7]

(3) Generalization is reduced if one of the classes is closed. In such a case new terms will be assigned to the open class regardless of the attributes of the referent. The effect of such a restriction would be to increase overlap between classes.

In some languages, new terms are assigned according to semantic criteria if they exist, but all the items without a semantic basis of assignment are put into one of the classes. In the Navaho system of stem classifiers of verbs, metaphorical terms are put into the "round object class." When one brings news or sorrow, the verb has the round object stem. For visible objects, however, there is semantic consistency. [8] The effect of such a rule is to decrease the proportion of semantically relevant items in the round object class, as described above in (1), but not to increase overlap.

(4) The larger the number of markers of gender in an utterance related to a given item, the greater the generalization will be. If there is a phonetic similarity between the linguistic cues in the various markers, then those markers become more strongly related to the semantic contrast. In Italian the fact that both adjectives and nouns use -o vs. -a to mark gender strengthens the association of each with sex. It is in fact improbable that speakers could sustain a system in which phonetically similar morphemes were associated with male referents in a nominal form and female referents in a modifier. A few high-frequency exceptions might be tolerated but the tendency would be towards consistency.

In addition, differential frequency of occurrence of particular modifiers with gender markers would modify the connotations of those markers. If delicata occurs more often than delicato, differential meaning accrues to the suffixes.

(5) The greater the cultural importance of the semantic distinction, the greater the generalization. Other factors being equal, more generalization might occur within a class correlated with sex differences than within one based on fine form properties of objects.

Our first set of hypotheses consists of a set of predictions about the variables that are related to degree of semantic generalization. The variations may occur between different languages, or between classifiers within one language.

Which aspects of meaning will be generalized? Taking gender as an example, there is an anatomical distinction, but we assign sex by these ultimate criteria only at birth or with animals. Most of the time we judge human sex on the basis of secondary, imperfectly correlated contrasts such as size, type of clothing, hair style, and voice. Finally, cultural experience and verbal practice differentiate the sexes and the masculine or feminine nouns which refer to them. We may therefore expect to find three different bases for meanings which might be generalized: (a) sexual symbolism associated with anatomical differences or sexual relations; (b) physical properties varying in their correlation with sex, such as size; (c) cultural associations such as contrasts in beauty, slowness, laziness, and stability. Within a given culture, we can predict systematic contrasts in meaning between masculine and feminine words with no animate referent.

Gender Assignment of Loan Words

How would one test such hypotheses? One source of evidence is the gender assignment of loan-words from a language without gender markers into a language with gender markers. In many American immigrant languages, English loan-words have been given gender markers. In analyses of loans into German, Norwegian, French, and Portuguese, certain common features have appeared: (1) Natural sex is usually pre-eminent. (2) If there is a virtual homonym, or if there is phonetic similarity between the English word as borrowed and the usual phonetic features of the gender markers in the borrowing language, the associated gender is assigned. Thus English -ing often yields French -ine (f.), German -ung (f.), and English -er often becomes German -er (m.), French -eur (m.), Portuguese -a (f.).[9]

(3) There may be a strong preference for one gender or the other. Thus in Norwegian and in Portuguese there is a bias toward masculine assignment, and in German towards feminine assignment of loanwords.

(4) The gender of the native word which best translates the borrowed word may be adopted. Sometimes whole semantic classes are thus affected, as in the French-Canadian preference for feminine gender for names of machines and masculine gender for cloth. Haugen has protested this principle. He argues that loanwords "were used precisely because the native word escaped the speaker or because he had never heard a native word for the idea in question. There is no reason to suppose that his subconscious should have whispered the gender of the native 'equivalent' to him when it failed to deliver the equivalent itself."[10] Haugen's objection to the principle does not seem to be valid. There are cases of semantic specialization, where both borrowed and native word are retained, and here gender transfer seems quite likely. Further, if gender produces particular semantic associations with words and their referents, it is possible that these associations might be recalled when the details of the word itself are momentarily lost. This is a common experience in the psychopathology of memory, when a proper name is temporarily forgotten, but certain letters, the number of syllables, or the ethnicity of the name may be recalled. Also, tachistoscopic perception research (or "subliminal" perception) shows that recognition or recall are by no means all-or-none affairs, but that partial aspects may be recalled when the whole cannot.[11] Whether such transfers actually occur is an empirical issue.

These factors represent a series of potential bases of assignment, which could conflict with each other. Ideally, they should be ordered in terms of relative strength so that unambiguous predictions can be made. Haugen's statement that "all nouns become masculine unless they were associated with a homophonous feminine or neuter morpheme or a female creature" represents a statement of priorities of factors that permits prediction.[12] If two factors of equal strength conflict, gender assignment may vacillate, which Haugen reports was

the case in 18% of the nouns he studied. [13] Some factors may be absolute; e.g. all female creatures may be called by feminine names without exception. On the other hand, the other three factors seem to be
matters of degree, and in the case of homophony the particular phonetic form in which a word is borrowed must be known. Our point
here is that the analysis of loans should approach as closely as possible to a perfectly predictive system. Until such an attempt is made,
and the exceptions can be isolated, it cannot be known either whether
the fourth factor is present, or whether any influence may be attributed to connotations.

Table 1
Bonfante's List of Matched Italian Words*

	gloss for Feminine	gloss for Masculine
buca	cave; grave; post office box; billiard pocket	narrow, round hole, quite deep; key hole; ear passage; small room
capana	hut, child's playhouse	small hut, cabana
cosa	thing	(pej.) vague thing, "stuff"
famiglia	family	servant
gamba	leg	stem of a plant, candlestick
pozza	puddle	well
sacca	soft bag for clothing, laundry bag	sturdy bag, often deep and narrow, for coal, potatoes, golf clubs; sleeping bag; type of dress
secchia	pail, pail-full	pail

*Bonfante, 847

Thus the available evidence on loanwords does not help us
to know whether gender markers carry any connotations which generalize. Bonfante has presented a more controlled source of evidence:
the analysis of items which share a common root and etymology but
which differ in gender. We will discuss only his examples in Italian,
which are presented in Table 1. [14] Gender in Italian is consistent,
with minimal overlap, agreement rules, and phonetically similar
markers for adjectives and nouns. Because there are only two genders and both classes are open, each class contains many items in
which sex is irrelevant. One would expect under such circumstances

that the connotations of sex difference would extend or generalize to these irrelevant items. The extent of generalization should be less than in an otherwise similar three-gender system.

Bonfante claims that these items reveal a strong size contrast: "The feminine in -a often indicates an object larger or more comprehensive than the corresponding masculine in -o."[15] Neither this list, nor a longer one in which we have added further items in Table 2, seems to present overwhelming support for this statement. Such evidence should be based first on systematic or complete selection of instances, and a method of size judgment by neutral native speakers. Neither of these precautions was taken. While Bonfante's method is considerably more controlled than the analysis of loan lists, both techniques omit an essential step, namely the assessment of the semantic judgments of the speech community, separately for each item, without knowledge by the informants of the hypothesis tested.

Connotations of Artificial Words

The following study represents a first step necessary in testing the hypotheses presented earlier—the use of a method giving an adequate range of instances and semantic judgments by native speakers. Nonsense words were presented to Italians. Because they were artificially constructed, it was possible to control the phonetic factors which influence connotations, and to make completely equivalent lists of masculine and feminine forms. Such a method may be considered an artificial and more systematic analogue of Bonfante's, and it permits assessment of connotations when the influence of denotations is completely removed.

Method[16]

Informants. Data were collected from 32 Italian bilinguals in Boston. They were given a test of language dominance, in which the difference in total time to name a set of 120 simple pictures in Italian and in English was measured. The Italian-dominant and the English-dominant on the test differed radically in their life histories. All of the Italian-dominant informants came to the United States after

Table 2

Matched Italian Words

	gloss for Feminine	gloss for Masculine
banca	bank (for money)	bench, counter
broda	(pej.) watery stuff	broth, juice
capotta	tent, car top of cloth	overcoat
fiasca	flat-sided flask	round-sided flask
fila	row, line	thread
faschia	band, bandage	bundle
folia	leaf	sheet of paper
fossa	grave, ditch	long ditch
frutta	piece of fruit, fruit in markets	fruit on a tree; fruits of labor
legna	pile of firewood, lumber	wood
mela	apple	apple-tree

(Many contrasts of the fruit and tree are similar)

pala	spade	pole, stick
pendula	pendulum clock	pendulum
piana	plain; window frame	plain; story or floor
picca	spade, pike, spear	pinnacle
pizza	pie	goatee; beak; pinnacle; lace
porta	door	port, harbor
posta	point of a sharp object	place, location; period (punctuation)
suffitta	garret, penthouse	ceiling
suola	sole of shoe	soil, earth
tavola	board	table
tela	canvas material	cloth panel, gore
torchia	large printing press	small press; typographical machine
tuba	musical instrument	pipe, tube
vela	sail	veil

the age of nine, whereas none of the English-dominant came after
six, and many were born in Boston.

Materials. A list of thirty root morphemes was prepared,
of consonant-vowel-consonant form, by systematically rotating vowels
and consonants. These were carefully checked against a dictionary
and a sample of informants to remove items that were meaningful or
reminded people of meaningful words. Two forms of the test were
constructed, so that the same root was given a masculine suffix on
one form and a feminine suffix on the other. Half the informants
received each form.

Instructions. "Some people think that you can guess what
words mean just by the way they sound. I have some words here
from a dialect of Italian that you don't know. Some of them are names
of strong things, weak things, good things, and bad things, and so
forth. See if you can guess the description from the way the words
sound. I will give you the word, and then ask you to choose which
description is better. For instance, GICA—buona o cattiva? If you
know any of the words, please tell me." Because of the dialectal
variations in the subjects, the instructions were given in English.

Procedure. Each of the thirty words was given with four
descriptive pairs in the appropriate gender: buono o cattivo, grosso
o piccolo, bruto o bello, delicato o forte. The informants who were
hesitant were encouraged to guess. These particular dimensions
were chosen because evidence obtained from American students had
suggested that there were different evaluations of man and woman on
scales involving either value (bad-good, pretty-ugly) or potency
(strong-weak, big-little). [17] Without prior testing of Italians, these
scales were selected as possibly related to physical and cultural sex
contrasts.

After the choices for the nonsense words, the informants
were asked to place gli uomini and le donne or le femine[18] on scales
representing each of these four dimensions. They were asked to
judge them on scales with seven points rather than two points, as for
the nonsense words. Half were asked to judge men first, and half
women, with the direction of the scales varied to avoid directional
preferences.

Results. Our assumption is that the judgments of the nonsense words are generalized from judgments of nouns with animate referents. Thus the first point to test is whether the informants thought men and women differed on the four scales. The statistical tests used on Table 3 compare the differences that actually appeared with those that might have occurred by chance among thirty people (two did not complete this part of the test). All the differences were too great to be due to chance. Le femine were consistently rated as prettier, weaker, and smaller than gli uomini. There was a slight tendency to rate women as better (buona) but it was smaller than the other differences, especially in the English-dominant informants.

Table 3
Rating of "Men" and "Women" on
Attribute Scales

Attribute poles[a]	gli uomini	(le femine) le donne	Difference	chance probability of difference[b]
Bello—bruto	2.53	1.57	0.96	< 0.01
Buono—cattivo	2.98	2.78	0.20	< 0.05
Delicato—forte	4.37	2.29	2.08	< 0.01
Piccolo—grosso	5.14	3.99	1.15	< 0.001

[a]Values have been corrected in direction so that the left attribute pole had a value of one and the right, of seven.
[b]Evaluated by correlated t-test, for thirty informants.

It is possible that people who regard women as bigger than men might also rate feminine nonsense words more often as grosso. For this reason, we separated the informants into two groups according to the direction of their ratings of gli uomini and le donne (le femine). The nonsense ratings were examined separately for the two groups. It did not appear that the individual rating was the important factor; even the deviant individuals went along with the majority in saying, for example, that masculine words more often were grosso. These idiosyncratic ratings of gli uomini and le donne (le femine) may come from thinking of particular persons while doing the ratings; evidently these idiosyncratic factors do not play a part in the nonsense ratings of the same informants.

Table 4

Differences in Number of Masculine and of Feminine Nonsense
Words with Specified Description by Italian–Dominant
Informants

Description	Average difference[a]	Chance probability[b]	Number of informants
Bruto	1	<0.005	12
Cattivo	1	<0.05	14
Forte	1	<0.001	12
Grosso	2	<0.05	13

[a]With 15 masculine and 15 feminine words, the differences could range between -15 and +15. The number of feminine words given the description was subtracted from the number of masculine words so described.

[b]Evaluated by the Wilcoxin Signed Ranks Test.

On Table 4, a few words were eliminated which an informant said sounded familiar. For this reason the number of informants is not the same for all words. For each informant, we subtracted the number of feminine words rated, e.g. grosso from the number of masculine words so rated. Theoretically, this value could range from -15, if no masculine and all feminine words were said to be grosso (-a) to +15 if the reverse obtained. If there is no systematic difference, the values would show a chance fluctuation around zero.

It can be seen on Table 4 that the average values differed slightly but systematically from zero, for the Italian–dominant informants. The difference was reliable for all four scales, but was most reliable for bruto and forte.

Such results might have occurred if the informants guessed our intent, and directed themselves to choose according to gender. However, there were no cases of sufficiently consistent patterns to suggest that this was the case.

We can conclude that there is a tendency to ascribe different connotations to masculine and feminine words in Italian, and that the differences are related to differences in the connotations of gli uomini and le donne (le femine).

Discussion

We have presented a simple technique for discovering the connotative contrast associated with a classifier by a given language community. The scales used were abbreviated versions of a more extensive mapping. Inspection of Tables 1 and 2 suggests other important dimensions which might show even stronger contrasts. We have merely shown the existence of a contrast, not its extent or magnitude. Also, we have assumed that testing of gli uomini and le donne (le femine) would give sufficient evidence of a contrast for nouns with animate referents, but perhaps some terms for familiar animals would give stronger contrasts.

What are the implications of the gender experiment for natural language and for meaningful words? Obviously, people do not regard apples or apple-trees as inherently masculine or feminine on the basis of grammatical gender. In everyday experience, the obvious attributes of objects far outweigh any increment of association derived from gender. While some speculations on the origins of gender have suggested that some inanimate objects were first viewed as animate (sun-moon, night-day, earth-sky), and assigned to contrasting genders,[19] still the great majority of everyday objects do not have these properties. Some shapes and substances do have sexual connotations. These features may in the past have had an influence on gender assignment.

Generalization of connotations is least important when the association of a word and a tangible referent is well-learned and automatic, and when the semantic referent is unambiguous and its properties are obvious. Probabilistic aspects of experience are more important when language is being learned, when a situation is ambiguous, or when active commerce with the environment is minimized and thought and feeling are maximized.[20]

There are certain points, therefore, where we may look for the reflection of connotations on natural language. One is during learning, when errors would tend towards consistency; in fact, learning of grammatical classes is probably facilitated considerably by any consistent semantic associates. Other points deserving of systematic investigation are borrowing and coinage, metaphor and slang, humor, poetry, and visual representation of abstractions. In this study we have taken only the first step, by showing that Italian gender carries meaning.

Modern linguists have rightfully been critical of semantic assumptions which are either untested or untestable. Yet there are certain points in linguistic contact and change and in stylistic differentiation where semantic influences may be significant, and where formal analyses may be supplemented. .We have shown that it is possible to test semantic statements about contemporary languages, believing that the systematic assessment of the semantic aspects of formal categories will prove to be important in the study of the uses of language.

NOTES

[1] R. W. Brown and E. H. Lenneberg, "A Study in Language and Cognition," Journal of Abnormal and Social Psychology XLIX (1954), 454-462.

[2] J. B. Carroll and J. B. Casagrande, "The Function of Language Classifications in Behavior," in Readings in Social Psychology, ed. by E. E. Maccoby, T. M. Newcomb, and E. L. Hartley (New York, 1958), pp. 18-31. Casagrande's study illustrates also the important point that classifiers in language provide only one form of training among many; two English-speaking control groups differing widely in cultural environment contrasted as sharply in performance as the Navaho-speaking and non-Navaho-speaking Navaho children.

[3] R. W. Brown, "Linguistic Determinism and the Part of Speech," Journal of Abnormal Social Psychology LV (1957), 1-5.

[4] A sophisticated analysis of the history of gender is available in I. Fodor, "The Origin of Grammatical Gender I, II," Lingua VIII (1959), 1-41, 186-214.

[5] S. A. Mednick and J. L. Freedman, "Stimulus Generalization," Psychological Bulletin LVII (1960), 169-200.

[6] For a discussion of semantic generalization, see C. E. Osgood, "The Nature and Measurement of Meaning," Psychological Bulletin XLIX (1952), 197-237, and Gregory Razran, "The Observable Unconscious and the Inferable Conscious in Current Soviet Psycho-

physiology: Interoceptive Conditioning, Semantic Conditioning, and the Orienting Reflex," Psychological Review LXVIII (1961), 81-147. Recent summaries of studies on the effects of language which include discussions of verbal mediation are S. M. Ervin and W. R. Miller, "Language Development" in the National Society for the Study of Education Yearbook, 1963: Child Psychology, and A. E. Goss, "Verbal Mediating Responses and Concept Formation," Psychological Review LXVIII (1961), 248-274, the latter being considerably the more extensive and technical.

[7]G. Bonfante, "Semantics, Language." In Encyclopedia of Psychology, Ed. by P. L. Harriman (New York, 1946), pp. 847-851.

[8]Whorf has stated that the Navaho category is only partially consistent semantically, citing the metaphorical extensions. B. L. Whorf, "Grammatical Categories," Language XXI (1945), 1-11. My own evidence in trying to predict stems used by informants for systematically varied referents and in eliciting word-associations accords more with the conclusions of Hoijer. Harry Hoijer, "Classificatory Verb Stems in the Apachean Languages," International Journal of American Linguistics XI (1945), 13-23. There is nearly a perfect semantic predictability for physical objects. The selection seems to be semantically rather than linguistically conditioned since a "rug" occurs both with a long object or flat flexible object stem, depending on its state, whether rolled or spread out.

[9]Leo Pap, Portuguese-American Speech (New York, 1949), p. 104; C. E. Reed, "Gender of English Words in Pennsylvania German," American Speech XVII (1942), 25-29; E. F. Haden and E. A. Joliat, "Le Genre Grammatical des Substantifs en Franco-Canadien Empruntés à l'Anglais," Publications of the Modern Language Association LV (1940), 839-854.

[10]Einar Haugen, The Norwegian Language in America (Philadelphia, 1953), v. 2, p. 449.

[11]Israel Goldiamond, "Indicators of Perception: I. Subliminal Perception, Subception, Unconscious Perception: An Analysis in Terms of Psychophysical Indicator Methodology," Psychological Bulletin LV (1958), 373-411.

[12]Haugen, op. cit., 448.

[13]Haugen, op. cit., 442.

[14]Bonfante, op. cit., 847. Bonfante states his agreement with a point made by Leo Spitzer in "Feminización del Neutro,"

<u>Revista de Filologia Hispanica</u> III (1941), 361, that the feminine is bigger because it embraces and envelops while the masculine penetrates: "es también lo que abarca al hombre, lo recibe en su regazo, es más amplio que él y lo contiene."

[15]Bonfante, loc. cit.

[16]These data were collected as part of a study sponsored by the Social Science Research Council Southwestern Project in Comparative Psycholinguistics, a project directed by J. B. Carroll. The services of David Arnold in recruiting informants and collecting the data are gratefully acknowledged.

[17]A complete description of data showing correlations with masculine-feminine of various scales, for American informants, can be found in C. E. Osgood, Charles Suci, and P. H. Tannenbaum, <u>The Measurement of Meaning</u>, Urbana, 1958. The technique has also been used cross-culturally (see the abstracts in <u>International Journal of American Linguistics</u> XXVII (1961), 260-263). Evidence obtained by the author from Navahos suggests that the size dimension should be divided into <u>tall-short</u> and <u>wide-narrow</u>. Men were rated as longer and narrower than women. The Italian term <u>grosso</u> like English <u>big</u> or <u>large</u>, does not distinguish height and breadth.

[18]It was ascertained first whether <u>le donne</u> or <u>le femine</u> was the informant's customary term.

[19]G. Bonfante, "L'animismo nelle lingue indoeuropee," <u>Sprachgeschichte und Wortbedeutung</u>, 1954, pp. 33-56.

[20]S. M. Ervin and G. Foster, "The development of meaning in children's descriptive terms," <u>Journal of Abnormal and Social Psychology</u> LXI (1960), 271-275, regarding learning. On gender, Roman Jakobson has collected some pertinent examples: "Ways of personifying or metaphorically interpreting inanimate nouns are prompted by their gender. A test in the Moscow Psychological Institute (1915) showed that Russians, prone to personify the weekdays, consistently represented Monday, Tuesday, and Thursday as males and Wednesday, Friday, and Saturday as females, without realizing that this distribution was due to the masculine gender of the first three names...as against the feminine gender of the others.... The fact that the word for Friday is masculine in some Slavic languages and feminine in others is reflected in the folk traditions of the corresponding peoples, which differ in their Friday ritual. The widespread Russian superstition that a fallen knife presages a male guest and a fallen fork a female one is determined by the masculine gender of...

'knife' and the feminine of ... 'fork' in Russian. In Slavic and other languages where 'day' is masculine and 'night' feminine, day is represented by poets as the lover of night. The Russian painter Repin was baffled as to why Sin had been depicted as a woman by German artists; he did not realize that 'sin' is feminine in German ..., but masculine in Russian .... Likewise a Russian child, while reading a translation of German tales, was astounded to find that Death, obviously a woman ...was pictured as an old man ... My Sister Life, the title of a book of poems by Boris Pasternak, is quite natural in Russian, where 'life' is feminine, but was enough to reduce to despair the Czech poet Josef Hora in his attempt to translate these poems, since in Czech this noun is masculine. " R. Jakobson, "On Linguistic Aspects of Translation, " in On Translation, Ed. by R. A. Brower (Cambridge, Mass. , 1959), p. 237.

[21]For other recent studies employing semantic differential ratings of nonsense words, see M. S. Miron, "A Cross-Linguistic Investigation of Phonetic Symbolism, " Journal of Abnormal and Social Psychology LXII (1961), 623-630, and N. N. Markel and E. P. Hamp, "Connotative Meanings of Certain Phoneme Sequences, " Studies in Linguistics XV (1960-1961), 47-61. The latter paper is concerned with phonesthemes, or sub-morphemic sequences with some meaningful associations.

12 | Navaho Word-Associations

In Collaboration with Herbert Landar

It has been found repeatedly with educated adults who speak
Indo-European languages that most responses in the word-associations are in the same grammatical class as the stimulus-words. [1]
Children's associations, on the other hand, are characteristically
sequential. The major shift, for both American and French children,
comes in the first few years of school. [2]

The current study of Navaho associations is principally designed to examine the role of grammatical classes in association.
First, the levels of paradigmatic responses, i.e. responses in the
same grammatical class, will be compared with those obtained in
other studies. Secondly, internal comparisons will be made, to see
whether classes occurring in final position in sentences have higher
frequencies of paradigmatic responses. Thirdly, the relation between contextual variety and sequential responses will be tested with
a Navaho system of classes with highly restricted contexts. Fourthly,
the level of commonality will be compared with the levels found in
other studies. The physical isolation of Navaho residences from
each other, and lack of mass-media should decrease commonality.
Finally, individual differences in schooling and Navaho dominance in
bilingual Ss will be related to associative behavior.

Method

Subjects. Nine cases were tested near Shiprock, New Mex-
ico, and 28 near Fort Defiance, Arizona. These areas are within
the Navaho reservation, and are surrounded by isolated clusters of
hogans where Navahos live in traditional style, herd sheep, and
congregate for rodeos, 'pow-wows,' and ritual purposes. Most Ss

were tested indoors in a room with modern furnishings. At least 8
of those tested were clearly monolinguals, 16 knew some English,
and 13 were English-dominant bilinguals, judging from their relative
speed in naming 120 pictured objects in the two languages. Ages ranged from 17 to 70 yr. Twenty-five were women.

Instructions. The instructions were tape-recorded in Navaho,
but an interpreter was present in case of misunderstanding.

Here is a sheet of paper with some words written on it. The
instructor will call out a word for you and he wants you to repeat the
word and add another word to it. The way you add another word is
something like this. The first word is 'cat.' Think of a cat, and
think that he drinks milk, and that he kills birds and mice, and he
likes to be near a fire, and he has whiskers. You can find a lot of
words connected with a cat. This is just an example. Find words
connected with the words that I say. Don't hold back, go right ahead.
I'm going to give three more words for you now. 'Wagon' : with a
wagon the first thing I think of is 'horse.' The next word is 'cloud' :
then I think of 'rain.' For 'money' I think of 'food.' You can say
any word, even though it's not connected with the thing; you can say
any word that comes to mind. As soon as you repeat the word, say
another word.

During testing, the Es called out the words, heard them
repeated to guarantee comprehension, and tape-recorded the responses. When the responses were too long, S was urged to shorten them,
and more examples were supplied.

Materials. One hundred and fourteen items were presented,
drawn in scrambled order from different grammatical classes. To
clarify later discussion, a brief description of Navaho grammatical
classes is necessary. [3]

Fifty stimulus-words were nouns or nominal compounds.
These words or compounds are defined partly by syntactic function
and partly by inflection. Nouns are single words which are inflected
for possession but not for number. Compounds and one-word nouns
usually lack inflectional suffixes to provide a basis for sound-simi-
larity, but 11 items referred to parts of the body, or relationships
('wife,' 'father') which require a possessive prefix (bi-má = 'his

mother,' qa-má='somebody's mother').[4] Such items tend to elicit responses in which either the base or prefix is repeated.

Nominal compounds have a diverse internal composition, and may be made up of various sequences of parts of speech, but they all occupy the position in sentences of ordinary simple one-word nouns. Nominal compounds may be formed of two nouns ('gas'= chidí bi-tooq= 'car its-water'), a noun with an enclitic ('grandmother' = qamá sání= 'somebody's-mother old'), or a noun with a verb ('sugar'= qáshį́įh Ləkan= 'salt it-is-sweet').

One word was a numeral, qashdlaq ('five'), a member of a nominal subclass defined by syntactic function.

Thirty-four stimulus-items were simple verbs. Verbs may be transitive or intransitive as in English. Translation of some intransitive verbs, however, reveals that adjectival meaning is involved. There is in fact no separate formal category of adjectives in Navaho, as there is in most Indo-European languages. The 50 simple verbs consisted of a prefix and stem. In addition, 4 verbs were more complex, including additional prefixes. The typical Navaho verb consists of a long string of prefixes plus a stem.

Six verbs exhibit a special property which has attracted attention in research on language and cognition.[5] To say 'hand it to me' one must select among eleven alternative stems. The selection is based on the physical properties of the thing you want. Many verbs of handling have a set of alternative stems. The six verbs used as stimuli were the six different ways of saying "it's sitting there," used respectively when one speaks of round bulky objects, fluffy things, flat flexible objects, things in containers, long rigid objects, and long flexible objects. As far as we could ascertain, this system is entirely consistent semantically, so that a child can use it correctly for new objects. Metaphorical extensions like "he brought the news," employ the round bulky object-stem. Necessarily these stems occur in comparatively restricted environments, since a noun that can occur with one will not usually occur with another. The exception is the name of an object that can change form: a rug unrolled is a flat flexible object but rolled up is a long object. Hereafter these 6 verbs will be called specialized verbs.

One stimulus-word was a particle, nishqnáájí ('right'), and four were relational expressions. These can be translated as 'high,' 'fast,' 'down,' and 'carefully' or 'slowly.' The last three end with an enclitic particle, -go. These terms tend to be used as modifiers before verbs.

A sentence may consist of merely one word, a verb (e.g. Lichííq, 'it is red,' or jiní, 'they say it') which may be translated with the subject included, or with both the subject and object included. A basic pattern of longer utterances, which contain nouns as well as the verb-stem and prefixes, is subject, object, and verb, in that order (e.g. gaLbáhí máqii dayiiLtsá, 'rabbit coyote they-saw-him').

Analysis. Two procedures were used for initial classification of responses. A Navaho informant identified which responses readily suggested a context in which they could substitute for the stimulus-word, and whether they could precede or follow the stimulus-word in utterances. Also, each word was classified as to grammatical class. In the subsequent analysis, a response is considered paradigmatic if (1) the item is in the same grammatical class as the stimulus-word, and (2) it does not contain the stimulus-word. An exception to the second rule was made in certain cases. Some very common compounds such as 'sugar' (qáshííh Lǝkan = 'salt it-is-sweet') and 'puppy' (Léécháági yázhí = 'dog young') contain their stimulus-words. It was decided that such compounds may be psychologically paradigmatic if the Navahos treated them as such. [6] Individuals who gave predominantly paradigmatic responses on unambiguous items, and others who gave predominantly syntagmatic responses were separated. These compounds were considered paradigmatic if the first group gave them as responses but none of the second group did. If some of each gave them, they were considered ambiguous and omitted from the computations.

Responses were considered sentences if they were quite long or included more than one basic constituent in addition to the stimulus-word. Except where indicated, sentence-responses were excluded. Both stimulus-and response-words which could be in more than one grammatical class were excluded. The paradigmatic score for each stimulus-word consists of the percentage of remaining responses which are paradigmatic. Exclusion of ambiguous or complex stimuli yielded 100 analyzable stimuli.

Results

Primary responses. The level of commonality for primary
responses was considerably lower than the level obtained on college
students. [7] If 47 items which correspond in the norms of Russell and
Jenkins and in the Navaho data are compared, the median commonality
for the Navaho items is 17% and for the English items is 45%. The
low level is not a result of the bias arising from selection of corresponding items from the Kent-Rosanoff list, since the median for the
total list of 100 words given to the Navaho was 17%.

A very large proportion of the primaries were paradigmatic.
Of the 47 corresponding words, 5 in English and 4 in Navaho produced
syntagmatic primaries, 2 in English and 5 in Navaho were ambiguous,
and the rest were paradigmatic.

It is of interest to compare the actual primaries of the translated terms, though there are, of course, artifacts in such comparisons. Twenty-four of the 47 items have corresponding primaries,
when ties are included if either corresponds. Correspondences seem
to be concentrated in certain types of words, chiefly terms which
have natural opposites, such as terms with adjectival meaning, nouns
with a contrasting mate (man-woman, boy-girl, hand-foot), and culturally corresponding pairs of tools (needle-thread, hammer-nail).
Discrepancies appear if a term has several meanings in one language
(foot and shoe are the same in Navaho), there are compounds containing one of the terms (sugar= sweet salt, and chili = bitter herb),
or there are cultural differences in the use of the referent. The latter
of course is the principal case here, and probably accounts for the
fact that correspondences were found to be less for Navaho and European languages than with the latter languages, as reported by Rosenzweig. [8] Some examples of culturally based differences seem to be
these: English bread-butter vs. Navaho 'bread' - 'fried bread', English
blossom-flower vs. Navaho 'blossom'-'pollen' (ritually important),
English house-home vs. Navaho 'house'-'hogan,' English whiskey-
drink vs. Navaho 'whiskey'-'it's no good,' (prohibited by the tribal
council on the reservation).

If we turn to the total list of 100 words, we find nearly all
the primaries to be paradigmatic. The exceptions are 'corn'-'white,'

'whiskey'-'it's no good,' 'noisy'-'children,' 'ripe'-'corn,' 'bitter'-
'chili' (bitter-herb), 'angry'-'cattle,' and the six specialized verbs.
These verbs, with their great restriction in permitted contexts,
all yielded syntagmatic primaries consisting of the nouns which most
typically precede each of them: 'stone,' 'wool,' 'blanket,' 'water,'
'log,' and 'rope.' In addition to the opposites and tools mentioned
above from the Kent-Rosanoff list, the words eliciting paradigmatic
primaries with the highest commonalities were terms of kinship,
parts of the body, natural pairs ('lightning'-'rain,' 'moon'-'sun'),
and 'five.'

Paradigmatic responses. The proportion of paradigmatic responses varied with class. The largest proportion occurred among
nouns, with a mean of 59% paradigmatic responses. Verbs had a mean
of 52% paradigmatic responses, modifiers 42%, and specialized verbs
29%. To the word 'five' 47% paradigmatic responses were given, if
only numerals are considered paradigmatic. These levels of paradigmatic response may be compared to other findings. Brown and
Berko reported means of 30%, 53%, 55%, and 81% paradigmatic
responses for first-, second-, and third-grade children and for
adults respectively, when mass-nouns are omitted.[9] Ervin, with a
list containing fewer adverbs, obtained 37% for kindergarten and
first-grade children, 62% for third-grade children, and 70% for
sixth-grade children.[10]

The principal syntagmatic responses to nouns and modifiers
were words which usually follow them in utterances. The principal
syntagmatic responses to verbs were nouns which could precede the
verbs. Since Navaho permits adjacent occurrence of nouns in sentences, some items classified as paradigmatic could occur contiguously
in discourse. In the second English study mentioned above, responses
in the same class which could be syntagmatic were omitted (e. g.
front-door). The prevalence of this pattern in Navaho made such
omissions impossible.

Class-analysis. It is conceivable that the levels of paradigmatic response obtained above could be derived from random responses to stimuli. In Table I it can be seen that this is not the case.
Nouns and specialized verbs tend to elicit nouns. Ordinary verbs
elicit verbs, and modifiers elicit both other modifiers (chiefly opposites) and verbs.[11]

Individual differences. There were very extreme differences in preferences for paradigmatic responses. Twenty-six individuals for whom data on schooling was available were chosen, and a sample of 55 responses was taken for each person. It was found that 3 persons had fewer than 6% paradigmatic and 3 had more than 94% paradigmatic responses. There was a small and unreliable tendency for those who had schooling or were English-dominant to give more paradigmatic responses.

Sentence-responses appeared in 9 of the 11 persons who were Navaho-dominant or monolingual and had no schooling, but only 3 of the remaining 15 people gave such responses. Thus the concept of the 'word' as a short unit seems to be acquired primarily through reading, even if it is reading in another language of quite different structure. Since the separation of the sentence-responses from the syntagmatic responses was somewhat arbitrary, there is some justification for pooling them. If this is done, the uneducated, Navaho-dominant group gives significantly fewer paradigmatic responses at the 2.5% level by the Mann-Whitney test.

Table I

Conditional Probability of Classes in Association

Stimulus-class

Response-class	Noun	Specialized verb	Verb	Modifier
Noun	.53	.51	.33	.11
Verb	.37	.38	.50	.43
Modifier	—	.01	.07	.39
Other	.02	.02	.01	.02
Sentence	.08	.08	.08	.06

Discussion

Paradigmatic responses. The level of paradigmatic responses is considerably lower for the Navaho than for educated adults in other cultures. The explanation is not obvious. Since a similar difference has been found in France between educated and uneducated samples,[12] it is probable that the educational process accounts for these differences among groups and for the changes with age.

But why might this be? One difference appears in this study as well as in the research on changes with age— education reduces the length of responses. Both sentence-responses and responses which include the stimulus-word are reduced. Paradigmatic responses are thus more possible because sentence-responses or phrase-responses containing the stimulus-word usually cannot be paradigmatic, or at least are not so judged in the analysis. But the differences remain when sentence-responses are omitted.

An explanation of group-differences must be based on a more general account of the development of paradigmatic preferences. It is clear that paradigmatic responses reflect possibilities of substitution in specific contexts. When English-speaking Ss have been asked to produce sentences and make substitutions for particular words (also used as stimulus-words for association), the substitutions they make correspond overwhelmingly to paradigmatic primaries. This is especially true of antonyms and other instances of high commonality.[13]

It may be expected that a prerequisite to the development of paradigmatic responses is sufficient contextual variety to reduce syntagmatic competition. The specialized verbs in Navaho provide a neat, grammatically defined test of this prediction. Since the 11 alternatives are contextually selective, the range of contextual variety is much less than that of ordinary verbs. The fact that all of these verbs produced primarily syntagmatic responses, and that these tended to be the nouns which usually precede the verbs, shows the importance of contextual variety.

If the difference between groups is based on an increase in size of vocabulary and hence in contextual variety with age or education, there should be more syntagmatic primaries offered by the children, the Navahos, and the uneducated Frenchmen. In fact, this was true only of the French sample. We have assumed that commonality in a group reflects frequency for an individual. This is not

necessarily the case. For children, and for the geographically
dispersed Navahos, idiosyncratic concentrations on certain sequences
may result in syntagmatic responses that are not reflected in primaries. In the case of the specialized verbs, the syntagmatic primaries reflected the fact that because of grammatical regularities
for all Navaho speakers the same contextual selectivity exists. Thus
we cannot rule out differences in the degree of contextual variety as an
explanation for differences among groups.

Given contextual variety, why do paradigmatic responses
occur? Several explanations have been offered, which are not necessarily mutually exclusive: (1) Paradigmatic responses may become associated with the stimulus through contiguity, while it would
not occur in normal overt speech, might appear when a listener an-
ticipates what another person says. Words which normally occur in
the same semantic and linguistic contexts would most often be erron-
eously anticipated, e.g. 'is the mattress . . . hard? soft?' This
explanation alone could not account for the differences among groups.
(2) Even though paradigmatic responses may not be the strongest
associates, the task may be interpreted as one of returning like for
like. Sometimes Ss are overt about self-instruction ("should I give
opposites?") and educational experience may give some practice in
similar tasks. The very marked individual differences in paradigmatic preferences suggest directing and monitoring of his own pattern of
response by some Ss. Even third-grade children ask whether there
is a right answer; they may thus hunt for some rule to follow. (3)
As language is learned, concept-formation may occur regarding
grammatical classes. This explanation may be appropriate in accounting for changes with age, in conjunction with the second point, but
it seems least satisfactory in accounting for differences among adults. [14]

There has been some suggestion of directional preferences
in syntagmatic responses in English. It now appears that this preference may reflect the structural properties of English. In most English sentences the antecedent to a verb is a pronoun in the subject
case. Since subjective pronouns do not usually occur in single-word
utterances in English, it is much more likely that a syntagmatic
response to a verb will be a word which follows the verb rather than
one which precedes it. It has been argued that the reason nouns show
paradigmatic dominance earlier than transitive verbs is that they

occur more often in final position in sentences and hence have occurred less often with a sequel. Yet it can also be argued that nouns are associated with more competing syntagmatic words, since they may follow verbs, and both follow and precede adjectives (in copular sentences). This competition may leave a paradigmatic response as the strongest possibility. A good example is the word <u>coffee</u>. It elicits many contexts: <u>drink</u> (preceding), and <u>good</u>, <u>hot</u>, and <u>black</u> (following). <u>Tea</u> is the primary association. <u>Game</u>, on the other hand, has only one frequent contextual word — <u>play</u>, and this is its most frequent associate although it normally precedes. [15] Brown and Berko's evidence that adverbs are slow in development of paradigmatic dominance, though they typically occur in final position, supports the argument that the basic principle is contextual variety rather than order. [16]

Now the Navaho data buttress this alternative. Navaho verbs strongly elicited the nouns which precede them. The particularly high frequency of syntagmatic responses in the case of the specialized verbs points to contextual variety as a fundamental variable in association.

Summary

The grammatical properties of Navaho word–associations have been examined for 100 stimulus-words. It has been shown that (1) commonalities were very low; (2) primaries tended to be paradigmatic except when contextual variety was limited; (3) with primaries, preferences for contrasts appeared as in English; (4) the proportion of paradigmatic responses out of total responses for each word was as low as among primary-school children; (5) the grammatical class of the response depended upon the class of the stimulus-word; (6) if a word had a restricted distribution, syntagmatic frequencies were especially high; (7) forward associations appeared to be no stronger than backward associations.

NOTES

This research was sponsored by the Southwest Project in Comparative Psycholinguistics of the Social Science Research Council. The second author did linguistic analysis while employed by the Department of

Public Health, Cornell University Medical College. We are grateful
to the Navaho staff of the Navaho-Cornell Clinic, and particularly to
William Morgan, Assistant in Anthropology of the Cornell-Navaho
Field Health Research Project, for services as linguistic informants,
and to Professor Harry Hoijer of the University of California for linguistic advice.

[1] The most detailed report was that of Arthur Wreschner, Die
reproduktion und assoziation von vorstellungen, Z. Psychol. Ergb.,
3, 1907, 329-599.

[2] R.W. Brown and Jean Berko, Word-association and the
acquisition of grammar, Child Develop., 1960, 31, 8; S. M. Ervin,
Changes with age in the verbal determinants of word-association,
Am. J. Psychol., 74, 1961, 361-372; M. R. Rosenzweig and R. Men-
ahem, Age, sexe, et níveau d'instruction comme facteurs détermi-
nants dans les associations de mots, Année psychol., 1962, 62, 45-61.

[3] Further information about Navaho is available in Harry
Hoijer, The Apachean verb, Part I: Verb structure prefixes, International J. Am. Linguistics, 11, 1945, 193-203; Part II: The prefixes for mode and tense, op. cit., 12, 1946, 1-13; Part III: The classifiers, op. cit., 51-59; Part IV: Major form classes, op.cit., 14,
1948, 247-259; Part V: The theme and prefix complex, op. cit.,
15, 1949, 12-22; Robert W. Young, The Navaho Yearbook, 1958,
197-228.

[4] The following conventions have been used for transcribing
Navaho sounds 'L' refers to a voiceless 'l', a lateral spirant; an
acute accent refers to raised pitch; double vowels are of longer dur-
ation; 'ə' refers to schwa, the vowel in 'gum'; 'q' refers to a glottal
catch; and ˜ above vowels refers to nasalization. All underlined words
are literal stimuli or responses, whereas words in quotation marks
are approximations or translations.

[5] Howard Maclay, An experimental study of language and
non-linguistic behavior, Southwestern J. Anthrop., 14, 1958, 220-
229; J. B. Carroll and J. B. Casagrande, The function of language
classifications in behavior, Readings in Social Psychology, 1958, 18-31.

[6] Similar constructions in English, such as 'table'-'table-
spoon,' or 'sweet'-'bitter-sweet' were omitted entirely in Ervin, loc.
cit., but were judged paradigmatic by Brown and Berko, loc. cit. and
Rosenzweig, loc. cit.

[7] W.A. Russell and J.J. Jenkins, The complete Minnesota
norms for responses to 100 words from the Kent-Rosanoff Word

Association Test, Studies in the role of language in behavior, Univer. Minn., Techn. Report No. 11, N8 onr 66216, 1954.

[8]Rosenzweig, Comparisons among word-association responses in English, French, German, and Italian, Am. J. Psychol. 74, 1961, 347-360.

[9]Brown and Berko, op. cit., 8.

[10]Ervin, op. cit., 367.

[11]Discrepancies from the paradigmatic percentages reflect the different base used in the two calculations.

[12]Rosenzweig, Année psychol., op. cit.

[13]Ervin, S. M. Correlates of associative frequency. J. Verbal Learning and Verbal Behavior, 1963, 422-431.

[14]The first explanation is discussed in Ervin, 1961, op. cit., and the third by Brown and Berko, op. cit., 1-4.

[15]Ervin-Tripp, S. M. Substitution, context, and association. Norms of word association, ed. by Leo Postman and Geoffrey Keppel. New York, Academic Press, 1970, pp. 383-467.

[16]Brown and Berko, op. cit., 8.

13 | Imitation and Structural Change in Children's Language

We all know that children's grammar converges on the norm for the community in which they live. How does this happen? One source might be through adult correction of errors and through operant conditioning reinforced by the responses of others. This is probably a relatively weak source of change in first language learning. We know, for instance, that children learn certain grammatical structures which nobody taught them explicitly, and we also know that often teachers try hard to eradicate some of them. All over the world children learn grammatical patterns whether or not anyone corrects their speech, and there have been cases in which children who were believed.for years to be mute have been found employing relatively mature grammatical patterns. A second source of change is maturation. Young children cannot learn grammatical and semantic concepts of a certain degree of complexity, and they produce sentences limited in length. Gvozdev (1961), in a book on child language development in Russian, has presented evidence that, when grammatical complexity is held constant, semantic difficulty is related to the age of acquisition of certain grammatical patterns. For instance, the conditional is learned late. Recent work by Roger W. Brown and his group supports this view. But maturation cannot account for the content of language nor for the particular structures acquired. A third factor affecting language development might be comprehension. We know that, typically, recognition precedes production. We know that people can understand many more words than they ever use. The number of cues for recognition is less than the information needed for accurate production, and in recognition we can often profit from redundancy.

Fraser, Bellugi, and Brown (1963) have recently found that children's imitation of grammatical contrasts regularly surpassed their comprehension, which in turn was superior to their freely generated speech. For instance, they would choose the right picture, or repeat "The sheep are jumping," or "The sheep is jumping," more often than they could speak the right name when a picture was pointed out.

The children in this study were asked to imitate. The real test as to whether imitation is significant as a source of progress in grammar should be based on spontaneous imitations, for children may imitate selectively.

The material to be reported here is merely suggestive. It consists of a study of only five children. It is unique in that I have the advantage of working from careful descriptive grammars for each of the children about whom I shall report. The crucial test is this: Are imitated utterances grammatically different from free utterances? If they are different, are they more advanced grammatically?

Ideally, one would write independent grammars for the imitated sentences and for the freely generated sentences and compare the grammatical rules. Since the number of imitations was far too small, grammatical rules were written only for the free sentences, and then the imitations were tested for their consistency with these rules. This method loads the dice against the similarity of the imitations to the free sentences.

First I shall describe what I mean by a grammar, then define what I mean by imitation, and finally test the hypothesis of similarity.

We collected 250 sentences of two words or more from Donnie (Table 1). At this time, when he was 2 years and 2 months old, his mother reported that he had just begun to put words together. The rule described here accounts for 198 of Donnie's sentences.

Another 16 sentences followed another rule, producing "what's that" and "what's this." There were 35 sentences which could be described by neither rule.

You will see that the following sentences were grammatically consistent:

Table 1. Sentence-Generating Rule for Donnie, Age 2:2

	Optional Classes[a]					Required Class
1	2	3	4	5	6	7
goodness					bead	bead(s)
oh	here(s)				blanket	blanket
oh oh	there(s)	go[b]			bow-wow	bow-wow
oh dear	where(s)		a		car	car(s)
				big	choochoo	choochoo
see			the		Daddy	Daddy
whee	this				kiddy-car	kiddy-car
	that(s)				ring	ring
					truck	truck(s)
					water	water
					etc.	etc.

[a] Classes 1 to 6, selected in that order, may precede 7.
[b] "This" and "that(s)" never precede "go."

Blanket water.   Oh, there's a bed.
Bow-wow dog.   Oh, car.
Here big truck.   Oh, dear, the truck.
Where go the car?   Where's a big choochoo car?

We could not account for 7 per cent of Donnie's sentences by any simple rules. These included the following:

Where the more bead?   Go bye-bye Daddy.
Naughty Donnie.   Here's it go.
Go get the truck.   Here's it goes.
What the choochoo car?

Three months later, Donnie's grammar had changed (Table 2). Some of the sentences that we could not account for at the earlier stage have now become more frequent and stable. We now find it necessary to set up a phrase rule for a nominal phrase, which you see in Table 2. Although all the regular sentences at the younger age contained at least one nominal, there are now more frequent sentences

Table 2. Nominal Phrase-Generating Rule for Donnie, Age 2:5

	Optional Classes[a]			Required Class
	1	2	3	4
NOMINAL	a	red	all-gone	all-gone
	the	big	ball	ball
		more	bead	bead(s)
			broken	broken
			bye-bye	bye-bye
			choochoo	choochoo
			green	green
			monkey	monkey
			truck	truck
			yellow	yellow
			etc.	etc.

[a] Classes 1 to 3, in that order, may precede 4.

without a nominal phrase (Table 3). We can conveniently divide Donnie's sentences into four types at this age. The largest number, 173, were declarative sentences like "there's a bus," "there's a green," "here's a broken," and "there's all-gone." Ninety-six were nominal sentences like "big yellow," "oh, broken," "yellow broken," or "monkey broken." Another 76 contained "go" or "goes" as in "car

Table 3. Sentence-Generating Rule for Donnie, Age 2:5

1	2	3[a]	4	5	6
oh boy	there(s)	it			
hi	where(s)	all	go	NOMINAL	have-it[c]
no	here(s)		goes		
don't	that(s)[b]				
etc.	this is[b]	NOMINAL			

[a] Multiword sentences contain at least one item from columns 3 to 6, with order as in the sequence of columns.
[b] That(s) and this (is) never precede columns 4 to 6.
[c] Columns 4 and 6 are mutually exclusive.

go broken," "goes the bubbles," and "there's it go." There were 20 sentences with "have-it," meaning "I want it." For example, "there beads, have-it" and "where the choo-choo, have it."

These are inductive or descriptive rules or grammars. Alternative descriptions might do as well: our criteria were brevity and completeness. We can test a grammar of an adult language by asking speakers if test sentences are acceptable; with so-called dead, literary languages we can cross-check different sources. With children, our descriptions must be more tentative. For these two-year-olds we found that between 77 and 80 per cent of the sentences could be described by our grammars.

Now we turn to the central issue. Are the spontaneous imitations of these children governed by the same rules as their freely generated sentences? To illustrate, here are some examples of Donnie's imitations at 2.5. You will find the first three are consistent, the last two are not.

"This is a round ring."	"This ring."
"Where does it go?"	"Where's it go?"
"Is Donnie all-gone?"	"Donnie all-gone."
"Is it a bus?"	"It a bus."
"Is it broken?"	"Is broken?"

We have confined this study only to overt, immediate repetitions. We have excluded imitations in which there were changes, as in "Liz is naughty," "He's naughty." We found that adult conversations are heavily threaded with such partial imitations and also that they are hard to separate from answers to questions. Judges might easily disagree in judging which were imitations. We kept the clear-cut cases, including exact repetitions, which were few, echoes of the final few words in sentences, and repetitions with words omitted. There were few cases of repetitions with changes in word order. Omissions bulked large in our cases of imitation. These tended to be concentrated on the unstressed segments of sentences, on articles, prepositions, auxiliaries, pronouns, and suffixes. For instance: "I'll make a cup for her to drink" produced "cup drink"; "Mr. Miller will try," "Miller try"; "Put the strap under her chin," "Strap chin." Thus the imitations had three characteristics: they selected the most recent and most emphasized words, and they preserved the word order.

When the imitations have been isolated, the next step is to identify the grammatically consistent sentences. These were of two types. Some used vocabulary that we had included in describing the grammars. As I have said, our rules included lists of words according to classes, or by positions they could occupy. Some of the imitated sentences included new words that were not on these lists. Any speech sample is selective in vocabulary, and since we were interested in structure and not vocabulary, we arbitrarily included as grammatical any sentences containing a single new word by treating these words as "deuces wild." That is to say, any new word could be assigned to a class so as to make a grammatical sentence. The same rule was used on the residual sentences which were freely generated. Some of these sentences were called ungrammatical simply because they included grammatically ambiguous words.

We used exactly the same rule of procedure for the imitated sentences and for the free sentences in deciding whether the sentence fit the structural rules or not. We made liberal, but equally liberal, provision for accepting new vocabulary in both samples. Thus we can see whether the rules of word arrangement were the same in the two samples (Table 4).

Table 4. Grammatical Novelty of Imitations

	Percentage Imitated	Percentage Grammatically Consistent	
		Freely Generated	Imitated
Susan (1; 10)	7	88	79
Christy (2. 0)	5	91	92
Donnie (2. 2)	6	93	100
Lisa (2. 3)	15	83	65
Holly (2. 4)	20	88	68[a]
Donnie (2. 5)	8	91	94
Donnie (2. 10)	7	92	91

[a] $X^2 = 9.4$

For all the children except one, Holly, the sentences in both samples were equally predictable from both rules. Donnie was studied at three ages, and there was no change with age in the consistency of his imitated sentences.

But what about Holly? We must move to our second question with her: Were the imitated sentences grammatically more advanced than the free ones, or simply more inconsistent? We shall use three criteria in judging the grammatical maturity of these sentences. These criteria are based on the changes that characterized the children's speech in the months following those we are considering. First, sentence length increased with age. Donnie's sentences at the three ages considered had an average length of 2.2, 2.4, and 2.7 words. Secondly, there is an increase in certain grammatical markers with age, including an increase in the use of articles and pronouns. Finally, there is an increase in adult-like sentence constructions consisting of imperative-plus-object, or subject-verb-object, or subject-verb-adjective, or subject-verb-partiple. Examples are "hold it," "he took it," "that's hot," and "they came over."

Using these three criteria, we examined all of Holly's residual sentences, both imitated and free, that did <u>not</u> fit the rules of arrangement we had called her grammar. The average length of the free sentences was three words, of the imitated sentences, two words. There were grammatical markers such as articles and pronouns in 62 per cent of the free sentences, and in 28 per cent of the imitated sentences. Half of the free sentences and a third of the imitated sentences were structurally complete, from an adult standpoint. There were no subject-verb-object imitated sentences, but there were six subject-verb-object free sentences, such as "I want play game" and "I don't see Heather car," Heather being Holly's sister.

We are left with a question about why Holly was so different from the other children. It was something of a <u>tour de force</u> to write a grammar for Holly. One class, identified as a class by the fact that its members occupied initial position in sentences, included "this-one," "see," "want" and "there." Another heterogeneous class, identified only by the fact that it followed the words just described, include "around," "pull," "raining," "book," and "two." No other child had such a bizarre system, if system it was. Probably Holly's imitations did not fit this system because these were not in fact rules governing her speech. Donnie's rules were far more simple, consistent, and pervasive. It is possible that the high percentage of imitations produced by Holly is related to the fluidity of her grammar. But if it is so, then her imitations were a disturbing rather than a productive factor in her grammatical development.

If we can rely at all on this sample of five children, there is an inescapable conclusion. Imitations under the optimal conditions, those of immediate recall, are not grammatically progressive. We cannot look to overt imitation as a source for the rapid progress children make in grammatical skill in these early years.

A word of caution. I have _not_ said that imitation is never important in language learning. In comprehension covert imitation may be important. Possibly imitation aids in the acquisition of vocabulary or of phonetic mastery. Perhaps overt imitation is indispensable in the special conditions of classroom language learning. All I have said is that there is not a shred of evidence supporting a view that progress toward adult norms of grammar arises merely from practice in overt imitation of adult sentences.

Fitting Theories to Facts

One may take several different approaches in accounting for child language development. We have already touched on one: the imitative view. According to this conceptualization the child makes errors and introduces abbreviations in his effort to approximate sentences he hears. Development is thought to consist of gradual elimination of such random errors.

This point of view is implied in the studies of grammatical development which have counted grammatical errors, omissions, and sentence length as criteria for developmental level. A second view assumes that children have sets of rules like those of adults, since they can understand adults, but that in speaking they have a combination of editing rules and random production errors. Development consists in eliminating the omissions and redundancies arising from these editing rules. A third view would assume that development can be described as the evolution of a series of linguistic systems increasing in complexity, with changes in behavior reflecting changes in the child's syntactical rules.

The data reported below have been collected in a collaborative study with Wick Miller, in which frequent texts were collected from seven monolingual oldest children, and monthly systematic tests were conducted on 24 children, during a period approximately from age 2 to 4.

In English plural inflection, the contrast dogs vs. dog might be learned as if the two words were unrelated, separate items of vocabulary. Each would be learned by imitation and by association with the appropriate semantic discrimination. Yet imitation will not account for the behavior of adults speaking English. If an adult hears a new word, say, the name of a new tool, such as a mindon, he will surely call two of them mindons, a word he has never heard. We might say that he has formed a new word by analogy. Such analogic extensions are not explainable as simple generalization, because they occur when both the referent and the word itself are new and clearly distinguishable from previously known words. We found that children formed new plurals in this way when they were between 2 and 3 years old.

We tested children systematically by showing them objects, first singly and then in pairs, and asking for a description. These tests were conducted at monthly intervals. Some of the things we asked about were familiar, such as "boys" and "oranges." Others were new objects, called such things as a bik, pud, or bunge.

If the child learns the plural first in terms of separate items of vocabulary, we would expect him to employ the plural suffix with some consistency with familiar words before he generalized to new words. In fact, this is just what happened. For nearly all the children, there was a time gap between the time when a familiar plural was used and the time when an analogous new word was given a plural. Thus, between the time when the child contrasted block and blocks and the time when he said that two things called bik were biks, there was a small but reliable gap of about two weeks. For car and boy and the analogous kie, the gap was about six weeks. For other words

the gap was greater. In all cases—pud, bik, kie, tass, and bunge—
the new contrast appeared later than the contrasts the children had
heard.

We would expect that this extension to new forms also would
occur for the irregular plurals. All of the children, over the period
we studied them, regularized the plural for foot and man. They said
man-mans, and foot-foots or feet-feets. Most preferred foot-foots.
Very few of the children fluctuated between foot and feet, so although
the word feet must have been heard by the children, we can clearly
see a regularizing influence. If imitation alone were at work, we
would have expected fluctuation between foot and feet.

There was a difference in the time of acquisition depending
on form. The English plural form is quite regular and has few
exceptions. Its form is governed by certain sound rules. Thus we
have mat and mats, but match and matches. We can describe this
difference by saying that words ending in sibilants, such as horse,
buzz, match, judge, marsh, or rouge, add a vowel plus s. Children
at this age frequently do not distinguish these sounds phonetically—
orange may be pronounced unpredictably as orinch, orinz, orints,
orins, orinsh by the same child. The children all shared the problem
of adding s to words ending in sibilant sounds. What they did was
omit a plural contrast for these words. The usual pattern in the earlier grammars was distinction of singular and plural except for words
ending in sibilants, which had the same forms for singular and plural.
Occasionally we would have analogies which removed the sibilant, as
in singular bun plural buns for bunges, and singular bok plural boks
for boxes.

At some point each child produced the regular plural for one
of these sibilant words. Quite often, when this happened, the plural
for other earlier forms changed. Thus when box-boxes first was given,
we found such forms as foot-footses, or hand-handses. Another pattern sometimes appeared. When tass-tasses came in, we found foot-
footiz or bik-bikiz.

These changes occurred with children who had previously
used the -s plural regularly, for foot, bik, and hand. Why did these
words change? If we examine the whole range of plurals employed

at one of these points in time, we might describe the system as involving two plural forms vacillating unpredictably from -s to -iz. Alternatively, -s or siz were both in unpredictable variation. Surely, at this point, it is clear that the child is employing some common response, whatever you may call it, in using all of these plural forms. A linguist would say the child had a plural morpheme with two allomorphs in free variation. How can a psychologist translate this behavior into terms familiar to him? This is most certainly not behavior learned by accumulated imitation. It is transitory, lasting at most two months, and then is resolved into a system of conditioned variation like that of adults.

There are two pieces of evidence here which will not fit a theory that inflection develops through imitation of familiar forms and extension by generalization to new items. One is the fact that foot and feet do not fluctuate as much as imitation of adults would lead us to expect. The other is that even highly practiced, familiar plurals may be temporarily changed in form by overgeneralization of new patterns. Both these data suggest that analogy in the production of sentences is a very important process and may outweigh the imitation of familiar forms.

Analogy is a familiar process to linguists. Formal similarity is the basis for the construct they call a morpheme. Yet overlaid on the child's systematic analogic forms, or morphemic patterns, we have a gradual accumulation of successful imitations which do not fit the stabilized pattern of the child, in such instances as oranges and boxes. Eventually these result in a change in the system, which becomes evident in the errors, from the adult standpoint, and in the analogic extensions to nonsense words. The conditioned allomorphs in the adult system—the different plurals in mats and matches—were imitated one by one at first. Then they produced random fluctuation between the two forms, and later stable responses conditioned by the same features in the phonetic environment as the adult plurals.

Now let us turn to past tense inflection. Our best data are from the group of seven children from whom we collected extensive texts in interviews over a period of time. It is, of course, much harder to elicit a contrast in tense than one in plurality. The semantic cues are less controllable. For this reason we relied on less systematic methods of testing. Now it happens that the English tense system has analogies to the system of plurals. Like the plurals, it has both a regular pattern and irregular forms. There is walk-walked, and there is go-went. As with the plurals, the specific phonemic pattern depends on the particular final phoneme of the simple verb—we have pack-packed and pat-patted, when a vowel is added in the suffix. As with plurals, the children used forms that indicated the difficulty of the pattern of adding a vowel—forms such as toasteded.

The major formal difference in English between plural inflection of nouns and tense inflection of verbs is the great frequency of irregular (or strong) verbs, whereas irregular nouns are relatively few. It was a surprise to me, in examining verb frequency tables for the children we studied, to find that verbs with regular inflection were few and infrequent in our earliest texts. Therefore, tense inflection begins with the irregular forms.

I looked for the first case of extension of the regular past tense suffix which could not have been imitated—for instance buyed, comed, doed. The odd, and to me astonishing thing is that these extensions occurred in some cases before the child had produced any other regular past tense forms according to our sample. In some cases the other past tense forms consisted of only one or two words of dubious significance as past tense signals.

Relatively rare was the extension of irregular patterns—though we did find tooken. With plurals we had found that extension to new instances followed considerable practice with the regular pattern. Of course, our texts must underestimate the frequency of regular verbs, since they are small samples, but the regularity with which we found such extensions occurring quite early suggests that it takes relatively few instances and little practice to produce analogic extension. Another interpretation is that such extensions can occur with little or no actual contrasts in the child's speech; he may base them on the variety of types employing the regular contrast in the language of the adult. That is, if he can comprehend the contrast in the adult language he may on that basis be led to produce analogous forms.

With plurals, the regular patterns were learned and extended first; children did not waver between <u>foot-feet</u> and <u>foot-foots</u> but employed <u>foot-foots</u> normally. With the irregular past tense forms, the children learned the unique, irregular contrasts as separate items of vocabulary first. Sometimes they were separate even contextually, as in the child who said <u>it came off</u> and <u>it came unfastened</u>, but <u>come over here</u> and <u>come right back.</u> Next, the children produced analogic past tense forms for these highly frequent words. At the same period in which a child said <u>did</u>, he might say <u>doed</u>; at the same age at which he said <u>broke</u>, he might say <u>breaked</u>, and so on. We do not know if there were correlated linguistic or semantic differences between these two versions of the past tense forms. At any event, these productive analogies occurred before we had evidence of practice on the familiar forms from which the analogies presumably stemmed. Whatever its basis in practice, it seems clear that the regularizing or analogizing tendency is very strong.

The learning of syntax is even more difficult to explain. Let us go back before the age of two. In the earliest examples we have obtained, we find that there are inconsistencies of order between words. A very simple system might be one that produces sentences like <u>all-gone book</u>, <u>read book,</u> and <u>book read.</u> Another said <u>snap on, snap off, fix on</u>. Notice that these sentences could not all be produced by simple abbreviation of adult sentences. Many of the children's sentences are such imitations, but some have a word order that cannot be explained by simple imitation. Children talk a great deal and they hear a great deal. It is improbable that they could produce the great variety of sentences they do produce from memorized strings of words.

When we introduced words to a child in controlled sentences, he put them into new and appropriate sentences. When told of a nonsense object <u>that's a po,</u> or <u>this is a po</u>, the child said <u>here's a po, where's a po</u>, <u>there's a po, the po go up there</u>, and <u>poz go up there.</u> When told <u>I'm gonna sib the toy</u>, he later said <u>I sib 'em</u>, indicating the appropriate gesture. Yet the form <u>wem</u>, in <u>this is a wem bead,</u> was not extended. Thus a noun form was productively utilized in many new contexts, a verb form in one, and an adjective form in none. However slight, at least here is an indication of an analogic extension at the syntactic level.

One explanation which has been offered by several different

observers of young children, for instance, Braine (1963), Brown
and Fraser (1963), and Miller and Ervin (1964), is that these early
systems indicate the beginnings of syntactic classes.

How do such classes develop? Two features of classes have
been noted to account for the development of regularities. In children's
language, there is greater semantic consistency than in adult language.
Brown (1957) has shown that by nursery school age children identify
verbs with action, nouns with things. Perhaps groupings into classes
of words that can occur in the same place in sentences rest at least
partly on semantic similarities. Another feature is that in all these
grammars there are some positions where only a few words can occur,
but that these words are very frequent. Thus one child started many
of her sentences with thats. Another ended many of her sentences
with on or off. The words that can occur following thats constitute
a class, in the same sense that nouns are identified as following the
for adults. This is not the only way we recognize nouns, but it is almost as useful as a suffix in marking the class. How do we know that
these words "go together" in a class for the child? We find that the
recorded bed-time monologues of a child described by Weir (1962)
were filled with instances of words substituting for each other: what
color blanket, what color mop, what color glass; there is the light;
here is the light; where is the light. Such practice, like the second-
language drill in the classroom, could make some words equivalent
counters in the game of rearrangement we call language. Thus, both
meaning and high frequency of certain linguistic environments seem
important in the evolution of syntactic classes.

Clearly, we have evidence that children are creative at the
very beginnings of sentence formation. They imitate a great deal,
but they also produce sentences which have both regularity and systematic difference from adult patterns. At the same time, within
these classes there are always statistical tendencies toward finer
differentiations.

As my last example, I will take the grammatical features
called transformations by Chomsky (1957). A good instance is the
rule for the purely syntactical use of do in English. This word appears
in a variety of sentence types: in elliptical forms, such as yes, they
do, in emphatic forms such as they do like it, in questions such as do
they like it? and in negatives as in they don't like it. According to

Chomsky's analysis, these uses of do are analogous and can be described by a single set of related rules in the grammar of adult English.

Let us see how children employ do. In the negative, a simple rule for the contrast of affirmative and negative would be simply to add no or not in a specified place. He's going vs. he's not going; he has shoes vs. he has no shoes. Another procedure would be to contrast is with isn't, can with can't, and so on. In both cases, the contrast of affirmative and negative rests on a simple addition or change, analogous to the morphological change for tense or for the plural. Neither rule presents new problems.

Some children had several co-existing negative signals. During the time period, one child had the following: (1) any in possession sentences, such as Joe has any sock and all the children has any shirt on; (2) not in descriptions and declaratives, such as Not Polly; (3) don't in most verb sentences, such as Don't eat that, and I don't like that. Note that all these utterances can be described in very simple terms without the use of more complex constructs than those needed to account for inflection, or simple syntactic classes.

But as the child acquires verb inflection, more complex rules develop. We say he goes, but we do not usually say he goes not. Simple addition of not is inadequate. We say he doesn't go. In the contrast he can go vs. he can't go there is only one difference. In the contrast he goes vs. he doesn't go there are two: the addition of the word don't in appropriate number and tense, and the difference between go and goes.

Usually children use don't quite early as a negative signal, but as inflections began we found sentences like Joe doesn't likes it and it doesn't fits in there. In these sentences inflections appeared, but in two places. In an analogous development, do appeared early in elliptical sentences as a verb substitute. Thus we find, in response to the remark there aren't any blocks in this book, the reply there do, and when Wick Miller said I'm Joe, the child said no you don't, you're Wick. Thus the child had not differentiated subclasses of words used in elliptical constructions, just as the subclasses of inflections of do with different number and tense did not appear until later. By age three, this child said it goes right here, doesn't it? and you're named "she," aren't you?, employing complex constructions which cannot be explained in terms of the simple semantic signals we found in <u>Joe has any sock</u>.

Chomsky has described the various uses of <u>do</u> in adult English economically as based on the same rule. Does the use of <u>do</u> appear concurrently in negatives, interrogatives, ellipsis, and emphasis? Quite clearly this is not the case. As we have seen, <u>don't</u> appears early in negatives. It is often the only negative signal. In interrogatives, the question is signaled by question words or by a rising pitch, and <u>do</u> is typically not present until months after it appears in negatives or in ellipsis. Thus we cannot infer the process of acquisition from an analysis of the structure of the adult language. Sentences that are described as generated through transformation rules in the adult grammar may be based on different, and simpler, rules in the early stages of the child's grammar. And a rule that may apply to a variety of types of sentences in the adult grammar may develop through quite separate and independent rules in the early stages of the children's grammars.

I have mentioned the development of tense and number inflection, simple syntax, and more complex syntactical processes called transformations. These have all raised certain similar problems of explanation.

In adult language, it has been found necessary to postulate such constructs as morpheme classes, syntactic classes, and grammatical rules. It is not inevitable that similar constructs need be employed in accounting for the earliest stages of language acquisition.

Three different theories of child language development were described earlier. The imitation view assumed that the child imitates adult sentences and gradually eliminates abbreviations and errors as he grows older. A second view assumes that children comprehend adult rules but make random errors in speaking. A third view sees language in children as involving successive systems, with increasing complexity.

In their simplest forms all these positions seem wrong. Let us review the evidence. We found that spontaneous imitations were syntactically similar to or simpler than nonimitations. In examining plural inflection, we saw that indiscriminate imitation would lead us to predict free variation of <u>foot</u> and <u>feet,</u> but, in fact, one form was usually preferred, and the plural contrast was based on analogic extension. We found it necessary to postulate a plural morpheme to account for the sudden and transitory appearance of forms like <u>bockis</u> and <u>feetsiz</u>. With verbs, mere frequency of use of a contrast was less important than the variety of types employing it, suggesting again the need for conditions giving rise to a past-tense morpheme, with varied environments for a particular form, before analogic extension can occur.

In children's early syntax, the data are still ambiguous, for it is hard to elicit and identify extensions to new cases. On the one hand, sentences like <u>fix on</u>, <u>all-gone puzzle</u>, <u>I not got red hair</u>, and <u>once I made a nothing pie</u> clearly involve processes of analogic extension. Here we see at least rudimentary classes. On the other hand, in any system we devised, there were indications of incipient subdivision, of statistical irregularities in the direction of the adult model, prior to shifts in the system.

In the use of <u>do</u> we found that the adult rule applies equally to the negative, interrogative, elliptical, and emphatic sentence. But among children <u>do</u> did not appear at the same time in these types of sentences. The pattern of development, and the rules that might describe usage at a particular point in time, differed for these different sentence types and differed for different children. Yet there were rules; errors were not random.

In all these cases, we find that children seem to be disposed to create linguistic systems. We have not examined the speech of twins, but it seems likely that we would find there a rich source of systematic creation of constructions. It is hard to conceive that children could, by the age of four, produce the extraordinarily complex and original sentences we hear from them if they are not actively, by analogic extensions, forming classes and rules.

At the same time we cannot wholly accept the third position presented—that of idiosyncratic systems. In every instance of systematic change I have examined, there has been some evidence of fluctuation, some evidence of greater similarity to adult speech than one would expect on the basis of the system alone. In addition, in the early stages of some complex rules—such as the use of <u>do</u>—we found that there were phases that seemed to rest on rudimentary acquisition of vocabulary. The use of <u>don't</u> as an undifferentiated negative signal could be so described.

The shift from one system to another may be initiated from several sources. One is the comprehension of adult speech, another is imitation. The relation of imitation to comprehension has barely been faced in discussions of child language, yet these two must account for the accretion of instances which eventuate in systematic changes.

In language, unlike other intellectual processes, the child can monitor his output through the same channel by which he receives the speech of others. If he knows how—if he can make discriminations and remember models—he can compare his own speech to that of others. Thus, language development involves at least three processes.

It is obvious that there is continual expansion in the comprehension of adult speech. Perhaps comprehension requires some ability to anticipate and hence, at a covert level, involves some of the same behavior that occurs in speech production. But this practice in comprehension alone is not sufficient to bring overt speech into conformity with understood speech. Consider again the phenomenon of so-called twin languages, for instance, or the language skills of second-generation immigrants who have never spoken the parents' first language but understand it, or of second-language learners who persistently make certain errors of syntax after years of second-language dominance, or of some children of immigrants who understand their age peers but speak the English of their parents. More than comprehension is involved.

Another process is the imitation of particular instances by children. What is entailed in hearing and imitation we do not know at this point. The fact that phrases may be uttered long after they are heard, without overt practice, suggests that our study of immediate, spontaneous imitation concerns only a fraction of actual imitation-derived utterances. Yet unless these utterances constitute a systematically simpler sample of all imitated utterances, it is obvious from our analysis of them that syntactical development at least cannot rest on imitation.

The third process is the building by analogy of classes and rules, a process which we infer from the child's consistent production of sentences he could not have heard. Of the three approaches which I offered earlier, I would suggest that the third is closest to the truth, but that the accrual of gradual changes under the influence of listening to adults lies at the base of the generalizations and analogies formed by the child. Any system of analysis which omits either the idiosyncratically structured and rule-governed features of children's language or the gradual changes within these rules is contradicted by evidence from all levels of the linguistic behavior of children.

NOTE

Conducted with the support of a grant from the National Institute of Mental Health and the facilities of the Institute for Human Development and the Institute for Human Learning at the University of California, Berkeley. The work was done in collaboration with Wick Miller, now Assistant Professor of Anthropology at the University of Utah.

REFERENCES

Braine, Martin D. S., The ontogeny of English phrase structure: The first phase. Language, 1963, 39, 1-13.

Brown, R. Linguistic determination and the part of speech. J. abnorm. soc. Psychol., 1957, 55, 1-5.

Brown, R., and Fraser, C., The acquisition of syntax. In C. N. Cofer and Barbara Musgrave (eds.), Verbal behavior and learning. New York: McGraw-Hill, 1963.

Chomsky, N. Syntactic structures. The Hague: Mouton, 1957.

Fraser, C., Bellugi, U., and Brown, R. Control of grammar in imitation, comprehension, and production. J. verb. Learn. verb. Behavior, 1963, 2, 121-135.

Gvozdev, A. N. Voprosy izucheniia detskoi rechi (Problems in the language development of the child). Moscow: Academy of Pedagogical Science, 1961.

Miller, W., and Ervin, S. The development of grammar in child language. In U. Bellugi and R. Brown (eds.), The acquisition of language. Child Developm. Monogr., 1964, 29, 9-34.

Weir, R. H. Language in the crib. The Hague: Mouton, 1962.

14 | Some Strategies for the First Two Years

Studies of children's texts and of such other performances as comprehension and imitation have given some basis for testing plausible generalizations about what is necessary for language processing in its early stages. In this paper, the prerequisites to language will be considered in the form of environmental circumstances, cognitive development, and children's information storage. On the basis of these considerations, we will examine the basic acquisition of regularities of order and inflection, the fundamental grammatical features found in the early performances of children.

Prerequisites to language learning

Languages consist of patterned surface signals which are correlated, under particular circumstances, with extra-linguistic events. In the adult language learner, who hears talk about abstract ideas, and about events at a distance in time and space, the meanings of utterances may appear to bear little relation to external events, except when he goes shopping. Yet, the learner must know the referent for learning of language to occur.

We shall consider here three categories of prerequisites to language learning. The first consists of what the environment must provide, the others the knowledge which language refers to and the processing skills which the child brings to the learning task. Where evidence is lacking, we hope in this way to draw attention to the need.

Environmental input

Since children learn to speak except under conditions of

radical isolation, we assume that the input conditions necessary are relatively simple:

a. Orientation towards the signals: If acoustic input is relatively random in relation to events of importance to the child, as is the case if it consists entirely of radio or TV broadcasts, the child may be unable to discover its structure. We have observed hearing children of deaf parents who had learned no speech from such input. The recurrence of signals at times of significance to the child, such as feeding, being changed, being held, being stimulated visually, may single out that channel, be it sound or gesture, for special attention.

b. Co-occurrence of speech with referential events: Let us suppose that parents held philosophical discourse in the presence of a baby, but never talked about the here and now. A child might in these conditions parrot gross features of their behavior, but the limitations would contain as many fortuitous as linguistically important features of speech. A significant portion of speech must refer to those relations, concrete objects, and events which are already attended to by the child.

Linguists argue that it is contrast of meaning which identifies which features of the sounds, or of the grammatical patterns, are significant; without such a criterion, the child would have no clue, except recurrence, to indicate which features must be stored as critical in absolute identification of items.

Is this to argue that nothing at all is learned from input devoid of meaning? Experiments with adults (see description in Ervin-Tripp, 1970, p. 340, 341, 348) suggest that meaningless material, even presented systematically so as to contrast acceptable and extraneous sounds, is destructive to language acquisition, possibly because the adults assign invented meanings to the forms. But these were adults. We do not know the extent to which hearing sentences without any referent can be in any way instructive about the structure of the sound system. The Hayes and Clark experiment (1970) with artificial sounds suggest that recurrent sequences may become salient and be stored even without the help of meaning, but their material lacked the phonetic diversity of actual speech since it was artificially produced.

It is certainly the case, however, that to learn syntax, reference must be present for the new learner. We do not always know, of
course, what the content of the recurrent reference is for the child,
what features of the environment, of his own states, or of the consequences of his speech he observes in storing words like "want", "all-
gone", and "more". "Reference" is not meant here in the simple sense
of observable objects, since it is clear that from the beginning children's interpretations are more complex.

If stability of interpretation is required, then a considerable
amount of the speech environment of children may be irrelevant to
the learning of grammar, because the interpretation of none of the
utterance is clear to him.

It may not be necessary that repetitive exposure occur, if
conditions are optimal. Asher (1965) has experimented with brief
learning trials in which second language input co-occurred with actions
by the learner to which the sentences or words referred. There was
a dramatic effectiveness in making the co-occurrence of signal and
referent optimal in time, in salience, in sensory richness. The rapid
fading of the acoustic signal may make simultaneity important.

c. Recurrence of vocabulary in diverse environments; moderate
vocabulary diversity: In order to identify the more abstract units,
starting with form classes, children must hear component units in
the diverse positions possible. Not all lexicon, obviously, needs to
meet this condition; once classes, or phrase markers for lexicon are
acquired, a single encounter can mark new vocabulary appropriately.
Conversely, varied entries in a fixed environment may be needed to
teach formal features. This is less clear, since if entries share
semantic features, they may be spontaneously grouped as a class,
without this requirement.

The issue of formal class learning, or phrase marker learning, is obviously central. Our point here is that characteristics of
the input may affect efficiency of learning. It could be argued that the
existing properties of languages have arisen because they create input
distributions which accelerate acquisition, a point which will be ex-
panded later in this paper.

In addition, observations of input in the United States have
shown that special conditions of parent and sibling style to infants may
contribute to the type of diversity experienced by the child. One feature is simplicity of structure, in the sense of brevity, few subordina-
tions, few passives, lack of false starts and intercalated material.
The result is a surface that maximizes the frequency of simple declarative, and of the constituent phrases that occur in answers.

The argument that input is degenerate, confusing, that the
surface orders in English are displayed in so many permutations that
simple order heuristics relating surface orders to meanings would be
impossible, must be produced from observations of speech styles at
conferences, not in family kitchens. Input simplicity and grammaticality do not remove the problem of later learning of complex orders,
but they do make the discovery of the first structures much less a problem.

Further, input to children is characterized by repetitiveness.
Contrary to linguists' belief that phrases are not repeated, in speech
to children they are repeated ad nauseam.

Kobashigawa (1968) found that it was common in speech to
children to maintain the same message across several sentences,
varying minor features which do not alter meaning, such as intonation,
rate, word order where non-critical, or optional deletions and contractions. In input to Finnish children, elements such as subject-verb-
object are permuted in such repetitions (Bowerman, 1971). In these
circumstances, the semantic equivalence of formal alternatives, given
maintenance of the external situation across the sentences, would be
apparent.

Several special styles which occur in some cultures as inputs
have theoretically possible accelerating effects. One is discourse
modelling, in which questions and answers are both supplied by the
interlocutor. Examples are given by Jean Berko Gleason (1971). The
"Where's the doggy", "There's the doggy" types of sentences found in
early child texts may reflect such input, in which replacements or discourse agreement is instructed.

In expansions, the child phrases his intention as an utterance, and the interlocutor alters the utterance in the direction of the presumed adult model. The effectiveness of expansions on changing language probably increases when

a) the interlocutor's interpretation matches the child's intention, and,

b) the child's deletions arise because he has not yet attended to the deleted elements, which are just "noisy" to him (Shipley, Smith and Gleitman, 1969).

In this case, the fact that he has already generated part of the sentence may free him to attend to the additional components.

In Cazden's experiment comparing expansions with modelling (supplying relevant comments in reply whenever the child spoke) the expansions were not controlled for either of these features, yet some gain in output mastery over controls occurred. The increment in output length or output developmental measures was greatest for the modelling condition. It seems likely that the experiments unwittingly supplied some structural repetition of the child's speech with added vocabulary diversity.

Prerequisite knowledge

In discovering the relation between utterance and meaning, the child must bring his knowledge of possible meanings to the analysis of input. Thus, a major issue for the study of the development of grammar is the assessment of knowledge through non-linguistic means. In the case of the child's communicative acts, the problem includes the study of intentions.

It is a striking finding of observers in a wide variety of languages around the world that the meanings in the early sentences of children seem to be confined to a relatively restricted and shared set. While it is true that some samples have not included all of this set, the omissions are slight, and could easily reflect sampling

deficiencies or cultural and situational biases which affect the child's
intentions while being taped.

Here are two sample lists:

List A	List B
Cigarette down.	Girl rides.
Give me candy.	Bring candy.
Candy mine.	Baby's eyes.
Hit you.	Baby fell.
Give me banana.	Put down.
You eat?	Baby walks.
I want water.	Wants sleep.
Ball there.	Keith there.
Go home.	Go there.
This visitor.	Your baby.

It is not obvious that List A was collected in Kenya from Luo children
(Blount, 1969), and List B in Samoa (Kernan, 1969).

Establishing early knowledge from a list of sentence meanings is obviously not the best route. It is too limited. As Bloom
(1971) points out, some utterances (her examples were away, there,
and more) are not in fact semantically richer when the noun is produced. The child's early one-word utterances in these cases may
arise from a poverty of naming lexicon. It is common, also, in the
case of possessives to find the named possessor used alone in the
same contexts as the later construction. There is no reason to assume
any enrichment of the child's intentions or knowledge at this point,
though linguistic skill has increased.

On the other hand, while many meanings in common early sentences may antedate sentence output considerably, sentences may deceive us. We do not know whether the production of actor-action sentences implies any abstraction of a concept of actor. Therefore, the following collection of examples is given to suggest that we need much richer studies of the intentional evidence concerning these relations using techniques which are not linguistic.

a. Modality refers to the contrast between asking, demanding, and commenting. This difference may be signalled by gesture and paralinguistic features before identifiable words begin. Gruber (1967) has claimed that one child whom he studied intensively with particularly rich extra-linguistic filmed information, did not make any comments in the earlier stages of multi-morphemic utterances. She always made demands, either that the listener look at or hand over.

Early sentences often contain explicit lexicon referring to questions (Where shoe ?), or to demand (I want dolly), but where a single noun occurs, it may not be obvious whether the utterance functions as a demand or as an identification or existence predication.

b. Vocatives occur early, but are not strictly speaking relations. In many early texts we have examples of attention-getters, whether gestural—by tugging on an arm—or vocal, by calling a name. The name of the addressee, or a vocative, is often included in sentences having other functions and is typically not integrated grammatically.

c. Identification and Existence. Statements naming referents may be one-term nominatives, like "dolly", or they may contain more elements like "See dolly", "This dolly". There is no evidence that these differences in surface representation represent semantic contrasts. This category is of course rich in cognitive antecedents since it requires isolation of objects and categories. Proper and common names appear undifferentiated at first, in the sense that in both cases the child supplies a generalization range.

Existence or "notice" utterances are situationally marked by a kind of discovery, but they do not appear to be marked by enough structural contrast to allow easy separation from demonstratives.

d. <u>Non-existence</u> and <u>negation</u>. "No page", "no rabbit", "all-gone puzzle", "car away", are examples, and of course single negators in isolation precede. In the text of a deaf child's early two-component sign utterances, Geballe found an absence of negators, but this may be idiosyncratic, or due to small sample size. In Park's text of a Korean child, there were substantial number of negatives, both of the refusal and non-existence type. "Train there-is-not", "No eat" (imp.).

e. <u>Recurrence</u> of objects or events appears in "more apple", "another toy", "more throw". These can be either descriptions or demands, and may occur without specification of object.

f. <u>Location</u>. Locational notions are among the earliest acquisitions of the child, and in the course of language development locational questions and adverbs precede temporal expressions of analogous structural difficulty by years. The questioned location, as in "Where shoe", to which the answer is pointing, is produced and understood from the beginning of questions. Early locational statements like "dolly car", or "go car" refer to places, on, or in which another thing or action is, or to destinations. Prolocatives like "here", or "there", appear in a variety of languages, but it is not evident that they are differentiated. Many forms used in English as verbs contain locational contrasts: "baby up" means to lift the baby up, "sweater off" to change the location of a sweater. "Fall-down" is an early English term requiring locational change in a specific direction. Given the presence of locations in identification and action sentences at Stage I, it is not surprising that at the next stage, when the surface structure is longer, locational information often is added to otherwise long strings, and that in the development of propositions, differentiation of location occurs relatively early.

g. <u>Possession</u>. In early sentences it is common to find utterances like "candy mine", "your baby", and "baby's eyes", which are very stable in the order of elements or locus of suffix. The constituents are a possessor, which usually is (+animate), allowing for metaphorical extension to dolls and stuffed animals, and an object consisting of a part of the body, clothing, or a concrete object not inherently possessed. In the ontogeny of these representations, we may find "Mommy" when pointing to Mommy's shoe, suggesting a loose associational relation.

But if all that the possessive relation involved for a child was a loose association of possessor often seen with possessed, the order stability in the surface representations would be impossible, since there would be no designation of an asymmetry in the relation to identify an order.

In one sense, the relation of possession is the first in English on which the components do not themselves specify the structural meaning, with the exception of possessive pronouns. Lois Bloom (1971), pointed out that "certain conceptions of experience are coded by particular word forms, function forms, which, however, make reference only by virtue of their contextual relations to other features of experience.... Certain conceptions of experience are coded by the interrelations among different categories of substantive word forms. Such categories are linguistic, and defined on the basis of relative occurrence of words in structural relationships that have distinctive meanings. Such structural meanings are independent of the lexical meanings of the forms within categories."

If the possessive construction, such as "Mommy glove" meets this criterion, it does not preclude the existence of what appear to be possessive assertions prior to two-word utterances. As Bloom points out, the conception of experience is separable from the form of codification, and could much antedate overt realization in language. Because of its structural interest, the contrast between acquisition of pronoun and nominal constructions of the possessive (using order, not inflection) provides a nice contrast for study of Bloom's ideas of alternative strategies for the acquisition of grammatical structures.

h. Conjunction. Pairing, usually of nominals without a marker. I do not know of any cases of pairing of other forms in hearing children. Possibly, sensory adjacence, even visual, is the only source at first for pairing. It may be that even a slight time delay on input, as in the case of successive acts, may impede coding at first, except in separate utterances. It certainly is the case that children can perceive and store successions of acts, since they can even perform integrated imitated sequences by the end of the second year.

i. Attribution. The ability to discern attributes obviously must be a fairly early feature of child cognition, but the eventual co-existence of attribute and head term in linguistic codification implies a further distinction, between the term which functions as head and a subordinated feature which is considered secondary to a primary class membership. It is not clear what the cognitive implications of the difference may be. In some cases, where there is feature intersection, the distinction would appear to be somewhat arbitrary or conventional, but in English at least, head terms tend to refer to the function class of an object rather than to its size, shape, color, or material, or to temporary conditions. The fact that changes of focus can lead to the shift of the head must make the surface difference somewhat opaque semantically to children in instances where the shift is common. In some of my early texts, such descriptive terms as "broken" had distributions identical to nouns, e.g. "See the broken".

Attributes are not among the most frequently coded aspects of child experience, except for possession and quantification, and one would guess that the differences which appear in the texts so far may reflect some differences in input to children. The common adjectives used in English are such terms as "big", "little", "pretty", "poor" (in the sense of injured), and "broken". Most commonly, these occur in pre-nominal rather than predicate position, suggesting that they are usually used either as identifiers or conventional parts of names, rather than as foregrounded predications by those who speak to children. In some cases, adjective-noun, or noun-noun sequences appear from the phonological forms to be unsegmented, as in the case of "mommycar" and "daddycar" in some texts of mine, the basis being a possessive noun used in the family as a conventional identifier and thus always present as part of the object name. In the case of Kathryn II, cited by Bloom (1970), the terms "bear book", "puppy book" and "tiger book" are quite possibly not invented by the child, since there is a series of books so titled.

j. Action-agent-object. Words describing actions occur early, though it is common to specify only one or two of the components of a three- or four-part predicate like "put" or "give", which have three nominal complements. Normally, the agent is (+animate) and the majority of objects, but not all, are inanimate. Bowerman found that subjects of action verbs might be vehicles. When expansion of noun phrases occurs, it is either in identification sentences or in objects. Perhaps inanimates more often have attributes as identifiers.

k. <u>States</u>. Stative verbs like "want", "like", "see", "have", appear
in the earliest sentences. It is not always obvious, of course, that they
are semantically clearly distinguished from active counterparts ("see
the book", "look at the book"). Nor do all children have such forms
in the texts we have seen. Both the Luo and Samoan, but not the Finnish texts had "want", the most common of these.

l. <u>Recipients</u>. Datives or indirect objects can be found in early texts,
though like attributives and states they may be sparse. Antinucci and
Parisi (1973) have pointed out a parallel between the complement
structure of verbs like "give" which require recipients, and "put"
which requires a locative complement. In these cases, languages im-
pose obligatory components which are already well within the cognitive
capacity of children.

However, the complexity of codification is increased by these
linguistic rules, and it is in the coding task that the children have
trouble. Parisi and Antinucci's system permits comparison between
development of coding in different languages or in different types of
sentences within a language, with the complexity of formal structure
controlled.

It is obvious that semantic development precedes its verbal
expression and continues to grow independently, as manifested, for
instance, in temporal categories. Slobin (1971) has asserted that
these cognitive relations are not affected by the learning of language,
which merely provides representations for them. This may well be
the case with universal categories, in which common conditions of
life or at least of the interaction of child and milieu have been such as
to guarantee development; in these cases it must be true that language
is merely a manifestation. On the other hand, in cases where particular languages have categories that are idiosyncratic, the presence
of the contrast might accelerate observation of a cognitive category
or relation. An example is the study by Carroll and Casagrande (1958)
of the shape of the categories codified by Navaho verb stems of handling
and placement. These are high frequency forms in child speech, and
strikingly correlated with concrete categories of shape like long rigid,
flat flexible, and so on. Navaho-speaking children choose shape over
color earlier than non-Navaho speaking children from the same milieu—
nursery school training in Boston—had the same impact in creating

form preference in English-speaking children, so there are other ways besides language to create dimensional saliency.

The requirement that the child be able to identify "sames" in the signal is simply one other aspect of isolating recurrences with many transformations in the environment, but the fact that these events are auditory, and involve changes related to features of the adjacent sounds rather than spatial and light transformations, may alter what properties of perception and storage are required. Bever's observation (1971) that long "jargon" utterances of a baby may be consistent situationally suggests that the first units may be fairly large. Since we are concerned here with grammatical acquisition, we will simply have to assume the child's ability to process speech sounds in such a way as to identify and store recurrent patterns.

Storage factors

If simultaneity of referential event and speech is a precondition of learning to understand speech, then it is necessary that one, or both, be stored for comparison. Young children's own speech tends to refer to on-going events like naming of time or locations, or to immediately past events, as in "dolly fall-down". When adults speak of distant events, they may over-tax the child's ability to match meaning and utterance.

But even when utterances refer to the present, the rapid fading of the acoustic signal may require a short term storage of acoustic information to allow work by the hearer in comparing the input with his referential knowledge. Given the small capacity in the immediate memory span, the selectivity of such storage is important in child language learning. Studies of imitation and of detection thresholds suggest the following generalizations about material with the highest probability of retention in short-term storage:

a) The most recent material. On the whole, spontaneous imitations draw selectively on the end of input material. Theories of memory would predict the strongest control of the most recent input, given the fluctuating attention of spontaneous imitations.

b) Initial words. There may be some slight advantage of onset

material over what is in the middle, for unanalyzed new input, providing the child is already attending.

c) Vowel quality of stressed syllables.

d) Intonational contour, level of pitch, and other gross paralinguistic
features.

e) Friction and nasality.

f) Order properties of sequential auditory material as described
above.

Since short-time storage is a prerequisite to building up
long-term information about language, there will be prior acquisition
of contrasts of the following types:

a) Prosodic contrasts and terminal juncture contrasts should be acquired early. In languages where modality contrasts can be signalled
by prosodic cues, these occur before segmental contrasts like question
words or inversions are used. In Japanese, Miyahara (1971) found
that prosodic cues were used before the postpositional -ka.

b) Particles, enclitics and items which are sentence final should be
learned early, before prefixes and other material earlier in utterances.

In Japanese, yo and ne, which are clause-final, are the first
functors (Miyahara, 1971).

c) Suffixes should be learned more easily than prefixes, and postpositions more easily than prepositions.

The most striking support comes from the Mikeš and
Vlahović (1966) study, in which bilinguals learned locatives in Hungarian before they used comparable prepositions making similar semantic
contrasts in Serbo-Croatian. Slobin quotes Pačesová (1968) on Czech
evidence that recency is stronger than stress as a determinant since
initial stressed syllables are often omitted in Czech child speech.

A beautiful example of the intersection of the two systems
in the long-term storage of a child is provided by Malmberg's 1945

account of the acquisition of Swedish by a Finnish-speaking child.
In this case, of course, we are examining the cumulative effects of
varying short-term storage experiences, in which the child was able
to juxtapose presumed meaning with whatever surface she stored.
Saliency of meaning obviously led to the retention of the noun stem,
but the rest of the material gives a good comparison between pre-stem
and post-stem order. The initial pattern of the child of course had a
Finnish noun stem followed by Finnish morphological material. The
replacement as she began to change her speech was in the following
order:

(1) Replacement of noun stem by Swedish noun.

(2) The Swedish noun stem receives a Swedish suffix, followed still
by the Finnish postpositional as before.

(3) The Finnish postposition is replaced by a Swedish preposition used
following the noun and its suffix.

(4) The preposition is correctly placed.

It can be seen here that the general order of putting in information in produced sentences is the hardest to change. The first
shift is in the lexical material, as we would expect, rather than in inflections. The Swedish suffix, rather than the preposition, is the next
most noticeable element, and is readily produced because it can replace
a Finnish suffix in the same position. The preposition was the last
feature, and curiously enough, though it was learned correctly, at
first it was produced in the position of the semantically corresponding
form in Finnish. The formal skeleton for the production of semantic
information still retained a Finnish syntactic programming, though
the morphophonemic content was Swedish. In terms of the order of
introduction of morphological elements, the order noun stem, then
suffix, and preposition last to be learned, is what we would expect on
the basis of semantic and perceptual salience.

d) Sentence-initial fixed-position forms should be learned more
easily than material in the middle of utterances. In English, question
words are learned very easily, as well as the demonstratives and
prolocatives which often initiate descriptions.

e) <u>Morphemes which are syllabic should be learned more easily than consonantal morphemes</u>. In the Mikeš and Vlahović study (1966), the suffix - <u>u</u> rather than -<u>t</u> was used in both languages, then -<u>ut</u>!

f) <u>Friction and nasal morphemes should be understood sooner than stop or glide forms</u>, though there could be articulatory problems in their production by the child.

g) <u>Relative order of stem and affix should not be altered</u>. There is no case in the child language data in which this has occurred.

h) <u>Relative order of high-frequency morpheme sequences should not be altered</u>.

i) <u>Where there is a dominant order for classes having structural meaning</u>, when that construction is acquired, it will reflect input order.

j) <u>Unstressed syllables may be lost in storage of words</u>. The Czech case cited earlier indicates that recency may be a stronger factor than stress.

Long-term learning

Braine has proposed that recurrence prevents the decay of stored information, and that certain properties of the stored surface string when repeatedly processed through short term storage will be preserved as the normal form of strings. Presumably, according to his model, this will happen whether or not the sentences have meaning, and his experimental work shows that adults can recognize novel but meaningless utterances conforming to a recurrent simple set of morphological rules.

Acquisition of affixes and function words

Like lexicon in particular sentences, functors differ in saliency. The factors which are likely to influence the frequency with which functors are kept in short term storage and become candidates for the discovery of relations to extra-linguistic conditions have been discussed earlier.

We can expect that if the semantic motivation for inflectional variation is not apparent, (e.g. in the gender variation instance) the child may store the most frequent lexical form. He may learn "shoes" before "shoe", but "dog" before "dogs". In Finnish, verbs are first represented in the third singular form, and locatives in the allative or directional case, in Bowerman's sample. Park, on the other hand, found action verbs more often in the Korean imperative.

The first appearance of contrastive inflections seems to depend on the obviousness of the semantic contrast as well as the salience of the morpheme. It seems plausible that as early as a child could semantically contrast subject and object orders productively in English, he might be able to use inflections for the same purpose, say in Garo (Burling, 1959), and we do learn that Burling's child used inflections simultaneously with syntactic contrast and that inflectional contrasts appear very early in Finnish (Argoff).

The importance of the semantic function of the morpheme rather than its frequency, is brought out by the example of wa and ga in Japanese. Wa occurs more frequently, yet it is ga that appears earlier in children's usage. Two differences in semantic function seem to account for the preference for ga. Wa can mark the subject, the object, or any phrase to which attention is drawn. It is often translated as "as for X", so one can say "As for the table, we ate on it", or "as for John, he left", or "as for Mother's, it was lost". Ga, on the other hand, only can mark a subject, so that it differs in marking a class with a unique grammatical function. Further, rather than re-foregrounding understood, often antecedent information, ga typically identifies new information, and in that sense is likely to be more focal and more important. "As for the glass, it was the boy who broke it". In this sentence, it is the boy, rather than the glass, which is new information to the hearer, and we have glass-wa, boy-ga. The glass has been mentioned before, is presumably implicit, or was an implied contrast to some antecedent. The phrase could in fact be omitted if the presumption is clear. Thus, both clarity of grammatical function, and novelty and focus would give preference to ga. With ga, there need be no ambiguity of subject and object; with only wa, there would be.

If the clarity of the correlation between the surface form and the meaning is obscured by the intersection of factors like gender which produce "noise", or by allomorphs related to phonological conditioning, then we would expect the most information-bearing minimal features for the contrast.

For example, in Serbo-Croatian, the contrast between locative and directional suffixes is complicated by gender, so we have -a̲, -i̲, and -u̲ as feminine case contrasts, and ∅, -u̲,and -a̲ or ∅ as masculine suffixes. In this system, -u̲ is ambiguous with respect to case, as is -a̲ . Only the feminine locative i̲ is unambiguous, and other things being equal, we would expect it to be preferred as a locative suffix over -u̲ when case distinctions begin. Thus we argue that clarity of contrast is more important than frequency, since -u̲ as accusative must be very frequent. In this argument, we follow Slobin's similar notion, in his analysis of Russian affix acquisition.

Most thinking about long-term storage of children has been focussed on grammatical rather than phonological issues. We know now that infants can make fine phonetic distinctions, and recognize change between adjacent inputs, but we do not know from this finding how selection is made for the long-term storage which makes absolute judgments possible. How the critical distinctive information could be selected in the absence of experience with meaning contrasts remains puzzling unless holistic, long-term auditory "eidetic imagery" is possible.

Analysis of children's speech confuses the articulatory regularities of the child's system with the perception and storage issue, though it certainly provides some minimal basis for judging what must be a core system. In Braine's characterization of Joan Velten's development, for example, it is clear that lexical storage must at least provide for the fully-controlled, non-redundant features, such as syllabic and coronal, and for some of the partially controlled features such as continuant and strident, since Joan could recognize words contrasted in these features and reproduce them at a later time. The notion that lexical storage is efficiently non-redundant does not necessarily correspond to the psychological facts.

Joan Velten clearly had some articulatory problems, since Velten reports that she produced / baza'/ as an output for / bada'/ , and shortly after produced / bada'/ and contrasted the two. His description gives the impression that the problem was one of production.

The phonotactic rules which affect her production can quite easily not affect her discrimination or recognition. For example, she had considerable consistency in producing final consonants, even nasals, without voicing, but if such a feature affected her receptive processing she should display recognition difficulties where voicing is an issue.

Messer (1967) and Menyuk (1968) have tried to find methods which locate phonotactic features of discrimination and recognition in children, and showed that children did react to violations of regular English phonotactic features. Children can also recognize accents. The extent to which this kind of learning could occur, apart from the acquisition of meaning, is not known. In addition, Menyuk and Messer did not provide the kind of stimuli which would allow the analysis of the order of acquisition of specific phonotactic rules, for comparison with the Braine characterization for instance.

While it is common for linguists to deplore the separation of analysis of heard from spoken material because they do not want to think there are multiple grammars, there is no reason to assume that processing strategies for heard material would be identical with the organization required for production. This contrast is most striking, of course, in phonotactics.

Learning order regularities

Potential strategies

Grammar-recognition learning involves recognizing relations between order or functor patterns and properties of meaning.

Braine's work has focussed on the recognition of order regularities and the conditions for such learning, without concern for the bearing that semantic correlates may have on facilitation of such learning. Semantic contrasts of course are only part of what is learned; it is a dramatic feature of both first and second language learning that they go further than intelligibility requires in the direction of learning of formal and stylistic correctness. In the case of children meaning contrasts do seem important in relation to determinants of order of acquisition.

The logical possibilities for a child faced with a signal which co-occurs with understood meanings are that the child simply ignore order features in the signal, that she store order in terms of invariant positions, and that she store the relative orders, in terms of probabilities when they are variable. These possibilities, and the relevant evidence, are considered below. A good deal of the evidence comes from sentence output by children, which, of course, has special characteristics relative to issues of recognition and storage.

Random order

It used to be thought [see Burling, (1959), for example] that children's first sentences were somewhat randomly ordered in terms of syntax. Suppose that the child discerns the relation between words and their meanings, but does not store any information about the orders of words, erasing what is in short-term memory about word order, but retaining order information as it affects morphemes within words. In the tests we have, we do not find random order. It seems unlikely that words are sufficiently distinct as units to children, especially in the typical repetitive input to allow such a radical contrast between the type of information stored in the lexicon and in the rest of the storage device.

Preserve features of invariant positions

If a fixed morpheme like a question particle occurs sentence final, the modality contrast it signals may be recognized early. In the case of English question words, a group of words have nearly invariant position; in child speech, question words are always sentence-initial, reflecting adult usage. We do not know whether relocating question words would interfere with their comprehension. In my work on answering questions, (Ervin-Tripp, 1970) the question word seemed rather like a dummy item with a fixed position for two-year-olds, in that children recognized that a question had been asked, but might answer as though a different question word had been used, the determinants of the choice depending on features of the rest of the sentence, like transitivity of the verb. The shared phonological features of question words in many languages may help in identifying them as such, at first, without any additional semantic features.

A storage device which marks certain lexical items as initial or final, or a sentence-producing device that is position-specified has quite limited utility. Speakers cannot in fact easily recall specific positions other than initial and final, so that only these positions could be indexed. The rest of the indexing would have to be relative rather than in terms of absolute position.

Store relative order

In languages where order carries semantic information, as in the contrast subject-object in English, the child must store specific instances like "pet the kitty" in order to allow him eventually to recognize that the item acted on normally follows the action word, and to abstract the relation between action and object, and match it with an order. In German, following modals the normal order is object-verb, and so it is common for children to learn object-action rather than action-object. Sentences with modals are frequent input to children, if our texts in English are appropriate examples. In Roeper's new data, the morphological evidence is clear, since in many cases the children preserve the infinitive suffix, as in examples: "Bleistift holen", and " Mama Schühchen anziehen".

The eventual result is the strategy which Bever has identified as a matching of an NVN surface with an agent-action-object interpretation, at a certain age. Sinclair (1972) reported that 37% of the 6-year-olds in her study still interpreted box-push-boy as agent-action-object. This strategy is found even later as well. We find that English speakers who firmly control passive structures in English use the NVN comprehension strategy at first on foreign language utterances, according to my evidence from French. Is this a reflection more strongly of relative noun positions, or the relation of one or both nouns to the verb? Sinclair's important study of French allows us to find that this strategy is much more complex in development than would at first appear.

She presented garçon pousser fille in six permutations. The form of this verb permits interpretation as a past participle (i.e., passive), imperfect, or imperative. Because French employs order rather than stress for foregrounding and contrast, it is likely that NVN order may be less common in input to children than it is in English. For example, one could say, "C'est la fille que le garçon a poussé," "il a poussé la fille, le garçon," or "poussez, les garçons et les filles!"

These were the following major types of response:

(a) Some of the youngest children themselves always acted as agents, disregarding completely the order of the words as though they heard only an imperative.

(b) Most of the children under 4 interpreted the sentences in terms of the dolls as agents. In particular, the noun just preceding the verb was likely to be treated as an agent, whether or not there was a transitive complement. Thus the subject-verb relation appears primary.

(c) The relative order of the two nouns played some role relatively early, so that the first of the two nouns in NNV might be interpreted as subject even though it did not immediately precede the verb. This strategy grew and dominated the choices of the 6-year-olds.

(d) Eventually some children began to attend to the action-patient relation. This strategy of attention to VO occurred at the same age as the reappearance of the child-as-agent but only for NNV. These children of five seemed to be interpreting the sentence as fille garçon poussés. We could call this descriptive or patient-focused strategy. Eventually, such sentences can lay the basis for passives.

One of the mysteries in Bever's studies of the development of the noun-verb-noun strategy was that he has reported that some very young children correctly gave passive interpretations. We might attribute such responses to patient focus or a descriptive orientation which sees the verb as a kind of participle or description. The most important finding in Sinclair's study is that the first order strategy is agent-action focus, and that action-patient focus is not as early in appearance. This directly goes counter to McNeill's view that the verb-object unit is elementary, because it comprises a fundamental sentence constituent, the verb phrase. It is probably necessary to

distinguish verbs with highly selective contexts from those, like
pousser selected because its object could in fact be animate or inanimate. Such sequences as drink milk might very well be primary units
of comprehension well before action-patient focus in reversible sentences.

If agent-action supplies the first order rule, the expectation
is confirmed that highly frequent and adjacent orders in the surface
structure will be learned quite easily, as we find in looking at pos-
sessor-possessed, agent-action, demonstrative-nominal in beginning
grammars. Sentences which deviate from adult order, like all gone
toy reflect semantic overgeneralization since the attribute-or quan-
tifier-head sequence of the sentence is quite suitable to the majority
of input cases.

Store probabilities of order

The surface order of units may not be consistent, either because it is affected by transforms unfamiliar to the child (e. g. the
English passive), or because the language does not in fact employ a
consistent syntactic order in signalling a semantic contrast, as in
the case of Finnish agent-action-object.

In such cases, the learner is evidently capable of storing a
probability record. In the case of English, we find children who make
occasional reversals of VO to OV, possibly reflecting passives or infinitive inputs, though passives are rare in input to most children in
our samples according to Drach (1968) and Pfuderer (1968). In
Finnish, Bowerman (1970) reported a rough correspondence between
the relative order for given structural types in the adult input and the
child's order.

The table makes clear that Rina's mother's most frequent
construction was prolocative-noun, and this dominated for the child
also. Seppo's mother's dominant type was SV, and this dominated
for Seppo. The lower frequency of Seppo's SVO relative to his
mother's is due to the fact he was at an earlier stage of language
development than Rina, and used more two-word than three-word utterances. In each set of alternative orders, the dominant order is

Structural Frequencies in Finnish Speech (Bowerman)

	Seppo	Seppo's Mother	Rina	Rina's Mother
	M. L. U.*		M. L. U.*	
	1.42-1.48		1.82	
Subject-verb	81	47	36	14
Verb-subject	27	5	1	2
Verb-object	24	16	16	14
Object-verb	7	3	5	–
SVO	13	32	27	11
SOV	–	1	3	1
OVS	2	1	–	–
OSV	1	–	2	–
VSO	–	1	1	1
VOS	–	–	–	–
Noun-prolocative	13	14	16	15
Prolocative-noun	19	41	97	31

_____

*Mean length of utterance in morphemes.

the same for adults and children, but the alternative orders, if adults use them, appear in child speech. It would take fine-grained contingency analysis of the texts to find if this order correspondence simply reflects some discourse echoing on a short-range basis, rather than any basic features of the child's grammar. In examining some order alternations in my own texts involving VO and OV changes, I found that what the adult said was often picked up by the child, and therefore produced the appearance of alternation. In this way, I might be able to alter the frequency of passives in the speech of an interlocutor by raising my own frequency in a conversation.

Adult repetitions and expansions define equivalence

Where adjacent synonymous repetitions in the input are order-preserving, whether the repetitions are of the speaker or are expansions of the child's speech, the child learns to preserve order in imitations, and to retain order specifications in determining structural meanings. Where the parental repetitions or expansions freely transforms order, as has been observed in Turkish and Finnish, children freely vary order in imitations. Whether there is a direct relations between this particular form of input and the child's processing of order information, we do not know. Such an experiment would require control over these varying types of input, including stability of order in all utterances of a given type addressed to the child.

Grammatical Storage

Word matrix storage

What is the nature of the storage device? What does it store? One possibility is that it stores a word matrix. We know that speakers have remarkably good knowledge of word frequencies in the language (Howes, 1957). On this basis, maybe higher order matrices are stored. The strongest argument against such a device is its weakness. Such a device is too weak to generate novel sequences, like "all-gone puzzle" which we know occur and have consistent grammatical properties.

If a word matrix existed, then the tallying of adjacent stressed words in texts of input to children would yield sentences like those found in children's speech. Here is a set of examples: "Does go", "Color my", "Want hold", "Come eat", "Happened know", "Going open", "Diaper for", "Animal this", "Here big". To anyone familiar with children's sentences these sound strange.

It seems clear that many "prepackaged" sequences must be stored by speakers, appearing as phrases, idioms, clichés, whose production and comprehension can partially bypass normal sentence processing routes.

Whatever storage device makes possible the retention of lexemes realized as words and phrases must also contain material which involves sequences heard more than once. In comprehension we have usually assumed that there is erasure or loss of surface information with retention only of semantic material. Sachs (1967) has shown that synonyms cannot be distinguished nor passives separated from actives after relatively small intervening material. But if it were the case that only semantic information is retained, language learning could not occur. There must be some storage of the phonological markers and semantic features inferred from the milieu of a new item for it to become part of the dictionary. It is not obvious that the device which accomplishes such storage has a strict word boundary and would refuse to store frequent sequences longer than words.[1] The nature of the abstracting process which allows some efficiency in this storage is unknown.[2]

Semantic feature storage

In order to account for novel utterances, Schlesinger (1971) has proposed that the child stores the semantic features of utterances and abstracts structural rules from a series of instances. When he hears "Mommy's shoe", "Daddy's shoe", "Daddy's hat", "Bobby's coat", he already knows that Mommy, Daddy and Bobby are people, and that shoe, hat and coat are moveable objects, and that in each case the specific object has a particular relation to the designated person. In this case, the child would learn that Possessive relation → (+human) + (+concrete object). The order, in this case, would be a feature of the rule. According to Schlesinger's formulation, the Intention (possessive relation) is realized by possessor + possessed. If I interpret Schlesinger correctly, the components of structural rules are semantic features, and the categories are classes of items sharing these semantic features.

It is clearly the case that there are such semantic unities in the structural classes in early sentences. In one of Braine's (1963) list of pivot classes, we find a grouping of many words which can follow "all": broke, buttoned, clean, done, dressed, dry, fix, gone, messy, shut, through, wet. They all share a common aspectual feature, and it is quite clear that the list is not interchangeable with a list of words following another pivot, "more": car, cereal, cookie, fish, high, hot, juice, read, sing, toast, walk.

Melissa Bowerman (1970) noted that all of the items with action verbs in her Finnish corpus were either (+animate) or (+vehicle).

In my opinion, the insight of Schlesinger's about the relatively large semantic homogeneity of early classes is very important,
in suggesting a major basis for acquisition; none of the early
grammars captured this property of child speech. McNeill's
analysis (1971) of early form classes allowed him to move directly
from formal classifications such as NVN to assumptions about
semantic relations— though it is possible that NVN could represent
location, not merely object, or a vocative rather than a subject.

There are several serious weaknesses in Schlesinger's
account as far as it goes, which also affect the attempts of Hebb,
Lambert and Tucker (1971) to subsume the ontogenesis of language
under traditional acquisition of conceptual categories.

From early on, there are classes which are not semantically homogenous, but which share considerable structural similarity.
For example, we find both "I want ball", and "Daddy throw ball."
It is clear that "throw" and "want" have very little, if anything, in
common semantically, and Fillmore (1968) would argue that "I" and
"Daddy" have quite a different role in the two sentences. Yet it would
clearly be inefficient to write a grammar of English which did not
subsume the two under the same major category, in view of their
common destiny in tense change, and under a variety of transformations.

There are complex patterns such as the auxiliary system in
English which are acquired in a relatively short period of time, obviously on the basis of transfer of patterns between items which do not
share semantic features. I think it would be very hard to find any
semantic communality between "can", "will" and "do", which would
be adequate to the rapid acquisition of the system by the two year
olds in Boston and Berkeley. Yet, Schlesinger's system, so far at
least, would require that formal classes all be defined in semantic
terms.

On the other hand, there are semantically related forms
which do not have the same formal functions, such as "eat", "eating"
and "food". It is hardly a surprise that we need some formal marker
systems, such as affixes and functors, to identify form classes, and
that semantic unity is not enough. It is true that there are children
like Park's (n.d.) who in learning Korean occasionally employed

words of appropriate semantic features in the wrong form-class position, such as "throw" for "ball" and "sit-down" for "bench". The
fact that these formal errors occur makes us wonder why such substitutions are not much more common, especially in languages without class-marking affixes.

Acquiring formal features

What could be the conditions for development of an abstract
formal marker for lexical members of form classes? Morphemes
and words and phrases which occur in the same environment, whether
defined by surface forms or classes of forms, acquire a common
formal marker. It is the case that those items occurring in the same
environment will often have some semantic features in common, by
virtue of the semantic co-occurrence constraints of the rest of the
sentence.

The point where grammatical features must have been
acquired is at the time when productivity occurs, and there is generalization from a semantically different item sharing distributional
properties. For example, a child may say "I'm knowing his name",
generalizing from action verbs to statives, because of common
distributions. It is the case, of course, that in most of the early
grammars it would be possible to characterize the form classes by
semantic features rather than a formal term. Once formal features
are acquired, many consequences follow— for example, the kind of
associative behavior that Brown and Berko (1960) attribute to formal
similarity of paradigmatic items.

McNeill (1971) has argued that some formal classes are
already present innately, like noun and verb. Since languages
differ in the formal classes required for their use, I should suppose
that we must find some means by which classes are discovered. It
is, of course, not necessary that the user of language, in fact, have
all the formal classes linguists think will simplify the grammar.
For example, many speakers may correctly employ verbal complements
by learning them as phrases, just as we used to learn the preposition
that followed French verbs, réussir à, and so on by rote. Unless there
is a fairly rich set of syntactic consequences, if the only property
shared by such covert classes is the particular structure or morpheme
that complements them there is, it seems to me, no need to abstract

a grouping. I suspect that some adult speakers have never done so, and if asked to generate lists of "paradigmatic" items would follow semantic and larger form class constraints, and not use the subclass list.

The richer the variety of structures in which a group of items occupies the same slot, the greater the likelihood that some formal marker will be generated, which in turn marks the lexicon and allows the structures to be organized as abstract rules, not low-level sequences.

Why functors?

It is a striking fact of spoken languages that there always are classes of affixes or function words which are relatively small in number and high in frequency. Frequently, these forms are not necessary for comprehension, as we find in listening to the telegraphic speech of children or of Japanese learning English. It seems to me that they have a function for comprehension, not for production, in marking form classes unambiguously, and it must be through these markers, whether or not the child at first reproduces them, that a considerable aid in generation of formal classes must come. The children in the Shipley, Smith and Gleitman experiment (1969) who spoke in telegraphic utterances but understood normal better than telegraphic sentences, were beginning to make use of this information.

Pidgin languages provide a natural experiment in the creation and preservation of fundamental features of languages. Under the social conditions in which pidgins arise, formalisms which mark social status are of minimal importance; concrete substantive communication and ease of acquisition for adults are the primary factors. What we might call transitory pidgins arise in many contact situations between monolinguals. The pidgins which have become conventionalized tend to share certain features, such as morphological simplicity and use of optional syntactic devices relying in order rather than inflection. But it is the more surprising that in such languages entirely new derivational affixes are sometimes created. In Neo-Melanesian, for example, the suffix [-felə] occurs for numerals, demonstratives, and one-syllable adjectives (Hall, 1966). Other affixes appear to have more obvious semantic functions. For example, the transitive verb suffix {-im} marks transitive verbs. {mi rid}=

I read, {mi ridim buk}= I'm reading a book, and {mi ridim}= I'm
reading something. The third person prefix provides a common
surface marker for singular and plural third person, which standard
English lacks. { all i-krosim }= they are angry at him, {ɛm i-fay-
tim jufelə }= he fights you-all.

     The implication is that oral languages must have surface
bench markers to make complex sequences easy to process for the
hearer. But we know that speakers do not in fact very well know
how to make their output pedagogically best. The assumption that
hearer needs affect the structure of output by the speaker requires
that one find some mechanism by which the speaker learns better
those strategies and those features which maximize comprehension.
We know from the Brown and Hanlon (1970) study that children, at
least, are not as speakers very sensitive to reinforcement contingen-
cies, and we know from Postovsky (1971), that one does not even have
to speak to learn fine features of language.

     Every speaker's primary role has been first as an under-
stander. He has had to make sense out of what he hears, and he has
only been able to interpret and store part of what he hears. If the
suffixes are simple structurally, providing a one-to-one match between surface and a conspicuous meaning, if they elucidate units
for comprehension, they are likely to enter storage as components
of simple processing rules, early on.

     Rather than a rule NVN = Agent-Action-Object, which
requires some kind of check to determine if a lexical item is marked
as V, the hearer can use [-im] as input to a simpler rule. That is,
the processing rule can short-cut the lexical check to the formal
marker. In storing new lexicon, the surface form may facilitate correct marking of the transitive verbs too.

     The morphological examples bear on the low-level marking of
form classes unambiguously, but it is also the case that functors may
allow surface marking of more complex units. Bever (1970), for
example, as well as Shipley and Catlin (1967) working with children,
have shown the importance of surface relative pronouns in facilitating
comprehension of relative clauses, in contrast to deleted pronouns.

Explanations that languages have the best of all structures tend to be tautological. If certain functors have facilitative effects in simple comprehension, then there probably are others which do not. It may not be necessary, for example, to have functors to identify semantically clear classes like the class of names of all concrete objects. Indeed, pidgins tend not to have such functors. At the other extreme, if the functors are structurally complex, as in the case of Russian inflection, the time required for acquisition might make them unavailable for the conditions of brief acquisition required of pidgins.

It is clear that at the onset of grammar in children, while surface markers of simple structure may facilitate the discovery of processing heuristics they are not absolutely necessary. The abstracting process which allows children to discover formal similarities, presumably from distributional features, is at least as early in development as the appearance of the auxiliary system in English.

Language Acquisition System (LAS)

A human Language Acquisition System (LAS) must be one that will develop typical ways of understanding and producing situated sentences. Such a system must include ways of changing stored knowledge and developed skills, on the basis of the types of input which are characteristic of human societies. We have discussed some of the properties of devices that at a minimum would need to be components of such a system:

a) Selective retention of features in short term memory, particularly including order of acoustic input.

b) Phonological and semantic selection and reorganization for retention in long-term memory.

c) Interpretation templates, providing interpretations of structures according to the formal and semantic properties of sequences.

d) Successive processing by alternative heuristics, allowing short-cuts for frequent phrases, instances where non-linguistic determinants are strong, and so on.

e) Formal feature generation, identifying abstract classes and providing marking of the lexicon.

These devices or processes need not be language-specific, though it appears at the moment that order retention may be stronger for acoustic than for visual signals. They may not be age-specific.

We can expect that age changes in acquisition will occur for three reasons, none of which affect the basic features in LAS. Input conditions are quite different for adults and children, because the external semantic reference of discourse may be reduced with age, and the linguistic complexity of input tends to be greater with age. Knowledge and availability of memory heuristics increases with age, making it easier to retain longer input and discover meanings. Often this knowledge is fairly specific; the knowledge of a larger vocabulary in one language may increase the probability of encountering cognates in the second language. The system in flux for the learner changes with age. By five, there is little important phonological change occurring other than style and register enrichment. At six, attention to phonological units is temporarily enhanced analytically by the acquisition of reading, if the system of orthography represents some morphophonological units. By ten, attention has shifted almost wholly to semantic and lexical expansion. Except in bilinguals, attention to phonetic nuances other than to those carrying social meaning will have been sharply reduced. We might expect that the processes which led to learning a phonological reorganization system suitable to the mother tongue, which must have required considerably more detailed and redundant retention of phonological information than is used later, would have long since been unused in most monolinguals.

NOTES

An earlier version of this paper appears as "The onset of grammar" in a memorial volume for Ruth Hirsch Weir edited by M. J. Hardman-de Bautista and V. Honsa. This version has been considerably enriched by the papers and the discussion at the Buffalo conference, as it was scheduled for the final day.

[1] During acquisition, early lack of segmentation may give the illusion of correct selection because a phrase is stored as a unit. When the units are segmented, the selection must be rewritten. An example is from data on French acquisition by English-speaking children who say regarde moi before they say regarde á moi, just as we find

children who say "comed" after saying "came." "Regarde à moi" of
course reflects a dictionary matching between French and English,
word-for-word.

[2]The superb study by Shipley, Smith, and Gleitman (1969),
among its other contributions, included the observation that children
after a certain point imitated the nonsense portions of sentences, instead of merely being disrupted in comprehension by nonsense. They
did not normally imitate what was said, so it could be that when the
surface features of the material do not lead to immediate, familiar,
easy interpretation the kind of erasure Sachs observed does not occur.

REFERENCES

Argoff, H.D. The acquisition of Finnish. Ph.D. dissertation, Univer-
        sity of California, Berkeley, in preparation.
Antinucci, Francesco and Domenico Parisi. 1973. Early language
        acquisition: a model and some data. Studies of child language
        development, ed. by C.A. Ferguson and D.I. Slobin. New
        York: Holt, Rinehart, and Winston.
Asher, J.J. 1965. The strategy of total response: an application to
        learning Russian. International Review of Applied Linguistics
        (IRAL) 3.291-300.
Berko-Gleason, Jean. 1971. Code-switching in children's language.
        Paper read at the conference on developmental psycholin-
        guistics, University of Buffalo, August.
Bever, T.G. 1970. The cognitive basis for linguistic structures.
        Cognition and the development of language, ed. by J.R. Hayes,
        279-362. New York: Wiley.
_____ 1971. Discussion. Language acquisition: models and
        methods, ed. by Renira Huxley and Elizabeth Ingram, p. 162.
        New York: Academic Press.
Bloom, L.M. 1970. Language development: form and function in
        emerging grammars. Cambridge, Massachusetts: The
        MIT Press.
_____ 1971. One word at a time: the use of single-word ut-
        terances before syntax. Paper read at the conference on
        developmental psycholinguistics, University of Buffalo,
        August.
Blount, B. G. 1969. Acquisition of language by Luo children. Work-

    ing Paper No. 19, Language-Behavior Research Laboratory, University of California, Berkeley.

Bowerman, M. F. 1970. Learning to talk: a cross-linguistic study of early syntactic development, with special reference to Finnish. Unpublished Ph. D. dissertation, Harvard University.

Braine, Martin D. S. 1963. The ontogeny of English phrase structure: the first phase. Language 39. 1-13.

_____ 1971. On two types of models of the internalization of grammars. The Ontogenesis of Grammar, ed. by D. I. Slobin, 153-188. New York: Academic Press.

Brown, Roger. In press. A first language. Cambridge, Massachusetts: Harvard University Press.

Brown, R. W. and Jean Berko. 1960. Word association and the acquisition of grammar. Child Development 31. 1-15.

Brown, R. W. and C. Hanlon. 1970. Derivational complexity and the order of acquisition in child speech. Cognition and the development of language, ed. by J. R. Hayes, 11-54. New York: Wiley.

Burling, Robbins. 1959. Language development of a Garo and English speaking child. Word 15. 45-68.

Carroll, J. B. and J. B. Casagrande. 1958. The function of language classifications in behavior. In Readings in social psychology, ed. by E. E. Maccoby, T. M. Newcomb, and E. L. Hartley. New York: Holt, Rinehart, and Winston.

Cazden, Courtney B. 1965. Environmental assistance to the child's acquisition of grammar. Unpublished Ph. D. dissertation, Harvard Graduate School of Education.

Drach, K. 1969. The language of parent: a pilot study. Language, society, and the child (Working Paper No. 14), Language-Behavior Research Laboratory, University of California, Berkeley.

Ervin-Tripp, S. 1970. Discourse agreement: how children answer questions. Cognition and the development of language, ed. by J. R. Hayes, 79-107. New York: Wiley.

Fillmore, C. J. 1968. The case for case. Universals in linguistic theory, ed. by E. Bach and R. T. Harms. New York: Holt, Rinehart and Winston.

Geballe, Carol. 1969. Early sentences of a deaf speaker. Unpublished term paper, Rhetoric 156, University of California, Berkeley.

Gruber, Jeffrey S. 1967. Correlations between the syntactic constructions of the child and the adult. Paper presented at the Society
for Research in Child Development, March 31.

Gvozdev, A.N. 1961. Voprosy izucheniia detskoi rechi. [Problems
in the language development of the child]. Moscow: Academy of Pediatric Science.

Hall, Robert A. 1966. Pidgin and creole languages. Ithaca, New
York: Cornell University Press.

Hayes, John R. and Herbert H. Clark. 1970. Experiments on the
segmentation of an artificial speech analogue. Cognition
and the development of language, ed. by J.R. Hayes, 221-
234. New York: Wiley.

Hebb, D.O., W.E. Lambert, and G.R. Tucker. 1971. Language,
thought, and experience. Modern Language Journal 15:4.
212-222.

Howes, D. 1957. On the relation between the probability of a word
as an association and in general linguistic usage. Journal
of Abnormal and Social Psychology 54. 75-85.

Kernan, Keith. 1969. The acquisition of language by Samoan children.
Unpublished Ph.D. dissertation, University of California,
Berkeley. Working Paper No. 21, Language-Behavior Re-
search Laboratory, University of California, Berkeley.

Kobashigawa, B. 1969. Repetitions in a mother's speech to her
child. Language, society, and the child, (Working Paper
No. 14), Language-Behavior Research Laboratory, University of California, Berkeley.

Leont'yev, A.A. 1969. Inner speech and the processes of grammatical
generation of utterances. Soviet Psychology 7:3. 11-16.

Malmberg, Bertil. 1945. Ett barn byter språk. Nordisk Tidsskrift. 21.
_____ 1964. Språket och människan. Lund: Aldus. 98-112.

McNeill, David. 1971. The capacity for the ontogenesis of grammar.
The ontogenesis of grammar, ed. by D.I. Slobin, 17-40.
New York: Academic Press.

Menyuk, P. 1968. Children's learning and reproduction of grammatical and non-grammatical phonological sequences. Child
Development 39. 849-859.

Messer, S. 1967. Implicit phonology in children. Journal of Verbal
Learning and Verbal Behavior 16:4. 609-613.

Mikeš, M. 1967. Acquisition des catégories grammaticales dans le
langage de l'enfant. Enfance 20. 289-298.

Mikeš, M., and P. Vlahović. 1966. Razvoj grammatičkik kategorija
    u dečjem govoru. Prilozi, proučavanju jezika, 2. Novi
    Sad, Yugoslavia.
Miyahara, Kazuko. 1971. Language development in a Japanese
    child. (Typescript).
Pačesová, J. 1968. The development of vocabulary in the child. Brno,
    Czechozlavakia: University J. E. Purkynš.
Park, Tschsng-Zin. Language acquisition in a Korean child.
    (typescript). Working Paper, Psychol. Inst., Univers.
    Münster.
Pfuderer, Carol. 1969. Some suggestions for a syntactic characteriza-
    tion of baby talk style. Language, society, and the child,
    Working Paper No. 14, Language-Behavior Research
    Laboratory, University of California, Berkeley.
Postovsky, Valerian. 1970. Effects of delay in oral practice at the
    beginning of language learning. Unpublished Ph. D. disser-
    tation, University of California, Berkeley.
Sachs, J. S. 1967. Recognition memory for syntactic and semantic
    aspects of connected discourse. Perception and Psychophysics
    2. 437-442.
Schlesinger, I. M. 1971. Production of utterances and language acqui-
    sition. The ontogenesis of grammar, ed. by D. I. Slobin,
    63-102. New York: Academic Press.
Shipley, E. R., C. S. Smith, and L. R. Gleitman. 1969. A study in
    the acquisition of language: free responses to commands.
    Language 45. 322-342.
Shipley, E. R., and J. C. Catlin. 1967. Short term memory for sen-
    tences in children: an exploratory study of temporal aspects
    of imposing structure. Technical Report No. 5, Eastern
    Psychiatric Institute, Philadelphia.
Slobin, D. I. In press. Cognitive prerequisites for the development of
    grammar. A survey of linguistic science, ed. by W. O.
    Dingwall. Admonton, Alberta: Linguistic Research, Inc.
Velten, H. V. 1943. The growth of phonemic and lexical patterns in
    infant language. Language 19. 281-292.

Part III. Sociolinguistics

15 | An Analysis of the Interaction of Language, Topic, and Listener

    In this paper we shall examine some of the characteristics of sociolinguistic research, and illustrate with a detailed example. The companion field of psycholinguistics (Osgood and Sebeok 1954; Saporta 1961) has concentrated heavily on individual psychology: perception, learning, individual differences, pathology. Social psychology has appeared primarily in attitude studies (Osgood et al. 1957: 189–216), not in psycholinguistic research concerning socialization and acculturation, or small-group and institutional behavior. Thus, in the very fields which overlap most with sociology and sociolinguistics, psycholinguistic research is least developed.

    Sociolinguists study verbal behavior in terms of the relations between the setting, the participants, the topic, the functions of the interaction, the form, and the values held by the participants about each of these (Hymes 1962: 25). Verbal behavior (talk and its equivalents) is the center of this definition, but of course a complete description of the system must include gestures or pictures when they are functional alternatives to linguistic signs. Verbal behavior is everywhere structured as a highly cohesive system, and therefore it is a convenient starting point. Others might want to deal with a larger set of communicative acts including, for instance, the dance and exchange of tangible objects.

Setting

    We shall use the term setting here in two senses, that of locale, or time and place, and that of situation, including the "standing behavior patterns" (Barker and Wright 1954: 45–46) occurring

when people encounter one another. Thus, situations include a family
breakfast, a faculty meeting, a party, Thanksgiving dinner, a lecture,
a date. Social situations may be restricted by cultural norms which
specify the appropriate participants, the physical setting, the topics,
the functions of discourse, and the style. Obviously, situations vary
as to which of these restrictions exist and the degree of permissible
variation, so that a sermon may allow less style variation than a
party. By altering any of these features, one might either create a
reaction of social outrage, change the situation to a new one (date
becomes job interview), or enter a situation lacking strong normative
attributes and allowing maximal variation.

        One of the major problems for sociolinguists will be the dis-
covery of independent and reliable methods for defining settings. The
folk taxonomy of a given society (Conklin 1962:120) might provide
lexical categories for the definition of settings. However, the folk
taxonomy may be too gross or too fine to indicate classifications of
value to the social scientist. The high degree of regularity of elliptical constructions in waiter-to-cook request forms suggests that
there is a setting class for which there is no common name in English; Thanksgiving and Christmas dinner behavior has common properties though we have no generally accepted superordinate term for both
events.

        Joos (1962:13) has given a classification of five major setting
varieties in his own cultural system; these he defines by style types
as intimate, casual, consultative, formal, and frozen. The fact that
only the first two correspond to common usage suggests that the folk
taxonomy may be inadequate for the level of generality Joos sought.
It would be desirable to couch the discriminanda of settings in terms
permitting cross-cultural comparisons. Joos's hypothesis (1962:10)
that all "national languages" have five styles is testable only if the
division of types he described is not arbitrary.

                              Participants

        For most sociolinguistic analyses the important features of
participants will be sociological attributes. These include the participants' status in the society, in terms such as sex, age, and occupation;

their roles relative to one another, such as an employer and his em-
ployee, a husband and his wife; and roles specific to the social situation, such as hostess-guest, teacher-pupil, and customer-salesgirl.

In any act of communication, there is a "sender" and a "receiver" (Hymes 1962: 25) who together may be called interlocutors.
In addition, there may be present an audience which is not the primary
addressee of the message. The role of sender, or speaker, is rarely
distributed in equal time to all participants. There appear to be four
factors which affect the amount of talking of each participant. One
factor is the situation. In informal small-group conversation the
roles of sender and receiver may alternate; in a sermon the sender
role is available to only one participant; in choral responses in a
ritual, or in a question period following a lecture, the role of sender
is allocated at specific times. A second, related, determinant of the
amount of talking is the role the participant has in the group and his
social and physical centrality. He may be a therapy patient, chairman, teacher, or switchboard operator, so that his formal role requires communication with great frequency; he may informally play
such a role, as in the case of a raconteur, or an expert on the topic
at hand. There is a personal constant carried from group to group.
The net effect of the second and third factors is that the sending frequency of participants in a group is almost always unequal, and has
been shown to have regular mathematical properties in informal discussion groups (Stephen and Mishler 1952; Bales and Borgatta 1955).
Because relative frequency of speaking is steeply graded, not evenly
distributed, in a large group the least frequent speaker may get almost no chances to speak. The "receiver" role also is unequally distributed even in face-to-face groups, being allocated to the most
central, the most powerful, those with highest status, the most frequent speakers, and under conditions where agreement is desired,
the most deviant (Hare 1962: 289; Schachter 1951).

Topic

The manifest content or referent of speech is here called
the topic. Topically equivalent sentences may be different in form
so that topic is maintained through a paraphrase or translation. Compare these two sentences paraphrased from Watson and Potter (1962:
253):

"Every episode of conversation has a focus of attention."

"There is a single topic in each homogeneous unit of inter-action." In the terms of Watson and Potter's definitions, these sentences are topically equivalent. Also equivalent are the following: "Shut up!" "Please be quiet." "Tais-toi."

Topic includes both gross categories such as subject matter (economics, household affairs, gossip), and the propositional content of utterances. It is the topic which is the concern of cognitive structure studies of kinship systems which differentiate "grandmother" and "mother" but not "mother" and "mommy."

Obviously some expressive speech (ouch!) and some routines (hi!) do not have a manifest topic. Such contentless speech could usually be replaced by gestures. In traditional treatments of language, topic is considered essential and typical because of its absence in most nonhuman and nonlinguistic communication. It seems more appropriate to consider referential speech as simply one subcategory of speech. Topically dissimilar utterances or utterances with and without referential content can be functional equivalents. From a functional standpoint, the following could be equivalents in some situations:

"I'm sorry" = "Excuse me."

"Hi" = "How are you."

Functions of the Interaction

Within a given setting, verbal discourse may vary in function. We use "function" to refer to the effect on the sender of his actions. Skinner (1957: 2) has pointed out that in its social uses language may be viewed as operant (rewarded or punished) behavior, which affects the speaker through the mediation of a hearer. The distinction between topic and function is similar to the one between manifest and latent content, as employed in content analysis. A difference is that since in many speech situations the addressee is known, and subsequent behavior of the sender is known, it is more often possible to delineate functions in ordinary speech than in the texts for which content analysis often is employed.

The following system was developed to account for the initiation of dyadic interactions. It is not intended to cover continuous discourse, but merely initiations. The criterion of classification was the hearer response which could terminate the interaction to the satisfaction of the initiator.

a. <u>Requests for goods, services, or information</u>. The overt behavior of the hearer is manipulated. E. g., "What time is it?" "Please pass the potatoes." "Slow down!"

b. <u>Requests for social responses</u>. The desired hearer reactions are often not explicit or even consciously known to the speaker. The subcategories often used are those derived from Murray's need system (1938:315) which includes recognition, dominance, self-abasement, nurturance, affiliation. Behaviorally, overt hearer responses which might be elicited are applause, sympathetic words, laughter, a hug, or an angry retort; but often hearer reactions are covert. E. g., "What a gorgeous dress you're wearing!" "A weird thing happened to me today." "You're a fool."

c. <u>Offering information or interpretation</u>. Spontaneous instruction evidently based on the belief that the hearer would be gratified to learn. Analogous to spontaneous offer of goods or services. E. g., "That's Orion." "Did you hear about the fire?"

d. <u>Expressive monologues</u>. Expressions of joy, sorrow, anger; talking to oneself, muttering. The sender reacts to an external stimulus, a feeling, or a problem without attending to the hearer's comments, which may be minimal or absent.

e. <u>Routines</u>. Greetings, thanks, apologies, offers of service by waitresses and salespeople, where the alternatives are extremely restricted, and hence predictable.

f. <u>Avoidance conversations</u>. Conversation is started only because the alternative activity is unpleasant or the sender is satiated; any hearer will do, and topics are highly variable. Water-cooler conversations in an office, coffee breaks during study sessions, bus-stop discourse.

A somewhat similar system was developed by Soskin and John (1963) to classify all the utterances in natural conversations. Their system, for instance, differentiates "signones," in which the speaker describes his own state or opinions, from "regnones," in which he tries to influence another's behavior. They point out that "signones" such as "I'm still thirsty" or "that tasted good" may in a benign and nurturant environment be used "as a consciously manipulative act." In purely functional terms, such "signones" are requests for goods, services, or information. Thus Soskin and John's classification seems in part to be formal. It is important to treat form separately from function just because there may be systematic discrepancies between manifest and latent function, as indicated in these examples. This point will be discussed further in the next section.

Because functions may not always be explicit, one way to discern latent functions is to examine the sender's reaction to various outcomes. The reason we know that "Got a match?" is sometimes a social demand rather than a demand for a match is that the speaker may go on chatting even if he fails to get a match. If he primarily wanted a match he would go elsewhere for one. Avoidance conversations are typically masked in the manifest content of other function classes. Small children at bed time may make plausible requests; these could be unmasked if a functionally equivalent alternative response were given—for instance, if one brought a cracker in response to a request for a glass of water. Certain conversational functions perhaps must always be masked in a given society; others must be masked for certain receivers or in certain settings. Masking permits functional ambiguity. A woman's remark to her escort, "it's cold outside tonight," might be either an expressive monologue or a request for his coat. Presumably such ambiguity may lead to social embarrassment because of differences in interpretation by speaker and hearer.

Formal Features of Communication

The form of communication may be viewed as having four aspects. The channel might be spoken language, writing, telegraphic signals, etc. As we have indicated, gestural signals on occasion may be systematic alternatives to speech and in such cases are part of the significant exchange. The code or variety consists of a systematic set of linguistic signals which co-occur in defining settings. For spoken languages, alternative codes may be vernaculars or super-posed varieties. Sociolinguistic variants are those linguistic alter-nations linguists regard as free variants or optional variants within a code, that is, two different ways of saying the same thing. Nonlinguis-tic vocal signals include the range of properties called paralinguistic (Trager 1958; Pittenger et al. 1960) which lack the arbitrary proper-ties of linguistic signals.

Linguists have been concerned primarily with codes rather than with the other three classes of formal variation. A discussion of code distinctions especially pertinent to social variations can be found in Gumperz (1961, 1962). He distinguishes between the vernac-ular (the speech used within the home and with peers) and the super-posed variety ("the norm in one or more socially definable communi-cation situations"). Superposed varieties include many types, from occupational argots to koinés used for trade and regional communica-tion, such as Melanesian Pidgin and Swahili. A special type of vernacular-koine relation exemplified in Greece, German Switzerland, Arab countries, and China, has been called diglossia by Ferguson (1959). These all are illustrations of code variations.

A speaker in any language community who enters diverse social situations normally has a repertoire of speech alternatives which shift with situation. Yet linguists have generally focused on relatively pure codes. They do this by trying to control the speech situation with the informant and to keep him from using borrowed forms without identifying them. They also may seek out monolinguals who have mastered only one vernacular, and whose speech constitutes therefore a recognizable norm (though not necessarily a highly valued norm in the larger community). Language communities label some alternative varieties, especially those which either are different enough to interfere with intelligibility, or are identified with specific social groups. "Folk linguistics" of dialect perception and of classi-fication into language and dialect taxonomies bears on the values attached to speaking in a certain way. As Weinreich has pointed out, "accent" perception is systematically biased (1953:21).

It may sometimes be difficult to isolate the features of superposed varieties, because they normally coexist in a single

speaker and therefore may interpenetrate. One must seek defining
situations demanding rigid adherence to a code (as in prayers) to
isolate the features of the code. These may be hard to find in societies like our own with great tolerance for stylistic variability in a
given situation. Where the formal difference in varieties is great,
as in some diglossias, interpenetration may be more effectively in-
hibited. Obviously, where code-switching and interpenetration or
borrowing are permissible, they become available to mark role and
topic shifts within a setting (Gumperz 1964a).

Sociolinguistic variants have received very little attention.
Examples are the systematic array of deletions available in answers
and requests, as in "Coffee," vs. "Would you give me some coffee,
please?"

Request sentences provide some excellent examples of formal
variation with functional and topical equivalence. If we use Soskin
and John's six categories (1963), we find that requests could take
any form, as in the following examples:

> "It's cold today." (structone)
> "Lend me your coat." (regnone) (Also "would you mind
>   lending... ?")
> "I'm cold." (signone)
> "That looks like a warm coat you have." (metrone)
> "Br-r-r." (expressive)
> "I wonder if I brought a coat." (excogitative)

We could also classify these utterances by more conventional grammatical terms, as declarative, imperative, and interrogative.

It is clear that the selection of these alternatives is not
"free" but is conditioned by both situational and personal factors.
Student observations have shown that the imperative form is used
most often to inferiors in occupational settings, and more often for
easy than difficult or unusual services. The yes-no question is the
most typical request form to superiors. Informants regarding cross-
cultural differences have reported great variation in the "normal"
request form to employees in such cases of alternatives as:

> "There's dust in the corner," vs. "Sweep the dust from
>   the corner."

"It's haying time," vs. "Start the haying tomorrow."

Morphological as well as syntactic options may be available as sociolinguistic variants, as illustrated by Fischer's analysis (1958) of the alternation between the participial suffixes /in/ and /iŋ/. Obviously the choice of referential synonyms (Conklin 1962) is socially conditioned, as anyone reflecting on English synonyms for body functions will recognize. In fact, the number of referential synonyms may be indicative of the complexity of attitudes towards the referent. Brown and Ford (1961) have observed that the number of terms of address in America is usually directly related to intimacy, nicknames and endearments permitting marking of attitude variations.

The intercorrelation of these variables has been demonstrated in a variety of studies. The following are illustrative:

(1) Participant-function-form. Basil Bernstein (1962) has discovered systematic differences between middle-class and working-class adolescent conversation groups in England. These may be summarized as greater emphasis on offering information and interpretation in middle-class groups and on requests for social responses in working-class groups. The effects on form of these function differences were great. The middle-class boys used fewer personal pronouns, a greater variety of adjectives, a greater variety of subordinate conjunctions, more complex syntax, and more pauses.

(2) Participant-form. Charles Ferguson (1964) has pointed out that in many languages there is a style peculiar to the situation of an adult addressing an infant. The common formal features may include a change in lexicon, simplification of grammar, formation of words by reduplications, simplifying of consonant clusters, and general labialization.

Brown and Gilman (1960) examined many aspects, both contemporary and historical, of the selection of "tu" and "vous" in French address, and the corresponding terms in Italian and German. They found that the selection was based primarily on the relation of sender and receiver, and that historically the selection had been based on relative power, whereas currently relative intimacy is more important. They found national differences, such as greater emphasis on kin-intimacy in Germany and on camaraderie in France and Italy. They also found that personality and ideology influenced individual differences in the sender's selection.

Joan Rubin (1962) found that the choice of Spanish or Guaraní for address in Paraguay was describable in terms of the same set of dimensions—"solidarity" and "power" or status, and sometimes setting. She gives the example of the use of Spanish by men courting women, and the switch to Guarani with marriage. Thus in a multilingual society a code shift can mark the same contrasts as a sociolinguistic variation in a single language.

Another kind of particpant-form study is illustrated by Putnam and O'Hern's analysis (1955) of the relation between social status, judged by sociological indices, and linguistic features of speech in a Negro community in Washington, D. C. This study has many similarities in method to dialect geography, but adds a procedure of judge's blind ratings of status from tapes, to make a three-way comparison possible between objective status, perceived status, and specific features. Labov (1964) gives a sophisticated analysis of a status-form relation.

(3) Function-setting. A comparison of interactions of a nine-year-old boy at camp and at home, by Gump, Schoggen, and Redl (1963) showed systematic functional changes even in such a subcategory as interactions addressed to adults. The percentage of "sharing" (which was primarily verbal) was higher at camp, and the percentage of "submissive" and "appeal" behavior toward adults was higher at home. Sharing included asking opinion, playing with an adult, competing, telling a story. The child's shifts in behavior may have been effects of the variations in adult-initiated interaction.

Soskin and John (1963:265) used a set of categories which were partially functional in analyzing tapes of a couple on vacation, and showed significant variations with setting. Explicitly directive utterances were most frequent by the wife in the cabin, and by the husband out rowing, where he gave her instructions. Informational utterances were most common for both at meal times.

(4) Topic-form. In a study of New England children, John Fischer (1958) collected evidence of several factors related to the

alternation of the participial suffix /iŋ/ vs. /in/. He found the
selection to depend on sender ("typical" vs. "good" boy), and on
topic of discourse. He heard "visiting," "correcting," and "reading"
vs. "swimmin," "chewin," and "hittin." The topical distribution suggests that behind the alternation by topic lies an alternation by participants, with /iŋ/ being heard from adults, especially teachers, and
/in/ being heard from peers.

John Gumperz (1964b) describes the effects of topic on the
alternation in Norway between a rural dialect and standard North
Norwegian. He found that the type of formal alternation depended
on the social properties of the group of addressees.

(5) Setting-form. Changes of form with setting have been
frequently described. Some excellent examples of a shift between a
spoken dialect and a superposed variety are provided by Ferguson
(1959), for example the shift from classical to colloquial Arabic
which accompanies a shift from formal lecturing to discussion in a
classroom. Herman (1961) has given a number of examples of the
influence of setting on code selection in Israel, pointing out that immigrants speak Hebrew more often in public than in private situations.

Sociolinguistic variations and paralinguistic features were
noted by Andrea Kaciff and Camille Chamberlain who compared children's speech in a pre-school playground with their role-playing in a
playhouse. The material was reported in an unpublished term paper.
They found certain lexical changes, such as the use of role-names in
address: "Go to sleep, baby, say goo-goo." They found that the
children playing the role of the mother adopted a sing-song intonation
especially when rebuking the play child. This intonation was not used
by the children except in imitative play, and had been observed by
another student in a study of adults' speech to other people's children.

In ordinary social life all of these interacting variables tend
to vary together. The public setting of the Israeli immigrants included a different audience than the private setting; the address of
adults to children is different in participants, topics, and form at
once. In using naturalistic situations, we can discern the critical
factors in determination of alternations only if we can find in nature
comparisons in which other possibly relevant factors are held constant.

An example is lecturing vs. class discussion in diglossia, where the topics, participants, and functions may remain the same but only the situation changes, and with it the form. Where it is not possible to find such orderly experimental situations, an appropriate sequel to the ethnographic method is the social experiment. We shall describe one below.

A Japanese Bilingual Experiment

Bilingual speech is convenient to study because the formal changes are vividly apparent. There are many forms of social relation between two language communities. American immigrants, for example, range through a wide spectrum in the diversity of function-language distributions. At one extreme might be an old storekeeper in Chinatown. He rarely needs any knowledge of English except to ask limited-response questions of his customers, or to tell the cost of an item. On the whole, he is like a tourist with request forms and a vocabulary limited to the goods or services exchanged. If he employs English in restricted settings, he may succeed in communicating with a minimum of knowledge of English grammar or phonology.

At the opposite extreme are immigrants who have married Americans and raised families here. They typically vary widely in the functional distribution of their use of English, frequently employing English for as many uses as their native language at home before. The limitations in their use of English occur in certain aspects of the code. They may have gaps in their English vocabulary, reflecting differential exposure, for instance, to rural life in the two countries. They may have difficulties learning a new sound system after adolescence; it is clear that aptitude, personality, and perhaps willingness to lose one's identity as a foreigner vary. Japanese women, for example, often do not respect Nisei, and may not wish to be taken for Nisei. Yet it is common to find women who have extensive mastery of the vocabulary and grammar of English, and whose English dominance is so great that they may be unable to speak their native tongue without intrusions at all levels from English.

The first step in the experimental study of Japanese-American speech in terms of the topic-audience-language correlations was an ethnographic description of their covariance, based on informant interviews. Thousands of Japanese women marry Americans every year, and come to this country to live and to raise their American offspring. In the San Francisco area, they are generally isolated socially from the American Japanese who seem un-Japanese to them, from the immigrant Japanese, who are older and of rural backgrounds, and from the temporary officials and business personnel from Japan. Usually they do not live in areas with Japanese shops. As a result of their isolation, they use Japanese in three situations: visits to Japan; jobs (for some) in Japanese restaurants; and talks with bilingual friends. The women who took part in the study usually had friends who were also "war brides." These were their confidantes, their recourse when worried. With these friends, in Japanese, they reminisced about Japan, discussed news from home, gossiped; Japanese was the language of social interchange and expressive monologues.

By contrast, the functions of English covered a varying range for different women. For all, it was the language for talking of goods and services, for shopping. In a few marriages, the husband was a companion and confidant, teaching a large variety of English words, teaching about American activities and values, discussing many topics. Such women had learned the subtleties of social interchange in English. In other families, the absence of the husband at sea, or his silence, left the wife with little occasion to use English at home. One woman who spoke little English at the time of her marriage reported that the couple "spoke the language of the eyes." It is quite clear that there was not an equivalent distribution of functions for Japanese and English for most of the women interviewed.

The women spoke English primarily with their husbands, children and neighbors. We would expect that when they spoke English the content would reflect the objects, experiences, and points of view encountered in this country. With their Japanese friends, language shifted with topic—American food, clothing, and husbands being discussed in English, and matters Japanese, or personal concerns being discussed in Japanese. Some reported never using English with Japanese friends except when the husbands were present, a situation presumably altering the topical distribution of conversations.

Language and Content

Our first hypothesis is that as language shifts, content will shift. This hypothesis was tested earlier for French and American content (Ervin 1964; Lambert 1963). In this case, we have the explicit hypothesis that wherever monolingual American women and Japanese women tested in Japan differ in content, the bilingual women will tend to show an analogous content shift with language, even though the situations are otherwise identical. A Japanese interviewer saw each woman twice in the same setting, and tape recorded the sessions. At the first, only Japanese was used, and at the second, only English. Verbal materials employed were word associations, sentence completions, semantic differentials, problem stories, and Thematic Apperception Tests.

Here are some illustrative examples, the speaker being the same for the Japanese and English. Where the American and Japanese monolingual comparison groups gave a particular item uniquely or more frequently than the other language group, the word is marked with (A) or (J).

> MOON: (Japanese) moon-viewing (J), zebra-grass (J), full moon (J), cloud (J)
> (English) sky (A), rocket (A), cloud (J)
> NEW YEAR'S DAY: (Japanese) pine decoration (J), rice-cake (J), feast (J), kimono (J), seven-spring-herbs (J), shuttlecock (J), tangerine (J), foot-warmer (J), friends (A)
> (English) new clothes, party (A), holidays (A)
> TEA: (Japanese) bowl (J), saucer (A), green (J), tea-cake (J), tea-ceremony (J)
> (English) teapot, kettle, tea leaf (A), party (A), green tea (J), lemon (A), sugar (A), cookies (J)

Similar contrasts may be illustrated with sentence completions. The informants heard (and read) the first half of the sentence. The same woman's responses in both languages are cited below:

> 1. WHEN MY WISHES CONFLICT WITH MY FAMILY...
> (Japanese) it is a time of great unhappiness.
> (English) I do what I want.

    2. I WILL PROBABLY BECOME...
        (Japanese) a housewife.
        (English) a teacher.
    3. REAL FRIENDS SHOULD...
        (Japanese) help each other.
        (English) be very frank.

On the last point, many women mentioned in attitude interviews that they particularly admired the frankness of American women.

It was found that when the sentences were weighted by their frequency in the American and Japanese monolingual comparison groups, the bilingual women's sentences were significantly less "Japanese" in content when the women spoke English. This change in content could not be simulated by women who did not change language but were instructed to give "typically Japanese" or "typically American" answers at the two sessions. Thus the change in the associations and the sentence completions is an effect of language, and not of self-instruction or set.

In the preceding experiment, everything was held constant except language, and the effects of a specified language on content were examined. It was expected that in the relatively abnormal situation of a Japanese woman forced to speak English to another Japanese woman, content typical of conversations between Americans would more often appear. This shift presumably would reflect English discourse with neighbors and husband and thematic materical from the English mass media.

Participant and Form

In a second experiment, the receiver was changed in each session, but the language was consistently English. The women were interviewed either by a Caucasian American or by a Japanese interviewer. Again, the women were in an abnormal situation when they were asked to speak English with another Japanese woman. The effects on the style of English were clear when the two situations were compared. With the Japanese listener, there was much more disruption of English syntax, more intrusion of Japanese words, and briefer speech.

A Japanese person provides an imperfect model of English, and as a listener is tolerant of and can understand Japanese intrusions. On the whole, the Japanese women are very tolerant of interpenetration of the two languages. We had found with French in the United States that those who had frequent discourse with other bilinguals had the highest incidence of borrowing of each language in the other (Ervin 1955). Thus we can say that bilinguals who speak only with other bilinguals may be on the road to merger of the two languages, unless there are strong pressures to insulate by topic or setting.

Topic and Form

In this experiment, it is possible to compare topics within each interview. In the word-associations, a stimulus word might be considered a topic. We know that some topics are more closely connected with life in the United States, others with Japan. For example, "love," "marriage," and "kitchen" have American associations for these women. On the other hand, "mushroom," "fish," and "New Year's Day" are strongly associated with Japanese life. When we weighted the English responses according to their frequency in the monolingual norm groups in Japan and the United States, it appeared that the war brides were closer to American women when associating to "love," "marriage," and "kitchen" but closer to Japanese women for the other three topics. This was true even though, as we have seen, these "Japanese" topics elicited less characteristically Japanese content when the language used was English, not Japanese.

In one part of the interview, the informants were asked to explain or describe, in English, a set of 14 topics. The topics designed to be associated with English were the husband's work and leisure activities, American housekeeping, American cooking, and shopping for food and clothing here. Another set of topics were designed to be more frequent in Japanese: Japanese festivals, Japanese New Year's Day, Japanese cooking and housekeeping, Doll Festival, and street story-tellers. The last two topics in each set were accompanied with photographs of the event to be described.

From this procedure we found that it was not the receiver alone, nor the topic alone, which affected speech but a specific

combination of the two. When the informants were instructed to
speak English, they had difficulty only when they spoke of Japanese
topics. The combination of a Japanese receiver and a Japanese topic
almost always demands the use of Japanese in a normal situation.
The effect of artificially violating this rule was that the women's
speech was disrupted. They borrowed more Japanese words, had
more disturbed syntax, were less fluent, and had more frequent hesitation pauses. Thus a simple change in the topic and listener had a
marked effect on the formal features of speech even though the most
obvious formal change, a switch of code, was not allowed.

In the analysis both of content and form changes, we had assumed that a bilingual is like two monolinguals with a single nervous
system. The differences in two settings or audiences of a bilingual
are viewed as extensions of the differences in monolinguals. But
there are limits to this simplified assumption. One is a cognitive
limit. There are reasons to believe that it is very hard to maintain
in one nervous system two category systems with only slight differences between them. This is true whether it be a semantic system
such as color terminology (Ervin 1961) or a phonemic system (Gumperz 1962). Thus there are pressures constantly towards a merger
of the two systems of the bilingual. Also, the very fact that a larger
repertoire of alternative behavior is available to the bilingual makes
him a victim of the special signs of response-competition, such as
hesitation pauses and less fluency.

The second limit to this assumption lies in the very functional
specialization we mentioned before. No bilingual, however fluent in
two languages, has exactly equivalent experiences in both language
communities. One may have been learned at home, one at school.
One may have been learned in childhood, the other in adolescence.
Perhaps now one is used at work and one in the family. Even in multilingual communities such as those of India and Switzerland, some
specialization exists. Robert Lowie, who grew up in a German-
speaking family in the United States, reported a deliberate effort to
keep an equivalent vocabulary (1945). He failed, for he could not
control the difference in frequency or social context for the lexicon
he acquired.

Thus, we cannot expect that a woman whose direct experience as a wife and mother was entirely in the United States would

have, even when speaking Japanese, quite the same content as a woman in Japan. Her familiarity with these domains of life will be
second-hand in some sense. In the same way, a woman who has
never raised children in the United States will have most of the domain of meaning involving childhood much more fully developed in
Japanese.

Finally, to the extent that the norms for Japanese and American monolingual behavior are current, they misrepresent the realities
of contact, for these Japanese women know the Japan of five or ten
years ago, not rapidly-changing contemporary Japan and its language.

Methods in Sociolinguistics

If we examine the research which satisfies our definition of
sociolinguistics, we find the methods used appear to be of four general types:

1. Studies of the speech of social groups. It has long been
a practice among linguists and sociologists to study certain properties
of the speech (usually the code) of predefined classes of speakers.
We have, for example, studies reporting homosexual jargon (Cory
1952:103-113) and thieves' jargon (Sutherland 1937). Dialect atlas
studies have selected code features such as special lexicon (e. g. ,
spider vs. frying-pan) and pronunciation (e. g. , / griysiy/ vs.
/ griyziy/). Traditionally, none of these studies takes the larger
social community as a unit; speakers are selected out of context,
and we may not know whether their speech varies with setting or
receiver. We might expect, for instance, that "criminals" might
use different speech to judges, parole officers, patrolmen, and cell-
mates, and Sutherland reports that this is the case (1937).

2. Ethnographic studies. A form of study discussed in detail by Hymes (1962) would employ traditional methods of observation and interview to study when speech is used at all, and variations
according to setting and participants. Naturalistic observations such
as those of Barker and Wright (1954), Barker (1963), Watson and
Potter (1962), Coser (1960) and Newman (1955) have ranged widely
over the intercorrelational problems we have mentioned earlier.

However, the drawback of such studies is that normally there is so much variation at once that we can find descriptive information about distributions but little definitive knowledge of which of the covarying features may be effective. Gump, Schoggen, and Redl (1963), for instance, compared a child's behavior in two social settings—but the settings involved different participants, different activities, and different physical surroundings. The authors point out that the child changed his forms of interaction, but it is not clear that this would have happened had his family been transported to a camp setting.

      3. Experimental studies. Inevitably, experiments set up artificial situations. That is just their purpose, for they allow artificial constraints on normal covariance, permitting us for example to control the social composition of juries (Strodtbeck et al. 1957), the size of a group (Bales and Borgatta 155), or the power relation of participants (Cohen 1958) without varying any other significant features. Such studies would normally be based first on ethnographic research to explore the distribution of speech in the natural community so that extrapolation might be made to the artificial situation.

      4. Distribution of forms. One can start with the analysis of formal alternatives and employ any of the above methods to study the determinants of the alternation. Fischer (1958), Brown and Gilman (1960), and Brown and Ford (1961) have done just this. This kind of study lends itself to a form of analysis we might call the description of equivalence patterns. For example, in some languages, the stylistic alternation which occurs when a man speaks to his superior rather than to a peer is similar to the alternation which occurs when a woman speaks to a man rather than to another woman. This is just a fragment of what is undoubtedly a wider set of corresponding alternations. If we looked at all societies in which such sets of correspondences occur, they might have common features, such as inferior ascribed status for women.

      Another example is suggested by the distribution of the features of baby talk. The alternation which accompanies speech to adults vs. speech to infants has some similarities to the alternations between neutral vs. affectionate speech between intimates. Should this relation turn out to be universal, we might hunt for manipulable variables to test the psychological basis of the correspondence. If it is not universal, we need to know what systematic differences between societies are related; frequently such societal differences have individual analogues that can be studied (the baby talk user vs. the non-baby-talk user).

These equivalence structures in verbal behavior are similar to the lexical classes which so interest cognitive theorists, for similarity in formal verbal behavior implies testable similarities in other types of behavior such as perception, memory, or emotional response.

This treatment of sociolinguistics has placed the face-to-face verbal encounter at the center of the definition. In contrast, a macroscopic approach to sociolinguistics might consider codes rather than finer formal contrasts, societal functions (such as education or law) rather than individual functions, institutionally classified settings (such as churches and mass media) rather than finer differentiations of setting in local communities, and values about language use as expressed in administrative actions and political behavior rather than merely in community norms and attitudes toward speakers of particular languages or dialects.

If one examines the generalizations in the studies we have cited, one finds that frequently they are special instances of more general social or psychological propositions. Brown and Ford (1961), for instance, noted that changes in address forms are expected to be initiated by the higher status participant; probably all respect behavior is so. Herman (1961) explicitly couched his study of multilingual code-switching in a broader framework of a theory of choice behavior.

Yet language is distinct in certain respects. Unlike other formally coded social behavior it can have semantic content. The internal imitations of external speech constitute a kind of portable society, both the voice of conscience and a categorization system, promoting socialization even of private behavior. Most of the uniquely human forms of social behavior are dependent on shared language, so that the structure of language use in society may be related to societal functioning in unique ways. If this is the case, sociolinguistics will contribute a new dimension to the social sciences rather than provide further exemplifications of the otherwise known.

NOTES

The point of view and the sources in this article have both been enriched by discussions with Dell Hymes and John Gumperz. The study of Japanese bilinguals mentioned below was supported by the National Science Foundation. The author is especially grateful to Yaeko Nishijima Putzar and Naomi Litt Quenk for their work on this project.

REFERENCES

Bales, R. F. and E. F. Borgatta. 1955. A study of group size: size of group as a factor in the interaction profile. In Small groups, Paul Hare, E. F. Borgatta and R. F. Bales, eds. New York, Knopf.

Barker, R. G. 1963. The stream of behavior. New York, Appleton-Century-Crofts.

Barker, R. G. and H. F. Wright. 1954. Midwest and its children. Evanston, Row, Peterson.

Bernstein, Basil. 1962. Social class, linguistic codes and grammatical elements. Language and Speech 5:221-240.

Brown, R. W. and M. Ford. 1961. Address in American English. Jornal of Abnormal and Social Psychology 62:375-385.

Brown, R. W. and Albert Gilman. 1960. The pronouns of power and solidarity. In Style in language, T. A. Sebeok, ed. New York, John Wiley.

Cohen, Arthur R. 1958. Upward communication in experimentally created hierarchies. Human Relations 11:41-53.

Conklin, Harold C. 1962. Lexicographical treatment of folk taxonomies. International Journal of American Linguistics 28:119-141.

Cory, D. W. 1952. The homosexual in America. New York, Greenberg.

Coser, Rose. 1960. Laughter among colleagues. Psychiatry 23:81-96.

Ervin, Susin M. 1955. The verbal behavior of bilinguals: The effects of language of report on the thematic apperception test content of adult French bilinguals. Ph.D. dissertation. University of Michigan. Microfilm Abstracts 55,2228.

Ervin, Susan M. 1961. Semantic shift in bilingualism. American Journal of Psychology 74:233-241.

Ervin, Susan M. 1964. Language and thematic apperception test content in bilinguals. Journal of Abnormal and Social Psychology 68:500-507.

Ferguson, C. A. 1959. Diglossia. Word 15:325-340.

Ferguson, C. A. 1964. Baby talk in six languages. In The ethnography of communication, J. J. Gumperz and Dell Hymes, eds., pp. 103-114. American Anthropologist 66:6, Part 2.

Fischer, John L. 1958. Social influences on the choice of a linguistic variant. Word 14:47-56.

Gump, Paul V., Phil Schoggen, and Fritz Redl. 1963. The behavior of the same child in different milieus. In The stream of behavior, R. G. Barker, ed. New York, Appleton-Century-Crofts.

Gumperz, John J. 1958. Dialect differences and social stratification in a North Indian village. American Anthropologist 60:668-682.

Gumperz, John J. 1961. Speech variation and the study of Indian civilization. American Anthropologist 63:976-988.

Gumperz, John J. 1962. Types of linguistic communities. Anthropological Linguistics 4:28-36.

Gumperz, John J. 1964a. Hindi-Punjabi code-switching in Delhi. In Proceedings of the International Congress of Linguists. Morris Halle, ed. The Hague (in press).

Gumperz, John J. 1964b. Linguistic and social interaction in two communities. In The ethnography of communication, J. J. Gumperz and Dell Hymes, eds., pp. 137-153.

Hare, A. Paul. 1962. Handbook of small group research. Glencoe, Free Press.

Herman, Simon. 1961. Explorations in the social psychology of language choice. Human Relations 14:149-164.

Hymes, Dell. 1962. The ethnography of speaking. In Anthropology and human behavior, T. Gladwin and W. Sturtevant, eds. Washington, D. C., Anthropological Society of Washington, pp. 15-53.

Joos, Martin. 1962. The five clocks. Supplement to International Journal of American Linguistics 28, Part V.

Labov, William. 1964. Phonological correlates of social stratification. In The ethnography of communication, J. J. Gumperz and Dell Hymes, eds., pp. 164-176. American Anthropologist 66:6, Part 2.

Lambert, Wallace E. 1963. Psychological approaches to the study of language, Part II; On second-language learning and bilingualism. The Modern Language Journal 47:114-121.

Lowie, Robert. 1945. A case of bilingualism. Word 1:249-260.

Murray, Henry A. 1938. Explorations in personality. Cambridge, Mass., Harvard University Press.

Newman, Stanley. 1955. Vocabulary levels: Zuni sacred and slang usage. Southwest Journal of Anthropology 11:345-354.

Osgood, C. E. and T. A. Sebeok. 1954. Psycholinguistics. Supplement to International Journal of American Linguistics 20, Memoir 10.

Osgood, C. E., George J. Suci, and Percy H. Tannenbaum. 1957. The measurement of meaning. Urbana, University of Illinois Press.

Pittenger, Robert E., C. F. Hockett, and John J. Danehy. 1960. The first five minutes. Ithaca, Paul Martineau.

Putnam, G. N. and Ettna M. O'Hern. 1955. The status significance of an isolated urban dialect. Language Dissertations No. 53.

Rubin, Joan. 1962. Bilingualism in Paraguay. Anthropoligical Linguistics 4:52-58.

Saporta, Sol. 1961. Psycholinguistics. New York, Holt, Rinehart, and Winston.

Schachter, Stanley. 1951. Deviation, rejection, and communication. Journal of Abnormal and Social Psychology 46:190-207.

Skinner, B. F. 1957. Verbal behavior. New York. Appleton-Century-Crofts.

Soskin, William F., and Vera John. 1963. The study of spontaneous talk. In The stream of behavior, R. G. Barker, ed. New York, Appleton-Century-Crofts.

Stephen, F. F. and E. G. Mishler. 1952. The distribution of participation in small groups: An exponential approximation. American Sociological Review 17:598-608.

Strodtbeck, F. L., Rita M. James, and C. Hawkins. 1957. Social status and jury deliberations. American Sociological Review 22:713-719.

Sutherland, E. 1937. The professional thief. Chicago, University of Chicago Press.

Trager, George. 1958. Paralanguage: a first approximation. Studies in Linguistics 13:1-12.

Watson, Jeanne and Robert J. Potter. 1962. An analytic unit for the study of interaction. Human relations 15:245-263.

16 | Children's Sociolinguistic Competence and Dialect Diversity

Comparative Studies of Language Development

Comparisons of social groups in the development of language and of cognitive functions mediated by or tested through language are common. These studies, to the extent that they focus on comparisons of underlying abilities, are only possible if the investigator has enough sociolinguistic knowledge to construct data-collecting situations which are comparable in a deep rather than superficial sense. These studies of children of varying social backgrounds can be contrasted with studies of sociolinguistic competence in pure form.[1] These need not be comparative at all. Their focus is the systematic relation of features of the children's language and the social milieu of speech, hearing, and talk about speech. Some of the major assumptions of this field have been developed in the works of Hymes (27, 28) and of Gumperz (20, 21) defining a field of ethnography of communication. In this chapter we shall focus on both comparative studies and developmental sociolinguistics and suggest some research problems which still face us, with particular attention to social dialects.

Problems of Bias

Linguistic bias. The first category of work, comparative studies, has attracted attention because American schools so often test and compare children's performances. But there has been great difficulty in finding ways of testing children's knowledge of language without using biased approaches. Most tests use communicative settings which are middle class, middle-class interviewers, middle-class kinds of tasks, middle-class language, and middle-class scoring

criteria. It is very easy to find bleak examples of ignorance of work
on social dialects and on social variation in the use of language, but
hard to find alternative approaches for those who think they have to
test.

One approach to the linguistic issue is to test development of
features common to different languages. Let us suppose, for example,
that we are concerned with the concept of location or of possession.
Both of these structures, and at least eight others, can be identified
in grammatical contrasts or classes in the earliest sentences of children in a variety of languages ranging from Samoan (31) to Luo in
Kenya (5). But if we are interested in the possessive, what approaches
can we take ?

1. The concept of possession is probably present well within the first eighteen months, but testing would require
   some nonverbal methods appropriate to the social group.
2. We might like to know how early children signal possession verbally by some distinct feature, any feature. Thus
   we might ask how early possession is a linguistically
   distinct feature.
3. We might ask how early a child comprehends specific linguistic contrasts as signalling possessive. The Torrey
   study (52) cited below asks this question, but in a non-
   comparative framework.
4. We might ask how early the child signals possessive with the
   adult linguistic contrast of his home milieu. If his parents
   and siblings speak a nonstandard dialect of English, this
   might mean using order alone, or order and prosodic
   features, but not a suffix.
5. We might ask how early a child can systematically signal
   possession with a linguistic feature of some dialect or
   language not used regularly in his home but sometimes
   heard. For English speakers in a bilingual community it
   might be the Spanish possessive. For lower-class East
   Coast blacks it might be a possessive suffix. For Standard English speakers it might be the nonstandard variants.

An appropriate example is the work of Osser, Wang, and Zaid
(43). This was a study of rates of development in core grammatical

transformations common to all dialects of English, such as relativization and passivization. The study compared middle-class white and lower-class black five-year-olds.

Many workers in child language question the likelihood of large differences in the average age of achievement of fundamental milestones (e.g., understanding verb-object, understanding relative clauses) or in ranges of variation in different social groups. There are two reasons for their doubt. One is the evidence of a considerable biological substrate for the maturation of language - learning abilities universal in humans (38), and the other is the evidence that the amount of direct reinforcement of language training seems to have little bearing, at least on grammatical development (7, 8). Short of biological abnormalities[2] or deviant social conditions in a particular family that are pathological in the society, this theory would lead one to suspect underlying similarity of competence. Thus those claiming differences must be particularly careful to use tests appropriate to the groups tested. There are many questions of interest in comparative studies outside of the hypothesis of difference, of course, such as universals of order and contingency for different features.

Osser, Wang, and Zaid developed some excellent methods for testing grammatical imitative skill and comprehension, aimed at specific grammatical features. But they made one serious mistake. The input was Standard English, so they used a type 4 test (like a parent's speech) for the middle-class children and a type 5 test (like the speech of the contact community) for the lower class children and assumed they could make them comparable by some scoring rules. Differences in familiarity with the testing dialect must have thoroughly confounded developmental results.

One solution to this problem has been proposed by Joan Baratz (1). She constructed a set of idealized sentences "translated" into uneducated variants (wherever possible in East Coast black speakers' phonology and grammar) and recorded by a middle-class white using a speech guise. Nobody speaks 100 percent nonstandard forms, so the input language was very artificial, but most of the children believed the speaker was black. The results show that whatever the unnaturalness of these materials, it was easier for

black urban children in the third and fifth grades to imitate them and
harder for white suburban children in relatively segregated areas to
imitate them than Standard English. Her study was not aimed at all at
studying development of specific grammatical features, but at a gross
test of grammatical competence and at showing that the surface structure of the test is highly relevant if one wants to make such comparisons. She is clearly right.

The Baratz test included an extremely stereotyped approximation of home dialect and outside dialect materials for both groups,
and she showed that for both it was easier to imitate pseudo-home
dialect materials. One could argue that until one is able to construct
materials with which the minority group does better (like the nonstandard section of the Baratz test) one does not understand the
unique features of the skills children acquire in those communities.
Of course it is also the case that no sharply circumscribed "Standard English" is in use by either children or their parents and that
both regional and class variation in "Standard" exists. For example,
we have found that preschoolers routinely change which to that in
working-class samples, and have noticed then that which is a relatively formal style not used much if at all with children. Out of an
appropriate balance of items known to be equally familiar to component groups one might construct a more language-fair test for
underlying structures than we now have.

Sociolinguistic bias. But sociolinguistic work has posed a
much more difficult challenge to those who wish to make comparisons
— one more difficult than equating familiarity with dialect features.
Each community, even subgroups within communities like teen-age
gangs, may develop its own pattern of language use, its own set of
speech events, its own valuing of skill. To take a simple example,
suppose one wants to compare fluency or active vocabulary size in
two groups. Presumably one can only assess fluency by discovering
the social situation in which the person talks the most. Labov (33)
has given a vivid example of a black child who was laconic with an
older black from the same community and only became talkative
when arguing with a friend. Assessment of vocabulary size in a
small sample of speech would require finding the speech events
within the culture of the children which maximally demand vocabulary diversity. An alternative might be to train the child to a new

task which interested him and in effect "resocialize" him, but then there would have to be some independent way of assessing success in this task. Jensen's comment (29) that the IQ of a lower-class black child might be raised ten points by spending many hours with him suggests that socialization to the task may be involved in a variety of ways which could be investigated.

An example of such an approach occurred to me while reading Labov's engrossing account of the rule structure for an insult game, "the dozens", involving Harlem males in the teen-age street culture (37). Playing the dozens requires sensitivity to syntactic patterns since success in the role of second party requires syntactic expansion, and in the role of third party some elements may remain constant but a semantic shift such as tense change or an anomalous but relevant lexical change can produce a successful effect. There is constant group evaluation and a high sense of skill.

Playing the dozens is not unique. "Rifting", "toasting", "rapping" are all speech events developed and labeled in black culture, all involving verbal creativity (32, 37). Kochman says (32) that "rapping is distinctively a fluent and lively way of talking, always characterized by a high degree of personal style. To one's own group, rapping may be descriptive of an interesting narration, a colorful rundown of some past event." One can only guess that the features of successful rapping are both modeled and rewarded in lower-class black children's experience. The autobiographies of such diverse figures as Rap Brown and Dick Gregory attest the importance of such early training.

If verbal skills are transferable, tests should tap these fundamental skills. They could be validated against the group's ranking of the person on the relevant speech events. An example of such an extension appears in the recent research of Susan Houston using story-retelling methods (26). She found that lower-class black children excelled white children in not just repeating the story elements but enriching them to make a more vivid narrative. While she did not use the group validation method, she did look for a performance which is a plausible derivative of values in the community.

The argument here is that the route out of our linguistic and

social myopia in constructing measures of language competence may
be to draw on the speech events and linguistic structures of minority
speakers. One problem of course is that the very fact that minority-
group members themselves may regard their informal style heard by
children as inappropriate to formal settings and tasks makes it harder to elicit "translations" or information about speech skills, except
by ethnographic work. In such cases it would be much easier to go
the other way, to first get materials, such as narratives, jokes, and
picture descriptions in the most informal milieu. To take a simple
case—Osser, Zaid, and Wang could get picture titles from speakers
of black nonstandard dialects asked to talk to their own children. One
cannot expect someone to sit in an office and be able to translate the
formal sentences of the test into colloquial style since the natural
vernacular style is usually not given to deliberate formal production.
In test construction, the appropriate direction would be to start by
searching for speech events, testing situations, and linguistic patterns familiar to the children to be tested. Full development and
independent validation of the testing materials should take place
within the reference population. It would be far easier to translate
materials into middle-class and Standard English than to go the other
direction.

In a recent comparison of standardized tests, Elsa Roberts
(46) pointed out that in four commonly used ability tests for children,
from 20 to 38 percent of the vocabulary items could be considered
potentially subculture-specific, and in the ITPA (Illinois Test of
Psycholinguistic Abilities) grammatical closure test, twenty-four
out of thirty-three items may have forms with dialectal variants.
The WPSSI (Wechsler Preschool and Primary Scale of Intelligence)
sentence imitation test is also subject to dialect-based errors.

Our current language competence tests are second dialect
tests for lower-class and especially for black children.[3] The ac-
cusations of bias that are being made are in many cases well founded. Whenever a test is supposed to assess fundamental linguistic
and intellectual competence, it must be oriented directly to the
speech community to be tested. Unless the speech skills and social
performances required by the test are equally familiar to all tested
children, the test is a biased estimate of underlying competence.

Developmental Studies

Assumptions

The development of tests for comparative work seems to be an example of applied developmental sociolinguistics. We have seen that adequate tests would have to draw on ethnographic developmental work. In basic research in developmental sociolinguistics, the principal assumption is that how people talk reflects directly both the regular patterns of their social networks and the immediate circumstances of speech. The first part is obvious; a child's interaction network is bound to influence his values about language and the repertoire he commands. The more we study speech in natural settings, the more we find systematic variation within every speaker, reflecting who he is addressing, where he is, what the social event may be, the topic of discussion, and the social relations he communicates by speaking. [4] The regularities in these features of speech make them as amenable to analysis as the abstracted rules called grammars. Competence in speaking includes the ability to use appropriate speech for the circumstance and when deviating from what is normal to convey what is intended. It would be an incompetent speaker who used baby talk to everyone or randomly interspersed sentences in baby talk or in a second language regardless of circumstance. It would be equally incompetent to use formal style in all situations and to all addressees in a society allowing for a broader range of variation.

With respect specifically to social dialects we assume that all varieties of English are alike in many underlying features. The child in a community with social dialects of English is in a very different situation from an immigrant. Even though he may not understand all details of Standard English, those he fails to understand or use may be relatively superficial from a linguistic if not a social standpoint. In casual discourse, intelligibility of Standard English to a nonstandard speaker is not likely to be the major problem, as it can be for a speaker of another language. Since gross unintelligibility is not present, motives for learning may be different.

As a result of mass media and education, as well as pressures towards "proper" speech in many homes, we assume that children who use many nonstandard features may often understand more of the surface features of Standard English than they reveal in their speech. In this sense a kind of bilingualism may exist at the comprehension level, as it does with those Spanish or Navaho speakers who can understand more than they produce.

Finally, we assume that social groups vary in the uses to which they most often put speech and in the value they attach to different uses, so that the range of uses of speech by a child is to be ascertained. On the other hand, certain values can be found universally in every social group. We ought to discover which speech events, for example, are evaluated aesthetically. We assume that aesthetic values are present in every society; whether they are focused on speech and, if so, on which kinds of speech is to be learned.

Previous Research

Systematic correlates of variations in dialect features. In speakers with a wide repertoire of language or dialect variation, the internal linguistic structure of that variation and its co-occurrence with semantic and social features can be examined. Sam Henrie (24) found that deletion of verb affixes by five-year-old black children was related to semantic features of the utterance and was not a random feature. It has been known for some time (59) that the form be as in "He be outa school" is semantically contrasted with is and carries meaning that Standard English cannot easily translate. Henrie found that by the age of five, children selected be most often for habitual actions ("they be sleeping") or distributed nontemporal states ("they be blue"), least often for momentary acts.

We have learned that the frequency of standard features may increase when (a) the child is role-playing doctor or teacher (30), (b) the child is in the schoolroom or being interviewed by an authority figure (25), (c) the child is interviewed alone rather than in a group (37), (d) the interviewer uses only Standard English rather than variable speech (58). Labov noted, for example, that in formal style black teen-agers used the plural suffix more, though the redundant third person verb marker remained infrequent. Since none of these studies except Labov's has focused on fine detail, we might be willing to pool them all as indicating a kind of formal-informal dimension. Fischer (14), for example, noted that New England three- to ten-year-old children increased their use of "-in" suffixes (fishin) over "-ing"

suffixes (fishing) in the course of an interview, presumably relaxing
into more casual style. Fischer noted, as others have, that girls in
his group used the more formal variant more; Kernan's examples of
formal features in role-playing usually involved girls.

This kind of variation corresponds to what Blom and Gumperz
call situational switching and Houston (25) calls "register," where
the primary determinants appear to be setting, situation, addressee,
and topic. Overlaid on these features, which in bilinguals often
generate sharp switching of languages, are variations in linguistic
features like "-in" and "-ing" which may or may not form coherent
styles. Gumperz calls these "metaphorical switching." These may
be viewed as reflections of changes of function or intent within the
particular interaction, that is, the variations between dialect features
can be considered linguistic devices for realizing intent or social
meaning. In a given conversation, different speech acts or structural
units within the conversation and different foci or speech episodes
often may be demarcated by changes in the frequency of socially
significant speech variables. Blom and Gumperz (4) describe these
phenomena with respect to dialect variation between a village dialect
in Norway and Standard Norwegian. The phenomena are analogous to
American dialect feature variation. [5]

An example of a simple analysis of classroom interaction
(under John Gumperz's guidance) with these concepts may illustrate
what I have in mind. Mary Rainey (45) studied a teacher in a black
Head Start class. She selected the alternation between "-ing" and "-in"
suffixes for observation, since they are related both to formality
(14, 34) and to dialect. The teacher regularly used "-ing" in formal
teaching and story reading but in these situations she used "-in" when
she was trying to get attention or closeness. Rainey calls "-ing" the
unmarked or usual form for formal teaching. On the other hand, the
unmarked form for informal or casual interaction was "-in" and in
these situations "-ing" was used for marked emphasis. ("Where are
you going, Ezekiel Cato Jones?") A contrast in register is the comparison of casual interaction with formal teaching; marking is the
change in meaning indicated by a shift from the normal features of
that register.

The notion that formality lies on a simple dimension seems
well founded empirically in Labov's studies. With addressee and

setting constant, he was able to accomplish style changes in "-ing" and in phonological alternatives by topical changes (e. g. , to a more emotional topic) or by task changes (to reciting a childhood rhyme, to reading) which affected the consciousness or "monitoring" of speech. Labov found in his Lower East Side New York study (34) that a full range of style variation in interviews was not adult-like until around fourteen or fifteen, but there is other evidence certainly that some variation exists before that time.   Typically, children use the more informal forms more often than adults (35, 48, 59) as one would expect from their exposure to informal home situations.

In contrast to Labov's unidimensional view of monitoring, Claudia Kernan (30) has used this term in speaking of "monitoring black" and "monitoring white. " These terms refer to speech which veers away from the normal expected, or unmarked vernacular. This monitoring is analogous to Blom and Gumperz's metaphorical switching. What are the social factors that go along with monitoring black? Some examples were parodying the speech of quoted persons to indicate their social characteristics. [6] On other occasions, speakers might be alluding to shared ethnic identity.

Many black public figures like Dick Gregory and Bobby Seale are skilled at these allusions to ethnic identity through "monitoring black. "[7] On the other hand, such allusions are common in everyday discourse, according to Kernan (30), and Gumperz has located instances in recordings made by a black-community worker of interaction between his wife and teen-age boys, for instance:

> You can tell me how your mother worked twenty hours a day and I can sit here and cry. I mean I can cry and I can feel for you. But as long as I don't get up and make certain that I and my children don't go through the same, I ain't did nothin' for you, brother. That's what I'm talking about. (19)

In speakers of Hawaiian pidgin, systematic register variation occurs between features of pidgin phonology, syntax, lexicon, and intonation and those features of Standard English known to the speaker, with social inputs such as age of addressee, relative status, familiarity, sex difference, and whether the addressee is an islander or mainlander. But within this registral variation, reference to shared, personal island experience even in a formal mainland setting can bring about style shift towards pidgin (42).

In a tape of Chicano bilingual interaction analyzed by Gumperz and Hernandez (19), loan words, exclamations, and sentence connectors were used as allusions to ethnic identity. These superficial items might even appear in relatively monitored speeches, such as political interaction. But in informal interaction where the speakers have no values deriding language switching, the bulk of the switching consists of changes in whole sentences or clauses underlying them. These code shifts have a social meaning similar to marking or style shifting in dialect variation. They can, for example, allude to ethnic identity, and depending on context carry special meanings of confidentiality or personal involvement. In these cases the switching is often quite unconscious and affects a deeper level in the sentence production process. In dialect style shifting, the parallel between these superficial and deep shifts would be the contrast between the isolated use of single features like be or exclamations and lexical items compared to more pervasive changes in paralinguistic and phonological features affecting longer units of discourse.

Labov has commented that if a speaker masters a fully consistent standard register, he may be unable to switch to the vernacular except through the use of markers whose frequency is not like that in an unmarked vernacular. He loses his fine sense of context-defined inherent variation. In some of the black monitoring observed by Kernan, forms were used that were caricatures and do not occur in any vernacular style.

The notion of marking or foregrounding information has been formally developed by Geoghegan (15). He has found, in working on alternations in address forms, that one can identify a regular, expected, reportable, unmarked form which is predictable from social features such as setting, age, rank, sex, and so on. This would correspond to register or situational or unmarked style as used above. Register does not carry meaning because it is predictable from known social features. Deviations from the unmarked alternatives carry social information such as positive and negative affect, deference, and anger. Thus "marking" is the same as Gumperz's metaphorical switches (4). Kernan's "monitoring" carries information to the listener because it deviates from the speaker's usual style in that situation. In her examples the information concerned attitudes toward addressees or persons referred to or quoted. Since these changes in speech are often unconscious, they can only be studied from taped natural conversations, not from informant reports.

Sociolinguistic development. I hope it is clear from this discussion of registers, styles, marking, and monitoring that these concepts are still being developed and changed and that attention to them will be fundamental in any research on children's understanding of the social aspects of language. Since work has been largely on adults, we do not know at how young an age and under what social conditions it is possible for speakers to show register or style variability in their speech.

My guess is that the first social features that will appear are major setting and addressee contrasts, since we find very early that bilingual children change language according to locations and persons. Martin Edelman, for example, examined the relation between reports of the expected language for given settings and language dominance as judged by fluency in emitting isolated words in a particular language associated with a given setting. The children were Puerto Rican bilinguals in New York, six to twelve. The pattern did not change with age, merely the amount of English dominance. Children knew significantly more English words for education and religion, but not for family and home. [8] Church, school, and home are unambiguous settings, for which dominant language was reportable by the children.

In addition, when nursery school children role-play they often adopt consistent speech patterns in accordance with the social categories involved—mothers and babies, doctors, cowboys, teachers, puppets. These situational patterns are relatively stereotyped but do reveal quite early use of language with consistent feature changes. What we do not know is what features change and what social cues can be generalized beyond particular persons.

The instances we have observed of speech variation for intent may not be socially conventionalized in young children. One can only surmise how the metaphor they seem to express has been learned. For example, children will use infantilized style as a marker for

dependency needs, but it is not clear whether this style is in fact
drawn from the child's own earlier repertoire or is some stereotype
of infant's speech. I have heard children of four years use telegraphic
sentences to a foreigner just learning English and thought it an imitation
but Eurwen Price reports that four-year-old English monolinguals in
a Welsh nursery school who assumed the Welsh teachers knew no
English spontaneously spoke telegraphically, e. g. , "Me cars now"
(44:34), yet they clearly had not heard such speech from the fully
bilingual teachers. The most striking feature of these style shifts
is that they are transitory and that within a given conversation they
may merely mark the onset before reversion to unmarked style.

We know that consistent code changes in second languages
can be learned early very rapidly. Edward Hernandez, in Berkeley,
has been studying a Chicano monolingual of three who became relatively bilingual within six months from nursery school exposure,
though his English at that time was considerably simpler than his
Spanish. We do not know how early or under what social conditions
completely consistent control over the situational selection of two
social dialects can be mastered. Part of the problem is that we know
relatively little about the linguistic features of such competence.
Greenlee, who observed bilingual five-year-olds, commented that
they already had learned not to speak Spanish before outsiders, but
that in her small sample of their own interaction there were code
shifts for marking emphasis, indicating addressee, and quoting (16).

Stylistic consistency. In the more formal types of situations,
bilinguals can learn relatively separated codes. Even metaphorical
switching tends to be at fairly high syntactic nodes if both lexical
alternatives are available to the speaker (i. e. , he doesn't have to use
vocabulary from one variety since he lacks words). Some bilinguals
even have a range of formal to informal styles in both codes (18).

One of the major differences between the variation found in
most bilinguals and in speakers with forms from various social
dialects has been argued by Kernan (30). She points out that there
is a lack of co-occurrence restrictions, or stylistic consistency,
in the samples of black speech. One changes register, or monitors,
by increasing or decreasing the frequency of certain variables, sometimes categorically. But if one examines the variables which show

stylistic variation, one finds the variants side by side. For example, "She has a morning class and a afternoon class, and she have their name taped down on a piece of cardboard" (30:52). She found the same variation in preschoolers: "They seen the bird, saw the ducks." For these reasons, she does not think that standard variants are dialect borrowings, but rather that they are integral to the dialect.

Labov, who has examined both individual and group styles in teen-age and adult Harlem speakers, has been impressed by the inconsistency of their formal style features, especially in the formal test situations typical of schools. "Whenever a subordinate dialect is in contact with a superordinate dialect, answers given in any formal test situation will shift from the subordinate towards the superordinate in an irregular and unsystematic manner" (37). Claudia Kernan also found, in classroom correction tests, that students had no stable notions of what the standard alternative was among the alternatives in their repertoire. Labov, McKay, Henrie, Kernan, and indeed everyone who has collected considerable samples of speech of dialect speakers have found that the full range of most standard forms will appear some time in their speech. That is, the problem of standard speech is in most cases not that the form is outside the repertoire but that the speaker cannot maintain a consistent choice of standard alternatives and not make slips. There is inadequate co-occurrence restriction between the standard forms whether they are dialect borrowings or not (59).

This is what we would expect if in fact the features that standard speakers use to identify standard and nonstandard speech are often used for metaphorical signalling by nonstandard speakers. They may hear a higher density of standard features as carrying a particular connotation in a given situation. But some features are not varied for this kind of meaning, and since various combinations of features co-occur there is no strong sense that any consistent style is required. In addition, there is considerable "inherent variation" according to Labov's work, which may not carry any connotations at all. In Standard English this inherent variation is not heard as marking the speaker as incompetent in Standard English, but since in any nonstandard English the variation includes features which are criterial to listeners' judgments of standardness, it appears to be socially inconsistent to outsiders.

In advising parents who rear bilingual children it is usual to point out that they should maintain consistency of speaker, occasion, and setting so that the child can be aided in predicting which form to use. But in the case of any nonstandard English the great bulk of the informal styles heard in the community by children contain a high degree of variability between standard and nonstandard features, since the variability is inherent in the dialect. A child who is to maintain a consistent choice of the standard alternative must mark it categorically in his storage, or at least have some linkages between forms which will make sequential occurrence of standard forms seem normal for him. If the child heard pure standard or nonstandard forms, this learning would not be a problem. He would learn the standard style as a second language with as brief and trivial interference as we normally find in immigrant children.[9] But this is not what he hears. He hears highly variable speech lacking in cooccurrence restrictions or predictability from segment to segment, at least at the grammatical level. Small wonder that many speakers are very uncertain as to which is standard and cannot do classroom correction tests comfortably.[10]

This line of thinking leads me to an outlandish proposal. If the problem is to identify "pure styles" and to store them with sufficient separateness to permit stylistic consistency, might it not be appropriate to help identify them by using "monitoring styles" of a sort, by having children role-play, parody, or use narrative styles in which a relatively extreme nonstandard without inherent variation in key features might seem appropriate and the other children could call them on failures? The converse would of course be role-playing a journalist, doctor, legislator, and so on, in Standard English grammar. The social appropriateness of such a move in a school might very well be questioned by parents who believe the school is the place for Standard English, but such games might enhance maximum adeptness in style switching. There is of course some precedent for permitting and encouraging a range of styles in dramatic play, even in school. In addition, there may be community tradition for such uses, as in the black speech act called "marking" (30) which parodies speech.

In courses helping adolescents to master register changes, Waterhouse (55) has found that even students who did not speak Standard English consistently were as a group critical of press releases in a role-played press conference if they contained non-standard features like copula deletion. The group itself, without pressure from the teacher, exerted constraints on role-players to keep a consistent register. The method saves the actor from being teased about speaking Standard English and potentially may be transferred to situations where the teacher is not present.

The practice of giving students drills in Standard English, which has developed in some schools, is based on the assumption that the variants do not exist in their repertoire. It also assumes that there may be massive problems of failure of communication. But studies of social dialects in fact show the frequency of non-standard forms to be small but socially important because of prejudice against nonstandard speakers. Where the standard variants exist in the child's repertoire already, and where some already are markers of social meaning, the teacher has a special objective quite different from that of basic second-language learning. The teacher needs to find the most effective way to give a child training in situational switching which will allow him to use the forms consistently in writing and in speech situations where he may be affected by fatigue, fear, and by concentration on the content of what he is saying. That seems to be what parents want to happen.

If a child is forced to speak only Standard English, he is robbed of an essential rhetorical tool. An example from Gumperz and Hernandez (19) illustrates deliberate use of style shifting:

> Student (reading from an autobiographical essay): This
> lady didn't have no sense.
> Teacher: What would be another way of saying that sentence?
> Student: She didn't have any sense. But not this lady; she
> didn't have no sense.

The child who is bilingual or speaks a nonstandard variant has style variation available which signals social meaning which may be unexpressible in Standard English. Where these meanings have analogues in style shifts within Standard English the teacher who is able to understand the child's intent can view it as part of his task to enlarge his own and the child's repertoire to include several ways of signalling these meanings, depending on the audience.

Comprehension of features. Interpretation of studies of the possibilities of variation in produced speech requires better evidence on what features children can hear. Because of the evidence that many variants occur freely if unpredictably in children's output, it is sometimes assumed that all children understand all features of Standard English. Jane Torrey's work (52) using comprehension tests such as choice of pictures is a model for studying these problems. She found that sibilant suffixes had markedly different probabilities of being understood or produced, depending on their grammatical functions. Almost all the black children in her Harlem sample understood a plural suffix and produced it regularly, almost none understood or produced a verb suffix marking number, as in "the cat scratches," vs. "the cats scratch," and about half understood and produced the copula, the possessive, and the verb suffix denoting tense, as in "the boy shut the door" vs. "the boy shuts the door." Torrey has not reported the performances of children who usually hear Standard English to see if some developmental factors are present. This study, of course, isolates the features from contextual redundancy by selecting sentences in which only the suffix must be the cue, as one must to discover whether a particular linguistic cue can be interpreted alone.

The kind of evidence that Labov, Kernan, Baratz, and others have obtained, showing that in imitation tasks children translate into their own dialect, may be insufficient indication of comprehension of particular features, since the sentences contain redundancy. For example, Baratz (1) found that white children translated "It's some toys out there" into "There are some toys out there," and black children often did the reverse. But this does not indicate that either group "understood" the first words, rather that the rest of the utterance made obligatory this form in their output. Error analysis of imitation materials with less redundancy would discover what syntactic and morphological features are employed. Torrey's findings are not inconsistent with the important fact that in everyday situations most Standard English may be intelligible grammatically to all black lower-class children, since in many situations language is redundant. [11]

A recent study by Weener (58) attempted to separate phonology from whatever semantic and syntactic sequential probabilities

are tested by memory for "orders of approximation" to English
by six- and seven-year-olds. From the standpoint of syntactic
differences, this method gives rather gross results and is unlikely
to be sensitive to whatever syntactic differences occur in the formal
output of lower-class black and middle-class white informants. The
interesting finding in this study was that when asked to remember
these strings of words, the lower-class black children and middle-
class whites did equally well with the materials read by a middle-
class speaker, but the whites had trouble remembering the same
materials read by a black speaker. That is, just as we might expect
on social grounds, black children have more exposure to middle-
class white phonology and can interpret it more easily than the suburban Detroit white children could interpret southern black speech. [12]

The Weener results remind us that the critical factors in
adjusting to phonological differences, as in adjusting to "foreign
accents," is likely to be experience and attitude toward the speaker.
Studies of the mutual intelligibility of speakers in varieties of social
settings allowing for both differences in contacts and in types of
speech exposure and for differences in social attitudes towards the
other group would inform us about factors causing changes in intelligibility in our pluralistic society. These studies need to focus
on comprehension as such, not output measures like the cloze
procedure, and it would be helpful if they would distinguish fine-
grained feature interpretation (as of the plural marker in Torrey's
work) from grosser referential intelligibility and the understanding
of allusion and metaphor.

One of the most significant findings in Kernan's work and in
recent studies of John Gumperz is that there is considerable informational or connotative content in choice among referential equivalents in the speaker's repertoire. A full competence in compre-
hending the speech of others includes these social interpretations.
So far, most research on information-transmission has been focused
on shapes, colors, and locations rather than on the equally systematic communication of hostility, affection, and deference. It is possible that the latter matters are of greater practical significance—
for example, in the classroom where teacher and pupil need to communicate respect for each other. If teachers cannot understand
when a pupil makes a conciliatory move, for instance, disaster could
follow.

Subjective reaction tests. Along with studies of comprehension, we need more information about children's attitudes towards speech varieties and their sense of norms of register and style. There have been numerous studies in which people rate voices out of context (except of topic) by Labov (34, 37), Tucker and Lambert (54), and Williams (57), for example. Such ratings necessarily tend to be of people or categories of people, since this is all the information the listeners can discover. It turns out to be the case, when specific features used in ratings are examined, that listeners tend to give "categorical" judgements, as Labov first pointed out. They will judge intelligence, ambition, and honesty just from "accent." They do not react to frequencies reliably but, as June McKay (40) has suggested, tend to pick out the "lowest" ranked social feature, even if it is rare, as an indicator of the speaker's social ranking—provided, of course, it is not contextually accounted for as "marking," such as parody, irony, humor. Williams has found that teachers tend to judge race from a few features. The work of Triandis, Loh, and Levin (53) and Lambert (39) implies that teachers will then treat the children by their group stereotype. From a practical standpoint, knowing which features are perceptually critical might help those who aim at giving the children the option of choosing when to be ethnically identifiable from phonology.

One of the fundamental ideas in sociolinguistics, as emphasized earlier, is that speech in fact and in its norms is context sensitive. We accept baby talk to infants but not to adolescents. As a measure of children's development of style norms, judgments of the sort just discussed need to be made where the social context is made clear in some way. It remains to be seen how children react to anomalies—by laughter, criticism, imitation perhaps. Children as young as five will criticize others who are doing role-playing for using the wrong terminology for the role, e.g., "You can't say 'honey'; you're the baby." Such studies are the judgmental analogue of the role-playing method of studying actually produced style and register changes, and the two kinds of studies should be paired to permit study of the extent to which judgments are finer than ability to produce the forms critical to the judgments. Labov (35) has found that by mid-teens speakers who did not themselves produce the most formal alternatives in New York phonology shared the opinion of the rest of the population on what variants were socially higher.

Claudia Kernan has commented that certain genres of folk
literature, such as songs, poetry, and narratives would be ludicrous
in Standard English, and Labov (34) found that childhood rhymes
often forced use of the most casual vernacular. It would be of great
value to know how sensitive are children to these social co-occurrence constraints, especially on genres brought into use from outside the school to enlarge the children's fluency in the classroom.
If they react to some kinds of performances as sounding wrong in
Standard English, or vice versa—if some require Standard English—
then efforts by the teacher to mismatch these types of discourse
with the wrong style may make the children uncomfortable and silent.
For these reasons studies of judgments may help guide teachers toward
culturally appropriate varieties of language.

<u>Functions of language.</u> One of the major issues that has come
to the fore in sociolinguistics and in applied work in education has
been the question of varieties of language function. Bernstein (3)
has pointed out that in England, middle-class parents train children
in a considerable amount of explicitness about referents, as though
they were talking to a stranger or blind person and no shared assumptions obtained. The result of this training (possibly through
the use of known-answer question drills) is that children perform
verbal tasks very well in test situations with minimal verbal stimulation. The difference in stress on overelaboration of detail vs.
terseness of description, based on shared assumptions, shows up in
a variety of studies. Hawkins (22) found that lower-class English
children described pictures with many "exophoric" pronouns, which
required that the listener see the picture, as indeed he did. Middle-
class pupils elaborated nouns and adjectives which specified information the examiner must already have known from seeing the picture.
Williams and Naremore (58) found that when children were asked to
be specific, class differences disappeared. But when terse questions
were asked, the middle-class children assumed they should give
complicated elaborate answers and the lower class, that only
minimal necessary responses were needed. Labov has cited examples illustrating the bewilderment of a child taken into a room by a
tester and told to "say what is in front of you" when both the tester and
the child could see quite well what it was.

The implication, of course, is that children may have learned that the function of such communication is to convey information.

If they have not been brought up on "known-answer" questions and taught to display their vocabulary and disregard whether the hearer knows the information, they may not understand the intent of such questions.

Claudia Kernan described such an incident during her study of the speech of Oakland black youngsters. She asked one child, "Where do you live?" and got a vague answer, "Over there," with a vaguely waved thumb. Shortly after, her husband asked the same question. The answer he got was, "You go down the stairs, turn left, walk three blocks..." What was the difference? Her husband had never been to the child's house— but she had picked the child up there.

Social-class differences in transmission of referential information may be a function of "set." If so, they can be easily changed by instruction or brief training. Studies by Cowan (10), Coulthard and Robinson (9), and Robinson (47) suggest that they are to some degree the effects of socially different ways of viewing the function of the act asked of them, or the "rules of the game." It is possible of course that skill in the particular domain of vocabulary or previous experience with materials might aid in such performances too.

Of considerable value to sociolinguistic work are studies of skills in language developed by children. For example, children often spontaneously play with sounds in the preschool years, and invent games transforming songs by simplified transformations like pig Latin. Where these skills become socially organized, they may develop into identifiable speech categories: nursery rhymes, songs, sounding, toasting, rifting, or rapping. These, in some cases, include oral traditions, knowledge of which is part of the developing competence of children. These may include not only general stylistic features but sequential rules. Children's skill is repeatedly evaluated by peers and highly appreciated. Houston (25) has even argued that in the rural poor that she studied, lack of toys resulted in more storytelling, language games, and placing more value on linguistic creativity, spontaneous narrative, and improvisation. She has shown that black lower-class children excel in story enrichment during retelling (26). Having recently seen a group of forty highly

educated adults and their children around a campfire without even
one person being skilled enough to carry on storytelling, I can believe education can produce cultural impoverishment!

Analysis of the structure of communication within communities could make us better able to draw events from children's
repertoire into the schools, better able to use them in testing competence to identify biologically based retardation, and better able
to understand how children interpret tasks they are given to do.
Within these speech categories, stylistic variations involving the
standard-nonstandard dimensions are important carriers of emotional significance. The ability to convey meaning depends on this
range of variation. We can expect that as children have contact
with members of varied social groups they will learn skill in a wider
range of speech categories, learn each other's oral traditions, and
learn devices for conveying information about social intent from
each other's dialects. We are already seeing these changes in
Berkeley children in integrated schools. Labov has pointed out that
the black children he studied valued language highly for cleverness
in besting others; this attitude, if fully understood by teachers, could,
he proposed, be a basis for enlarging language competence.

Needed Research

Testing milestones. Tests were developed in schools to
predict success in schools as they were constituted and to assess
achievements of the school. The need to compare the achievements
of school entities and to pass the blame for failures onto the child
probably will unfortunately guarantee that tests will continue to be
used even when they are not needed for fundamental diagnosis. Diagnosis of biologically based retardation, assuming we have means of
pedagogically treating such retardation, is an important function of
tests. If this is to be done well, there need to be tests of basic
milestones in competence which contain materials equated in dialect
and social biases for the populations to be tested.

In contrast to previous attempts at culture-free testing,
sociolinguistic research gives hope of finding how to create communicative settings, tasks, language, and scoring criteria that are
fully compatible with the experience of the tested children and are

validated within their own social group in cases of fairly clear group
differences. Of course, ethnic and class categories do not bound
homogeneous groups, so it is not clear in a diverse classroom which
one it is appropriate to choose from a package of tests labeled lower-
class black, middle-class black, Chicano, and so on. But at least
such a pluralistic set might take us beyond the current middle-class-
white package!

As an example of the improvements of testing and teaching
materials which might be gained from a realistic orientation to children's language use, we might cite the weaknesses of reading work-
books and tests. Items which rest on "comparing initial sound" or
"rhyming words" depend on the probabilities that children will produce a very specific item of vocabulary for a given picture. They
don't work as teaching materials or as valid tests unless the children
do in fact "mediate" with these vocabulary items. Sensitive teachers
have noticed repeatedly that a large proportion of these items do not
elicit the expected names. The differences may be even larger where
environmental and social differences exist. Such items are useless
for teaching or testing without specific individual tutoring. Another
example is the section in reading-recognition tests of word lists
which are to be matched to pictures. Even if the words are read
aloud, the items in some cases cannot be matched. But in this situation children rely on a single mediated name of the picture more than
adults do. Probably such tests are often not tests of reading. In
paragraph comprehension items, the syntax and content is often such
that even if it were read aloud the child could not understand it. Such
a test is not a pure test of reading skill. The evidence that children
speaking social dialects cannot read may be largely based on invalid
measures of reading ability. Of course, the effects of this evidence
may be self-fulfilling if teachers believe dialect speakers have trouble
learning to read.

Speech variation. We need much more work on the social
conditions which alter the frequency of social variants in speech. We
need work with children to see what are the social factors which increase and decrease ethnic identity markers in their speech at different ages. [13] It is not clear whether the monitoring of ethnic solidarity which Kernan describes has parallels in social categories
like "working class" where there are no sharp socially defined

boundaries. But there probably are parallels in all groups to the increase in vernacular usage under excitement that Labov has found.

Wider target populations. We need to extend sociolinguistic
work to a wider variety of regions and groups. The problems of
urban schools have for practical reasons led to lower-class black,
Puerto Rican, and Chicano groups being at the focus of recent work.
However, developmental sociolinguistics is appropriate to any child;
upper-class children, both black and white, have stylistic variation
in their speech, too, and can be studied to gain basic information
about age changes in the structure and function of speech variation.
Any groups speaking nonstandard English are equally appropriate for
the study of the relations between standard and nonstandard; areas of
regional migration allow for group identity-marking through speech
variables (e. g. , migrants from Appalachia in Detroit). Since the
social and the linguistic factors are slightly different in each of these
groups, better generalizations about basic processes would be available if the range of groups studied was extended. There is a practical
factor; such work is always contingent on collaboration or principal
direction by ingroup members.

Code-switching training. We need to explore teaching
methods for increasing competence in code switching and to find out
the ages at which different methods are suitable for teaching. At
present, unfortunately, most research on second-language learning
has been so atheoretical and ad hoc that we know very little of basic
relevance to questions of how different features of language can be
learned. Role-playing and developing of tasks with appropriate
registers that the children themselves recognize and reinforce (e. g. ,
Waterhouse) are examples of possible methods to use. It is not
clear when formal instruction, drills, individual tutoring, peer
group learning, and teaching by older children from the same social
group might be most effective. How does one learn appropriate
frequencies where there is inherent variation vs. the learning of
categorical features ?

One of the problems in suggesting changes in educational
methods is the lack of close study of actual classroom interaction.
Teachers are not conscious of the methods they use. Tapes and
videotapes can provide a way to locate the effective features of

current methods, methods chosen post hoc as most effective, or methods used in experimental studies. Since communication is not merely verbal, videotapes may considerably enrich our ability to interpret what happens in the classroom.

Comprehension. We need far more studies like Torrey's, exploring fully the range of comprehension of specific features of various types of English for various types of listeners. It would be of value to know whether teachers understand their pupils, for example, in terms of specific grammatical features.

Ethnography of literacy. We need to explore the place of reading and writing in the linguistic life of the child. Labov found Harlem teenagers who did not know if their close friends were literate. Literacy was not necessary for the activities of the boys. Exploration of children's values about language might lead to ways of devising uses of language and, specifically, reading for beginners that are relevant to interests they already have; later one hopes that new interests arising from what they read will carry them further.

It is not clear how important type of language is in reading; adults frequently have strong attitudes that only Standard English is appropriate for reading. Navahos were for many years not especially receptive to efforts to make a written language of Navaho; English is for writing. Schools, of course, are not immune from adult community pressures; if it could be shown that literacy in the vernacular clearly aids literacy in Standard English, then the adults might be persuadable. Indeed, in community-controlled Navaho schools vernacular education and vernacular literacy have spurted recently.

Learning to read. We need to explore in detail the structural relations between the child's oral comprehension skills, his speech, and reading and writing. I know of no evidence that learning to understand written language (as contrasted with reading aloud) is generally affected by the child's dialect of English. In a recent study of third-graders, Melmed asked them to read sentences containing key items, and then to choose the appropriate picture. For example, a sentence might be, "I have six cats," or "He fell and tore his pants," and the picture items contrasted six-sick and tore-toe. Although in reading aloud, they used black English phonology in 28 percent of the pairs, they chose the wrong picture in only 5.4 percent of cases for the same pairs. Thus their comprehension was not affected by the homonyms. Although black and white pupils differed significantly in both phonetic output and phonological discrimination in listening, they did not differ in oral and silent reading comprehension tests built around the hypothesis of homonym confusion.

We might expect there would be problems in spelling to the extent that spelling relies on phonological rather than visual memory. Phonological features like l-lessness and consonant cluster simplification affected auditory discrimination in Melmed's subjects and could affect the information they had stored about their aurally-learned vocabulary. These items will have to be acquired by rote, visual, whole-word learning rather than completely rule-governed production, like knife and would.

Labov has pointed out that the underlying form is in many cases the same for standard and nonstandard words and only deletion rules apply. All children need to learn the relation between deletion and the spelled form; all English speakers learn there is no one-to-one relation between spelling to sound and to depend to some extent on some sight vocabulary or contextual guessing. In other parts of the world where children speak a highly valued local dialect, learning to read a standard is no problem.

Two directions of research need exploration. One might be to explore the relation between common features in varieties of Standard English and the child's comprehension and production. We could test the child's specific feature knowledge as Torrey and Melmed have done and build materials related in systematic ways to this knowledge. I am not persuaded that social or regional dialects are related to having difficulties decoding inflectional suffixes in listening or reading. Labov has evidence that white boys as well as blacks do not readily interpret the -ed suffix in reading as a past tense indicator, especially in early adolescence and preadolescence. In cases where such grammatical features are not readily understood, they may not normally interfere with comprehension, given the redundancy of most texts, but they clearly are important in marginal cases and in writing. Specific instructional materials could focus on these issues.

A second possibility would be better investigation of the issues of teaching comprehension apart from reading aloud (which has to be unlearned later anyway). If part of the problem is the social one of punishment by teachers who do not recognize when speech is the child's equivalent of what is written, the teacher's judgment either must be changed or bypassed. In effect one would teach children to decode written symbols to their meanings via the path of hearing spoken words with what they read at first. Children would of course engage in sotto voce articulation while reading but they would not be directly punished or rewarded by the teacher for this vocal behavior.

Joan Baratz and William Stewart have proposed that children will learn to read faster if the grammatical structures used in primers are derived from their own output (2) or are structurally similar. Such materials could of course be prepared by teachers from stories told by the children with lexical normalization of spelling but not of syntax. We need detailed research with appropriate controls. With content and vocabulary controlled, does a child learn faster if the grammatical structures used come from his own output? What if they are like his most standard forms? His most nonstandard forms (as in the Baratz materials)? Variable, as verbatim materials would be? It is clear that different content, [14] different grammar but conventionalized orthography, different vocabulary and concept familiarity might all be at issue and should be studied separately. In these studies there needs to be knowledge of the spontaneous story-producing style of pupils, since a number of studies have shown relatively low frequencies of nonstandard variants and considerable variation between pupils.

Case histories of learning to read with details of teacher-child interaction might help us locate points of difficulty, identify over-generalization stages, and develop better theories of the reading process, and, more important, better teacher training methods. It is to be hoped that detailed recordings will be available of children's performance as they learn to read the Baratz-Stewart materials.

It is quite possible that the structural features of the materials in terms of dialect are not important in themselves, given that children understand most Standard English structures and that many

differences are superficial. Teachers and supervisors who have
worked in many schools with minority pupils complain that the fundamental problem is that many middle-class teachers do not believe
that poor children, especially nonstandard speakers, can easily
learn to read. I could list a variety of types of observed behavior
toward lower-class children that could be the kinds of discouraging
cues that children emotionally understand or that more directly reduce the opportunity of the child to learn (19). There are dramatic
examples of teachers who have brought below-average IQ slum children to the third-grade level in reading while in first grade. We need
to identify and videotape the teaching methods of such teachers and
locate by experiment what are the key features of their methods, and
then teach with these videotapes.

If the Baratz-Stewart materials do result in faster learning,
one reason might be their effects on teacher attitudes. If teachers believe the child has a language and a culture of his own that they themselves do not fully understand, they are less likely to treat him as
"deficient." This may be a key difference in attitudes toward immigrant children and native ethnic minorities. One cannot teach this
lesson by exhortation; teachers who begin to realize that the children know something they don't know may respect the children more.
Therefore, research on the effects of teaching materials should include work on some sensitive indices (perhaps of the Lambert speech-
guise type) of changes in social attitudes towards dialect speakers on
the part of teachers and administrators.

Judgments. We need more research on the development of
children's subjective reactions to language. How early, and by what
features, do they identify categories of speakers? Are there sex
differences, as so many studies have suggested, in the direction of
greater preference for and use of formal variants in girls? How early
can children, depending on their social experience, differentiate the
Standard English of various ethnic groups? How do they evaluate it?

Speech norms. How do norms of appropriateness of speech
variables to situation and meaning develop? While we know that
children produce "baby-talk intonation" to babies when they are no
more than twenty months old, we do not know how soon they react
to misplaced baby talk as anomalous, or judge meanings on the basis
of speech variables.

Teacher training. We need to explore for practical as well
as theoretical reasons ways of training teachers to understand nonstandard speech. Gumperz has made two proposals along these lines.
One is that systematic nonstandard dialects be taught as second languages to teachers. The purpose would not be that the teachers produce these forms in the classroom, but that by learning them as
"second languages" teachers would be brought to recognize their
systematic character and their variability and to understand how they
convey meaning. I believe also, from work on second-language teaching, that there might be a very strong attitudinal impact on the teachers.
Learning a second language through methods of close imitation of
native speakers is a dramatic personal experience. Success in imitation (within the range of adult articulatory rigidity) might be a sensitive measure of intergroup attitudes.

The second method proposed by Gumperz would be similar
to some "sensitivity training" methods. Taped interaction between
two groups of pupils or of teachers and pupils would be selected to
show misunderstanding of the meaning of linguistic features and/ or
stylistic variation. For instance, suppose an excited child used more
dialect features and the teacher heard these as hostile. Two groups
of listeners could separately be asked to make judgments about the
social meaning of each utterance. The differences in these judgments
would bring to light systems of meaning that are not the same in the two
groups and allow some learning about humor, irony, and insult. The
significance of pitch changes, of marking of allusions, could begin to
be apparent to trainees.

Teacher vernacular. We need to know more about the impact
on children's attitudes of the teacher's use of the vernacular in the
classroom. Some programs are already systematically teaching, for
instance, "Pocho" to teachers. [15] In the case of nonstandard black
features, Kernan's work suggests that nonstandard features out of
context may have implications of ridicule, as for example if nonstandard grammar is used without associated phonological and paralinguistic features. Yet Baratz's method of teaching reading implies
that the teacher knows how to speak nonstandard English appropriately.

Style consistency. We need to know how stylistic consistency
can be learned, since children hear speech which is variable at home

and among their friends. A good deal needs to be known about whether
roleplaying can increase consistency, and whether a bipolar contrast
between two relatively consistent "codes" is required or optimal for
developing separately stored features, lexically, phonologically, and
syntactically. The practical implications of more work on the learning of style rules are considerable.

Linguistic vs. social emphasis. Teacher training materials
emphasizing formal categorial linguistic differences could have some
negative effects on attitudes and educational practices. The formal
differences between regional and social dialects are trivial and superficial in terms of the basic goals of the schools. The real educational
problems may lie in the structure of the school and the operating
classroom, in failures of social communication in the classroom, in
strong beliefs about the knowledge, abilities, and attributes of speakers
judged by their regional or social dialect (53). If teachers mistakenly
conclude that dialects are related to thought processes, that nonstandard
speakers are like new immigrants and lack Standard English in their
repertoire, or that all members of a given ethnic group are alike and
have the same range of linguistic skills, then linguistically oriented
materials will have reinforced social stereotypes and diverted attention from the real failures of the schools. For these reasons a
high priority research area should be ethnography of classroom
communication, and training about social dialects should include a
sociolinguistic rather than formal perspective.

Glossary

Categorial shifting. Definition of a register, code, or style contrast
in terms of presence or absence rather than relative frequency of speech features.

Co-occurrence constraints. Rules governing the predictability of
linguistic features of one part of an utterance from another
part, to produce consistency of style or code.

Copula deletion. Absence of is or are in speech in some contexts in
black English in environments where contraction is possible,
according to specific conditioning factors in the linguistic and
semantic context.

Exophoric pronouns. Pronouns with an extralinguistic "antecedent".

Inherent variation. Variable frequency of certain speech features like contraction, consonant deletions, syllable deletions contingent on linguistic and social determinants.

Lexical alternatives. Different vocabulary identical in reference but varying with code or register, e.g., bathroom vs. head.

Metaphorical switching. Style changes which have social meanings derived from the similar register or situational variation, e.g., baby talk has a metaphorical meaning that the addressee is loved like a baby or that the speaker is a baby.

Monitoring. Labov: Self-conciousness about speaking, which alters the relative frequencies of socially stigmatized or valued features. Kernan: Speech styles with ethnic identity allusions.

Paralinguistic. Concerning features outside of the conventional linguistic channel, e.g., pitch, rate, loudness, nonspeech vocalizations like laughter and coughs.

Phonology. The sound system of a language or dialect.

Register. (See Unmarked register.)

Relativization. Creation of a relative clause out of two independent predications.

Speech acts. Cultural units in interaction, such as greetings, jokes, requests, demands, praise.

Speech episode. Unit in ongoing interaction demarcated by change in participants, locus, activity, topic, or focus of attention.

Speech event. Cultural unit involving patterned sequences of speech acts, such as a church service, a class, a telephone conversation, a bridge game, storytelling.

Surface structure. The word or sound sequence of a sentence as uttered in contrast to the underlying meaning or the semantic and grammatical relations the surface represents.

Syntactic nodes. In phrase-structure parsing of a sentence into constituents, nodes are superordinate units which are realized by units closer to the surface. A predicate or verb phrase is a higher node than a preposition or noun.

Unmarked register. The normal, usual speech pattern for a given constellation of setting, participants, and topic.

NOTES

The ideas in this paper have been influenced considerably by discussions with John Gumperz to whom I have not always given due
credit. Participants in the conference on Social Dialect Studies in
Educational Research held at the Center for Applied Linguistics,
October 1969, for which this paper was prepared as "Social Dialects
in Developmental Sociolinguistics", will find that many suggestions
made and ideas expressed during the discussion have been incorporated here in the interests of preserving them. They were so much
group products that I am not sure how to attribute them. Claudia
Kernan's remarks as discussant particularly influenced me. I have
received many insightful suggestions about primary school classroom problems from teachers and former teachers, including particularly Eileen Green, Louisa Lewis, Herbert Kohl, Mary Jamieson,
and Mary Suzuki.

[1] For theoretical discussions of communicative competence,
see Hymes (28). For some research suggestions regarding developmental sociolinguistics, see Slobin (49). The term sociolinguistic
rather than communicative is used here to exclude the many forms
of skill in nonlinguistic communication which also undergo development and show up at an earlier age than conventional linguistic
communication.

[2] With biological abnormalities we include birth damage,
damage arising from malnutrition in gestation or infancy, damage
from malnutrition of the maternal grandmother during pregnancy,
damage from chronic illnesses, as well as genetically based brain
deficiencies. From a social engineering standpoint it is important
of course to differentiate these sources since something can be done
about the systematic violence to the poor which results in malnutrition, illness, and the higher incidence of birth damage.

[3] Stewart (51) in particular has argued strongly that the
number and importance of grammatical differences between nonstandard black English and any form of standard English is greater,
for historical reasons, than other social dialect differences.

[4] For further discussion of these points see Hymes (27) and
Ervin-Tripp (12). The furthest development of the importance of
repertoire in social meaning has been in the work of John Gumperz
(4, 17, 18).

[5] A striking finding of this study was that speakers valued the local vernacular highly and <u>could not believe</u> that they employed Standard Norwegian words and features for certain kinds of speech. The relation between the vernacular and a standard has been an educational issue in many parts of the world; studies in other places might often be relevant to developmental issues in the United States.

[6] A vivid example of completely unconscious marking which was not a direct imitation appeared in Labov's study of Lower East Side New York speech (35:97). A Negro without ethnically distinctive speech told a story about a dangerous experience. In the dialogue he included, he represented his own speech in his typical unmarked casual style, but he also represented the speech of the person he feared, since that person was supposed to have threatened someone with a gun. This voice was rasping and rapid, with "country" southern Negro features. He later reported that the other person was—a Hungarian!

[7] An example from Bobby Seale, an expert at such monitoring, in a speech at a "Free Huey" rally: "If the United States government and the courts... did this they would have to choose black people from the black community to sit on their juries. They would have to choose some of them mothers who been working twenty years in Miss Ann's kitchen scrubbing floors like my mother done. They have to choose some of the hard-working fathers. They have to choose some of them brothers standing on the block out there wondering where they gonna git a gig!" In the discussion of press reports of the Black Panther Party, he says "the paper's going to call us thugs and hoodlums... but the brothers on the block... gonna say, them some out-of-sight thugs and hoodlums up there, and the brother on the block is going to say, who is these thugs and hoodlums. In fact, them dudes look just like me. In fact, I know John, George, Paul. In fact, I know Bobby Hutton. Hey, man, I know that dude, over there. Hey man, what you cats doin with them rods?" Voice quality and intonation change demarcates the quotation as well as the style shift apparent in a transcript (6). This monitoring style was found in a rally with a largely black audience but not in a radio interview on the same subject matter.

[8] The discrepancy between the children's report about neighborhood language, which they rated as predominantly Spanish, and their word-fluency scores, which were significantly higher in English for the task of naming objects in the neighborhood, illustrates the problems of using tests rather than recordings of natural conversation.

It is possible that most "doorstep conversations" common in the
Puerto Rican neighborhoods were in Spanish but that vocabulary for
nameable shops and objects was primarily English, and likewise that
considerable English was in fact used in conversations which speakers believed were in Spanish. John Gumperz (18) has particularly
emphasized the difference between questionnaire answers and actual
behavior.

[9]Here we distinguish immigrant children from children in
those bilingual communities where the same conditions of admixture
of English and other forms may obtain in some cases. Many instances
have been observed in which bilinguals cannot identify the language of
the provenance of a form because it is used in both their codes.

[10]Kernan developed a method for identifying when speakers
knew the "proper" standard form. She asked teenagers to correct
nonstandard sentences. She found that such forms as deleted copula,
negative inversion (can't nobody jump), "ain't" and "done" plus
participle, and hypercorrect verb suffix (they runs) were consistently identified, but the students were uncertain about many other forms.
Labov (37) has had the same results, showing that some forms are
stigmatized and are identified as nonstandard, but others are not.

> Six-year-old: She done ate up all of my potato chips.
> Mother: Done ate! She has...have ate up all my potato
> chips. (30)

[11]This statement may sound overoptimistic. There are many
registers outside of the everyday experience of most people. In the
more open enrollment in universities, there may be many students
encountering for the first time, with discouraging results, not only
new vocabulary and subject matter but also lecturers who use complex nominalizations and unusual types of sentence embeddings. The
assumption that syntactic learning ends in childhood is not socially
realistic, but there has been little systematic study of complex
registers.

[12]In studies which disconnect syntax from phonology, there
is a serious confounding because of the likelihood of some co-occurrence rules or rules of style consistency between the two levels. Nonstandard syntax with "standard" or media-announcer phonology is
bizarre and quite different in meaning from nonstandard syntax and
congruent phonology. In the same way, the standard syntax and stereotyped stage nonstandard phonology employed by Stern and Kieslar (50)
was so bizarre a combination that black children could not understand

it very well. In the Weener study the syntax had no clear identity and the black speaker's phonology was a natural formal reading style.

[13]In some features there is a slight increase during adolescence (37) and greater register effect. We can expect that the peer culture will alter norms and that the progress from childhood to adult status will be affected not only by increasing knowledge (in relation to which children become more like adults with respect to formal style), but also by strongly age-graded attitudes about in-group communication and by generational changes in norms that remain with the teen-agers when they are adults.

[14]Some primers have simply painted the faces of children for minority readers. A deeper change might entail using names and nicknames actually in use, culture content of interest to the children, but, most important, thematic cores that engage them. Teaching of minority folklore could have both properties of interest to ethnic identity and thematic relevance; on the other hand, folklore whose themes arise from social conditions which are critically different can be as irrelevant as Dick and Jane and become a historical study but not personally engaging.

At the Social Dialect Conference, it was pointed out that black children like the Five Chinese Brothers because they were rewarded for cleverness, which is highly valued in black culture. It was mentioned that Ping, about a duck lost from his flock on a Chinese junk, appealed to Navahos. Possibly the metaphor of the duck parallels the flock in Navaho reservation experience. At least, one should not assume that such superficial features as geographical location or skin color in pictures determine the power of materials to engage a child's interest. Verbal games and folklore known to the parents and community resource people who can help develop school materials are not only a direct source of educational content, they can be a springboard to creative parallels to draw on for themes, formal structure, or interactive motives.

[15]For instance, a current program for Chicano teachers at Sacramento State College.

REFERENCES

1. Baratz, Joan C. "A Bidialectal Task for Determining Language
        Proficiency in Economically Disadvantaged Negro Children."
        Child Development 40 (1969): 889-902.

2. Baratz, Joan C., and Shuy, Roger W., eds. Teaching Black
       Children to Read. Washington: Center for Applied Lin-
       guistics, 1969.
3. Bernstein, Basil. "A Socio-linguistic Approach to Socialization:
       With Some References to Educability." In Language and
       Poverty: Perspectives on a Theme, edited by Frederick
       Williams, pp. 25-61. Chicago: Markham Publishing Co.,
       1970.
4. Blom, J. P., and Gumperz, J. J. "Some Social Determinants of
       Verbal Behavior." Directions in Sociolinguistics, edited by
       J. J. Gumperz and D. Hymes. New York: Holt, Rinehart
       & Winston, 1972.
5. Blount, B. G. "Acquisition of Language by Luo Children." Lan-
       guage-Behavior Laboratory Working Paper No. 19. Berkeley:
       University of California, 1969.
6. Brooks, Sammie. "A Study of the Rhetorical Styles of Bobby
       Seale, Chairman of the Black Panther Party for Self-Defense."
       Term paper, Rhetoric 152, University of California, Berk-
       eley, 1971.
7. Brown, R., Cazden, C. B.; and Bellugi, U. "The Child's Gram-
       mar from I to III." In Minnesota Symposia for Child Psycho-
       logy, Vol. II, edited by J. P. Hill, pp. 28-73. Minneapolis:
       University of Minnesota Press, 1969.
8. Cazden, Courtney. "The Neglected Situation in Child Language
       Research and Education." In Language and Poverty: Perspec-
       tives on a Theme, edited by Frederick Williams, pp. 81-101.
       Chicago: Markham Publishing Co., 1970.
9. Coulthard, R. M., and Robinson, W. P. "The Structure of the
       Nominal Group and the Elaboratedness of Code." Language
       and Speech II, (1968): 234-50.
10. Cowan, P. "The Link between Cognitive Structure and Social
       Structure in Two-Child Verbal Interaction." Symposium
       presented at the Society for Research on Child Development
       meeting, 1967.
11. Edelman, M. "The Contextualization of Schoolchildren's Bilin-
       gualism." Bilingualism in the Barrio, edited by Joshua A.
       Fishman, Robert L. Cooper, Roxana Ma, et al., pp. 525-
       37. Final Report, Yeshiva University, Contract OEC-1-7-
       062817-0297, U. S. Department of Health, Education, and
       Welfare, 1968. [= Bloomington: Indiana University, Center
       for Research in Language Sciences, 1971.]

12. Ervin-Tripp, Susan M. "An Analysis of the Interaction of Language, Topic, and Listener." In "The Ethnography of Communication," edited by J. J. Gumperz and D. Hymes. American Anthropologist 66 (1964): 86-102. (Pt. 2, No. 6.)

13. _____ "Sociolinguistics." In Advances in Experimental Social Psychology, Vol. 4, edited by Leonard Berkowitz, pp. 91-165. New York: Academic Press, 1968.

14. Fischer, J. L. "Social Influences in the Choice of a Linguistic Variant." Word 14 (1958): 47-56.

15. Geoghegan, W. "The Use of Marking Rules in Semantic Systems." Language-Behavior Laboratory Working Paper No. 26. Berkeley: University of California, 1969.

16. Greenlee, Mel. "Rules for Code-Switching: A Pilot Study of Natural Conversation in Bilingual Children." Term paper, Rhetoric 260, University of California, Berkeley, 1971.

17. Gumperz, J. J. "Linguistic and Social Interaction in Two Communities." In "The Ethnography of Communication," edited by J. J. Gumperz and D. Hymes. American Anthropologist 66 (1964): 137-53. (Pt. 2, No. 6.)

18. _____ "On the Linguistic Markers of Bilingual Communication." In Problems of Bilingualism, edited by J. Macnamara, pp. 48-57. Journal of Social Issues 23 (1967): pt. 2, pp. 48-57.

19. Gumperz, J. J., and Hernandez, Edward. "Bilingualism, Bidialectalism, and Classroom Interaction." In Language in the Classroom, edited by C. Cazden. New York: Teacher's Press, in press.

20. Gumperz, J. J., and Hymes, D. "The Ethnography of Communication." American Anthropologist 66 (1964): pt. 2, no. 6.

21. _____ Directions in Sociolinguistics. New York: Holt, Rinehart & Winston, 1972.

22. Hawkins, P. R. "Social Class, the Nominal Group and Reference." Language and Speech 12 (1969): 125-35.

23. Heider, E. "Style and Effectiveness of Children's Verbal Communications within and between Social Classes." Ph.D. dissertation, Harvard University, 1969.

24. Henrie, S. N. "A Study of Verb Phrases Used by Five Year Old Nonstandard Negro English Speaking Children." Ph.D. dissertation, University of California, Berkeley, 1969.

25. Houston, Susan. "A Sociolinguistic Consideration of the Black English of Children in Northern Florida." Language 45 (1969): 599-607.

26. Houston, Susan. "Syntactic Complexity and Information Trans-
      mission in First Graders." Child Development, in press.
27. Hymes, D. "Toward Ethnographies of Communication." In "The
      Ethnography of Communication," edited by J. J. Gumperz and
      D. Hymes. American Anthropologist 66 (1964): 1-34. (Pt.
      2, No. 6.)
28. _____ On Communicative Competence. Conduct and Communica-
      tion, no. 4. Philadelphia: University of Pennsylvania Press,
      in press.
29. Jensen, A. R. "How Much Can We Boost IQ and Scholastic
      Achievement?" Harvard Educational Review 39 (1969): 1-124.
30. Kernan, Claudia M. "Language Behavior in a Black Urban
      Community." Monographs of the Language-Behavior Labo-
      ratory, no. 2. Berkeley: University of California, 1969.
31. Kernan, Keith. "The Acquisition of Language by Samoan Chil-
      dren." Language-Behavior Laboratory Working Paper No.
      21. Berkeley: University of California, 1969.
32. Kochman, Thomas. 'Rapping' in the Black Ghetto, Transactions
      (February 1969): 26-34.
33. Labov, W. "The Logic of Nonstandard English." In Language and
      Poverty: Perspectives on a Theme, edited by Frederick
      Williams, pp. 153-87. Chicago: Markham Publishing Co.,
      1970.
34. _____ The Social Stratification of English in New York City.
      Washington: Center for Applied Linguistics, 1966.
35. _____ "Stages in the Acquisition of Standard English." In
      Social Dialects and Language Learning, edited by Roger
      Shuy, pp. 77-103. Champaign, Ill.: National Council of
      Teachers of English, 1965.
36. _____ "The Study of Language in its Social Context." Studium
      Generale, in press.
37. Labov, W.; Cohen, P.; Robins, C.; and Lewis, J. A Study of
      the Non-Standard English of Negro and Puerto Rican
      Speakers in New York City. Final Report, OE-6-10-059.
      Columbia University, New York City, 1968.
38. Lenneberg, E. Biological Foundations of Language. New York:
      John Wiley & Sons, 1967.
39. Lambert, W. "A Social Psychology of Bilingualism." In Prob-
      lems of Bilingualism, edited by J. Macnamara. Journal of
      Social Issues 23 (1967): pt. 2, pp. 91-109.

40. McKay, June Rumery. "A Partial Analysis of a Variety of Non-standard Negro English." Ph. D. dissertation, University of California, Berkeley, 1969.

41. Melmed, Paul. "Black English Phonology: The Question of Reading Interference." Ph. D. dissertation, University of California, Berkeley, 1970.

42. Oishi, Jaynie, and Dorothy Kakimoto. "Pidgin and Pidgin Speakers." Term paper, Speech 164, University of California, Berkeley, 1967.

43. Osser, H.; Wang, M.; and Zaid, F. "The Young Child's Ability to Imitate and Comprehend Speech: A Comparison of Two Sub-cultural Groups." Child Development 40 (1969): 1063-75.

44. Price, Eurwen. "Early Bilingualism." In Towards Bilingualism, edited by C. J. Dodson, et al., p. 34. Welsh Studies in Education, vol. I, edited by Jack L. Williams. Cardiff: University of Wales Press, 1968.

45. Rainey, Mary. "Style-Switching in a Headstart Class." Language-Behavior Laboratory Working Paper No. 16. Berkeley: University of California, 1969.

46. Roberts, Elsa. "An Evaluation of Standardized Tests as Tools for the Measurement of Language Development." Unpublished paper. Cambridge, Mass: Language Research Foundation, 1971.

47. Robinson, W. P. "Social Factors and Language Development in Primary School Children." In Mechanisms in Child Language Development, edited by Renira Huxley and Elizabeth Ingram. London: Academic Press, 1971.

48. Shuy, R.; Wolfram, W.; and Riley, W. K. Linguistic Correlates of Social Stratification in Detroit Speech. Final Report, OE-6-1347, 1967.

49. Slobin, D. I., ed. A Field Manual for Cross-Cultural Study of the Acquisition of Communicative Competence. University of California, Berkeley, Associated Students' Bookstore, 1967.

50. Stern, Carolyn, and Keislar, E. An Experimental Investigation of the Use of Dialect vs. Standard English as a Language of Instruction. OEO Project IED 66-1-12, 1968.

51. Stewart, W. "Toward a History of American Negro Dialect." In Language and Poverty, edited by F. Williams, pp. 351-79. Chicago: Markham Publishing Co., 1970.

52. Torrey, Jane. "Teaching Standard English to Speakers of
     Other Dialects." Second International Congress of Applied
     Linguistics, Cambridge, England, 1969.
53. Triandis, H. D.; Loh, W. D.; and Levin, Leslie. "Race, Status,
     Quality of Spoken English, and Opinions about Civil Rights as
     Determinants of Interpersonal Attitudes." Journal of
     Personality and Social Psychology 3 (1966): 468-72.
54. Tucker, R., and Lambert, W. "White and Negro Listeners'
     Reactions to Various American-English Dialects." Social
     Forces 47 (1969): 463-68.
55. Waterhouse, J. "Report on a Neighborhood Youth Corps Summer
     Language Program, July 1-August 2, 1968." University of
     California, Berkeley. Mineographed.
56. Weener, P. D. "Social Dialect Differences and the Recall of
     Verbal Messages." Journal of Educational Psychology 60
     (1969): 194-99.
57. Williams, F. "Psychological Correlates of Speech Characteris-
     tics: On Sounding Disadvantaged." Journal of Speech and
     Hearing Research, in press.
58. Williams, F., and Naremore, Rita C. "On the Functional
     Analysis of Social Class Differences in Modes of Speech."
     Speech Monographs 36 (1969): 77-101.
59. Wolfram, W. Detroit Negro Speech. Washington: Center for
     Applied Linguistics, 1969.

17 | The Structure of Communicative Choice

Group therapy session:

Joe: Ken face it, you're a poor little rich kid.
Ken: Yes, Mommy. Thank you.

— Harvey Sacks Class Notes No. 11

Classroom scene:

Mrs. Tripp: Miss Hayashijima?
Student: Yes, sir.

Insult and humor must be based on agreement about the
underlying rules of speech and on the social meaning of linguistic
features. Linguistic selection is deeply enmeshed in the structure of
society; members can readily recognize and interpret socially codified deviations from the norm. While one can use sociolinguistic
data to learn about social structure, or to learn about linguistic rules
which otherwise defy analysis, it is the purpose of this essay to examine some aspects of sociolinguistic rules as a domain of structured behavior to be studied on its own terms.

The focus here will be on micro-sociolinguistics, the study
of the components of face-to-face interaction as they affect or are
affected by the formal structure of speech. These components may
include the personnel, the situation, the function of the interaction,
the topic, the message, and the channel. Many of the factors that
influence face-to-face communication are strongly affected by larger
events such as conquest, and official policies affecting immigration,
schooling, publication rights, employment, and housing. But macro-

sociolinguistic relationships can in fact contain diverse linguistic consequences. Studies which treat "language spoken" as a unitary variable, for instance, risk masking the phenomena of shifting, and of co-occurrence of features which have produced language change as a consequence of group contact. The dynamism of change requires both the larger and the detailed perspective. When diverse linguistic possibilities exist in the community, one can examine the structure of diversity both between and within individuals. Social contacts and their content obviously have a bearing on the range of diversity between individuals. In turn, an individual can allude to this existing range as a communicative device in his own individual repertoire. For example, in racially integrated schools from the first day of contact we have observed students using dialectal feature-shifting as an expressive device; their repertoire of communicative means has been enlarged. Communicative choice by an individual can be seen in terms of structured alternatives on a variety of time scales. At certain points in their life history people may make major changes in linguistic knowledge and commitments— for example at school entry, or when they emigrate. Within a shorter time span, we find that participation in speech events such as church services, commercial transactions, and social conversations may commit them to code or register changes, and so on down to smaller units like greetings and insults. These alternations are structured.

During the sixties, psycholinguists were persuaded that both verbal output and comprehension were guided by rules which allowed unique sentences to be produced and understood. Recently, performance or processing models are being developed, (Morton 1970, Morton and Smith 1971) to account for a variety of performances which depend on language, such as speech, verbal imitation, comprehension, and verbal memory. Various aspects of rehearsal, storage, and processing strategies have been studied from this perspective.

We have evidence in this essay to suggest that rules of verbal output and comprehension must be so written as to specify social features and the embedding of utterances in speech events and social contexts. The fact that rules of address involve discrete selections between these social features is encouraging, for it shows that the non-linguistic world of human action is structured and hence accessible to rules. Indeed, these sociolinguistic rules provide an approach to what that structure is, and lead us to non-arbitrary units.

Linguists have begun to find that some linguistic problems cannot be resolved without attention to the pragmatic features of situated discourse. We can assume that processing models for sentences are only a beginning. Sentence processing models translate the structural description of the linguist's grammar into a model of real-time events in a speaker or hearer; we can expect to find models of sociolinguistic processing bearing an analogous relation to sociolinguistic rules. We can also expect to see studies of the development of sociolinguistic competence in children (e.g. Slobin 1967) and migrants to new societies, and research on sociolinguistically deviant behavior. But the first step, of course, is to develop an extensive set of studies of sociolinguistic rules.

ALTERNATION RULES

American Rules of Address

A scene on a public street in the contemporary United States:

"What's your name, boy?" the policeman asked....
"Dr. Poussaint. I'm a physician...."
"What's your first name, boy?..."
"Alvin."
— Poussaint 1967:53

Anybody familiar with American address rules can tell us the feelings reported by Dr. Poussaint : "As my heart palpitated, I muttered in profound humiliation.... For the moment, my manhood had been ripped from me.... No amount of self-love could have salvaged my pride or preserved my integrity.... [I felt] self-hate." It is possible to specify quite precisely the rule employed by the policeman. Dr. Poussaint's overt, though coerced, acquiescence in a public insult through widely recognized rules of address is the source of his extreme emotion.

Brown and Ford (Hymes 1964) have done pioneering and ingenious research on forms of address in American English using as corpora American plays, observed usage in a Boston business firm, and reported usage of business executives. They found primarily FN (first name) reciprocation, or TLN (title plus last name) reciprocation. However, asymmetrical exchanges were found where there was age difference or occupational rank difference. Intimacy was related to the use of multiple names.

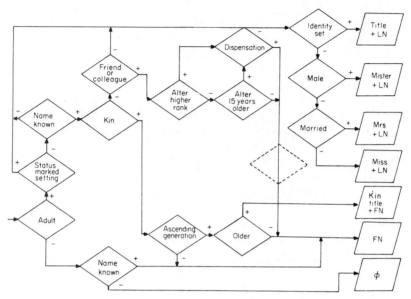

Fig. 1. An American address system.

Expanding their analysis to account for details from my own rules of address, I have found the structure expressed in the diagram in Fig. 1. The advantage of formal diagramming is that it offers precision greater than that of discursive description (Hymes 1967). The type of diagram presented here, following Geoghegan (1971), is to be read like a computer flow chart. The entrance point is on the left, and from left to right there is a series of binary selectors. Each path through the diagram leads to a possible outcome, that is, one of the possible alternative forms of address.

Note that the set of paths, or the rule, is like a formal grammar in that it is a way of representing a logical model. The diagram is not intended as a model of a process, of the actual decision sequence by which a speaker chooses a form of address or a listener interprets one. The two structures may or may not correspond.

In any case, the task of determining the structure implicit in people's report of what forms of address are possible and appropriate is clearly distinct from the task of studying how people, in real situations and in real time, make choices. The criteria and methods of the two kinds of study are quite different. Just as two individuals who share the same grammar might not share the same performance strategies, so two individuals might have different decision or interpretation procedures for sociolinguistic alternatives but have the identical logical structure to their reports of behavior.

The person whose knowledge of address is represented in Fig. 1 is assumed to be a competent adult member of a Western American academic community. The address forms which are the "outcomes" to be accounted for might fit in frames like "Look, ____, it's time to leave." The outcomes themselves are formal sets, with alternative realizations; for example, first names may alternate with nicknames, as will be indicated in a later section. One possible outcome is no-naming, indicated in Fig. 1 by the linguistic symbol for zero [∅].

The diamonds indicate selectors. They are points where the social categories allow different paths. At first glance, some selectors look like simple external features, but the social determinants vary according to the system, and the specific nature of the categories must be discovered by ethnographic means. For example, "Older" implies knowledge by the range of age defined as contemporary. In some southeast Asian systems, even one day makes a person socially older.

The first selector checks whether the addressee is a child or not. In face-to-face address, if the addressee is a child, all of the other distinctions can be ignored. What is the dividing line between adult and child? In my own system, it seems to be school-leaving age, at around eighteen. An employed sixteen-year-old might be classified as an adult.

Status-marked situations are settings such as the courtroom, the large faculty meeting, and Congress, where statuses are clearly specified, speech style is rigidly prescribed, and the form of address of each person is derived from his social identity, e.g., "your honor"

or "Mr. Chairman." The test for establishing the list of such settings is whether personal friendships are apparent in the address
forms or whether they are neutralized (or masked) by the formal
requirements of the setting. There are, of course, other channels
by which personal relations might be revealed, but here we are concerned only with address alternations, not with tone of voice, connotations of lexicon, and so on.

Among nonkin the dominant selector of first-naming is
whether alter is to be classified as having the status of a colleague or
social acquaintance. When introducing social acquaintances or new
work colleagues, it is necessary to employ first names so that the
new acquaintances can first-name each other immediately. Familiarity is not a factor between dyads of the same age and rank, and there
are no options. For an American assistant professor to call a new
colleague of the same rank and age "Professor Watkins" or "Mr.
Watkins" would be considered strange, at least on the American west
coast.

Rank here refers to a hierarchy within a working group, or
to ranked statuses like teacher-pupil. In the American system, no
distinction in address is made to equals or subordinates since both
receive FN. The distinction may be made elsewhere in the linguistic
system, for example, in the style of requests used. We have found
that subordinates outside the family receive direct commands in the
form of imperatives more often than equals, to whom requests are
phrased in other ways, at least in some settings.

A senior alter has the option of dispensing the speaker from
offering TLN by suggesting that he use a first name, or tacitly accepting the first name. Brown and Ford (Hymes 1964) have discussed the ambiguity that arises because it is not clear whether the
superior, for instance a professor addressing a doctoral candidate
or younger instructor, wishes to receive back the FN he gives. This
problem is mentioned by Emily Post: "It is also effrontery for a
younger person to call an older by her or his first name, without being
asked to do so. Only a very underbred, thickskinned person would attempt it" (Post 1922:54). In the American system described in Fig.
1, age difference is not significant until it is nearly the size of a
generation, which suggests its origins in the family. The presence

of options, or dispensation, creates a locus for the expression of individual and situational nuances. The form of address can reveal dispensation, and therefore be a matter for display or concealment in front of third parties. "No-naming" or ∅ , is an outcome of uncertainty among the options.[1]

The identity set refers to a list of occupational titles or courtesy titles accorded people in certain statuses. Examples are "Judge," "Doctor," "Professor," and so on.[2] A priest, physician, dentist, or judge may be addressed by title alone, but a plain citizen or an academic person may not. In the latter cases, if the name is unknown, there is no address form (or zero, ∅) available, and we simply "no-name" the addressee. The parentheses used here refer to optional elements, the bracketed elements to social selectional categories.

[Cardinal]: Your excellency
[U. S. President]: Mr. President
[Priest]: Father (+ LN)
[Nun]: Sister (+ religious name)
[Physician]: Doctor (+ LN)
[Ph. D., Ed. D.], etc. : (Doctor + LN)
[Professor]: (Professor + LN)
[Adult] etc. : (Mr. + LN)
                (Mrs. + LN)
                (Miss + LN)

Wherever the parenthetical items cannot be fully realized, as when LN is unknown , and there is no lone title, the addressee is no-named, by a set of rules of the form as follows: Father + ∅ → Father, Professor + ∅ → ∅, Mr. + ∅ → ∅, etc. An older male addressee may be called "sir" if deference is intended, as an optional extra marking.

These are my rules, and seem to apply fairly narrowly within the academic circle I know. Nonacademic university personnel can be heard saying "Professor" or "Doctor" without LN, as can schoolteachers. These delicate differences in sociolinguistic rules are sensitive indicators of the communication net.

The zero forms imply that often no address form is available to follow routines like "yes," "no," "pardon me," and "thank you." Speakers of languages or dialects where all such routines must contain an address form are likely in English either to use full name or to adopt forms like "sir" and "ma'am," which are either not used or used only to elderly addressees in this system.

One might expect to be able to collapse the rule system by treating kin terms as a form of title, but it appears that the selectors are not identical for kin and nonkin. A rule which specifies that _ascending generation_ only receives title implies that a first cousin would not be called "cousin" but merely FN, whereas an aunt of the same age would receive a kin title, as would a parent's cousin. If a title is normally used in direct address, and there are several members of the kin category, a first name may also be given (e.g., Aunt Louise). Frequently, there are additional features marked within a given family, such as patrilineal vs. matrilineal, near vs. distant. Whenever the address forms for an individual person's relatives are studied, this proves to be the case, in my experience.

Presumably, the individual set of rules or the regional dialect of a reader of this chapter may differ in some details from that reported in Fig. 1; or a better formulation is possible. Perhaps sociolinguists will begin to use a favorite frame of linguists — "In my dialect we say ..." — to illustrate such differences in sociolinguistic rules. For example, I have been told that in some American communities there may be a specific status of familiarity beyond first-naming, where a variant of the middle name is optional among intimates. This form then becomes the normal, or unmarked, address form to the addressee.

> "What's your name, boy?"
> "Dr. Poussaint. I'm a physician."
> "What's your first name, boy?"
> "Alvin."

The policeman insulted Dr. Poussaint three times. First, he employed a social selector for race, in addressing him as "boy," which neutralizes identity set, rank, and even adult status. Addressed to a white man, "boy" presumably would be used only for a child, youth, or menial regarded as a nonperson.

Dr. Poussaint's reply supplied only TLN and its justification.
He made clear that he wanted the officer to suppress the race selector, yielding a rule like Fig. 1. This is clearly a nondeferential
reply since it does not contain the FN required by the policeman's
address rule. The officer next treated TLN as failure to answer his
demand, as a nonname, and demanded FN; third, he repeated the
term "boy," which would be appropriate to unknown addressees.

According to Fig. 1, under no circumstances should a stranger address a physician by his first name. Indeed, the prestige of
physicians even exempts them from first-naming (but not from "Doc")
by used-car salesmen, and physicians' wives can be heard so identifying themselves in public so as to claim more deference than "Mrs."
brings. Thus the policeman's message is quite precise: "Blacks are
wrong to claim adult status or occupational rank. You are children."
Dr. Poussaint was stripped of all deference due his age and rank.

Communication has been perfect in this interchange. Both
were familiar with an address system which contained a selector
for race available to both blacks and whites for insult, condescension,
or deference, as needed. Only because they shared these norms could
the policeman's act have its unequivocal impact.

Comparative Rule Studies

The formulation of rules in this fashion can allow us to contrast one sociolinguistic system with another in a systematic way.
We can assume that a shared language does not necessarily mean a
shared set of sociolinguistic rules. For instance, rules in educated
circles in England vary. In upper-class boarding schools, boys and
girls address each other by last name instead of FN. In some universities and other milieux affected by the public school usage, solidary address to male acquaintances and colleagues is LN rather
than FN. To women it is Mrs. or Miss + LN by men (not title + LN),
and FN by women. Thus sex of both speaker and addressee is important.

In other university circles the difference from the American
rule is less; prior to dispensation by seniors with whom one is acquainted, one may use Mr. or Mrs. rather than occupational title

as an acceptably familiar but deferential form. Note that this is the
usage to women by male addressees in the other system. The two
English systems contrast with the American one in allowing basically
three, rather than two, classes of alternatives for nonkin: Occupational title + LN, M + LN, and FN/ LN. M + LN is used for intermediate cases, the familiar person who must be deferred to or treated with courtesy.

Two Asian systems of address have been described recently.
The pioneering work of William Geoghegan (1971) describes the naming
system of a speaker of Bisayan, a Philippine language. As in most
systems, children routinely receive the familiar address form. The
Bisayan system, like the American and English, chooses on the basis
of relative rank, relative age, and friendship. But there are important differences. In the United States, all adult strangers are addressed with deference; in the Bisayan system, social inferiors
do not receive titled address. In the American system for nonkin,
added age, like higher rank, merely increases distance or delays
familiar address; in the Bisayan system inferiors or friends who
are older receive a special term of address uniting informality and
deference.

The Korean system is more unlike the American (Howell
1967). In Korea, relative rank must first be assessed. If rank is
equal, relative age within two years is assessed, and if that is equal,
solidarity (e.g., classmates) will differentiate familiar from polite
speech. This system differs both in its components and its order
from the American and Bisayan rules. Both inferiors and superiors
are addressed differently from equals. Many kinds of dyads differ
in authority— husband-wife, customer-tradesman, teacher-pupil,
employer-employee. In each case, asymmetrical address is used.
Addressees more than two years older or younger than the speaker
are differentially addressed, so that close friendship is rigidly age
graded. Solidary relations arise from status, just as they do between equal colleagues in the American system, regardless of personal ties. There are more familiar address forms yet to signal
intimacy within solidary dyads. If the English system has three levels, there are even more in the Korean system. Since the criteria
were multiple in the Howell study, not a single frame, the comparison
is not quite exact.

As Howell points out, the Korean system illustrates that the dimension of approach that Brown and Gilman (1960) called solidarity may in fact have several forms in one society. In the Korean system intimacy is separable from solidarity. This separation may also exist in the American system, but in a different way. One is required to first-name colleagues even though they are disliked. As Brown and Ford (Hymes 1964) showed, however, nicknames may indicate friendship more intimate than the solidarity that requires or is shown by FN. They found that various criteria of intimacy, such as self-disclosure, were related to the <u>number</u> of FN alternates, such as nicknames and sometimes LN, used to an addressee, and proposed that greater intimacy creates more complex and varied dyadic relations which speakers may opt to signal by a greater number of address variants. Thus in the American system two points of major option for speakers exist: the ambiguous address relation between solidary speakers of unequal age or status, and intimacy.[3] We can expect that systems will vary in the points where address is prescribed or where options exist; Brown and Ford suggest a universal feature, however, in saying that in all systems relatively more frequent interaction should be related to more address variation. This they suggest is related to a semantic principle of greater differentiation of important domains.[4]

Two-Choice System

The brilliant work of Brown and Gilman which initiated the recent wave of studies of address was based on a study of T and V, their abbreviation for familiar vs. formal second person verbs and pronouns in many European languages. In English the same alternation existed before "thou" was lost. The contrast is realized in German by <u>du</u> and <u>sie,</u> in French by <u>tu</u> and <u>vous,</u> and in Russian by <u>ty</u> and <u>vy</u>.

One might expect two-choice systems to be somewhat simpler than a system like Bisayan, which in Geoghegan's (1971) description gives nineteen output categories. But the number of outcomes can be few, though the number of selectors is many or the kinds of rules relating them complex. Figure 2 gives a description of the nineteenth-century rules of the Russian gentry, as I derive them from the excellent analysis by Friedrich (1972), which gives sufficiently full detail to permit resolution of priorities. Special statuses refers to the tsar and God, who seem not to fit on any status continuum. Status-marked settings mentioned by Friedrich were the court, parliament, public occasions, duels, and examinations. Rank inferiors might be lower in social class, army rank, or ethnic group or be servants. Solidarity applied to classmates, fellow students, fellow

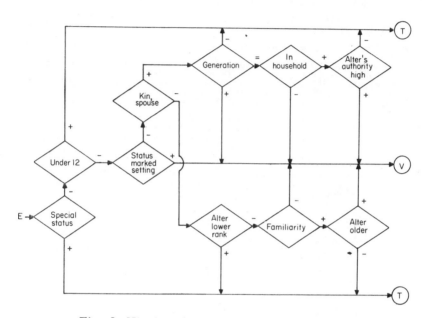

Fig. 2. Nineteenth century Russian address.

revolutionaries, lovers, and intimate friends. Perhaps it is more properly called familiarity or intimacy since there does not seem to be the prescription present in the Korean and American solidary relation. A feature of the system which Friedrich's literary examples illustrate vividly is its sensitivity to situational features. Thus T means "the right to use ty" but not the obligation to do so. Within the kin group, household is of considerable importance because of the large households separated by distance in traditional Russia.

A slightly later eastern European system described by Slobin (1963) is given in Fig. 3. The Yiddish system, as described by immigrants, is somewhat more like the American than like the

Russian system in that deference is always given adult strangers, regardless of rank. However, an older person received deference,
despite familiarity, unless he was a member of the kin group. In the
American system familiarity can neutralize age.

How have these systems changed? We have some evidence
from the Soviet Union. The Russian revolutionaries, unlike the
French, decreed V, implying that they wanted respect more than
solidarity. The current system is identical to the old with one exception: Within the family, asymmetry has given way to reciprocal T,
as it has in most of western Europe, at least in urbanized groups.
For nonkin in ranked systems like factories, superiors receive vy
and give ty:

> When a new employee is addressed as "ty," she says, "Why
> do I call you 'vy' while you call me 'ty'?" Kormilitzyn
> gleefully shoots back a ready answer: "If I were to call every-
> one 'vy' I'd never get my plan fulfilled. You don't fulfill plans
> by using 'vy'" (Kantorovich 1966:30).

Evidently, the upper-class habit of using vy until familiarity
was established (a system reflecting the fact that the T/ V contrast
itself came in from above as a borrowing from French) has seeped
downward. "A half-century ago even upon first meeting two workers

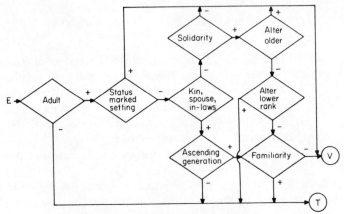

Fig. 3. Yiddish address system.

of the same generation would immediately use 'ty.' Today things
are different. Middle-aged workers maintain 'vy' for a long time,
or else adopt the intermediate form which is very widespread among
people within a given profession: 'ty' combined with first name and
patronymic" (Kantorovich 1966: 81).

Kantorovich, true to the 1917 decree, complains about three
features of the current system: ty to inferiors regardless of age, ty
to older kin, and first names alone among young acquaintances. Thus
he favors the more deferential alternative in each case. Social change
in Russia has been relatively slow in sociolinguistic rules, has affected family life more than public life, and has spread the practices
of the gentry among the workers.

The Puerto Rican two-choice system shown in Fig. 4 is
quite simple, either because it is a system of children or because my
analysis is based on statistical tables not individual interviews. The
data were generously supplied by Wallace Lambert and his collaborators from a large-scale study of comparative address systems in
several cultures. Elementary and high school students filled in ques-
tionnaires about the forms of address given and received. In this
chart, interlocale and intersubject differences have been suppressed.
The striking feature of this system is that it requires only three
discriminations. It is likely, of course, that adult informants would

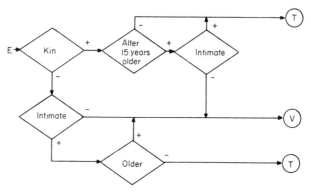

Fig. 4. Puerto Rican address system (children).

elaborate further details. Intimacy in this system refers to close ties of friendship, which can occur with others of widely varying age, e. g. , with godparents, and is quite distinct from solidarity, which arises from status alone. Adolescent girls, for example, do not give tu to a classmate unless she is a friend.

Lambert and his collaborators have collected slightly less detailed data from samples of schoolchildren in Montreal, from a small town in Quebec, from Mayenne, France, and from St. Pierre et Michelon, an island colony with close ties to France, much closer than to nearby Canada.

The system of kin address varies considerably. In both Mayenne and St. Pierre, all kin and godparents receive tu. In Quebec, the urban middle class is moving in this direction, but the urban lower class and the rural regions from which it derives retain an address system like Puerto Rico's in which distance (including age) within the family is important. In some families, even older siblings receive vous. For kin address, of course, the sanctions are intrafamily, so one would expect between-family differences to be greater during social change than in nonkin address. Generally, "intimate" means parents, then aunts, uncles, and godparents, then grandparents. Some interfamily differences might be accounted for by finding which family members live in the household, which nearby , and which far away.

Sex of addressee appears to be a feature of adult systems, or may influence the probabilities of intimacy where there is a selector. In Quebec, adults generally give tu to children and young men regardless of familiarity. In St. Pierre (except with upper-class girls, who are less likely to receive tu under any conditions) acquaintance legitimizes tu and is necessary even in addressing children. In Mayenne, middle-class little boys said they received tu from everyone (and reported often reciprocating to strangers), but otherwise familiarity seems to be required, as in Puerto Rico, in the Mayenne system. Boys generally receive T from employers, and in the country and the urban lower class they receive T from service personnel. It should be noted that the analysis from the children's standpoint of what they think they receive is an interesting reflection of the fact that people know what they should say themselves, and they also expect some standard form from others. In analyzing the adult rule systems, however, the children's data are not the best; the adults of rural or lower class background may have different rules (e.g., service personnel?) than others.

Elsewhere Lambert (1967b) has discussed the development of address rules with age. There are several interesting problems in the learning of these systems, such as the visibility of the various social selectors. One can assume the rank gradations in an adult system might be learned late (at least in terms of generalizability to new addressees), as would generation differentiations not highly related to age.

A second problem emphasized by Lambert is the structure of alternation itself. Children in most language communities learn fairly early to employ the asymmetry of first and second person (for a case study, see McNeill 1963). Thus if they always received T and gave V, there might be less difficulty; however, they see others exchanging reciprocal V and T as well as asymmetrical address, and they give T to some alters. Comparative research should be done in natural language communities where the language structure provides different category systems and social selectors (Slobin 1967).

The compressed presentation here of Lambert's work has indicated several directions for research on social criteria of address selection. Lambert has shown that these rules are sensitive indicators of differences between social groups, and of social change. One must look beyond the address system for independent social features correlated with address systems of a defined type. In order to do such studies, a clear-cut formal system for typologizing properties of address systems (like language typologies) is necessary.

Brown has already suggested that the dimensions of power and solidarity are likely to be present in all address systems since they are the basic dimensions of social behavior. If these are universals, we can look elsewhere for ways of typologizing systems, as suggested here, according to:

1. The order of universal selectors in the rule;
2. The location of personal options (such as dispensation, located at rank and age in the rule on Fig. 1);
3. Outcome types (for a given social selector, what lin-

guistic or paralinguistic features most commonly realize
the contrast?);

4. Formal features of the informational system (e.g., the
relation of input alternatives to outcomes, or the amount
of neutralization);

5. Formal type of rule for realizing insults, condescension,
deference, and so on by operations on the output of rules
for normal, unmarked address (or on the rules themselves)
(see the last section of this chapter).

Socialization

Adults entering a new system because of geographical or
occupational mobility may have to learn new sociolinguistic rules.
A contrastive analysis of formal rules, in combination with a theory
of social learning, would allow specification of what will happen.

First, we can predict what the speaker will do. We can
expect, on the basis of research on bilinguals, that the linguistic
alternatives will at first be assimilated to familiar forms, to "diamorphs." Thus a Frenchman in the United States might start out by
assuming that monsieur = Mr., madame = Mrs., and so on.

However, the rules for occurrence of these forms are
different in France. In polite discourse, routines like "merci," "au
revoir," "bonjour," and "pardon" do not occur without an address
form in France, although they may in the United States. One always
uses "Au revoir, madame" or some alternative address form.
Madame differs from "Mrs." in at least two ways. Unknown female
addressees of a certain age are normally called madame, regard-
less of marital status. Further, Mrs. + $\emptyset$ = $\emptyset$; madame + $\emptyset$ =
madame. As a matter of fact, the rule requiring address with
routines implies that when LN is not known, there cannot be a "zero
alternant" — some form of address must be used anyway, like the
English "sir." As a result of these differences in rules, we can
expect to hear elderly spinsters addressed: "Pardon me, Mrs."

How do listeners account for errors? Shifting at certain
points in sociolinguistic rules is regularly available as an option.
Normally, it is interpreted as changing the listener's perceived identity, or his relation to the speaker. The result may be complimen-

tary, as "sir" to an unknown working-class male, or insulting, as "Mommy" to an adolescent male. If the learner of a sociolinguistic system makes an error that falls within this range of interpretable shifts, he may constantly exchange predictably faulty social meanings. Suppose the speaker, but not the listener, has a system in which familiarity, not merely solidarity, is required for use of a first name. He will use TLN in the United States to his new colleagues and be regarded as aloof or excessively formal. He will feel that first-name usage from his colleagues is brash and intrusive. In the same way, encounters across social groups may lead to misunderstandings within the United States. Suppose a used-car salesman regards his relation to his customers as solidary, or a physician so regards his relation to old patients. The American using the rule in Fig. 1 might regard such speakers as intrusive, having made a false claim to a solidary status. In this way, one can pinpoint abrasive features of interaction across groups.

Another possible outcome is that the alternative selected is completely outside the system. This would be the case with "excuse me, Mrs.," which cannot be used under any circumstances by rule 1. This behavior is then interpreted by any additional cues available, such as the face, dress, or accent of a foreigner. In such cases, if sociolinguistic rules are imperfectly learned, there may be social utility in retaining an accent; wherever the attitude toward the group of foreigners is sufficiently benign, it is better to be so designated than to risk insulting or offending addressees.

Integrated Sociolinguistic Rules

The rules just given are fractional. They are selective regarding the linguistic alternations accounted for. They define only specific linguistic entries as the universe of outcomes to be predicted. If one starts from social variables, a different set of rules might emerge. This is the outlook of William Geoghegan (1971), Ward Goodenough (1965), and Dell Hymes (1964), who suggests taking "a specific or universal function, such as the distinguishing of the status or role of man and woman, derogation, respect, or the like, and investigating the diverse means so organized within the language habits of the community,... [rather than] looking for function as a correlative of structure already established." This is the point of view taken in the last section of this paper.

Using such an approach, Goodenough examined behavior toward a range of statuses and found that it was possible to rank both the statuses and the forms of behavior into Guttman scales and equivalence classes, grouped at the same scale point (1965). In this way, various kinds of verbal and nonverbal behavior can be shown to be outcomes of the same social selectors.

Deference, the feature studied by Goodenough, may be indicated by pronoun alternations, names or titles, tone of voice, grammatical forms, vocabulary, and so on (Capell 1966:104ff; Martin, in Hymes 1964). Rubin suggests even language change may serve the same purpose (1962). Deferential behavior as in the Spanish-Guaraní choice in Paraguay may in some systems only be realized in special situations such as in introductions or in making requests. If one compares an isolated segment of two sociolinguistic systems, it cannot legitimately be concluded that a given social variable is more important in one system than the other. It may simply be realized through a different form of behavior.

It is not clear how the different realizations of social selectors might be important. Language, address terms, pronominal selection, or consistent verb suffixing (as in Japanese) can be consciously controlled more readily, perhaps, than can intonation contours or syntactic complexity. Frenchmen report "trying to use tu" with friends. Such forms can be taught by rule specification to children or newcomers. Forms which allow specific exceptions, or which have options so that too great or too little frequency might be conspicuous, cannot be taught deliberately so easily. Such rules can be acquired by newcomers only by long and intense exposure rather than formal teaching.

Some alternations are common and required; others can be avoided. Howell reports that in Knoxville, Tennessee, Negroes uncertain whether or not to reciprocate FN simply avoided address forms to colleagues (Howell 1967:81-83), just as Brown and Ford noted in the academic rank system. In a pronominal rank system, like French or Russian, such avoidance is nearly impossible. Among bilinguals, language switching may be employed to avoid rank signaling (Howell 1967; Tanner 1967). The avoidable selector can be considered a special case of the presence of options in the system. Tyler (1965) has noticed that morphological deference features (like the Japanese) are more common in societies of particular kinship types, such as lineage organization.

This description is primarily made from the standpoint of predicting a speaker's choice of alternatives in some frame. It is also possible to examine these rules from the standpoint of comprehension or interpretation, as have Blom and Gumperz (1972) in their discussion of <u>social meaning</u>. Just as one can comprehend a language without speaking it, as actors we can interpret the social meaning of the acts of others without necessarily using rules identical to our own. The relation between production and comprehension rules remains to be studied.

Co-occurrence Rules

Types of Rules

"How's it going, Your Eminence? Centrifuging OK? Also have you been analyzin' whatcḧunnertook t'achieve?" The bizarreness of this hypothetical episode arises from the oscillations between different varieties of speech. It violates the co-occurrence rules that we may assume English to have.

In the preceding section, we were concerned with the selection of lexical items, pronouns, or inflectional alternatives. We conceived of each instance as involving social selectors. Once a selection has been made, however, later occurrences within the same utterance, conversation, or even between the same dyad may be predictable. Whenever there is predictability between two linguistic forms, we can speak of co-occurrence rules (Gumperz 1967).

Co-occurrence rules could be of two kinds. The instance of predictability through time might be called horizontal since it specifies relations between items sequentially in the discourse. Another type might be called vertical, specifying the realization of an item at each of the levels of structure of a language. For instance, given a syntactical form, only certain lexicon may normally be employed, and a particular set of phonetic values may realize the lexicon. If one has learned political terms in New York and gardening terms in Virginia, the phonetic coloring of the lexicon may reflect their provenance in the individual's history. The most striking case

lies in the well-practiced bilingual who uses French syntax and pronunciation for French vocabulary and English syntax and pronunciation for English vocabulary.

In the example, the following are violations of vertical co-
occurrence:

a. "How's it going" is a phrase from casual speech, but
the suffix "-ing" is used, rather than "-in'," which is normal for casual speech;
b. An elliptical construction is used in the second utterance,
which contains only a participle, but the formal "-ing" appears again;
c. A technical word, "centrifuge," is used in the elliptical
construction;
d. The "-in'" suffix is used with the formal "analyze";
e. Rapid informal articulation is used for the pedantic
phrase "undertook to achieve".

Horizontal co-occurrence rules refer to the same level of
structure, and might be lexical or structural. The vocabulary in
the example oscillates between slang and technical terms, the syntax
between ellipsis and parallel nonellipsis. In bilingual speech one
may find structural predictability independent of lexicon, as in an
example of Pennsylvania German: <u>Di kau ist over di fens chumpt.</u>
Here the syntax and grammatical morphemes are German, lexicon
English. Horizontal co-occurrence rules governing selection of
grammatical morphemes are common, with lexical switching and
phrase switching allowed. Diebold (1963) also gives examples in
which Greek-Americans who can speak both Greek and English with
"perfect" co-occurrence rules, if they employ English loan words in
the Greek discourse, realize them in the Greek phonological system.
This would suggest that for these speakers horizontal, or syntagmatic,
phonological rules override vertical realization rules.

One of the startling aberrations in the example is the use of
slang to a cardinal. We would expect to find that deferential address
forms would be co-occurrent with formal style. One pictures a cardinal in a microbiology laboratory addressed by a janitor who knows
technical terms but cannot fully control formal syntax and phonology!
Like ungrammatical sentences, sociolinguistically deviant utterances

become normal if one can define setting and personnel to locate them. This, of course, is the point. Wherever there are regular co-occurrences, deviant behavior is marked and calls attention to its social meaning.

The most extreme forms of sanctions for co-occurrence specification are likely to be found in ritualized religious speech in traditional societies. Here it would be blasphemous to utter the wrong speech. Indeed, Gumperz has suggested that linguistics first began with the Sanskrit scholars' efforts to identify the formal features of religious texts and transmit them unchanged. Thus from the special social constraint on alternations sprang the concept of "language."

At the opposite extreme are the conditions in American college lecturing, where technical terms, slang, and informal and formal syntax alternate to some extent. Friedrich also gives examples (1972) of delicate communication of changing relationships by shifts within conversations.

Style

Formal Style. Style is the term normally used to refer to the co-occurrent changes at various levels of linguistic structure within one language. The vertical properties of such shifts have been pointed out by Joos (1962). Hymes (1964) has commented that probably every society has at least three style levels: formal or polite, colloquial, and slang or vulgar.

If Hymes is right about a polite style which contrasts with the unmarked or "normal" colloquial, it might be proposed that this is the style preferred in public, serious, ceremonial occasions. Co-occurrence restrictions are particularly likely because of the seriousness of such situations. The style becomes a formal marker for occasions of societal importance where the personal relationship is minimized. We would expect that the distant or superior form of address and pronoun is universally employed in public high style. In Fig. 1 and 2 "status-marked situations" which call for titles and V may also call for polite style. Thus speakers who exchange colloquial style normally might change to this style in certain public occasions such as funerals or graduation ceremonies.

It might in general be the case in English that in otherwise identical situations, an alter addressed with TLN receives polite style more than one addressed with FN. Howell (1967:99) reported such correlations in Korean.

In Geertz' (1960) analysis of prijaji speech etiquette in Java, a distinction is made between affixes and function morphemes controlled by co-occurrence rules, and honorific vocabulary (like "sir"), which is sporadic and which is governed in effect by rules of frequency rather than categorical co-occurrence. Since a single selection is made in the first case, he refers to a "styleme."

Formal lexicon and "-ing" should be related. Fischer (Hymes 1964) found that criticizing, visiting, interesting, reading, and correcting and flubbin', punchin', swimmin', chewin', and hittin', occurred in a single speaker's usage. It is not clear here whether it is lexical style or topic that is at issue since there were no examples of denotative synonyms realized through different vocabulary. Such examples, of the sort given in Newman (Hymes 1964) and found plentifully in English lexicon for body functions (e.g., urinate vs. weewee), provide clearer evidence for co-occurrence restrictions between lexicon and structure.

Labov (1966b) did include the "-ing" vs. "-in" variation in his study of style contrasts in different social strata, and found it worked precisely as did the phonological variables. Polite style in a speaker might require a certain higher frequency (Figs. 5 and 6) of postvocalic [r] or of [θ] rather than [t] in, e.g., "thing," and of "-ing." While the variables differentiating polite from casual style tended to be the same in different classes, the precise frequency reached for each variable was a function of class too (Labov 1966a). Thus his evidence suggests co-occurrence rules for grammatical morphemes and phonology. Labov (1966b) and Klima (1964) consider the formal description of phonological and syntactic style features, respectively.

Informal Style. In trying to sample different styles while interviewing, Labov made the assumption that speakers would use a more formal style during the interview questioning than at other times. He used several devices for locating such shifts contextually: speech outside the interview situation, speech to others usually in

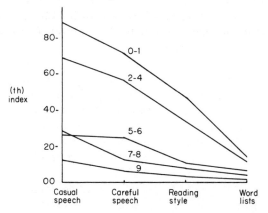

Fig. 5. Class and style of stratification of [th] in thing, three, etc., for adult native New York City speakers (Labov, 1966).

the family, rambling asides, role playing (specifically, getting adults to recite childhood rhymes), and answers to a question about a dangerous experience. He found that when "channel cues" (changes in tempo, pitch range, volume, or rate of breathing) indicated a change to casual or spontaneous speech within a speech episode, the phonological features changed. In the examples illustrating the shifts, lexicon and syntax changed too.

It is commonly the case that as one moves from the least deferent speech to the most, from the informal to the ceremonial, there is more structural elaboration and less abbreviation. Probably, this difference is a universal, for two reasons. One is that elaboration is a cost, and is therefore most likely in culturally valued situations or relationships (Homans 1958). The other is that a high degree of abbreviation is only possible in in-group communication. While ceremonials may be confined to a sacred few, wherever they have a public function and must communicate content, we assume that this principle of elaboration holds. Elaboration could be defined with respect to a surface structure, or to the complexity of imbedded forms in the syntax, or some such criteria. A very brief poem might, in fact, in terms of rules and "effort" of compression, be more complex than a discursive report of the "same" content. Some forms are

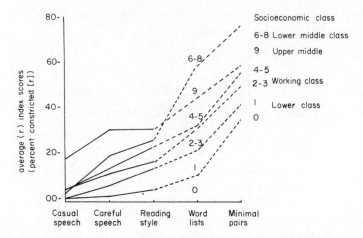

Fig. 6. Class stratification of [r] in guard, car, beer, beard, etc., for native New York City adults (Labov, 1966).

unambiguous: suffixed versus unsuffixed forms, as in Japanese honorifics or polite verb suffixes; titles versus nontitles; and so on.

From a formal grammatical standpoint, ellipsis is more complex than nonellipsis since the grammar must contain an additional rule. It is not clear how ellipsis might be handled in a performance model. However, ellipsis in the syntactical sense is clearly more common in informal speech.

From Soskin and John's (1963) text of a married couple we find the following:

> Bet you didn't learn it there.
> Your name?
> Want me to take it...
> Wanna take your shoes off?
> Not that way!
> Directly into it.

The formal rules for sentence contractions and ellipsis are readily written.

Another form of ellipsis is that used in conversational epi-

sodes in second-speaker forms or to complete one's own earlier utterances. From Soskin and John (1963):

> That fish, Honey.
> Like this?
> Undulating!
> Towed!
> With both of them!
> Well, I could.

These forms of ellipsis are learned. Brent and Katz (1967)
found that anaphoric pronominalization is rare in young children; it
is obligatory in adult second-speaker rules. Bellugi (1967) found
also that contractions occur later than uncontracted forms in children, except as unanalyzed morphemes.

Semantic compression is also available, in casual speech
among intimates (see Ervin-Tripp 1968). In slang the alternates
are primarily lexical. As Newman (Hymes 1964) has pointed out
the actual forms used are not necessarily different, but in sacred
or slang contexts they take on a different meaning, so in speaking of
slang vocabulary one must include both form and its semantic features. Since slang is highly transitory by definition, it will be understood and correctly used only within the group or network where it
developed or to which it has moved at a given time. One might predict that the selection rules for slang should restrict it to addressees
to whom one claims a solidary relation. Thus a college lecture laced
with slang is a claim on the identification of the audience.

Phonetically, a form which occurs in casual speech more than
in polite styles is rapid speech, which entails horizontal changes.

What are you doing?	[hwədar ju 'duwiŋ]
Whaddya doing?	[hwədji 'duwiŋ]
Whach doon?	[wəč 'dun]

There are regular phonetic alternations related to rate, e.g.,

1. Retention of syllable of major stress and peak pitch
2. As degree of speeding increases, loss of weakest stress
3. Loss or assimilation of semivowels

[r] in postvocalic position lost
[d] + [j] → [ǰ]   e.g., Whadja do?
[t] + [j] → [č]   e.g., Whatcha doin?[5]
4. Possible loss of marginal phonological distinctions like
/hw/ vs. /w/, perhaps as part of casual speech style
5. Centralization of unstressed vowels

There is a reverse set of rules available to speakers used
to these alternations. The extra-slow style may be employed in
sounding out for a dictionary or over the telephone. Thus normal
"school" may become slow [sɨkuwɨl]. Many of these rules derive
from the rules of English stress (Chomsky and Halle 1968).

Styles Related to Occupation. Language changes related to
work arise for three reasons. One is that any activity brings with
it objects, concepts, and values which are talked about by specialists
in that activity, and indeed may be known only to them. Another is
that whatever solidarity an interacting work group may achieve, or
whatever identification a reference group (e.g., psychologists or
transformational linguists) may stimulate, it can be alluded to by
selection of appropriate alternatives in speaking or writing. Many
instances of abbreviations in factories, or of work-group slang, or
of technical terminology synonymous with colloquial vocabulary,
must have this second feature. Further, the particular communicative conditions might give rise to some features — signal tower
communication, headline style, the special syntax of short-order
restaurant speech. While the slang and lexical features of restaurant speech can be found in kitchens, fast unambiguous oral communication needed between waiter and cook alone may lie behind the
special syntax Brian Stross reported (see Ervin-Tripp 1969). Examples are the structure (number) + (category) + (modifier) which
he found in such orders as "two bacon and " for bacon and eggs and
"LT plain" for lettuce and tomato sandwich. Virtually all registers,
including that of social science writing, have syntactic as well as
lexical features. The details of the co-occurrence rules for such
styles remain to be studied.

Baby Talk. In many languages a special style is employed
in talking to infants, which changes its features with the age of the
child. A cross-linguistic comparison has been made by Ferguson
(1964). In English, baby talk affects all levels of structure.

Most speakers are likely to be conscious of baby-talk lexicon, as they often are of the lexical features of styles. Baby lexicon includes words like potty, weewee, bunny, night-night, mommy, and daddy. Many other words in adult speech become appropriate for speaking to infants when the suffix "-ie" is added. Drach and his colleagues (1969) found that speech to children is syntactically simpler and more repetitious, and contains fewer errors and hesitation pause and more ellipsis resulting in shorter sentences than speech to adults.

Phonological effects and paralinguistic features are especially conspicuous. Samples of talk to infants show certain general phonetic changes such as palatalization. Most striking is the higher pitch the younger the infant, and the use of a singsong, wide-ranging intonation. Observations of the social distribution of this style show it more common in addressing other people's children than one's own. For instance, nurses use the paralinguistic features at least in persuading children; and in cooperative nurseries, comparison of own-child and other-child addressees indicates a distinct shift to more age attribution with own child.

Children themselves use many of the features of adult baby talk very early. In addressing younger siblings they may adopt lexical and paralinguistic features of the adult baby talk as early as age two. In role play they use phrases and address terms from baby talk, e.g., "Goo-goo, little baby," and freely employ the sing-song intonation in addressing "babies." In other respects their role play is stereotyped rather than strictly imitative, for example in the frequent use of role names, and it may be that the use of the intonational and lexical features of baby talk may function simply as role markers in their play.

Linguistic Repertoire. Co-occurrence rules refer to the selection of alternates within the repertoire of a speaker in terms of previous or concomitant selections. The range of possible alternates should be known in such a study. In an American monolingual, the range is likely to include the styles just discussed, and perhaps an occupational register. Labov has pointed out, however, that it is rare to control a very wide stylistic range unless one is a speech specialist and that upwardly mobile persons usually lose the "ability to switch 'downwards' to their original vernacular" (1964: 92).

In many parts of the world, a code that is relatively distinct from the casual vernacular is used in formal situations. This
condition, called "diglossia" in Ferguson's (1959) classic article,
may, because of the greater code difference, be accompanied by more
co-occurrence restriction than is style shifting, where the common
features of the styles may outweigh their differences. Examples
where the codes are related are Greece, German Switzerland, Haiti,
and Arab countries. Standard languages coexisting with local dialects
are somewhat less perceptually separable; historically, the dialect
does not usually maintain itself except phonetically, though there
may be ideological resistance to borrowing from the standard
(Blom and Gumperz 1972). Differential access to the everyday use
of the standard, in combination with valued social meanings of a
dialect, as in the case of nonstandard urban English or creoles such
as those of Hawaii and Jamaica, may preserve variation.

Where diglossia takes the form of bilingualism (Fishman
1967), one might at first assume that the co-occurrence rules would
primarily govern situations requiring the high form. Such a condition exists in many American bilingual communities, with English
as the high form. However, these are not usually pure cases since
English is the vernacular if there are casual contacts outside the
immigrant community. Under these conditions there can be considerable interpenetration (Gumperz 1967).

Co-occurrence rules in common-sense terms refer to "language mixing." Some bilingual communities have strong attitudinal
opposition to switching (usually they mean lexical co-occurrence).
Blom and Gumperz (1972) found that in a Norwegian village speakers
were unconscious of the use of standard forms and were very upset
to hear tapes showing lack of co-occurrence restrictions in behavior.
In practice, the maintenance of coordinate or segregated systems depend on social factors. Coordinate bilingualism is possible if there
is a complete range of equivalent lexicon in both systems, and social
support for the bilingualism. If this is not the case, some topics
cannot be discussed, some emotions cannot be conveyed, and borrowing, perhaps surrounded by a routine disclaimer frame, will occur.
The other social condition permitting such segregation in diglossia are
the closed network circumstances reported by Blom and Gumperz
where certain topics and transactional types simply would not occur
in casual discourse. Thus American researchers can find rich

grounds for the study of behavioral support or loss of co-occurrence rules, either in English style, registers, dialects, or multilingualism.

Shifting within Discourse

Situational Shifting. The social features alluded to in the alternation rules so far discussed have primarily been features of situations or personnel present. Sociolinguistic alternations based on these kinds of "situational shifting" (Blom and Gumperz 1972) can be seen in the two-year-old's use of baby-talk intonation to his baby sister, the multilingual child's selection of language for a new servant, the slum Afro-American child's loss of classroom copulas when on the playground, the Hawaiian college boy's selection of standard lexicon when a mainland stranger arrives, and replacement, in addition, of the creole's intonation if the stranger is a girl. These consistent behavioral shifts may or may not be related to normative rules of the type shown in Figures 1 to 4 derived from informant's reports.

Speech Acts. In addition, however, such shifts can occur within occasions. They might be related to functions, speech acts, or topics. "What did he say?" "He asked her for a match." "Why did he do that?" "He wanted to meet her, talk with her." The first characterization describes a speech act, request. The second refers to the function of the act. We assume that all members of social groups can identify speech acts, that they are units in the cultural system. "What are you talking about?" "We were just saying hello." "We were telling jokes." "I was introducing Joe." Saying hello, telling jokes, and introducing are speech acts subordinate to organized exchanges like parties and joint work, often located within them by sequencing rules (Schegloff 1972) or rules of propriety (e. g., one introduces guests at a formal dinner, but not the waitress).

In these examples, the speech acts are labeled units. It is possible that some consistencies in rules of behavior imply the existence of a unit, though it may not appear in the folk taxonomy of speech acts. For example, suppose that one cannot say to a stranger on the street, "My name is George Landers. What time is it?" or "Hello, sir. Where is the post office?" Then to formulate the rule, one needs a category of information requests addressed

to strangers in order to indicate that greetings and self-introductions
are excluded. Another indication that such units may exist is that
they commonly occur in bilingual interaction; there may be a language shift between two different speech acts.

There is no reason to assume that speech acts are the same
everywhere. Certain special forms of discourse, like poetry and
speechmaking, may have components known only to specialists.
Whether and why there are labels used in the teaching of these performances is itself an interesting cultural study.

Speech acts in English include greetings, self-identification,
invitations, rejections, apologies, and so on. The ones identified so
far tend to be routines, but we can expect to find other more abstract
units as research proceeds.

Topics. When conversations have an explicit message with
informational content, they can be said to have a topic. "What are
you talking about?" "Nothing." "Gossip." "Shop talk." "The weath-
er." "The war." "We were having an automobile discussion about the
psychological motives for drag racing in the streets." In everyday discourse, the question of topic is most likely to occur in invitations or
rejections so that the answers are such as to exclude a new arrival
or give him enough information to participate. Besides selecting
personnel for participation, topics may be governed by a continuity
rule. In a formal lecture in a university there is a constraint on
continuity and relevance, just as there is in technical writing, where
editing can enforce the constraint. Evidences of constraint are apologies for deviation: "That reminds me ..." "Oh, by the way..."
"To get back to the question ..." "To change the subject..." Cultural rules regarding speech events may include constraints as to the
grounds for relevance.

Kjolseth (1967) has found in analysis of some group interaction that topical episodes are key factors in speakers' tactics.

A performer's tactic may be to direct his episode as a probe
into the preceding episode. In contrast, in another situation
his tactic may be to extend and elaborate some antecedent
episode. On still another occasion his tactic may be to
close off and limit a previous episode.... These tactical

types are based on, or defined in terms of, two qualities abstracted from the performances: (a) the episode locus of relevances drawn from the existent conversation resource, and (b) the purpose of the episode with respect to surrounding episodes.

The three examples given by Kjolseth would involve topical continuation, recycling, or change, respectively. These general features of speech events require that members be able to identify relevance but not necessarily to label topics.

There is yet a third form of evidence that topic may be a cultural unit. Bilinguals can frequently give reliable accounts of topical code switching, and their behavior often corresponds in general to their accounts (Erivin-Tripp 1964).

We can thus argue that topic, like speech act, must be a basic variable in interaction on the grounds that speakers can identify topical change as generating code shift, that speakers can sometimes report what they are talking about, and that topical continuity, recycling, and change may be normative features of speech events, or at least relevant to values about good conversations. One might, in fact, find that there are rules for topic selection just as there are for address.

Messages. The analysis of messages refers to two-term relationships, whereas topic is a single term allowing for simple taxonomies. Here we intend to refer only to the manifest or explicit message. Our reason for the distinction is that latent content categories typically refer to intent (see, e.g., Dollard and Auld 1959; Katz 1966; Leary 1957; Marsden 1965). Our position here is that intent or function is part of the constellation of social features out of which interaction is generated. It can be realized in a variety of ways, of which verbal interaction is only one. We seek regular rules by which one can relate underlying categories to their formal realizations, or the formal features of interaction with their social meanings. Failure to discover such rules has led to considerable discouragement with the evident arbitrariness of content classifications in studies of natural discourse.

The manifest message, however, is the product of the social

features of the situation as well as of intent, and is therefore insepa-
rable from the interaction product. All the selections made in realization of the functions of communication can carry some kind of information, whether about the speaker, the situation, the hearer, or the topic. In detail, given alternations cannot do all at once, though they may
be ambiguous as to which is intended. In this case, we intend the message only to refer to what is said or implied about the topic. There
have been numerous summaries of ways of classifying messages (e.g.,
Pool 1959). A recent innovation is logical analysis (Véron et al. 1965).
The underlying structure of logical linkages between terms in utterances was analyzed, then semantic relations were described in terms
of logical relations between pairs of units (e.g., equivalence, inference, conjunction, specification of conditions, sequential relations,
explanation, opposition, causes, ...). A Markov semantic analysis
revealed very large and consistent differences between subject groups,
which were, in the study reported, clinical categories, but could be
texts in a different society.

Function of Interaction

Criteria. If sociolinguistic alternation rules have intents or
functions as their input, then one strategy in identifying such rules is
to isolate a functional category and examine its realizations. We assume that the theory of functions itself must lie outside of sociolinguistics, in another social science. However, an examination of the
various functions realized by speech is of considerable importance in
view of the evidence that these functions change with age and vary with
culture.

Firth (1935) was among many who sought to identify the
functions of speech. He included phatic communion (creating solidarity or alluding to it); pragmatic efficiency (accompanying work);
planning and guidance; address; greetings, farewells, adjustment of
relations, and so on; speech as a commitment, (courts, promises).
Primarily, his view of function was the social value of the act.

Function is likely to be viewed by a psychologist from the
standpoint of the interacting parties, either the sender or the receiver. Soskin has played tapes to listeners and asked them to report what they would say and what they would think. This method
assumes that function is effect. It is close to Blom and Gumperz '
(1972) criterion of social meaning.

A second method is to analyze actual instances of acts, and infer whether the receiver's response satisfied the speaker, either from his overt behavior or by questioning him. This method includes action, response, and reaction. It is derived from Skinner's (1957) theory that speech is operant behavior which affects the speaker through the mediation of a hearer. Feedback and audience consistency presumably "shape" effective speech in the normal person. In this method, function is identified by classes of satisfactory listener responses.

If intent is imputed to a speaker on the basis of some features of the content or form of his speech, a third form of functional analysis appears. This, of course, is the method of latent content analysis (e.g., Katz 1966).

A set of function categories was devised to account for the initiation of dyadic interaction, on the basis of a corpus of instances of action, response, and reaction (Ervin-Tripp 1964). The list includes eliciting goods, services, and information; implicit requests for social responses; offering of information or interpretations; expressive monologues; routines, and speech to avoid alternative activities.

Mands. One of the simplest functional categories to examine is one which Skinner (1957) called the mand since it is defined by the fact that normally it elicits goods, services, and information. One could broaden the definition by specifying that the intent is to obtain these since it is clear that under some conditions, the actor does for himself.

Soskin and John (1963) devised a category system, intermediate between the strata suggested here, which will serve to illustrate the breadth of possible realizations of mands. Suppose the actor wants the loan of a coat:

> "It's cold today" (structone).
> "Lend me your coat" (regnone).
> "I'm cold" (signone).
> "That looks like a warm coat you have" (metrone).
> "Br-r-r" (expressive).
> "I wonder if I brought a coat" (excogitative).

It is immediately obvious that these ways of getting a coat are socially distributed in a nonrandom way and would be quite ineffective under many circumstances.

If we look at the category which most explicitly realizes a a mand, and can be said to be pragmatically unambiguous, the regnone, we find that there are a variety of speech acts that might be regnones, including requests and orders: "Ask him to close the window" vs. "Tell him to close the window." "Shut the window!" vs. "Would you mind closing the window?"

At a lower stratum, the syntactical, the request often involves some kind of speech act neutralization. For example, one can joke by misinterpreting a speech act, by saying "yes" to "Would you mind closing the window?" or to "Do you have a match?" or "Do you know where the post office is?" or to "Is George there?" on the phone, and doing nothing further. In each of these cases, the request is realized through a yes/ no question. From the standpoint of syntax, such a response is quite appropriate. Under specifiable social conditions, however, these become the normal, unmarked form for realizing requests in the mature speaker. When one does not in fact want to speak to George but merely to know whether or not he is home, some other form must be chosen, or a fast footnote added.

These instances are highly stabilized cases of an apparent neutralization which has become the normal form for request and therefore would in fact be described by many speakers as "asking X to close the window" and so on, if they were told to convert these into indirect speech.

In addition, one finds many instances of the selection of the normal form for realization for some other function to represent a mand. Quite possibly, of course, in closed networks these become as usual as the "asking" examples.

Bessie Dikeman and Patricia Parker (1964) found that within some families mands were neutralized between equals most of the time, less than half the time from seniors to juniors, and in a minority of cases when juniors spoke. Examples from their papers were these:

"Where's the coffee, Dremsel?" (it is visible) (to wife)
[gloss: bring me the coffee].
"Is that enough bacon for you and Thelma?" (to husband)
[gloss: save some for Thelma].
"It's 7:15" (to daughter) [gloss: hurry up].
"Mother, you know I don't have a robe. Well, we're having
a slumber party tomorrow night" [gloss: buy me a robe].
"Oh dear, I wish I were taller" (to adult brother) [gloss:
get down the dishes].

In factory settings, subordinates usually received commands,
sometimes requests. Carol Pfuderer (1968) found that in a university office commands were reserved for familiar peers. Within this
category of addressee, however, if the speaker was within the ter-
ritory of the receiver, requests were used instead. If distance separated them, a command might be altered by a tag question making
it a request ("Ask Marcy, why don't you?"), "please," address
terms, or rising pitch. If the addressee was not a peer, requests,
pragmatic neutralizations, or displacement of addressee occurred.
Pragmatic neutralizations included information questions ("Has anyone
gone to the accounting this week?" "Whose turn is it to make coffee
this week, Ruby?") and statements ("It's stuffy in here." "Someone has to see Dean Smith."). In cases where the obvious receiver
was much higher in rank, there might be displacement to a peer addressee but use of a highly deferent request form ("Joan, would you
please get the stapler for me?"). In this example the nearest person
to the stapler was a standing senior professor, not Joan, who was
seated farther away.

Mands require action on the part of the alter so that the
obligations and privileges inherent in the social relations of the personnel are likely to result in different linguistic realizations of the
same function. We might expect displacement where possible in
cases of extreme deference, perhaps pragmatic neutralization allowing the receiver an option of interpretation. In situations of high
mutual nurturance where intimacy makes interpretability likely, as
in many families, the basis for pragmatic neutralization may be
quite different, perhaps serving to mask mands outside the normal
duties of the receiver. In the same way, Stross (1964) found that
"please" was used only for requested acts extraneous to duties.

We can expect that where variant address forms exist,
they might alternate in mands. Milla Ayoub (1962), in a discussion
of bipolar kin terms in Arabic, points out that in addition to proper
names, a mother can call her son by either of two terms that also can
mean "my mother." When a parent wishes to cajole or placate a
child, but not command him, he uses these bipolar terms. This is
particularly the case with sons. They are never used in direct
commands.

In discussing current address practices in the Soviet Union,
Kantorovich (1966) mentions that friends might switch from ty to vy
with first name and patronymic when help is asked for.

Episodes. Watson and Potter (1962) used the term episode
as a unit of analysis, which can terminate whenever there is a change
in the major participants, the role system of the participants, the
focus of attention, and the relationship toward the focus of attention.
This term, rather than topic, was chosen to differentiate cases
where a similar apparent topic might be within a person's own experience, part of an ongoing activity, or an abstract referential category, as in a discussion.

The different episodes that Watson and Potter's units identify
probably will find some reflections in formal changes. These shifts
arise from:

> a. Sequencing rules concerning speech acts within a speech
> event.
> b. Changes in the activity, if any, accompanying the inter-
> action (e.g., a ball game or dinner preparation).
> c. Disruptive events such as the arrival of new personnel,
> accidents like bumps or sneezes, and phone calls, which
> require routines to right the situation.
> d. Shifts arising from unexpected responses of alter, leading
> to changes in function.
> e. Function satiation. Presumably, functions oscillate in
> patterned ways in stable groups.
> f. Topic-evoked shifts in functions. Under the impact of in-
> structions or of associative dynamics, the topic may change
> in the course of the conversation. These changes can alter
> the available resources for the participants and thereby

change their intent. If the topic shifts from child rearing to economics, e.g., a bachelor may find he has greater resources for displaying knowledge and receiving recognition. He may speak more, use more technical vocabulary, perhaps even to the point that listeners do not understand. There were many such instances in studying the speech of bilinguals, in which topic and language were controlled by instructions (Ervin 1964; Ervin-Tripp 1964, 1967).

Blom and Gumperz (1972) found that among university-trained villagers, many features of standard Norwegian appeared when topics shifted from local to nonlocal. In the offering of information, speakers with a large repertoire of speech alternatives can maximize credibility by adopting the most suitable role. Thus discussion of university structure might elicit use of more standard Norwegian forms than would gossip about instructors, where student speech features would be adopted, especially those shared with addressees.

As functions change, address too may change through a conversation. David Day described in a term paper changes when an argument occurred in a class regarding an instructor's views of a student's beliefs. Address progressed from FN to Dr. LN to Professor LN. In comments with other students as addressee, LN was used in reference to the instructor, in front of him. Concurrently, slang decreased.

When there is agreement about the normal, unmarked address form to alters of specified statuses, then any shift can convey intent. Friedrich (1972) gives convincing cases of momentary shifts at times of personal crises. He points out that in a public setting friends would mask their intimacy with V; in talking of personal topics they would invoke their friendship with ty and remove it for impersonal topics with vy.

Kantorovich (1966:43) gives similar examples in current practice:

> I say "ty" to my subordinates, but certainly don't do this
> in order to belittle them. I know that they'll answer me
> with "vy," but this isn't grovelling — it's a mark of respect....

Somebody I call "ty" is somehow closer to me than someone
I have to call "vy " ...If I get mad at one of my workers,
and he needs a bawling out, I frequently switch to "vy."

When cursing, many people who customarily use "ty" suddenly switch to "vy," and many who are on a mutual "vy" basis switch
to "ty" (Kostomarov 1967).

In systems with age or rank asymmetry of address, the use
of the more deferential form to an equal or subordinate can either
mean that they are receiving respect or being put off at a distance.
To account fully for the interpretation of such actions by the receivers,
we need to know the other signals, such as tone of voice, other address
features, and the available ambiguities of the relationship. In the
case of courtship, e.g., the important dimension is closeness or
distance, and address changes would be so interpreted.

Rules for Switching. I have emphasized throughout this chapter that linguistic interaction is a system of behavior in which underlying functions are realized through an organized set of output rules
within a social situation. If the function requires conveying an explicit message with informational content, some semantic information
is presented in the alternatives selected. Other alternatives require
the representation of social information.

In addressee-dominated rules like those in Figures 1 to 4,
effects of function switching can be represented as transformations
upon the unmarked outputs of the addressee rules. They may take
the form of simple replacements, e.g., if familiarity exists, different
names may be employed as a direct representation of varied functions.
Thus a node or selector for familiarity and for function is added to
the branching rules. Tyler's (1966) rules are of this type.

Blom and Gumperz (1972) have suggested that metaphorical
switching simply consists of treating the addressee as though his
social features were different. In this case, the rule acts upon the
selection points. In the case of Dr. Poussaint, hostile intent was
represented in the selection of "adult- " rather than "adult+ " at the
first selection point. Presumably, this possibility suggested itself
by the existence of a traditional southern system of address to Blacks
in which all but the very old (aunty) were addressed as children. When

Harvey Sacks asked his UCLA students to play the role of boarders with their families in vacation, their silence, politeness of address and requests, and withdrawal from gossip and semantic ellipsis in conversation were interpreted by their families as evidence of sickness or hostility.

The Russian example implies that a simple transformation upon the output forms can express hostility; however, the inversion may be a consequence of transformation of selection features, making the friend a nonfriend, and the formal associate an inferior. Such general rules are a necessity if familiarity is absent since they permit the interpretation of new instances on the basis of the hearer's general knowledge of the system of sociolinguistic rules.

"Rules" could refer to structures for generating or interpreting speech, to reports of beliefs about practices, or to standards of correctness. We have given examples of all three kinds of rules, not always clearly distinguishing them. Labov's (1966b) index of linguistic insecurity compared the last two.

Behavioral rules and reports about behavior are likely to be systematically different. If the norms contain a probability or frequency factor, speaker's beliefs are, instead, categorical (Labov 1966b). Beliefs about the social selectors in sociolinguistic rules are more likely to include features of personnel, since categorization devices realize these (Sacks) features, than to note functional variation. Syntactical variables are not remembered (Sachs 1967) beyond the time needed for decoding unless they are markers, helping us classify the speaker. In multilingual communities phonological, syntactic, and semantic shifting is often not observed (Gumperz 1964a, 1967). Even borrowed vocabulary is unnoticed by members if values oppose borrowing (Blom and Gumperz 1972). Some speakers cannot remember the language in which they just spoke, let alone report it to an interviewer.

These phenomena are not merely grounds for distrusting members' reports. Just as reference to a relative (Tyler 1972) is affected by more than the semantic dimensions of reference, so the act of describing, even to oneself, is a product which could realize a variety of functions. Member's reports are likely to be as sensitive to social variation as any speech act mentioned in this chapter, and

therefore prove as amenable to study. We expect then that rules
based on report will have a systematic relation to behavioral consistencies, but not a one-to-one correspondence.

LINGUISTIC DIVERSITY

A. The Fundamentals of Communication

The fundamental fact about language is its obvious diversity.
Moving from country to country, region to region, class to class, and
caste to caste, we find changes in language. Linguistic diversity apparently is related to social interaction.

Linguistic similarity must be explained, for it is clear that
separated sets of speakers will develop different languages. Two
quite different bases for similarity can be examined: the fundamental
requirement of mutual intelligibility among people who belong to the
same social community, and the consequences of variability in overt
behavior in terms of social values.

A test for mutual intelligibility might be the Two Person
Communication game. First used by Carroll (1958), it has recently
been revived (Maclay and Newman 1960; Krauss and Weinheimer
1964; Brent and Katz 1967). A hearer out of sight of a speaker
selects, constructs, or in some way responds to instructions from a
speaker regarding a set of materials. Feedback may or may not be
allowed. The advantage of this method is that one can examine the
relation between success in the objective task and various speech
features, and that the social relation of speaker and hearer can be
controlled. For our question about the degree of similarity required
for intelligibility, we shall assume optimal social attitudes (Wolff
1959) and simply concern ourselves with features of linguistic structure. No feedback is allowed, and we shall ask what the bare minimum of linguistic similarity might be that would allow successful
transmission of messages about referents.

(1) There must be shared categories of meaning so that
speakers will attend to the same features of the referent materials.

(2) There must be shared lexicon identifying the significant
referents, attributes, relationships, and actions, and shared central

meanings for this lexicon. Languages which are related and have many cognates are instances.

(3) The shared lexicon must be recognizable. Thus its morphophonemic realizations must be similar, and the phonological and phonetic systems must be sufficiently alike to allow recognition of the similar items. Precisely what these limitations entail is not clear. Wurm and Laycock (1961) have shown that both phonetic and phonemic differences can lead to asymmetrical intelligibility of cognates among related dialects. They have found instances where A understood B but not vice versa. They suggested use of a phonetic hierarchy of rank to account for such cases. For instance, they found that the speaker using a stop could understand a speaker using a homologous fricative, but not the reverse. This suggestion is important and needs further testing. I would have predicted the reverse, on the grounds that a speaker's repertoire in comprehension includes child variants, which tend to be of 'higher rank' phonetically than their adult models.

A second point they make is that the phonological system relationships, i.e. , those found in contrastive analysis, may allow predictions. We can suppose that one-to-one high frequency substitutions might be easy to recognize where the phonetic realization, but not the phonological system, is affected. Comprehension of foreign accents is easiest in such cases. O'Neil (in press) found that Faroese could understand Icelanders, but not vice versa, because of many-to-one conversion rules.

Further, there must be some similarities in phonotactic rules so that the lexical forms can be related. In instances of children's renditions of adult words, we often find that adults cannot comprehend because of the radical alteration in the word formation. Thus [mana] and [ŋ ən] are unlikely to be recognized as "banana" and "gun", and [me] and [ni] in another child are even less likely to be recognized as "blanket" and "candy", although each arises from regular replacement rules (Ervin-Tripp 1966). In each case, the initial consonant is nasal if a nasal occurs anyplace in the adult word, and it is homologous with the initial consonant of the model word. Other word length and syllable-forming canons differ for these two children.

(4) There must be shared order rules for the basic gram-

matical relations. By basic relations (McNeill 1966), we mean sub-ject-verb, verb-object, and modifier-head. Unless these minimal structures can be identified, the communication of messages is not possible, although topics or labels could be listed. Of course, these order constraints do not apply where the lexical items could only express one of these relations, as often is the case.

There has been, to my knowledge, no research raising pre-cisely the above structural questions and using the Two Person Com-munication game. Esper (1966) studied the transmission of linguistic forms through a series of speakers experimentally, employing refer-ents and artificial languages but in a different procedure. He found surprisingly rapid morphological regularization, which suggests that this is the "natural" tendency historically, within socially isolated groups.

Stewart (1967) has commented on two natural instances of cross-language communication where precisely these factors might impair intelligibility. "Ah 'own know wey 'ey lib", he argued, con-tains sufficient changes in phonetic realizations, word-formation rules, and so on, to seriously impair recognition of "I don't know where they live". "Dey ain't like dat" is likely to be misunderstood as "They aren't like that" rather than "They didn't like that." The dialect translation of the first would be "Dey not like dat" or "Dey don't be like dat," depending on a semantic contrast, not realized in standard English, between momentary and repeated conditions. This second example indicates that the basic grammatical relations may be the same, but misunderstanding still remains possible. Of course, Stewart was not discussing the highly restricted referential situation of our experiment.

The fascinating permutations on this experimental procedure would permit testing many analogs of natural language change and language contact. We have predicted that when speaker A addresses listener B, under optimal social conditions, the success of the ini-tial communication depends on structural relations between languages a and b. If B has had earlier experience with other speakers of a, we might expect him to have learned to translate features of a into b, to some extent. It must take some frequency of instances to rec-ognize structural similarities. We already know that A will provide better instructions, even without any feedback, with time (if he is old enough) (Krauss and Weinheimer 1964). Where exchange is always unidirectional, B learns to understand language a to some degree, and becomes a 'passive bilingual'. Note that B is not just listening but is required by the task to perform actions; thus he is not like a television watcher.

If give-and-take can occur, it is conceivable that a third language, c, might develop, with shared properties drawn from a and b. Such a development would be like the growth of a pidgin between two monolinguals under the press of trade or other limited encounters (Reinecke 1938). One test of the degree to which c is actually intermediate between the other two, or a composite, is to test whether when c is the code, A can communicate more successfully with B than he first did with B. That is, we assume that if c is closer to b than was a, it should be a more efficient means of communication, even to a neophyte listener.

The encounter of speakers from different language communities has had a variety of outcomes in natural conditions, including mutual bilingualism, the evolution of a pidgin, and one-way bilingualism (Reinecke 1938; Weinreich 1953). It might be possible to explore the social conditions yielding these varied results by controlled manipulation of conditions.

An important feature of this procedure is that it can allow separate assessment of comprehension and speech similarity. If system a is understood or perhaps translated into b by the listener, there is no implication that B necessarily can speak language a. It is quite a separate issue whether features of a enter into the speech of B; under some social conditions, features could perhaps be transmitted without comprehension.

Several recent studies of intergroup 'comprehension' make the issue of objective measurement of intelligibility important. Peisach (1965) has studied replacement of omitted items (the Cloze procedure) in passages of children's speech. She found that middle class children do better than lower class children in replacing every nth word verbatim in the middle class samples of speech, and on the lower class speech they do as well as the lower class children. When similarity of grammatical category alone is considered, she found Negro speech replaceable equally by all, but white speech easier

for the middle class children (and for white children). The Cloze
procedure requires actual emission of the appropriate response. It
can be considered a form of comprehension test only if one believes
in the "analysis-by-synthesis" theory of comprehension; it is not,
on its face, a comprehension measure. Another way of stating the
results is that middle class children can predict and imitate lower
class and Negro speech, but lower class and Negro children are un-
willing (or unable) to produce middle class and white speech by the
fifth grade. Harms (1961) found the opposite among adults, who
"understood" speakers of high social rank best, or of their own level
when using Cloze.

       Labov and Cohen (1967) have some striking evidence suggest-
ing that many Negro children, also in New York, can comprehend
but not produce standard English. Many of the children highly motivated to imitate sentences gave back "I asked Alvin if he knows how to
play basketball" as "I aks Alvin do he know how to play basketball."
These translations are regarded by the children as accurate imitations.
Likewise "Nobody ever saw that game" would become "Nobody never
saw that game". For the grammatical differences not arising by
deletion rules out of the standard grammar, the children frequently
understood but were not able to produce the standard forms. Nor
did they notice the difference, going directly to the meaning (Jacqueline Sachs 1967).

       Two groups can communicate extremely well, indeed per-
fectly, though they speak different languages. Multilingual conversations are an everyday occurrence in many social milieux. There
may be interspersed lexical borrowings in both languages, but if
there is a common semantic core, mutual communication can survive
very different realization rules.

       If it is the case that the social life of a community could be
carried on without speech similarity, then we cannot explain language similarity solely by the demands of basic communication.
A more profound account is needed.

B. Communicative Frequency

       A common explanation for the evidence of linguistic similar-
ity and its distribution is the frequency of communication between

speakers. The most obvious determinants of frequency are proximity, work, power, and liking. If one undertakes to write a rule predicting who will speak to whom, with a given intent, proximity always enters into the rule. Thus in housing projects, people at positions near high-traffic points are talked with more; in classrooms, neighbors become acquainted; and in small groups, seating controls interchange frequency (Hare and Bales 1963).

Some selection factors may make proximity secondary, except as a cost component, so that we find people commuting hours to a place of work or flying six thousand miles to a conference. In small groups, resources or status, assigned or assumed, may increase frequency of interchange (Bales et al. 1951). Considerable research suggests that people select "similar" addressees for social interaction, which, in turn, increases their liking. Homans, in fact, pointed out that the interaction arising from sheer proximity could create "sentiments" (1950) and thereby increase liking. All of these features which measurably increase interaction in studies of face-to-face groups have cumulative effects that are visible sociologically.

These features of face-to-face interaction compounded over many individuals should be evident in the geographical distribution of linguistic features. One of the oldest forms of sociolinguistics is dialect geography. The distribution of particular speech features is mapped, the boundaries being isoglosses. Normally these are not identical for different speech features. Extensive studies have been made of such distributions in Europe and in the United States— for instance, of bag vs. sack, grea/ s/ y vs. grea/ z/ y. In general, linguistic features reveal the patterns of migration, intermarriage, and transportation routes. If there are natural barriers or social barriers to marriage or friendship, isoglosses may appear. Thus, McDavid (1951) noted that the rise of the large northern ghettoes in the past 40 years has led to an increase in the linguistic distance between northern whites and Negroes. Individual lexical items may follow the salesman: 'tonic' is used in the Boston marketing area for soft drinks, and 'chesterfield' for couch or sofa in the San Francisco wholesale region.

The political boundaries between communities are sharp but may not seriously affect interaction frequency over time. This we can infer from the fact that isoglosses do not match political boundaries. Isoglosses often do not even correspond with each other; that is, individual features may not diffuse at the same time or in the same way. Changes, as one would expect on a frequency model, are gradual. Gumperz (1958), in a study of phonemic isoglosses, found that changes were gradual even within the isoglosses. The functional load or practical importance of the contrast gradually decreased until it disappeared, and the phonetic distinctiveness also decreased.

The most extreme test of the argument that frequency of communication reduces speech diversity occurs in bilingual contacts. Gumperz (1967) located a border region between Indo-Aryan and Dravidian speaking sectors of India in which speakers were bilingual, using Marathi and Kannada in different settings. These border dialects have become increasingly similar in centuries of bilingualism. They have the same semantic features, syntax, and phonology, and differ only in the phonemic shape of morphemes, what we might call the vocabulary and function words. Each dialect is essentially a morpheme-by-morpheme translation of the other. However, other speakers of Kannada still identify this dialect as a form of Kannada because they recognize its morphemes— it is simply a deviant form, as Jamaican Creole is a deviant form of English.

This example illustrates both convergence of speech with high interaction frequency, and the maintenance of contrast. The convergence occurs at those levels of language we believe are least conscious and least criterial for the identification of the language. Speakers tend to identify languages by the shape of the morphemes, by the vocabulary, but even more by its function words and inflectional and derivational morphemes. The Kannada-Marathi example demonstrates that in spite of high contact frequency, speakers may insist on maintaining linguistic diversity, and that they may, in fact, believe it to be greater than it is.

There are many instances, to be discussed later, where frequency is high but speech distinctiveness is maintained. Castes in India interact with high frequency; Negro servants in the United States interact with employers; lower class pupils interact with teachers; and Spanish-speaking grandmothers interact with English-speaking grandsons— yet diversity persists.

High frequency of communication is a necessary but not a sufficient condition for increased linguistic similarity. High frequency of communication must result, at a minimum, in passive bilingualism of both parties, active bilingualism of one party, or a lingua franca. The only necessity is that each understand the speech of the other.

We do not yet know what the consequences of passive control of two systems must be. Active control typically leads to convergence at certain levels, starting with semantic boundaries and frequency of syntactic options (Earle 1967; Ervin 1961; McNeill 1966; Ervin-Tripp 1967). We have argued that there are cognitive reasons for such fusions and that they tend to take place when social conditions, such as contact with monolinguals, reading, and strong values about co-occurrence restrictions, do not provide strong support for system separation. Presumably, passive control of a second language has less impact.

Only one study has directly related the communication frequency of individual persons who all communicate to speech similarity. Hammer et al (1965) measured the observed centrality of individuals, and also the person-to-person frequency for every pair in a New York coffee shop with a regular clientele. They obtained speech samples and used the Cloze procedure. Central persons were most predictable, and each person most successfully predicted the omitted items from the speech of persons with whom he interacted most.

It is not quite clear what is measured in Cloze. All phonological features are missing. What is included are semantic factors that influence collocations, vocabulary, and perhaps some aspects of grammar. This study at first seems to support frequency as a critical variable in similarity, but it may not actually meet the critical limitations. The study was done in a social setting, interaction was social, and the members were parts of friendship networks. That is, some third variable may have determined both interaction frequency and similarity on Cloze. The hidden variable seems to be cohesiveness.

C. Cohesiveness and Linguistic Diversity

It seems that people talk like those with whom they have the closest social ties. We do not know precisely why this is the case;

it may be that the features of social relationships which bring about
this result are not the same for all types of speech similarity. In
social networks and groups, there is a high frequency of interaction.
The high attraction of others in the group or network means that
they not only serve as models but can also act as reinforcing agents
in their responses to speech, affecting attitudes toward features in
the community repertoire. In addition, there might be secondary
reinforcement in sounding like a valued person.

All levels of speech appear to be affected. With respect to
the phonetic realization of phonemes, age may constrain changes in
the system. Even under optimal conditions, many persons over 12
years old seem to have difficulty changing their phonetic realization
rules except under careful monitoring.

Labov (1966) has argued that the everyday vernacular is
stabilized by puberty on the basis of the peer model. Cultures where
peer ties are weaker (if any exist) would provide a valuable comparison.

The functions of communication in cohesive networks necessarily include a high frequency of requests for social reinforcement,
and of expressive speech. The social group may or may not be concerned with information and opinion exchange for its own sake.
Davis (1961), in a study of the maintenance or dissolution of 'great
books' discussion groups, found that if there were many members of a
social network in such a group, its durability was enhanced for col-
lege-educated members and decreased for noncollege-educated. He
suggested that for the latter there might be a conflict between interaction practices in the network and the constraints of the discussion
group. Bossard (1945) commented on large differences between
families in the extent of information-exchange in dinner table conversation.

The most ingenious work on interfamily differences in communication has been conducted by Basil Bernstein. He has pointed
out (1968, 1972) that communicative patterns and socialization methods
within families are related to occupational roles and to the character
of a family's social network. Empirical support was found in mothers'
reports of use of appeals to children, emphasis on different functions
of language, and encouragement of interaction. In turn, London five-

year-olds differed by social class (and by mothers' reports) in the
variety of nouns and adjectives, use of relative clauses, use of pronouns with extraverbal referents, and in ability to switch style with
task.   That some of these differences may reflect performance customs rather than capacity is suggested by the report of Cowan (1967)
that American working class children, though less successful than
middle class children on the Two Person Communication game,
learned fast when paired with middle class partners.

Hess and Shipman (1965), who observed actual mother-child
interaction in Negro preschool families, found considerable social class
variation and between-family variation in the extent to which mothers
used the situation to elicit labeling and informational communication
from the children.   The measures correlated two years later with
oral comprehension.   Schatzmann and Strauss (1955) found social
class differences in oral narratives that may be related to Bernstein's
distinction.   See also Lawton (1964).

There has been too little study of natural interaction <u>within</u>
social groups to extricate what the important differences are— whether
they lie in the amount of interaction of children with adults vs. peers
and siblings, whether there are differences in encounters with
strangers and training of children in competence with outsiders, or
whether there are differences in emphasis in intragroup speech
functions.

Because evidence about the verbal skills of lower class
Negroes came from formal testing situations and classrooms, there
have been widespread misconceptions about "verbal deprivation" in
American society, with expensive educational consequences.   Recent
investigators such as Labov and Cohen (1967) in Harlem and Edding-
ton and Claudia Mitchell in San Francisco and Oakland have recorded
natural interaction.   All have found that Negro lower class speakers
are highly verbal in terms of speech frequency.   Both adolescents
and children engage with great skill in verbal games for which they
have complex traditions.   "Controlled situations" may, in fact, obscure
the very skills which have been most developed within a particular
group.

"General verbal deprivation" could conceivably exist.   It
most probably would be found in unusual social isolation, or in cases

of social marginality, particularly where a language has been lost
but there has not been full access to a range of functions in a second
language. For further detailed discussion of research on this point
and some new data, see Cazden (1966, 1967).

Topics of discourse are likely to be different in cohesive
networks as a result of differing values and interests. This produces
considerable impact on the semantic structure and lexicon.

One way of studying differences in messages arising from
communication is to examine content shifts, under acculturation,
where there may be radical changes in social allegiances. A study
of this phenomenon in Japanese women married to Americans showed
that there was considerable difference between women who gave messages typical of their agemates in Tokyo and those who were more
like American women, even when speaking Japanese (Ervin-Tripp
1967). Word associations, sentence completions, TATs, story completions, and semantic differentials were all used in both languages.
In general, the women who remained more Japanese in response content would rather be Japanese than American, preserve more Japanese
customs, and keep up strong ties to Japan. The chief characteristics
of the women who shifted to American responses were that they identified with American women, had close American friends, read American magazines, and met somewhat less opposition to their marriage
from Japanese friends and family. The last point implies that in
Japan they may have been less conservative. Though both sets of
women would seem, on the surface, to have had a cohesive tie to an
American partner, the interviews revealed striking differences.
Marriages in Japan involve far more social separation of husband and
wife than here; for example, there is little joint socializing with nonkin. Many of the Japanese women in this country do not regard their
husbands as confidants in trouble, and may, indeed, seldom see them.
When either the husband or an American friend was regarded as a
close confidant, the messages were more American. It is, in fact,
not easy to give 'typically American' responses on many of these tests,
so their ability to do so represents a considerable degree of subtle
learning.

Semantic innovation is one of the striking features of cohesive
groups. There may be new activities requiring new names; there
may be finer discriminations required along continua; and there may

be new conceptual categories. These are realized by lexical innovations which spread within the network. Examples are "she's in high
drag" in the homosexual network, referring to a male homosexual in
women's clothing (Cory 1952); "prat", "breech", "insider", "tail
pit", and "fob", pickpocket jargon for pockets (Conwell 1937); "cooling the mark out" by the confidence man (Goffman 1952); and "trivial" or
"motivated", and "reflexive", terms used among transformationalists
and ethnomethodologists respectively, with special meanings. Many
examples can be found in Mauer (1962).

A glimpse of the working of this process can be seen in the
Two Person Communicative game.

Krauss and Weinheimer (1964) found that reference phrases
became abbreviated with practice. Given the limitation on necessary
referential distinctions, abbreviated coding is efficient. The result
is not merely a change in the external shape of the form but a semantic
shift, since the simplest term comes to have the specific meaning of
the highly qualified phrase. The authors mention analogies like "hypo"
among photographers and "comps" among graduate students.

Brent and Katz (1967) made comparisons of types of coding
of drawings by middle class whites and by Negro Job Corps teenagers.
Unfortunately, they used geometric shapes, which gives a distinct
advantage to subjects who are formally educated. They found that the
Negro subjects were relatively successful although they used nontechnical names like "sharp-pointed piece", "a square wiggling", and
"the funny looking piece". It would be an advantage to use materials
equally strange or equally familiar to both groups and to control network features of the speaker and listener. We have strong evidence
that members of the same social group prefer nontechnical communication. Where materials are neutral (e.g., nonsense forms), nontechnical, highly metaphorical communication is most efficient in
terms of both brevity and success in a nonfeedback condition.

Even though the semantic distinctions made are not new,
group jargon or new morphophonemic realizations for lexical categories are common in cohesive groups. Occasionally, such terminology arises to allow secrecy before outsiders (though Conwell and
Mauer commented that secrecy is better served by semantic shift
employing conventional morphemes). New morphemes are the most

apparent mark of an ingroup, whether or not they realize novel semantic distinctions. In fact, the best test for the symbolic value of the
marker is whether it has referential meaning and, if so, whether it
is translatable. Conwell (1937) pointed out that the pickpocket's terminology is not used before outsiders, but it is used to test the trust-
worthiness of a member of the network and to find how much he knows.
In simple terms, the use of such terms can symbolize membership if
the group is large or boundary maintenance is important; if the group
is small, like a family, and its members known, the terms are used
to indicate solidarity. Bossard (1945) cited examples of family words;
many baby words or nicknames survive with such social meanings.

Where the incidence of social or regional dialect difference
coincides with density of friendship network, the structural dialect
features, including syntax and phonology, may come to be markers
of cohesiveness. Blom and Gumperz (1972) found that the local dialect of Hemnisberget, Norway, had this significance to its residents.

Labov (1963) observed that the rate of dialect change was
different in Martha's Vineyard among young men, depending upon
their social loyalties. There was a change in progress very markedly
differentiating young men from their grandparents. The men who
went along in this direction were those who had the strongest local
ties and did not want to move off-island. It is not clear whether or
not interaction frequencies were also affected by the different values.
The effects showed up in articulation.

Strong social ties affect all aspects of linguistic systems;
our evidence suggests that the most quickly affected are the semantic
system and lexicon — in short, the vocabulary. The structural morphemes evidently are not as sensitive to the forces of cohesion as
are other morphemes.

D. Identity Marking

Every society is differentiated by age and sex; in addition,
rank, occupational identities, and other categories will be found.
Since the rights and duties of its members are a function of these identities, it is of great social importance to establish high visibility for
them. Sometimes this has been done by legislation controlling permissible clothing, house type, and so on. Everywhere it seems to

be the case that information about social identity is contained in speech variables. In urban societies, the social function of such marking is greater, since it may be the only information available; on the other hand, the social sanctions for violation may be reduced. McCormack (1960) has noted the spread of upper caste dialect features in urban lower caste speakers in India.

In some cases, there may be more frequent communication within, rather than between, categories. Clearly, this is not always the case; within the western family, communication occurs with high frequency across both sex and age categories. Therefore, something other than frequency of communication or group cohesion must account for the preservation of speech diversity which marks social identity.

It is not precisely clear what features of speech mark sex in the United States. In some languages (Haas 1957; Martin, in Hymes 1964) lexicon, function words, and phonological rules are different for males and females. The study of the training of boys by women in such societies would be enlightening. There are clearly topical differences arising from occupational and family status and, therefore, possibly semantic differences and differences in lexical repertoire. Masculinity-femininity tests have leaned heavily on differences in lexicon, particularly in the meanings realized, or in collocations. Sociolinguistic rules are probably not the same; e.g., speech etiquette concerning taboo words. Men and women do not use terms of address in quite the same way, and young women, at least, use more deferential request forms than young men. In fact, it is commonly the case in many languages that women employ more deferential speech, but one can expect that such differences are related to other indicators of relative rank. For example, in jury deliberations (Strodtbeck et al. 1957), women are several steps lower in social class, in terms of their speech frequency and evaluation by fellow jurors. Labov (1966) and Levine and Crockett (1966) found more situational style shifting by women; Fischer (1958) recorded the formal "-ing" suffix relatively more often from girls than boys.

Age differences in speech arise both through language change and age-grading. Though grandparent and grandchild may communicate, they are unlikely to have the same system. Labov (1963, 1966a) related several such changes to current distributions. For instance, he points out the spread of "r" in New York City. In the top social class, in casual speech, "r" was used by only 43% of the respondents over 40 years old but by twice as many of the younger respondents. Changes like ice box-refrigerator (for the latter object), and victrola-phonograph-record player-stereo are apparent to all of us.

In addition, certain lexicon or structures may be considered inappropriate at a particular age. Newman (1954) remarked that slang is for the young Zunis. Children over a certain age are expected to stop using nursery terms like "bunny", "piggy", "potty", and "horsie", except in addressing infants. Pig Latin and other playful transforms (Conklin 1959) may be age-restricted. Stewart has claimed that a form he calls "basilect" is learned among Washington, D.C. Negroes from their peers in early childhood and begins to disappear, under negative sanctions, around age 7 or 8. Adolescents studied in New York (Labov and Cohen 1967) had forms similar to the adolescent speech of some Washington D.C. speakers, including two features absent in standard English: a completive or intensive-perfective "I done seen it" or "I done forgot it" (semantically contrasted with the simple past or perfect); and a distinction with be analogous to the distinction between habitual use and momentary or ongoing action (a distinction made in the standard language only for other action verbs): "He be with us all the time", vs. "He with us right now" (He walks every day vs. He's walking right now).

Many statuses entail the learning of specialized languages or superposed varieties. The Brahmin, for example, is likely to have studied English and to have many more borrowings in his speech than the non-Brahmin. Brahmins can sometimes be identified by such borrowed forms or by literary vocabulary (McCormack 1960), just as psychologists' occupational register can identify them. In addition, the functions and topics imposed by occupations can alter the speech of parents in the home, and in "anticipatory socialization" the children from different occupational milieux may be affected.

One way to differentiate similarity arising from cohesion from difference arising from identity marking is the presence of negative sanctions. Ramanujan pointed out (1967) that Brahmin parents specifically reject non-Brahmin items or use them with pejorative connotations. The Brahmins show, in several respects, that they value the preservation of markers of their identity. They consciously borrow more foreign forms and preserve their phonological deviance so that their phonological repertoire is very large. They have maintained more morphological irregularities (like our strong verbs) in their development of various inflectional paradigms, even though the evidence suggests that the earlier language (now written) was more regular. The evidence from the Esper experiment (1966) and the evolution of the non-Brahmin dialects is that regularization is the more normal destiny unless some factor interferes. In cases of phonological difference from the non-Brahmin dialects, in the realization of cognates, they have, in morphemes where the realizations fall together in the two dialects and would thus be indistinguishable, innovated a distinction. The semantic space is far more differentiated, as is the lexicon. The learning of a language full of irregularities is obviously more difficult — every child spontaneously regularizes. Like the Mandarin learning Chinese characters, the Brahmin puts additional effort into the maintenance of an elite dialect because the reward is its distinctive marking of his identity.

One might assume that lower castes would adopt prestige speech, and there is, as cited earlier, some evidence of such tendencies in urban milieux. One way of preventing such spread is the use of a non-Brahmin style when addressing non-Brahmins which, of course, reduces frequency of exposure. In addition, there are sanctions against such emulation.

American Negro speech may provide an example of identity marking although the evidence is ambiguous. Stewart has argued (1967) that Negro speech is based on creoles used in the early slave period, and that this history accounts for some of the basic semantic and syntactical differences Labov and Cohen (1967) have recently cited, which appear in various black communities all over the country. Labov has suggested that working class casual speech features connote solidarity, reducing the impact of standard English heard in school on casual style.

Certainly the clearest evidence of the identity-marking function of language is language maintenance during contact. Fishman (1966) has extensively discussed various features of language maintenance programs. Although the dominant groups in the United States have strongly favored language shift by immigrants, to the point of legislating against vernacular education, some groups continued to resist the loss of their language. Those who succeeded best, according to Kloss (in Fishman 1966), did so either by total isolation (like the Canadian Dukhobors) or by living in sufficiently dense concentrations to allow a high frequency of ingroup communication and the use of their language for the widest range of social functions. In particular, many maintained their own educational facilities, e.g., Chinese, Japanese, and Russians, promoting in-group cohesion among the children. A critical turning point lies in the speech practices of teen-agers. Where they are forced to mix with outsiders in large urban schools or consolidated rural school districts, the group language tends to disappear.

In parts of the world where there is a stabilized condition of great language diversity, as in Africa and Asia, it is quite normal to retain the group vernacular as a home language but to be bilingual for wider communication. Probably the degree of language distance in these cases is relatively small, as Gumperz has pointed out (1967). In these instances, the shape of morphemes is an important identity marker; shifting between co-occurrent sets of morphemes by such bilinguals is merely a more extreme instance of the small group vocabulary of the family, stabilized through time by endogamy and by the high value placed on group identity markers.

An extreme case in the opposite direction occurs in initial invention of pidgins. Here values of identity may be unimportant, and the practical need to communicate dominates. In fact, pidgins tend to develop when the norms which sustain co-occurrence rules are missing. Thus they appear in the transitory encounters of traders away from home, in the fortuitous combination of diverse speakers in the setting of work—in plantations, mines, and harbor cities. In this respect, African urbanization and slavery shared a feature, and we may guess that earlier circumstances of urbanization also gave rise to pidgins. Pidgins are characterized structurally by morphological simplification and regularization, and by use of material from more than one language. At first, they are spoken with the phonetic features of the respective mother tongues. Of course, with time the pidgin can come to symbolize the subordinate-employer relation. Temporary communication systems much like pidgins occur widely in contact conditions in the United States. These situations have never been given the serious study they deserve.

When a pidgin becomes the mother tongue of its speakers (and thereby technically a creole), it may acquire all the values of group identity of other vernaculars. Meredith (1964) quoted a speaker of Hawaiian Pidgin (a creole language) who was subjected to a university requirement of mastery of standard English: "Why you try change me? I no want to speak like damn haole!" Meredith reported "hostility, disinterest, and resistance to change" in the remedial class. The changes in the functions and structure of pidgins which become mother tongues can be studied by comparing second-language speakers with their children for whom it is a mother tongue (Sankoff and Laberge 1971).

E.   Attitudes Toward Speech Diversity

In studying phonological diversity in New York City speech, Labov (1966) identified three different categories of social phenomena arising from diversity. These he called "indicators", "markers", and "stereotypes"

Indicators are features which are noted only by the trained observer. For example, few people are aware that "cot" and "caught" are distinguished in some areas and not in others. Indicators are features which are functions of social indices like class or region but neither vary with style in a given speaker nor enter into beliefs about language.

Markers, in Labov's system, vary with both group membership and style of the speaker, and can be used in role-switching. In the New York City system, he found that "r", "oh", and "eh" were very powerful markers, in that they changed radically according to the self-monitoring of the speaker. In Fig. 5, the use of less [t] and more [th] with increased self-monitoring is shown by the slopes. A speaker who in rapid excited speech might say, "It wasn't a good day but a bid one", or "Ian saw tree cahs goin by," might in reading say "bad", and "Ann saw three cars going by".

Stereotypes, like their social counterparts, may or may not conform to social reality, and tend to be categorical. Thus, although a working class man might use [t] or [d] only 40% to 50% of the time, he will be heard as always saying "dis", "dat", and "ting". Evidence suggests that children notice differences like "bath" vs. "baf", and "window" vs. "winda", though they may ignore simple phonetic shifts.

Hypercorrection involves the spread of a speech feature from a higher prestige group to another, with overgeneralization of the feature based on a categorical stereotype. In Fig. 6, the upper middle class used "r" considerably less in self-conscious speech than did the lower middle class, who believed it to be characteristic of the best speech. A more common example can be seen in the contrast between standard English "He and I came" and nonstandard "Him and me came". Hypercorrect versions can be found which yield "She wrote to him and I" or "She wrote to he and I". Lexical examples were given by Ian Ross (1956) and even by Emily Post (1922); usually these are instances of the extension of formal, literary, or commercial vocabulary into casual speech. Labov (1966) has shown that hypercorrection is greatest among speakers who score high on a Linguistic Insecurity Index, derived from comparison of what they report they say and what they select as correct in pairs which, in fact, are not markers. Levine and Crockett (1966) also found that the second highest group shifted most with style.

Blau (1956) has observed a very similar phenomenon among upwardly mobile persons in quite different measures of insecurity: These people report more nervousness, are more likely to discriminate against Negro neighbors than any other types, and in these respects the members of high and low social classes are more alike than the intermediate people, provided they are mobile.

Labov (1966) has suggested that there may be "unconscious" stereotypes which account for borrowings which are not from prestige groups. He suggested that the masculinity connotation of working class casual speech might be such an instance. His measure of subjective reaction to speech samples required subjects to rank the speaker occupationally, thus, clearly asking for social class stereotypes rather than features implying some other social meaning.

The richest variety of work along this line is that of Lambert (1963, 1967a) and his collaborators, who have had the same speaker use "guises" to produce samples. These then are rated for a great range of features like personality, intelligence, and physical traits. French Canadians, he found, rated a "French guise" as less intelligent and less a leader than the English-Canadian guise. In a study in Israel (Lambert et al. 1965), on the other hand, it was found that Arabic-speaking and Hebrew-speaking subjects had mutually hostile stereotypes when judging the guises. Tucker and Lambert (1967) found that evaluation by northern white and southern Negro college students differed in that Mississippi Negro college speech was least favored by the whites, and southern educated white speech least favored by the Negroes. Top-valued forms were the same for both groups.

Harms (1961) recorded speech from different social classes and found that 10-15 second samples could be differentiated by listeners. Regardless of their own class, they rated high-ranked speakers as more credible. This method, like that of Lambert's, does not allow isolation of the critical linguistic features. Lambert, on the other hand, has been able to identify a far wider range of social meanings in the speech variations than did the single scales of Labov and of Harms.

Triandis et al. (1966) tried to balance various sources of judgment by counterbalancing race, messages (on discrimination legislation), and standard vs. nonstandard grammar. Slides were shown while a tape was played. College students who were uninfluenced by race as "liberals" were still much influenced by grammar, even more than by the message, in their judgment of the man's character, ideas, value, and social acceptability. Three-fourths of the variance on admiration and evaluation is carried by the linguistic contrast. A new test for liberals might be this: "Would you want your daughter to marry a man who says ain't?"

Some consequences of these stereotypes about language can be seen in Rosenthal and Jackson's (1966) finding that IQ scores of pupils during a year rose 15 points when teachers were told arbitrary children were "fast gainers". Linguistic variables may convey the same message.

F. Rules for Diversity

William Labov has begun to use his large collection of material on speech of different New York City groups to discover rules accounting both for stylistic and intergroup diversity quantitatively.

He has been able to use quantitative functions because he has been measuring articulation ranges and frequencies of occurrence as speech variables, as well as using quantitative measures of social variables. Thus the rules he can find are not categorical in structure like those in an earlier section.

Figure 5 shows that a phonetic feature is a linear function both of social class and of style. Because of the apparently regular change with style, Labov hypothesized that there is a single dimension he called "self-monitoring" underlying the style differences. Obviously, the relationship can be expressed by a linear equation in which the phonetic variable = $\underline{a}$ (class) + $\underline{b}$ (style) + $\underline{c}$.

In the case of hypercorrection of the kind shown in Fig. 6, the measure of linguistic insecurity can be used as a function of style, increasing its slope. For such phonetic variables, the function is $\underline{a}$ (class) + $\underline{b}$ (style) (Linguistic Insecurity Index) + $\underline{c}$. Some adjustments are made for age as well, since there is an interaction of age, class, and norms.

These rules are important innovations. They treat linguistic phenomena as continuous variables. Whether the use of continuous measures is possible except at the phonetic and semantic edge of linguistics is not clear; frequencies certainly are quantifiable for discrete categories too. The rules, like those in an earlier section, introduce social features as integral components. Normally, social features are mentioned in linguistic descriptions as a last resort, such as in a few style variations like those in Japanese where morphological rules must consider addressee. Finally, they include, in a single formal description, the differences between speakers and the differences within speakers. The fact that this is possible is impressive evidence of the existence of an over-all sociolinguistic system larger than the cognitive structure of members individually. As Labov has pointed out, a single member sees the system only along the coordinates of his own position in it; he only witnesses the full style variation of his own social peers. In fact, the possibility of writing rules which transcend class suggests a new criterion for a speech community.

We have argued that the distribution of features of speech and of mutual intelligibility across people shows discontinuities, and that these are based on social cohesiveness in networks and on boundary-marking to maintain group identity, as well as on frequency of interaction. These same forces must affect the distribution of sociolinguistic rules. A particular greeting form may be used uniquely in a particular group; the conditions determining when greetings shall occur could also vary, and serve as boundary markers. One suspects, however, that these rules are somewhat less subject to conscious control than vocabulary selection, and may be considerably harder for an outsider to learn.

Such delicate differences as whether one can say "Yes, Professor" without a last name can indicate group membership as surely as features of accent or vocabulary. This address form is impossible under the rule in Figure 1, and could be used only by an outsider, or as an allusion to outsiders.

Performance in speech events which are special to a group may be a kind of test of membership, of secret knowledge. Members who disseminate cultural knowledge to outsiders could be viewed by some as displaying the group's prowess, or by others as betraying secrets useful for defining boundaries. The attitude of members to cooperation on research on sociolinguistics thus becomes itself a datum about the functions of those rules in the group.

Just as alternation rules and the structure of speech events must be learned, so code and register shifting is not random. The linguistic features available for shifting, the types of co-occurrence rules, and the social meaning of various kinds of shifting could vary in various networks since shifting is used for communicative purposes (Gumperz and Hernandez-Ch. 1971).

Linguistic features provide us with new and sensitive indices of class or group identification, socialization and role-shifting. The precision with which these features can be specified makes them valuable for the study of on-going interaction. Linguistic interaction is deeply embedded in nearly all our social processes, in socialization in the family, into new occupations, and into a new social community. Sociolinguistic rules are central to, even if they do not totally compose the organized structure which generates our social acts and through which we interpret others. Just as the study of linguistic structure is seen by many as a penetrating route to cognitive structure in the speaking human, so may sociolinguistic rules lead to rules for social action. Through these rules we may be able to identify the acts which are the functional units of interaction, since rules, unlike arbitrary coding schemes, reflect the actor's own natural system.

NOTES

I am deeply indebted to John Gumperz and to William Labov for detailed commentary on a draft of this article, and to Dell Hymes and other members of the Sociolinguistics Committee of the Social Science Research Council, as well as to our work group in Berkeley, for discussions which have radically altered my view of this field. This article was written with the support of the Institute of Human Development and some aid from the Laboratory for Language-Behavior Research of the University of California. Elizabeth Closs Traugott provided some address data. Student work contributing to generalizations in the text included studies by Reneé Ackerman, Lou Bilter, Camille Chamberlain, Judith Horner, Andrea Kaciff, Terrence Keeney, Jane Logan, Dana Meyer, Paula Palmquist, Elaine Rogers, Joan von Schlegell, Elisabeth Selkirk, and Billi Wooley. Soviet material was provided by Dan Slobin. The major sections of this article have appeared before with minor revisions as: On sociolinguistic rules: alternation and co-occurrence, in Directions in sociolinguistics: the ethnography of communication, edited by J.J. Gumperz and Dell Hymes, New York, Holt, Rinehart and Winston, 1971, 218-250, and in Sociolinguistics, in Advances in experimental social psychology, edited by Leonard Berkowitz, New York, Academic Press, 1968, 4. 91-165.

[1]Reference rules involve additional considerations such as the relation of the addressee and referent. If the addressee is of lower rank or age than both the referent and the speaker, then the speaker in Figure 1 employs the addressee's address term, e.g. Mrs. Jones may refer to her husband to addressees who know him as "Charles" to a friend, "Mr. Jones" to a servant, or "Daddy" to his child.

[2]English occupational titles usually neutralize sex. The first woman appointee to the British High Court of Justice produced an address crisis because the traditional occupational titles contained terms that in other contexts are selected by sex. "Mrs. Lane, like

the other justices, were by the lord chancellor's decree to be called
'My Lord' and 'Mr. Justice Lane.' His Lordship, Mr. Justice Lane,
is also entitled by ancient judicial tradition to a bachelor knighthood.''
(Time, August 27, 1965.) Justices in British law wear wigs and
robes, elaborating the status marking of the settings in which they
act. The decision shows that to members, the terms are not sex
indicators, and that the alternatives, "My Lady" and "Mrs. Justice
Lane," would be sex marked rather than neutral, just as "chair-
woman" is.

[3]In the system shown in Fig. 1, it is possible to create asymmetrical address by using FN to a familiar addressee who cannot
reciprocate because of rank or age difference and lack of dispensation,
e.g. a domestic servant. Everett Hughes has noted a shift from TLN
to FN by physicians whose patients moved from private fees to Medi-
care. Since this usage cannot be accommodated on Fig. 1, the patients
have no recourse but to feel demeaned like Dr. Poussaint.

[4]William Geohegan has proposed that under very high conditions of familiarity as in village families, paralinguistic and other
non-lexical cues are used, not lexical alternatives.

[5]These rules will not account for the devoicing of $[\check{c}]$ in
ellipsis of underlying "what are" but not of "what did", so it is
clear that rate rules should be rules operating on the realization of
underlying features rather than surface changes as described here.

REFERENCES

Ayoub, Milla. 1962. Bi-polarity in Arabic kinship terms. In H. G.
    Lunt (ed.), Proceedings of the Ninth International Congress
    of Linguists (The Hague: Mouton), pp. 1100-1106.
Bales, R. F. and E. F. Borgatta. 1955. Size of groups as a factor
    in the interaction profile. In A. Hare, E. F. Borgatta, and
    R. F. Bales (eds.), Small Groups (New York: Wiley), pp.
    396-413.
Bales, R. F., F. Strodtbeck, T. Mills and Mary E. Roseborough.
    1951. Channels of communication in small groups. Ameri-
    can Sociological Review 6. 461-468.
Bellugi, Ursula. 1967. The acquisition of negation. Ph. D. disser-
    tation, Harvard Graduate School of Education.

Bernstein, Basil. 1964. Elaborated and restricted codes: their
     social origins and some consequences. In John J. Gumperz
     and Dell Hymes (eds.), The ethnography of communication.
     American Anthropologist 66. 6/2.55-69.
_____ 1968. Language, Primary Socialization and Education
     (London: Routledge and Kegan Paul).
_____ 1972. A socio-linguistic approach to socialization:
     with some references to educability. In J.J. Gumperz and
     D. Hymes (eds.), Directions in Sociolinguistics (New York:
     Holt, Rinehart and Winston), 465-497.
Blau, P. 1956. Social mobility and interpersonal relations. Ameri-
     can Sociological Review 21. 290-295.
Blom, J.P., and J.J. Gumperz. 1972. Some social determinants of
     verbal behavior. In J.J. Gumperz and D. Hymes (eds.),
     Directions in Sociolinguistics (New York: Holt, Rinehart,
     and Winston).
Bossard, J.H.S. 1945. Family modes of expression. American
     Sociological Review 10. 226-237.
Brent, S.G., and Evelyn W. Katz. 1967. A study of language devia-
     tions and cognitive processes. OEO-Job Corps Project 1209,
     Progress Report No. 3 (Wayne State University).
Brown, Roger W. and Marguerite Ford. 1961. Address in American
     English. Journal of Abnormal and Social Psychology 62.
     375-385.
Brown, R.W., and A. Gilman. 1960. The pronouns of power and
     solidarity. In T. Sebeok (ed.), Style in Language (Cambridge,
     Mass.: MIT Press), pp. 253-276.
Capell, A. 1966. Studies in socio-linguistics (The Hague: Mouton).
Carroll, J.B. 1958. Process and content in psycholinguistics. In
     R. Glaser (ed.), Current Trends in the Description and Anal-
     ysis of Behavior (Pittsburgh, Penn.: University of Pitts-
     burgh Press), pp. 175-200.
Cazden, Courtney B. 1966. Subcultural differences in child language:
     An inter-disciplinary review. Merrill-Palmer Quarterly
     12. 185-219.
_____ 1967. On individual differences in language competence
     and performance. Journal of Special Education 1. 135-150.
Chomsky, Noam and Morris Halle. 1968. The sound pattern of
     English. New York: Harper and Row.
Conklin, Harold C. 1959. Linguistic play in its cultural context.
     Language 35. 631-636.

Conwell, C. 1937. The Professional Thief (Chicago, Ill.: University of Chicago Press).

Cory, D. W. 1952. The Homosexual in America (New York: Greenberg).

Cowan, P. 1967. The link between cognitive structure and social structure in two-child verbal interaction. Symposium presented at the Society for Research on Child Development meeting.

Davis, J. A. 1961. Compositional effects, systems, and the survival of small discussion groups. Public Opinion Quarterly 25. 574-584.

Diebold, A. R. 1963. Code-switching in Greek-English bilingual speech. Georgetown University Monograph Series on Languages and Linguishes 15.

Dikeman, Bessie and Patricia Parker. 1964. Request forms. Term paper for Speech 160B, University of California, Berkeley.

Dollard, J. and F. Auld Jr. 1959. Scoring Human Motives: A Manual (New Haven, Conn.: Yale University Press).

Drach, K., B. Kobashigawa, C. Pfuderer, and D. Slobin. 1969. The structure of linguistic input to children. Language-Behavior Research Laboratory, working paper No. 14, Berkeley, University of California.

Earle, Margaret J. 1967. Bilingual semantic merging and an aspect of acculturation. Journal of Personality and Social Psychology 6. 304-312.

Ervin, Susan M. 1961. Semantic shift in bilingualism. American Journal of Psychology 74. 233-241. [In this volume, pp. 33-44.]
_____ 1964. Language and TAT content in bilinguals. Journal of Abnormal and Social Psychology 68. 500-507. [In this volume, pp. 45-61.]

Ervin-Tripp, Susan M. 1964. An analysis of the interaction of language, topic, and listener. American Anthropologist 66, No. 6, Part 2, 86-102. [In this volume, pp. 239-261.]
_____ 1966. Language development. In Lois and Martin Hoffman (eds.), Review of Child Development Research, Vol. 2 (New York: Russell Sage Foundation), pp. 55-106.
_____ 1967. An Issei learns English. Journal of Social Issues 23. No. 2, 78-90. [In this volume, pp. 62-77.]
_____ 1968. On becoming a bilingual. In L. G. Kelly (ed.), The Description and Measurement of Bilingualism 26-35. (Toronto: University of Toronto Press). [In this volume, pp. 78-91.]

Esper, E. A. 1966. Social transmission of an artificial language. Language 42. 575–580.

Ferguson, Charles A. 1959. Diglossia. Word 15: 2.325–40.
_____ 1964. Baby talk in six languages. American Anthropologist 66, No. 6, Part 2, 103–114.

Firth, J. R. 1935. The technique of semantics. Transactions of the Philological Society 36–72 (London).

Fischer, J. L. 1958. Social influence in the choice of a linguistic variant. Word 14. 47–56.
_____ 1965. The stylistic significance of consonantal sandhi in Trukese and Ponapean. American Anthropologist 67. 1495–1502.

Fishman, J. A. 1966. Language Loyalty in the United States (The Hague: Mouton).

Fishman, J. A. 1967. Bilingualism with and without diglossia; diglossia with and without bilingualism. Journal of Social Issues 23, No. 2, 29–38.

Friedrich, Paul. 1972. Social context and semantic feature: the Russian pronominal usage. In John J. Gumperz and Dell Hymes (eds.), Directions in sociolinguistics, 270–300. New York: Holt, Rinehart and Winston.

Geertz, C. 1960. The Religion of Java (Glencoe, Ill.: Free Press).

Geohegan, W. 1971. Information processing systems in culture. In P. Kay (ed.). Explorations in Mathematical Anthropology. Cambridge, Mass.: MIT Press.

Goffman, E. 1952. Cooling the mark out. Psychiatry 15. 451–463.

Goodenough, W. H. 1965. Rethinking 'status' and 'role': toward a general model of the cultural organization of social relationships. In M. Banton (ed.), The Relevance of Models for Social Anthropology (London: Tavistock), pp. 1–24.

Gumperz, J. J. 1958. Phonological differences in three Hindi dialects. Language 34. 212–224.
_____ 1964 a. Hindi–Punjabi code-switching in Delhi. In H. G. Lunt (ed.), Proceedings of the Ninth International Congress of Linguists (The Hague: Mouton), pp. 1115–1124.
_____ 1964 b. Linguistic and social interaction in two communities. In John J. Gumperz and Dell Hymes (eds.), The Ethnography of Communication. American Anthropologist 66. 6/2.137–154.
_____ 1967. On the linguistic markers of bilingual communication. Journal of Social Issues 23. 2.48–57.

Gumperz, John J. and Eduardo Hernandez-Ch. 1971. Bilingualism, bidialectalism, and classroom interaction. In Courtney Cazden, Dell Hymes, and Vera John (eds.), The Function of Language in the Classroom. New York: Teachers College Press.

Gumperz, J.J., and D. Hymes (eds.), 1964. The Ethnography of Communication. American Anthropologist 66, No. 6.

_____ 1972. Directions in Sociolinguistics (New York: Holt, Rinehart, and Winston).

Haas, Mary R. 1957. Thai word Games. Journal of American Folklore 70. 173-175.

Hammer, Muriel, Sylvia Polgar, and K. Salzinger. 1965. Comparison of data-sources in a sociolinguistic study. Paper presented at American Anthropological Association meeting, Denver, Colorado.

Hare, A.P. and R.F. Bales. 1963. Seating position and small group interaction. Sociometry 26. 480-486.

Harms, L. S. 1961. Listener comprehension of speakers of three status groups. Language and Speech 4. 109-112.

Hess, R.D., and Virginia Shipman. 1965. Early experience and the socialization of cognitive modes in children. Child Development 36. 869-886.

Homans, G.C. 1950. The Human Group (New York: Harcourt, Brace, and World).

_____ 1958. Social behavior as exchange. American Journal of Sociology 62. 597-606.

Howell, R.W. 1967. Linguistic choice as an index to social change. Ph.D. dissertation, University of California, Berkeley.

Hymes, Dell. 1964. Language in Culture and Society (New York: Harper and Row).

_____ 1967. Models of the interaction of language and social setting. Journal of Social Issues 23, No. 2, 8-28.

Joos, M. 1962. The Five Clocks. International Journal of American Linguistics 28, Part 5.

Kantorovich, V. 1966. Ty i vy: Zametki pisatelya (Ty and Vy: a Writer's Notes) (Moscow: Izd-vo pol. lit.).

Katz, Evelyn. 1966. A content-analysis method for studying themes of interpersonal behavior. Psychological Bulletin 66. 419-422.

Kjolseth, J.R. 1967. Structure and process in conversation. Paper at American Sociological Society meeting, San Francisco.

Klima, E. S. 1964. Relatedness between grammatical systems.
　　　Language 40. 1-20.
Knutson, A. L. 1960. Quiet and vocal groups. Sociometry 23.
　　　36-49.
Kostomarov, V. G. 1967. Russkiy rechevoy stiket (Russian speech
　　　etiquette). Russkiy yazyk za rubezhom 1. 56-62.
Krauss, R. M., and S. Weinheimer. 1964. Changes in reference
　　　phrases as a function of frequency of usage in social interaction;
　　　a preliminary study. Psychonomic Science 1. 113-114.
Labov, W. 1963. The social motivation of a sound change. Word
　　　19. 273-309.
　　　_____ 1964. Phonological correlates of social stratification.
　　　American Anthropologist 66, No. 6, 164-176.
Labov, W. 1966a. Hypercorrection by the lower middle-class as
　　　a factor in linguistic change. In William Bright (ed.), Soc-
　　　iolinguistics (The Hague: Mouton), pp. 84-113.
　　　_____ 1966b. The Social Stratification of English in New York
　　　City (Washington, D. C.: Center for Applied Linguistics).
Labov, W. and P. Cohen. 1967. Systematic relations of standard
　　　and nonstandard rules in the grammars of Negro speakers.
　　　Project Literacy Reports, No. 8, Cornell University, Ithaca,
　　　New York.
Lambert, W. E. 1963. Psychological approaches to the study of
　　　language. II. On second-language learning and bilingualism.
　　　Modern Language Journal 47. 114-121.
　　　_____ 1967 a. A social psychology of bilingualism. Journal
　　　of Social Issues 23, No. 2, 91-109.
　　　_____ 1967 b. The use of tu and vous as forms of address in
　　　Canada: a pilot study. Journal of Verbal Learning and Ver-
　　　bal Behavior 6. 614-617.
Lambert, W. E., M. Anisfeld, and Grace Yeni-Komshian. 1965.
　　　Evaluational reactions of Jewish and Arab adolescents to
　　　dialect and language variations. Journal of Personality and
　　　Social Psychology 2. 84-90.
Lawton, D. 1964. Social class language differences in group dis-
　　　cussions. Language and Speech 7. 183-204.
Leary, T. 1957. Interpersonal Diagnosis of Personality (New York:
　　　Ronald Press).
Levine, L., and H. J. Crockett, Jr. 1966. Speech variation in a
　　　Piedmont community: Postvocalic r. Sociological Inquiry
　　　36, No. 2, 204-226.

Maclay, H., and S. Newman. 1960. Two variables affecting the
    message in communication. In Dorothy K. Wilner (ed.),
    Decisions, Values, and Groups (New York: Pergamon
    Press), pp. 218-219.
Marsden. G. 1965. Content-analysis studies of therapeutic inter-
    views: 1954-1964. Psychological Bulletin 63. 298-321.
Martin, Samuel E. 1964. Speech levels in Japan and Korea. In Dell
    Hymes (ed.), Language in Culture and Society (New York:
    Harper and Row), pp. 407-415.
Mauer, D.W. 1962. The Big Con (New York: New American Li-
    brary).
McCormack, W. 1960. Social dialects in Dharwar Kannada. Inter-
    national Journal of American Linguistics 26, No. 3, 79-91.
McDavid, R.I. 1951. Dialect differences and inter-group tensions.
    Studies in Linguistics 9. 27-33.
McNeill, D. 1963. The Psychology of You and I: A case history of
    a small language system. Paper presented at American
    Psychological Association meeting.
_____ 1966. Developmental psycholinguistics. In F. Smith
    and G.A. Miller (eds.), The Genesis of Language (Cam-
    bridge, Mass.: MIT Press), pp. 15-84.
Meredith, G.M. 1964. Personality correlates of pidgin English
    usage among Japanese-American college students in Hawaii.
    Japanese Psychological Research 6. 176-183.
Morton, John. 1970. A functional model for memory. In Models of
    Human memory, 203-354. New York: Academic Press.
Morton, John and Neil V. Smith. Some ideas concerning the acquisi-
    tion of phonology. In proceedings of the conference of the
    Centre National de Recherches Scientifiques, Paris 1971.
Newman, Stanley S. 1954. Vocabulary levels: Zuni sacred and
    slang usage. Southwestern Journal of Anthropology 11.
    345-354.
O'Neil, W.A. In press. Transformational dialectology. Proceed-
    ings of the Second International Congress of Dialectologists,
    Marburg.
Peisach, Estelle C. 1965. Children's comprehension of teacher and
    peer speech. Child Development 36. 467-480.
Pfuderer, Carol. 1968. A scale of politeness of request forms in
    English. Term paper for Speech 164A, University of
    California, Berkeley.

Pool, I. 1959. Trends in Content Analysis (Urbana, Ill.: University of Illinois Press).

Post, Emily. 1922. Etiquette (New York: Funk and Wagnalls).

Poussaint, A. F. 1967. A Negro psychiatrist explains the Negro psyche. New York Times Magazine, August 20, 52ff.

Ramanujan, A. K. 1967. The structure of variation: A study in caste dialects. In B. Cohn and M. Singer (eds.), Social Structure and Social Change in India (New York: Aldine), pp. 461-474.

Reinecke, John. 1938. Trade jargons and creole dialects as marginal languages. Social Forces 17. 107-118.

Rosenthal, R. and Lenore Jackson. 1966. Teacher's expectancies: Determinants of pupil's I. Q. gains. Psychological Reports 19. 115-118.

Ross, I. 1956. U and non-U: An essay in sociological linguistics. In Nancy Mitford (ed.), Noblesse Oblige (New York: Harpers), pp. 55-92.

Rubin, Joan. 1962. Bilingualism in Paraguay. Anthropological Linguistics 4. 52-58.

_____ 1968. National Bilingualism in Paraguay (The Hague: Mouton).

Sachs, Jacqueline S. 1967. Recognition memory for syntactic and semantic aspects of connected discourse. Perception and Psychophysics 2. 437-442.

Sacks, H. On some features of a method used in selecting identifications: An exercise in the formal study of natural social activities. Unpublished talk.

Samarin, W. J. 1967. Field Linguistics: A Guide to Linguistic Field Work (New York: Holt, Rinehart and Winston).

Sankoff, Gillian and S. Laberge. 1971. On the acquisition of native speakers by a language. Northeastern Linguistics Society meeting, October.

Schatzman, L. and A. Strauss. 1955. Social class and modes of communication. American Journal of Sociology 6. 329-338.

Schegloff, E. 1972. Sequencing in conversational openings. In J. J. Gumperz and D. Hymes (eds.), Directions in Sociolinguistics (New York: Holt, Rinehart, and Winston).

Skinner, B. F. 1957. Verbal Behavior (New York: Appleton-Century-Crofts).

Slobin, D. I. 1963. Some aspects of the use of pronouns of address in Yiddish. Word 19. 193-202.

Slobin, D. I. (ed.), 1967. A Field Manual for Cross-Cultural Study
    of the Acquisition of Communicative Competence (University
    of California, Language-Behavior Laboratory).
Soskin, W. F., and Vera John. 1963. The study of spontaneous talk.
    In R. G. Barker (ed.), The Stream of Behavior (New York:
    Appleton-Century-Crofts).
Stewart, W. A. 1967. Sociolinguistic factors in the history of American
    Negro dialects. The Florida FL Reporter 5, No. 2, 1-4.
Strodtbeck, F. L., Rita James, and C. Hawkins. 1957. Social
    status and jury deliberations. American Sociological
    Review 22. 713-719.
Stross, B. 1964. Waiter-to-cook speech in restaurants. Term paper,
    Speech 160B, University of California, Berkeley.
Tanner, Nancy. 1967. Speech and society among the Indonesian
    elite: A case study of a multilingual community. Anthropo-
    logical Linguistics 9, Part 3, 15-40.
Time, August 27, 1965.
Triandis, H. C., W. D. Loh, and Leslie Levin. 1966. Race, status,
    quality of spoken English, and opinions about civil rights as
    determinants of interpersonal attitudes. Journal of Person-
    ality and Social Psychology 3. 468-472.
Tucker, G. R. and W. Lambert. 1967. White and Negro listeners'
    reactions to various American-English dialects. Paper
    presented at Eastern Psychological Association meeting.
    [Social Forces 47. 463-468.]
Tyler, S. 1965. Koya language morphology and patterns of kinship
    behavior. American Anthropologist 67. 1428-1440.
_____ 1972. Context and alternation in Koya kinship. In John
    J. Gumperz and Dell Hymes, (eds.), Directions in sociolin-
    guistics, 251-269. New York: Holt, Rinehart, and Winston.
Véron, E., C. E. Sluzki, F. Korn, A. Kornblit, and R. Malfe. 1965.
    Communication and Neurosis (University of Buenos Aires
    Inst. Sociologia.). Mimeo.
Watson, Jeanne and R. J. Potter. 1962. An analytic unit for the
    study of interaction. Human Relations 15. 245-263.
Weinreich, U. 1953. Languages in Contact (New York: Linguistic
    Circle of New York).
Williams, Marion. 1964. Restaurant syntax. Term paper, Speech
    160B, University of California, Berkeley.
Wurm, S. A. and D. C. Laycock. 1961. The question of language and
    dialect in New Guinea. Oceania 32. 128-143.

Author's Postscript

When Anwar Dil honored me with an invitation to participate in this series my unfinished work and unreached goals loomed up. But looking back has been an unexpected pleasure. What follows is a somewhat rationalized reconstruction of the course of this work, which leaves out two incentives—the great joy of listening to children and bilinguals, and the excitement of learning, throughout my life, from innovators in the study of language. My sensitive and supportive editor has helped this recall.

The work in this volume, because of the accidents of personal history, reflects several major currents in the development of psycholinguistics and sociolinguistics. As a social psychologist, I was first drawn to work on bilingualism by the dramatic personal experience of bilingual friends who said they were troubled by a sense of multiple identity, of multiple personality. My explanation was that language is acquired in a social milieu and enters strongly into a speaker's internal representation of his society and of himself. In pursuing this question through several studies (chapters 1, 5, 6) I found that the selection of language by bilinguals might commit them to social content as well.

But the compelling vision both of the dominant linguistics of the era and of the founders of psycholinguistics was that language was predominantly mental, private, that the topic was "the nature of the mind", not the structure of communication, internal and external. Whether the concepts used were associations, mediating responses, or transformations, the locus was the mind. In the extreme, the child seemed to develop language virtually without benefit of milieu. The integration of these polar perspectives has been a major problem of these years.

The stimulation of the 1953 summer seminar on psycholinguistics left its younger participants, new to the field, charged with ideas for years of research. In a series of studies of bilinguals (chapters 2, 3, 4) the theory of mediating responses was used to predict semantic boundary shifts in bilinguals, efficiency in memory storage and retrieval, and the degree of meaning contrast between "translation-equivalents" as a consequence of a bilingual's learning history in a semantic domain. The use of a few variables seemed enough to account for a good part of the occurrence of lexical interference—but as soon as I turned to continuous texts, as I did in my dissertation, the structural cohesion of the text worked havoc with theories restricted to lexical factors alone.

Associations, another major area of research at the time, seemed to have no bearing at all either on grammar or on connected speech. So, to attempt to bring the force of the many new findings to bear on issues of language structure, a theory of the learning of associations was developed and tested (chapters 10, 12, and "Correlates of Associative Frequency", 1963) which based the development of associative responses first on contiguity in connected speech, and later, with the development of increased sequential variety—especially in the early school years—on substitution probabilities and thus on similarity of semantic and syntactic features. In this view associations did not generate but resulted from experience with speech.

But the linguists' challenge to account for structure was really inadequately met by these psychological approaches. When Chomsky's 1957 book on syntax appeared, it was immediately obvious that child grammatical development should show changes reflecting the development of the integrative rules he had found. With linguist Wick Miller work was begun in 1960 on what we thought would be the first study of sequential stages in generative syntax in young children. This large study, of which only a part (chapter 13) is included here, showed very clearly that children's grammars had some but not all of the features of adult grammars, that they were indeed highly structured and creative, and that their properties could not be explained by rote learning or imitation.

The freshness of the discoveries of structure in early syntax, and continuing wonder at the complexities that children incorporate productively into their language use from an early age kept driving all

of those working on child grammar to seek a fuller account. It took me
surprisingly long to realize that the process of acquisition bore fundamental similarities to the learning I had observed in bilinguals (chapters 7, 8). The emphasis usually placed on biological critical periods,
and on interference, had blocked the recognition of the similarity of
process; it was only in reorganizing my perspective on first language
development, to see it as a series of stages in a changing language
acquisition system that selects and alters what it absorbs (chapter 14),
that suddenly I could see that interference was no different from the
enduring structure of a monolingual child's own prior language. This
insight allowed two of my lines of interest to converge. It also brought
to the fore the fact that the differences between first and second language acquisition in reality are often just those factors of intent, motive, social milieu, communicative choice which are left unexamined
in first language acquisition as irrelevant to structure.

During these years I felt uneasy at having left aside the major
issues of language as a social act which first drew me into psycholinguistics. At the same time, the other fundamental property of language,
its intricate and orderly structure, was equally compelling. It seemed
difficult to map onto language systematically social and motivational
variables which are ambiguous and often assigned by social scientists
to arbitrary categories. It was obvious, in examining the material
from the Japanese bilingualism study and other work on language in
society (chapter 15) that there was highly systematic co-variation
between variables in the speech situation.

For these reasons the most important contribution in the
new field of sociolinguistics appeared to be the discovery of new strata
of structure in language. A variety of instances of choice among alternatives, of which address term selection (chapter 17) is a very
simple case, have been shown to have as orderly a structure as any
syntax. Yet they have as features in the rule non-linguistic determinants such as rank or age of addressee, as well as in some cases features of the linguistic context. The structure of these rules and their
acquisition (chapter 16) all lie before us as problems. But the fear that
the real world is too unstructured to be incorporated into the study of
language use can be laid to rest, for it would seem that in the use of options of communication, people have developed natural categories just
as they did with the acoustic continua. The discreteness of language
provides us with a route to discovery of these natural categories.

Bibliography of
Susan M. Ervin-Tripp's Works

Compiled by Anwar S. Dil

1948   (With Eve Borsook). Kaiser Friedrich Art Collection.
            Vassar Brew 36 (April). 11, 12, 19.

1949   Mannerist aspects of modern painting. Vassar Review 1:
            5. 9-12.

1952-3   (With Robert T. Bower). Translation problems in interna-
            tional surveys. Public Opinion Quarterly 16. 595-604.

1954 a.   Identification and bilingualism. Paper presented at a Social
            Science Research Council Committee on Psycholinguistics
            Conference on Bilingualism. [In this volume, pp. 1-14.]
     b.   Some relationships between cognition, feeling and speech.
            Paper presented at a conference on bilingualism, May,
            sponsored by the Social Science Research Council Commit-
            tee on Psycholinguistics.
     c. d. Information transmission with code translation (pp. 185-192);
            (With C. E. Osgood). Second language learning and bilingual-
            ism (pp. 139-145). Psycholinguistics: a survey of theory
            and research problems, ed. by C. E. Osgood and T. A.
            Sebeok. Journal of Abnormal and Social Psychology 20.
            [Reprint edition: Bloomington: Indiana University Press,
            1965.] [In this volume, pp. 15-23.]

1955   The verbal behavior of bilinguals. The effect of language
            of report on the Thematic Apperception Test content of
            adult French bilinguals. Microfilm AC-1, No. 12, 571.
            University of Michigan Microfilm Library, Ann Arbor.

1958 a.   Review of Intelligence in the United States, by H. Miner.
              Psychometrika 23. 388–390.

      b.   Review of Certain language skills in children, by Mildred
              Templin. Contemporary Psychology 3. 128–129.

1960 a.   (With Garrett Foster). The development of meaning in
              children's descriptive terms. Journal of Abnormal and
              Social Psychology 60. 271–275. [Reprinted in The psychol-
              ogy of language, thought, and instruction, ed. by John P.
              DeCecco, 276–283. New York: Holt, Rinehart and Win-
              ston, 1967. In Semantic differential technique: a source-
              book, ed. by C. E. Osgood and J. Snider, 332–339.
              Chicago: Aldine, 1969. In Research readings in child
              psychology, ed. by D. S. Palermo and L. P. Lipsitt,
              344–350. New York: Holt, Rinehart and Winston, 1963.]
              [In this volume, pp. 130–138.]

      b.   Cognitive effects of bilingualism. Proceedings of the
              Sixteenth International Congress of Psychology, Bonn, 1960.
              Amsterdam: North-Holland Publishing Company, 1962,
              pp. 703–704.

      c.   Experimental procedures of children. Child Development
              31. 703–719.

      d.   (With H. J. Landar and A. E. Horowitz). Navaho color
              categories. Language 36. 368–382.

      e.   Training and a logical operation by children. Child Develop-
              ment 31. 555–563. [Reprinted in The causes of behavior:
              Readings in child development and educational psychology,
              ed. by J. Rosenblith and W. Allinsmith, 229–231. Boston:
              Allyn and Bacon, 1962.]

      f.   Transfer effects of learning a verbal generalization. Child
              Development 31. 537–554. [Reprinted in Readings in
              learning and human abilities, ed. by R. Ripple, 443–461.
              New York: Harper and Row, 1964.]

      g.   Review of Verbal categories in child language, by H. Kahane,
              R. Kahane, and Sol Saporta. Romance Philology 14. 45–48.

1961 a.   Changes with age in the verbal determinants of word-associ-
              ation. American Journal of Psychology 74. 361–372.
              [Reprinted in Readings in the psychology of language, ed. by
              L. Jakobovits and M. Miron, 530–540. New York:

Prentice-Hall, 1967.] [In this volume, pp. 139-155.]

b. Learning and recall in bilinguals. American Journal of
Psychology 74. 446-451. [In this volume, pp. 24-32.]

c. Semantic shift in bilingualism. American Journal of Psychology 74. 233-241. [In this volume, pp. 33-44.]

d. Review of Speech and the development of mental processes
in the child, by A. R. Luria and F. Ia. Yudovich. Contemporary Psychology 6. 20.

1962   The connotations of gender. Word 18. 249-261. [In this
volume, pp. 156-172.]

1963 a.   (With Wick Miller). Language development. National
Society for the Study of Education Yearbook, ed. by H.
Stevenson, 108-143. [Reprinted in Readings in the sociology
of language, ed. by J. A. Fishman, 69-98. The Hague:
Mouton, 1970.]

b. (With J. Sawyer, Shirley Silver, Joanne D'Andrea, Haruo
Aoki). The utility of translation and written symbols during
the first thirty hours of language study. International
Review of Applied Linguistics (IRAL) 1. 157-192.

c. (With H. Landar). Navaho word associations. American
Journal of Psychology 76. 49-57. [In this volume, pp. 173-
184.]

d. Review of Variations in value orientations, by F. Kluckhorn
and F. Strodtbeck. American Journal of Psychology 76.
342-343.

e. Review of Psycholinguistics, ed. by Sol Saporta. American
Anthropologist 65. 750-752.

f. Correlates of associative frequency. Journal of Verbal
Learning and Verbal Behavior 1. 422-431.

1964 a.   An analysis of the interaction of language, topic, and listener. The ethnography of communication, ed. by J. J.
Gumperz and D. Hymes, 86-102. American Anthropologist
66:6, Part 2. [Reprinted in Readings in the sociology of
language, ed. by J. A. Fishman, 192-211. The Hague:
Mouton, 1970. In Readings in social interaction, ed. by
Michael Argyle. Chicago: Aldine, 1971.] [In this
volume, pp. 239-261.]

b. (With Wick Miller). The development of grammar in child
language. The acquisition of language, ed. by U. Bellugi
and R. Brown, 9-34. Monographs of the Society for Research
in Child Development 29.1. [Reprinted in Cognitive development in children; five monographs of the Society for
Research in Child Development. Chicago: University of
Chicago Press, 1970, 309-334. In Child language: A book
of readings, ed. by A. Bar-Adon and W. F. Leopold, 322-
339. Englewood Cliffs, N. J.: Prentice-Hall, 1971. In
Studies in child language development, ed. by C. A. Ferguson
and D. I. Slobin. New York: Holt, Rinehart, and Winston,
1973.]

c. Imitation and structural change in children's language.
New directions in the study of language, ed. by E. H.
Lenneberg, 163-189. Cambridge: The MIT Press, 1964.
[Reprinted in Structuralism, a reader, ed. by M. Lane,
57-72. London: Cape, 1970. In Studies in child language
development, ed. by C. A. Ferguson and D. I. Slobin.
New York: Holt, Rinehart, and Winston, 1973.] [In this
volume, pp. 185-203.]

d. Language and TAT content in bilinguals. Journal of Abnormal and Social Psychology 68. 500-507. [Reprinted
in Cross-cultural studies of behavior, ed. by I. Al-Issa
and Wayne Dennis, 415-428. New York: Holt, Rinehart
and Winston, 1970. In The psychosociology of language,
ed. by Serge Moscovici, 369-383. Chicago: Markham,
1972.] [In this volume, pp. 45-61.]

e. Language and thought. Horizons of anthropology, ed. by
Sol Tax, 81-91. Chicago: Aldine Publishing Company,
1964. [= Language in human psychology. Voice of America
Forum Lecture Series.]

f. Review of Language in the crib, by R. H. Weir. International Journal of American Linguistics 30. 420-424.

g. Abstracts on psycholinguistics. International Journal of
American Linguistics 30. 90-93, 184-193.

1966 a. Language development. Review of child development
research, ed. by Martin and Lois Hoffman 2.55-105.
New York: Russell Sage Foundation.

b. (With Dan I. Slobin). Psycholinguistics. Annual Review
of Psychology 17. 435-474. [Italian version in Rassegna

Italiana di sociologia 9:2. 383-425 (1968).]

c. Discussion. Speech, language, and communication, ed. by
E. C. Carterette, 58-60, 245-246. Los Angeles: University
of California Press.

1967 a. Introduction, phonology, communicative routines, contrastive analysis, informal education, introduction to styles,
natural conversation. Field manual for cross-cultural study
of the acquisition of communicative competence, ed. by
D. I. Slobin. Berkeley, California: ASUC Bookstore.
Introduction (ix-xv), Linguistic Development: Phonology
(11-14), Linguistic Development: Vocabulary (With Dan I.
Slobin, 15-17), Communicative Routines (46-49), Contrastive Analysis (61-69), Theoretical Considerations and Possible Subsidiary Studies: Phonology (93-103), Informal
Education (137-148), Usage and Styles (155-156), Natural
Conversation (172-175).

b. An Issei learns English. Problems in bilingualism, ed. by
John Macnamara, 78-90. Journal of Social Issues 23:2.
[In this volume, pp. 62-77.]

c. Navaho connotative judgments: The metaphor of person
description. Studies in southwestern ethnolinguistics, ed.
by D. Hymes and W. E. Bittle, 91-116. The Hague: Mouton.

d. On becoming a bilingual. Language-Behavior Research
Laboratory, University of California, Berkeley, Working
Paper No. 8. [Slightly revised version in The description
and measurement of bilingualism, ed. by L. G. Kelly,
26-35. Toronto, Canada: University of Toronto Press.]
[Final revised version in this volume, pp. 78-91.]

e. Breakthrough: the genesis of language. The Daily Cali-
fornian, November 22.

1968 a. Language development. International Encyclopedia of the
Social Sciences, ed. by David L. Shills, 9. 9-14. New
York: The Macmillan Company & The Free Press.

b. The acquisition of communicative competence by children
in different cultures. Proceedings of the VIIth International
Congress of Anthropological and Ethnological Sciences
3. 406-408.

c. Sociolinguistics. Advances in experimental social psychology,

ed. by L. Berkowitz, 4.91-165. New York: Academic
Press. [Reprinted in Advances in the sociology of language,
ed. by J. A. Fishman, Volume I, 15-91. The Hague:
Mouton, 1971.]

1969   Summer workshops in sociolinguistics: Research on children's acquisition of communicative competence. Items
(Social Science Research Council), May, pp. 22-26.

1970 a. Discourse agreement: How children answer questions.
Cognition and language learning, ed. by R. Hayes, 79-107.
New York: Wiley and Sons.

    b. Structure and process in language acquisition. Monograph
Series on Languages and Linguistics 23, ed. by J. E. Alatis,
pp. 313-353. Washington, D.C.: Georgetown University
Press. [In this volume, pp. 92-129.]

    c. Substitution, context, and association. Norms of word
association, ed. by L. Postman and G. Keppel, 383-467.
New York: Academic Press.

    d. The academic mythology. The Daily Californian (University
of California, Berkeley), January 27.

1971 a. An overview of theories of grammatical development. The
ontogenesis of grammar: some facts and theories, ed. by
D. I. Slobin, 189-212. New York: Academic Press.

    b. Social backgrounds and verbal skills. Language acquisition:
models and methods, ed. by R. Huxley and E. Ingram,
29-39. London/New York: Academic Press.

    c. Social dialects in developmental sociolinguistics. Socio-
linguistics: a cross-disciplinary perspective, ed. by R.
Shuy, 35-64. Washington, D. C.: Center for Applied
Linguistics.

    d. (With Elisabeth Colson and Elizabeth Scott). Report of the
subcommittee on the status of academic women on the
Berkeley campus. Academic Senate, University of California. [Reprinted in Discrimination against women, Part
2, pp. 1143-1221. Washington, D. C.: U. S. Government
Printing Office.]

    e. "What a girl can do". The Daily Californian (University of
California, Berkeley), February 12.

    f.   Discriminatory hiring practices. Science 174.1281.

    g.   Origins of language. Developmental psychology today,
        163-179. Del Mar, California: CRM Books.

1972 a.   On sociolinguistic rules: alternation and co-occurrence.
        Directions in sociolinguistics: the ethnography of commun-
        ication, ed. by J. J. Gumperz and Dell Hymes, 218-250.
        New York: Holt, Rinehart and Winston.

    b.   Children's sociolinguistic competence and dialect diversity.
        Early childhood education; The seventy-first yearbook of
        the National Society for the Study of Education, ed. by Ira
        J. Gordon, 123-160. Chicago: University of Chicago
        Press. [In this volume, pp. 262-301.]

    c.   The onset of grammar. Papers on linguistics and child
        language: Ruth Hirsch Weir memorial volume, ed. by
        V. Honsa and Hardman de-Bautistia. The Hague: Mouton,
        in press.

    d.   Language learning. To appear in Encyclopedia Brittanica.

    e.   Some bases for early features of production. Paper pre-
        sented at the C. N. R. S. Colloque International sur les
        Problèmes Actuels de Psycholinguistique, Paris, December
        13-18, 1971. To appear in the Proceedings.

    f.   Some strategies for the first two years. Cognitive develop-
        ment and the acquisition of language, ed. by T. Moore.
        New York: Academic Press, 1973. [In this volume, pp.
        204-238.]

    g.   The structure of communicative choice. [In this volume,
        pp. 302-373.]

    h.   Susan M. Ervin-Tripp on language acquisition and commun-
        icative choice. Perspectives in Linguistic Education: Con-
        versations with Language Scholars, by Anwar S. Dil.
        Abbottabad: Linguistic Research Group of Pakistan, in
        press.

Tables 1 and 2 are referred to on pp. 134-35.

TABLE 1

PROPORTION ASCRIBING CORRELATED ATTRIBUTE DIFFERENCES TO OBJECTS

Stimulus Differences	Response	First Grade			Sixth Grade			
		Boys	Girls	Total	Boys	Girls	Total	Differences
Heavy	BIG	40.6	36.0[a]	38.6[a]	16.7	25.0	20.8	17.8
Strong	BIG	31.2	52.0	39.7	30.6	25.0	27.8	11.9
Strong	HEAVY	37.5	46.2	41.4	33.3	33.3	33.3	8.0
Big	STRONG	50.0	53.8	51.7	36.1	38.9	37.5	14.2
Heavy	STRONG	56.2	76.9	65.5	41.7	47.2	44.4	21.1
	N[b]	16	13	28	18	18	36	

[a] The number of cases in this cell is reduced by one owing to loss of data.
[b] The Ss reported were those who correctly differentiated the stimulus attribute for all three attributes on all materials.

TABLE 2

PROPORTION ASCRIBING CORRELATED ATTRIBUTE DIFFERENCES TO FACES

Stimulus Differences	Response	First Grade			Sixth Grade			
		Boys	Girls	Total	Boys	Girls	Total	Differences
Happy	CLEAN	12.5	5.9	9.1	0.0	11.1	5.6	3.5
Pretty	CLEAN	28.6	7.7	18.5	5.6	5.6	5.6	12.9
Clean	HAPPY	37.5	47.0	42.4	5.6	22.2	13.9	28.5*
Pretty	HAPPY	85.7	91.7	88.5	67.1	38.9	50.0	38.5*
Clean	PRETTY	100.0	82.4	90.9	50.0	50.0	50.0	40.9*
Happy	PRETTY	81.2	82.4	81.8	83.3	66.7	75.0	6.8
Clean	GOOD	50.0	70.6	60.6	27.8	33.3	30.6	30.0*
Happy	GOOD	100.0	94.1	97.0	77.8	55.6	66.7	30.3*
Pretty	GOOD	78.6	50.0	65.4	44.4	22.2	33.3	32.0*
	N[a]	16	17	33	18	18	36	

[a] Changes in $\underline{N}$ due to failure to name stimulus difference correctly: first-grade boys for PRETTY stimulus 14, girls 12; sixth-grade boys, 17, and girls, 16.
*Significant at the .01 level.